THE EARLY ESSAYS

THE HERITAGE OF SOCIOLOGY

A Series Edited by Donald N. Levine

Morris Janowitz, *Founding Editor*

TALCOTT PARSONS
THE EARLY ESSAYS

Edited and with an Introduction by
CHARLES CAMIC

THE UNIVERSITY OF CHICAGO PRESS

Chicago and London

CHARLES CAMIC is professor of sociology at the University of Wisconsin, Madison. He is the author of *Experience and Enlightenment: Socialization for Cultural Change in Eighteenth-Century Scotland,* also published by the University of Chicago Press.

The University of Chicago Press, Chicago 60637
The University of Chicago Press, Ltd., London
© 1991 by The University of Chicago
All rights reserved. Published 1991
Printed in the United States of America

00 99 98 97 96 95 94 93 92 91   5 4 3 2 1

ISBN 0-226-09236-4 (cl.).—ISBN 0-226-09237-2 (pbk.)

Library of Congress Cataloging-in-Publication Data

Parsons, Talcott, 1902–
    The early essays / Talcott Parsons : edited and with an introduction by Charles Camic.
        p.   cm.—(Heritage of sociology)
    Includes bibliographical references and index.
    1. Sociology—Philosophy.   2. Social action.   I. Camic, Charles.
    II. Title.   III. Series.
HM24.P2833 1991
301'.01—dc20   90-19213

Contents

Acknowledgments   vii
Introduction: Talcott Parsons before *The Structure of
Social Action,* by Charles Camic   ix

I Capitalist Society and Its Origins

1   "Capitalism" in Recent German Literature: Sombart
    and Weber   3
2   Review of *Modern Capitalism: Its Origin and Devel-
    opment,* by Henri Sée   39
3   Jean Calvin   41
4   Samuel Smiles   45
5   Service   47
6   Thrift   51
7   H. M. Robertson on Max Weber and His School   57

II Studies in the Development of the Theory of
   Action

8   Economics and Sociology: Marshall in Relation to the
    Thought of His Time   69
9   Review of *An Introduction to the Study of Society,* by
    Frank H. Hankins   95
10 Review of *Einführung in die Soziologie,* by Ferdinand
    Tönnies   97
11 Thomas Robert Malthus   101
12 Vilfredo Pareto   105
13 Society   109
14 Review of *Max Webers Wissenschaftslehre,* by Alexan-
    der von Schelting   123
15 Pareto's Central Analytical Scheme   133

III   The Foundations of Analytical Sociology

16   Some Reflections on "The Nature and Significance of
        Economics"   153
17   Sociological Elements in Economic Thought   181
18   The Place of Ultimate Values in Sociological Theory   231
19   On Certain Sociological Elements in Professor Taus-
        sig's Thought   259
20   Review of *Economics and Sociology*, by Adolf Löwe   279

     Appendix: A Word from Amherst Students
                 (with Addison T. Cutler)   287
     Index   293

Acknowledgments

Preparation of this volume was facilitated by generous help from several persons and institutions. For information pertaining to Talcott Parsons's early career, I am grateful to Jeffrey C. Alexander, Harold J. Bershady, William Buxton, Victor Lidz, Charles O'Connell, Charles D. Parsons, and Bruce C. Wearne. I would also like to thank Clark A. Elliott of the Harvard University Archives for his helpfulness in numerous matters relating to the Talcott Parsons Papers. I have benefited as well from the cooperation of the staffs of the Archives and the Registrar's Office of Amherst College, the Special Collections Department of the University of Chicago Library, the British Library of Political and Economic Science of the London School of Economics and Political Science, and the library of the Federal Bureau of Investigation. Acknowledgment is also due to G. Steven Lybrand for research assistance and to Mary-Ann Twist for expert secretarial assistance. Bernard Barber, Warren Hagstrom, Robert Alun Jones, Donald N. Levine, and John Riley kindly read and commented on the Introduction, and I greatly appreciate their valuable advice.

Introduction: Talcott Parsons before *The Structure of Social Action*

Talcott Parsons's early intellectual career has long lain in the shadows, eclipsed by his enormous output in the period running from the publication in 1937 of his first book, *The Structure of Social Action,* until his death in 1979. The scholarly effort required to come to terms with the large corpus of work that he produced during this period, as well as the magnitude of *The Structure of Social Action,* has deflected interest from what came before, creating the widespread belief that Parsons's oeuvre commenced with his first book and, insofar as it underwent development, did so from this point of departure.

Given this belief, scholarly understanding of the "early Parsons" lags well behind the understanding of figures like the early Marx, the early Freud, the early Durkheim, and the early Weber, for there was, in fact, a substantial body of work before *The Structure of Social Action.* In the decade prior to the book's release, Parsons published nearly thirty items, approximately the same number as in the decade *after* publication of the book. The quantity of early unpublished work is equally impressive, and selections from this are gradually appearing in print. The present volume brings together and reproduces in full the majority of Parsons's early published writings. These cover the period from the autumn of 1923, the start of Parsons's senior year in college, until November 1937, the month and year of the publication of *The Structure of Social Action.* Together they chart the decisive initial phases of the process by which one of this century's major approaches to sociological theory took shape. This process was intimately tied to biographical and intellectual-historical circumstances that form part of the early history of American social science.

Starting Points

With the advantage of hindsight, it is not difficult to recognize Talcott Parsons's early life experiences as conditions particularly fertile for a bold young man of ideas.[1] Parsons was born on 13 December 1902 in Colorado Springs, Colorado, the fifth and last child of Edward Smith Parsons and Mary A. Ingersol Parsons (both born in 1863). His parents had migrated westward to Colorado in the late nineteenth century, when his father, an ordained Congregational minister who had already broken from the mold of his Yankee merchant forebears to attend Yale Divinity School, was posted there as a home missionary.

In later life, Parsons remembered the home environment in which he grew up as a liberal one for its time. His mother was a suffragist and backer of various progressive causes, while his father was a "social gospel" Protestant, committed to the same reformist social-service orientation that spurred the early development of American sociology. From 1892 until 1917, the senior Parsons was also head professor of English at Colorado College, then a small coeducational institution connected with the Congregational church. His intellectual interests, however, extended well beyond the field of literary studies. Not Milton and Lowell alone, but various contemporary social issues were what occupied his attention, as well as the foreground of his published works. The hallmark of these works was a forward-looking brand of turn-of-the-century Christian opinion: alarm over the moral consequences of the modern "industrial system," with its selfishness, economic individualism, exploitation of labor, and tendency toward social "disorder"; receptivity to improvements that might emerge from "scientific investigation, higher criticism, rationalism, philosophical speculation" and even "Christianized Socialism"; and hope that partisans of the divergent ethical viewpoints would unite around a "common store of truth and principle" to work with the church, "the inspirer of all life," for progress toward a "perfect humanity."[2]

1. A full intellectual biography of Parsons remains to be written. At the present time, the chief sources of information are Bernard Barber, "Biographical Sketch," in *Essays in Sociological Theory Pure and Applied,* by Talcott Parsons (Glencoe: Free Press, 1949), 349–52; Martin Martel, "Parsons, Talcott," in *Biographical Supplement,* vol. 18 of *International Encyclopedia of the Social Sciences,* ed. David L. Sills (New York: Macmillan, 1979), 609–30; and Talcott Parsons's own statements, especially "Short Account of My Intellectual Development," *Alpha Kappa Deltan* 29 (1959): 3–12, and "On Building Social Systems Theory: A Personal History," *Daedalus* 99 (1970): 826–81. Throughout the Introduction, matters of fact not otherwise attributed are drawn from these accounts.

2. Edward Parsons, "A Christian Critique of Socialism," *Andover Review* 11 (1889): 601, 610–11; Edward Parsons, "The Church and Education," *Colorado College Publication, Language Series* 2, no. 21 (1908): 92, 94–95, 97.

As an adult, Talcott Parsons spoke frequently about how much he owed to his parents and "to the values they stood for";[3] but apart from this recollection (and the fact that he attended local schools and spent a year of his youth in Germany), little is yet known about his childhood. Perhaps the most dramatic period was immediately before his family's departure from Colorado Springs. During his years at Colorado College, Edward Parsons had been given a large administrative role, serving for more than a decade as dean of the Department of Arts and Sciences and, concurrently, as vice president of the college. In connection with these positions, he became a central figure, from late 1915 until 1918, in a controversy that rocked the college—and presumably, too, the Parsons household (a site of late-night faculty conferences)—over charges that the college president had engaged in "indiscreet and improper conduct" toward some of his female employees. Edward Parsons's conduct during the episode commanded wide faculty and student support, but brought him into serious disfavor with the local board of trustees, which summarily dismissed him from the college in the summer of 1917. Reporting on the episode a few years later, a committee of the American Association of University Professors issued a sharp condemnation of the trustees' "arbitrary and unjust" behavior and a thorough vindication of Parsons's actions.[4] But the deed was done, and in 1918 Edward Parsons resettled his family in New York City and accepted a position with the YMCA. (The following year he became president of Marietta College in Ohio.)

As a result of this move to New York, Talcott Parsons spent his last two years of high school at the Horace Mann School for Boys, which was affiliated with Columbia Teachers College and renowned at the time for making available "the very best American education had to offer to high-ability children who planned academic and professional careers."[5] From there he proceeded in the fall of 1920 to Amherst College, which his father and two older brothers had previously attended. In following the family tradition, however, the young Parsons began a run of intellectual luck that would carry him over the course of the next decade—and with relatively little design on his own part—

3. John Riley, remarks on the occasion of the retirement banquet for Talcott Parsons, 18 May 1973, ed. Martin Martel and Mark Shields, in *Essays on the Sociology of Talcott Parsons*, ed. G. C. Hallen (Meerut, India: Indian Journal of Social Research, n.d.), 439.

4. Committee on Academic Freedom and Tenure, "Report of the Sub-Committee of Inquiry for Colorado College," *Bulletin of the American Association of University Professors* 5 (1919): 51–130.

5. Lawrence Cremin, David Shannon, and Mary Townsend, *A History of Teachers College, Columbia University* (Morningside Heights, N.Y.: Columbia University Press, 1954), 104.

to some of the great academic centers of the interwar period. This trajectory had considerable significance for the development of his thinking. Not only did it plunge Parsons directly into several vigorous streams of contemporary thought, it stamped his thinking with a peculiarly self-referential quality, or tendency to regard the ideas he personally encountered in local surroundings as those ideas most worth engaging and vesting with epochal import.

When Talcott Parsons entered Amherst, the college was experiencing the fruits of its dramatic transformation from a small New England college, suffering from falling admissions standards and low faculty salaries, into a nationally recognized institution, hailed by *The New Republic* as richer in "intellectual life" than any other American college.[6] The change followed the appointment in 1912 of the philosopher Alexander Meiklejohn as Amherst's president. One of the period's leading educational reformers, Meiklejohn brought to Amherst his belief that human knowledge was becoming "a collection of scattered observations about the world rather than an understanding of it" and his deep conviction that "the time has come for a reconstruction, for a new synthesis" that would infuse "industrial civilization" with the meaning and purpose that had been lost "amidst the . . . doubts and differences [of] men . . . today."[7] To promote his objectives, Meiklejohn replaced Amherst's electives-based curriculum with a program of requirements, urged its prosperous students to consider socialist alternatives to capitalism (and its faculty to offer workers' classes in surrounding industrial areas), and took bold steps to develop the social sciences, so that the student would "see and appreciate what is intended, what accomplished, and what left undone by such institutions as property, the courts, the family, the church, the mill."[8]

6. D[ouglas] W[ilson], "The Story in the Meiklejohn Files," part 1, *Amherst,* Fall 1982, p. 12.

7. Alexander Meiklejohn, "What the Liberal College Is," in *Alexander Meiklejohn: Teacher of Freedom,* ed. Cynthia Stokes Brown (Berkeley, Calif.: Meiklejohn Civil Liberties Institute, 1981 [original date of speech 1912]), 75; Meiklejohn, "What Does the College Hope to Be during the Next One Hundred Years," in *Reprints of Two Addresses Delivered at the Amherst College Centennial Celebration* (Holyoke, Mass.: Alden Press, 1921), 30.

8. Meiklejohn, "What the Liberal College Is," 77. On these aspects of Meiklejohn's transformation of Amherst, see Cynthia Stokes Brown, "Alexander Meiklejohn," in *Alexander Meiklejohn: Teacher of Freedom,* 1–56; Lucien Price, *Prophets Unawares: The Romance of an Idea* (New York: Century Co., 1924); Wilson, "Meiklejohn Files," part 1, 8–15, 28–31; Wilson, "The Story in the Meiklejohn Files," part 2, *Amherst,* Spring 1983, pp. 8–16, 53–65.

To what extent Meiklejohn's views—in their concern with industrial society, openness to social science and socialism, and forecast
of a new synthesis of divergent opinions—recalled to the young Parsons the ideas of his father is a matter of speculation. Beyond question, though, are his commitment, while at Amherst, to the educational experiment launched by Meiklejohn (who was also Parsons's
sophomore-year philosophy professor) and his bitter disappointment
when Meiklejohn too fell victim to a college board of trustees and was
forced to resign his position in June 1923. This event, which occurred
at the end of Parsons's junior year, immediately became "the biggest
controversy in the college's history" and commanded such broad interest that news reporters from all over the nation (Walter Lippmann
among them) were sent to cover the story.[9] Many years later it was
revealed that the trustees' decision was precipitated by Meiklejohn's
private financial indiscretions; but at the time the indiscretions were
concealed and emphasis laid on his increasing inability to govern the
Amherst faculty, which had been torn into a small pro-Meiklejohn
camp and a large group opposed to his innovations.[10] Meiklejohn still
retained great popularity with students in the college, however, and
upon his forced resignation, and the protest resignations of eight faculty supporters, many juniors in particular suddenly "felt as if the
gates of life had been slammed shut."[11] With this group the young
Parsons strongly sympathized, and his reaction to the "Meiklejohn
affair" forms the subject of his first known publication (reprinted as
the appendix to this volume), an article coauthored with classmate
Addison Cutler for *The New Student,* a magazine that constituted
America's "chief expression of campus protest [during] the 1920s."[12]
In it Parsons, declaring his identity as a young "intellectual," comes
out unequivocally for Meiklejohn, the New Guard faculty, and "the
cause of liberal education."

But Parsons's political awareness during his college days was not
confined to local controversies. As he later wrote: "I was certainly
attracted by . . . a mild political activism and by movements stemming
from the Left. Many of us at Amherst . . . were enthusiasts for the
Russian Revolution and for the rise of the British Labor Party, and we

9. Wilson, "Meiklejohn Files," part 1, 8; Wilson, "Meiklejohn Files," part 2, 57.
10. Wilson, "Meiklejohn Files," part 1, 8–15, 28–31; Wilson, "Meiklejohn Files,"
part 2, 8–16, 53–65.
11. Brown, "Alexander Meiklejohn," 19.
12. Seymour Martin Lipset, "Political Controversies at Harvard, 1636 to 1974," in
Education and Politics at Harvard, by Seymour Martin Lipset and David Riesman (New
York: McGraw-Hill, 1975), 157.

were firmly in the opposition to the current United States regime during the presidencies of Harding and Coolidge." [13] In this connection, he joined the national Student League for Industrial Democracy, a prominent organization of Social Democrats, and thus brought himself to the attention of the Federal Bureau of Investigation, which began a file on his activities in late 1923. [14]

The academic side of Parsons's Amherst years was no less consequential. Entering college with the idea of pursuing graduate work in biology or, like his older brother, a career in medicine, Parsons took four semesters of chemistry and six of biology, apparently acquiring, in the process, a thorough grounding in the natural sciences. [15] In later life, he remained proud of this, recalling with pleasure that he "was even an assistant in the laboratory of a general course in biological evolution and [worked] for a whole summer [at] Wood's Hole, the famous marine biological laboratory," and reporting Curt Stern's comment that "at Amherst, biology was taught at a very advanced, even a graduate level, [by] highly distinguished people." [16] Outside the natural sciences, Parsons concentrated in two areas. The first of these was philosophy, where his course work included a seminar on *The Critique of Pure Reason* and a seminar on modern German philosophy, the latter taught by Otto Manthey-Zorn, a professor of German who would become instrumental in Parsons's early career. As to the second area in which Parsons concentrated: befitting the Meiklejohn era, this was the social sciences.

Here Parsons's introduction came during his first semester in the course "Social and Economic Institutions" (which is favorably described in the Cutler-Parsons article). Taking the place of conventional introductory courses in government and economics, "S. and E. I." (as it was known) was, in contemporary eyes, "the most dramatic single innovation" of Meiklejohn's presidency: "a frank examination of merits, defects, and alternatives, [an experience that] turned out boys who at the end of their freshman year had at least some elementary knowledge of the why and wherefore of the social scheme in

13. Parsons, "Clarence Ayres's Economics and Sociology," in *Science and Ceremony,* ed. William Breit and William Patton Culbertson, Jr. (Austin: University of Texas Press, 1976), 176.

14. Federal Bureau of Investigation, file HQ 100–390459 (hereafter, FBI file).

15. This and the information reported below on Parsons's course of study are drawn from his college transcript, Office of the Registrar, Amherst College; and from the 1920–24 issues of the bulletin entitled *Amherst College Curriculum,* Amherst College Library.

16. Parsons, "My Intellectual Development," 3; Parsons, "Building Social Systems," 875 n. 16.

which they lived."[17] This was followed in Parsons's junior year by a course entitled "The Economic Order" with Walton Hamilton, at the time America's foremost exponent of "institutional economics," and a companion course entitled "The Moral Order" with Clarence Ayres, a philosopher who would soon become an institutional economist himself.[18] This year-long encounter with institutional economics proved significant. To it Parsons ever afterward attributed his intellectual conversion from biology to the social sciences.[19]

But what did the encounter mean? In terms of the course with Hamilton, it meant close study with an eclectic thinker vitally concerned with the epoch of "modern industrialism" and the "social control" of the problems that characterized it (inefficiency, business cycles, population growth, capitalist monopoly, poverty, etc.), problems that "represent a lack of harmony . . . between the many and various aspects of social life—between institution and institution, between activity and custom, between practice and ideal." A well-read student of the history of economic thought, Hamilton continually criticized orthodox, neoclassical economics for having abandoned these epoch-specific issues in the interest of building abstract theories premised on "extreme individualism, rationality, and utilitarianism." In his view, the time had come for economics to expand beyond "formulas explaining the processes through which prices emerge" to the study of "institutions," understood as "the conventions, customs, habits of thinking and modes of doing which make up" the economy. In this category, Hamilton included "institutions [such] as the market, trade, contract, property, and competition which give . . . character to current economic life," as well as the state agencies, community organizations, "usages," "codes of ethics," and "rules of the game" without which an "economic order . . . cannot maintain itself." To treat this subject matter, he recommended that economists adopt a "genetic method," which looks to the past "to explain what a thing is in terms of how it came to be," and urged special attention to "the process by which modern industrial culture has come to be what it is" and to possess its unique "spirit, values, activities and institutions."[20]

17. Price, *Prophets Unawares*, 33, 38.

18. Wilson, "Meiklejohn Files," part 2, 12.

19. Parsons, "Building Social Systems," 826; Parsons, "Dialogues with Parsons," ed. Martin Martel, in *Essays on the Sociology of Talcott Parsons* (transcript of interviews given 1973–74), 3; Parsons, "Clarence Ayres," 176.

20. Walton Hamilton, *Current Economic Problems*, 3d ed. (1925; reprint, Chicago: University of Chicago Press, 1927 [1st ed., 1915]), xi, 1, 2, 65, 904, 905; W. Hamilton,

Parsons's coursework with Ayres reinforced these teachings and exposed him to several other major currents of early twentieth-century thought. Under Ayres, he read from Cooley and Dewey, Veblen and Sumner, Maine, Morgan, Sapir and Lowie, and even Emile Durkheim, and became familiar with some of the pressing issues in American social science at the time: the relationship between the individual and society, the role of culture in shaping inherited psychological attributes, the nature of biological evolution, the stages of social and moral evolution, the extent of intersocietal differences, and the contributions to these questions of recent work by behaviorists, anthropologists, sociologists, and others.

Parsons laid out his own views on such matters in two term papers for Ayres's course which he preserved all his life, "The Theory of Human Behavior in Its Individual and Social Aspects" and "A Behavioristic Conception of the Nature of Morals," both of which display analytical powers in advance of his years and opinions in accord with the contemporary avant-garde. The object of the papers was both to criticize thinkers who would reduce human life to psychological, biological, or other natural-scientific forces and to insist that "the individual . . . is inevitably a member of a social group, and that he begins that membership in a plastic, unformed state in which every influence will have an almost unbelievable effect on him." [21] Accordingly, it was Parsons's view that "culture," rather than nature, is the decisive factor, with different societies exhibiting "almost infinite variation" in their cultural arrangements or "moral order." He argued, further, that the structure of a "moral order" is related to a society's technology, to its regulative institutions (which are necessary to prevent individual "impulses and whims" from igniting "conflict"), and to its religious rites and ceremonies—the last being significant because (as he wrote, quoting Durkheim) "in any society that has existed to date, ritual has always been one of the most important elements in the mores." [22] But Parsons rejected the assumption of "the unilinear theory of moral evolution" that "a culture advanced in technology is also advanced in morals, in institutions, [and] in ritual." [23] To him, the relationship

Industrial Policy and Institutionalism: Selected Essays (Clifton, N.J.: Kelley, 1974 [essays originally published 1915–18]), no pagination.

21. Parsons, "The Theory of Human Behavior in Its Individual and Social Aspects" (1922), 7, Talcott Parsons Papers, Harvard University Archives, Cambridge, Mass. (hereafter cited as Parsons Papers).

22. Ibid., 13; Parsons, "A Behavioristic Conception of the Nature of Morals" (1923), 1–5, Parsons Papers.

23. Parsons, "Nature of Morals," 20–21.

among social phenomena is more complex and will only be unravelled through an application of the genetic method that would seek to understand the distinctive moral patterns of "modern industrial civilization" by tracing them "back to early enough stages to . . . account for the peculiar character they may bear." [24]

In 1924, Parsons graduated from Amherst magna cum laude, closing his college career with a commencement-day speech that is said to have advanced proposals for social and economic reform in the United States.[25] Thereafter, finding himself little attracted to American graduate programs, he accepted an offer from his uncle to finance a year of study abroad and attended the London School of Economics (as a nondegree student) from October 1924 until June 1925. While there, he met another American economics student, Helen Walker, who became his wife in 1927. He also encountered one of the most distinguished and productive social science faculties in contemporary Europe.[26] This encounter was somewhat fortuitous, since Parsons was initially attracted to the LSE by the presence there of two leading Social Democrats, Harold Laski and Richard H. Tawney.[27] But the courses that he audited offered him far more than expected. During his stay, he did attend Tawney's lectures, as well as those of the proto-institutional economist Edwin Cannan, a noted historian of economic thought and critic of the work of Alfred Marshall; and the two were presumably the sources of the background he recalled acquiring at the LSE "on the industrial revolution in England and hence, more generally, [on] the antecedents of modern industrial society." [28] At the same time, he received his first "formal" introduction to sociology, learning "a great deal" about the subject from L. T. Hobhouse, Britain's first professor of sociology, and Morris Ginsberg, his protégé.[29] Through Ginsberg, Parsons also became aware of the great functionalist anthropologist Bronislaw Malinowski, with whom he then took two courses, including one that formed the basis of Malinowski's *Magic, Science, and Religion.*

"It was a very fruitful academic year," as Parsons later put it, and

24. Parsons, "Theory of Human Behavior," 12; Parsons, "Nature of Morals," 12.
25. FBI file.
26. William Beveridge, *The London School of Economics and Its Problems, 1919–1937* (London: Allen and Unwin, 1960), 50–51; Abraham Flexner, *Universities: American, English, German* (New York: Oxford University Press, 1930), 240.
27. Martel, "Parsons, Talcott," 610.
28. Parsons, "Richard Henry Tawney (1880–1962)," *American Sociological Review* 27 (1962): 888; Parsons, *Social Systems and the Evolution of Action Theory* (New York: Free Press, 1977), 18.
29. Parsons, "My Intellectual Development," 4.

one that reinforced "the Hamilton-Ayres point of view." [30] Malinowski's treatment of "primitive" societies, in particular, seems to have
strengthened in him both the idea that cultures are systems of inter-
connected parts, irreducible to biological forces, and the belief that
societies exhibit wide institutional variation and therefore elude
simple evolutionary formulas, especially those assuming the decline of
religion and rise of scientific rationalism. [31] But interesting though this
work in anthropology was, even more attractive to Parsons was the
field of sociology, where he was "impressed by [Hobhouse], both personally and intellectually, especially through his writings." [32] According to Parsons, "Hobhouse was the first model of 'the sociologist' conspicuously presented to me when I became an apprentice aspiring to
professional status in that field." [33] This was during the last phase of
Hobhouse's career, the phase associated with his *Social Development,*
a work distinguished by its anti-Spencerian approach to social evolution and conceptualization of social progress not as an automatic, unilinear process, but as one dependent on a complex configuration of
conditions, among them the guidance of human will. In Hobhouse's
view, sociology actually "has the web of human purpose as its main
subject"; it thus confronts the fact that "there must be some unity
which holds the jarring elements [of social life] together." [34] Taking
this starting point, he defined "the social factor" as human "interac-
tions [and] their consequences" (viz., institutions, ideas, and religious
and moral beliefs) and then argued that "orderly society . . . rests on
a system of common rules of behavior." [35] To suit this broad view of
the social, he proposed an expansive vision of sociology as including
both "social philosophy" and the study of "the various forms of interaction [that are] the subject-matter of several special sciences. Competitive industry [gives] rise to economics, and the action and interaction of political institutions, organized parties, and unorganized
individuals to modern political and social psychology. All such spe-

30. Parsons, "An Approach to Psychological Theory in Terms of the Theory of Ac-
tion," in *Psychology: A Study of a Science,* vol. 3, ed. Sigmund Koch (New York:
McGraw-Hill, 1959), 620; Parsons, "Dialogues with Parsons," 4; Parsons, "Clarence
Ayres," 177.
    31. Barber, "Biographical Sketch," 349; Martel, "Parsons, Talcott," 610; Parsons,
"Malinowski and the Theory of Social Systems," in *Social Systems and the Evolution
of Action Theory* (original date of article 1957), 83–85.
    32. Parsons, *Evolution of Action Theory,* 18.
    33. Ibid.
    34. L. T. Hobhouse, *Social Development* (1924; reprint, London: Allen and Unwin,
1966), 12, 37.
    35. Ibid., 41, 210–12.

cialisms belong to the field of sociology which ideally would . . . be their synthesis. . . . That is to say, sociology is concerned with the relation of the parts in a whole," [36] with "the general character of social relations [as well as] the nature and determining conditions of social development." [37]

This viewpoint made sociology, or social philosophy, similar to what the institutionalists at Amherst had called economics—or so Parsons apparently observed to Walton Hamilton, who responded in May 1925, "as you remarked in your last letter, the various social studies are all tangled together, and it doesn't matter particularly what one calls himself. I think that one can do almost anything in economics that one can do in philosophy. . . . Economics, too, has one advantage in giving a somewhat surer claim to an income." [38] Whether or not this was useful advice, the whole matter was soon further complicated for Parsons by experiences resulting from a decision he had recently reached to go from England to Germany. The decision, as he explains it, was made possible by "a German-American exchange fellowship program, which had been instituted just during that year [as] a gesture of reconciliation after the first World War. One of my Amherst teachers, Professor Otto Manthey-Zorn, was a member of the American committee and [proposed that] I should apply. I did so and was awarded a fellowship and without having any personal say in the matter, was assigned to [the University of] Heidelberg." [39] Of the wisdom of remaining abroad, Edward Parsons was apparently dubious; as Manthey-Zorn reminded the younger Parsons, "your father evidently thinks that it would be more advantageous for you to spend a year or two teaching so as to give you time to shake down your ideas, especially as to the problem that you would like to study." [40] But despite this (and the meagerness of his fellowship), Talcott Parsons persisted, proceeding to Heidelberg in June 1925, then to Vienna for an intensive summer course in German, then back to Heidelberg for the 1925/26 academic year.

This sojourn took place during what was, of course, a period of mounting internal and external crisis in German higher education. It

36. Ibid., 213.

37. Hobhouse (1916) as cited by Philip Abrams, *The Origins of British Sociology: 1834–1914* (Chicago: University of Chicago Press, 1968), 135.

38. Walton Hamilton to Parsons, 15 May 1925, Parsons Papers.

39. Parsons, "The Circumstances of My Encounter with Max Weber," in *Sociological Traditions from Generation to Generation*, ed. Robert K. Merton and Matilda White Riley (Norwood, N.J.: Ablex, 1980), 38.

40. Otto Manthey-Zorn to Parsons, 25 February 1925, Parsons Papers.

was Parsons's luck, however, that although the University of Heidelberg was not entirely insulated from the growing tensions, it "was still
the major intellectual center of the German academic world" and preserved, in the relatively democratic sociopolitical atmosphere of
Baden, many of the traditions of the prestigious small-town university
composed of a community of scholars.[41] This is certainly how Parsons
saw it: "At Heidelberg I came into contact with what most would
regard as the very best of German culture in the early part of this
century, building on the great traditions of the German universities of
the nineteenth century. . . . The dangers which eventuated in the Nazi
movement were simply not evident at the time."[42] What was evident
was an unanticipated store of intellectual offerings, which further "reinforced" the interests that he had formed at Amherst.[43]

Integral to this was his discovery of Max Weber, who had died five
years earlier but whose ideas still dominated the local intellectual
scene. While unaware of Weber prior to arriving in Heidelberg, Parsons was captivated immediately by reading his work, especially *Die
protestantische Ethik und der Geist des Kapitalismus,* in part no
doubt because of the book's relevance in the light of Parsons's own
Protestant upbringing. Accenting this exposure to Weber's work was
Parsons's encounter with surviving members of the Weber circle, including Marianne Weber and Else von Jaffe-Richthofen (into whose
salons Parsons was invited on several occasions), younger thinkers like
Alexander von Schelting and Karl Mannheim, and such distinguished
figures as Weber's younger brother, the political sociologist Alfred Weber, and the philosopher Karl Jaspers.[44] From the latter three, Parsons
actually took courses, including a seminar on Max Weber with Mannheim, and another on Kant with Jaspers, whose own thinking already
rested on the idea of various antinomies positioned in irreconcilable
conflict and yet moving toward "convergence" and "synthesis." Chief
among these antinomies was the opposition of "positivism and idealism" (Jaspers's terminology) and of "two irreducible and contrasting
methods, explanation from established causes and explanation from
intelligible motives."[45]

41. Edward Shils, "Mannheim, Karl," *International Encyclopedia of the Social Sciences,* ed. David L. Sills (New York: Macmillan, 1968), 9:447; Michael Stephen Stein-
berg, *Sabers and Brown Shirts: The German Students' Path to National Socialism,
1918–1935* (Chicago: University of Chicago Press, 1973), 23–24, 27, 44–45.

42. Parsons, *Politics and Social Structure* (New York: Free Press, 1969), 59–60.

43. Parsons, "Approach to Psychological Theory," 620.

44. Parsons, "Encounter with Max Weber," 37–43.

45. The quotations are from the analysis of Jaspers by Dieter Henrich, "Karl Jaspers:
Thinking with Max Weber in Mind," in *Max Weber and His Contemporaries,* ed. Wolf-

In addition, Parsons studied with Emil Lederer, "the leading academic socialist of Germany of the 1920's,"[46] who apparently encouraged his reading of Marx, and with Edgar Salin, a young economist who had recently published a brief volume entitled *Geschichte der Volkswirtschaftslehre*.[47] In this, he offered a sweeping examination of economic thought through the ages, which paid particular attention to the classical and neoclassical theorists (e.g., Malthus, Ricardo, Pareto, Marshall) and to historicist and socialist thinkers, and then culminated in an appreciative treatment of two men, Werner Sombart and Max Weber. According to Salin, the field of economics was "divided between two diametrically opposed points of view giving rise to two essentially different types of theory": on the one hand, "the individualist, rationalist, analytic, natural science approach [deriving from] English utilitarianism and atomism" and, on the other hand, an approach (which he preferred) that gave expression to an "organic theory of society, the state and economic life" and was rooted in German romanticism's emphasis on the "organic growth . . . of symbols and cultures, and [on the tradition's tendency] to oppose the conception of a developing and living whole to the notions of causally linked atoms and of rationally grouped individuals."[48] When Parsons realized that Heidelberg's course requirements were modest enough that he could make substantial progress, during the tenure of his fellowship, toward a doctor of philosophy degree (something he had not originally intended to seek), he chose Salin as his advisor for a dissertation on the concept of "capitalism," a topic in line with much of his work during the preceding five years. Upon Salin's advice, he confined this project to an examination of German literature on the subject, especially the writings of Marx, Sombart, and Weber.[49] Writing from Amherst in February 1926, Manthey-Zorn backed the plan, commenting to Parsons that "Sombart is probably quite well known here; but there ought to be especial value in a good introduction to Weber's work. At all events I would go for the thesis just as hard as I could.

gang Mommsen and Jurgen Osterhammel (London: Allen and Unwin, 1987), 533–36. For Jaspers on "positivism" and "idealism," see his *Philosophy*, 3 vols., trans. E. B. Ashton (London: University of Chicago Press, 1971 [original date 1932]), vol. 1, chap. 4, and vol. 3, pp. 188–92. For Parsons's view of Jaspers, see Parsons, "Jaspers, Karl," in *Biographical Supplement* to *The International Encyclopedia of the Social Sciences*, 18:341–45.

46. Joseph A. Schumpeter, *History of Economic Analysis*, ed. Elizabeth Boody Schumpeter (1954; reprint, New York: Oxford University Press, 1966), 884 n. 10.

47. Edgar Salin (Berlin: Springer, 1923).

48. Edgar Salin, "Romantic and Universalist Economics," in *Encyclopaedia of the Social Sciences*, ed. Edwin R. A. Seligman (New York: Macmillan, 1931), 5:385, 387.

49. Parsons, "Dialogues with Parsons," 4.

[I]f you threw [it] away . . . and the push that Salin evidently is giving you toward it, you would be letting go the best of your opportunities." [50]

That Parsons did not do. By the summer semester of 1926 he presented two of the three planned chapters of his thesis to Salin, who evidently approved them. He then returned to America, where Manthey-Zorn had arranged a one-year instructorship in the Amherst Department of Economics. Here Parsons served as a tutor in freshman economics and taught his own senior course, "Recent European Social Developments and Social Theories," the announcement for which advertised the examination of "the leading problems and principles of sociology . . . in light of . . . changes in Europe since the industrial revolution, [with] special attention [to] England and Germany." [51] Parsons found that this pair of assignments "allowed time for a good deal of work on [the] dissertation" and apparently also for preparing for his upcoming oral examinations in Heidelberg, in the two "minor" fields of modern European history and modern philosophy, and in the two "major" fields of economic theory and sociological theory. [52]

Not surprisingly, it is to this period—when he was teaching an economics and a sociology course and studying for orals in both fields— that Parsons subsequently traced the emergence of his concern with "the relations between economic and sociological theory." [53] During the same period, Parsons also decided to pursue additional graduate work in the United States, and in early 1927 he considered the programs of several major economics and sociology departments in the East and Midwest. [54] By this point, though, he was involved in discussions with his department chairman, Richard Meriam, who had recently arrived from the Harvard economics department. Through these discussions, Parsons became convinced that his prior training in economics "was way off the main track." He was therefore quick to accept when Meriam arranged for Harvard to offer him a nonfaculty instructorship, a position that would make it possible to earn a modest income while attending graduate courses as a nondegree candi-

50. Otto Manthey-Zorn to Parsons, 21 February 1926, Parsons Papers.

51. Ibid.; George D. Olds to Parsons, 15 April 1926, Parsons Papers.

52. Parsons, "Building Social Systems," 827; Parsons, "Encounter with Max Weber," 40.

53. Parsons, "My Intellectual Development," 5; Parsons, "Building Social Systems," 827; Parsons, "Encounter with Max Weber," 40–41.

54. Paul Douglas (of the University of Chicago) to Parsons, 14 February 1927; John M. Gaus (of the University of Minnesota) to Parsons, 8 February 1927; Walton Hamilton (then of the Robert Brookings Graduate School) to Parsons, 25 January 1927; L. C. Marshall (of the University of Chicago) to Parsons, 24 January 1927—all in Parsons Papers.

date.[55] Before assuming the position, however, Parsons briefly returned to Heidelberg to finish his degree requirements, earning on 29 July 1927 the grade of "sehr gut" for his oral and written work from his examining committee (Salin, Alfred Weber, Jaspers, and the historian Willy Andreas), and receiving on Salin's written report the prediction that "this author is guaranteed to bring honor to this university in the U.S.A."[56] In the fall of 1927, with all this behind him, Talcott Parsons arrived at the center of orthodox economic thought in America, the Department of Economics at Harvard University.

Phase I. Capitalist Society and Its Origins

The writings that Parsons published in the decade between his arrival at Harvard and the appearance, in late 1937, of *The Structure of Social Action* fall into three overlapping but relatively distinct thematic areas or clusters, which may also be viewed as approximate chronological phases in the early development of his thinking. These are not discrete phases, however, for Parsons was already at work on the second while the first was underway and was likewise at work on the third before his writings in either of the other two areas were completed. Consequently, some of the last-written items from the first two thematic clusters diverge noticeably from earlier-written items, differing in ways indicative of the path along which his ideas were moving during the period. All three phases reveal the deep embeddedness of Parsons's thought in his immediate sociointellectual experiences, though the base of those experiences expanded over the course of the decade as his years at Harvard, which are discussed in the next section, presented opportunities and problems beyond those associated with his upbringing, college education, and initial postgraduate work.

While the impact of these earliest experiences persisted throughout the whole decade, it was most direct during the first phase of Parsons's work. The chief characteristic of this phase was Parsons's embrace of the "institutionalist" project, as implanted at Amherst and reinforced in London and Heidelberg: that is, his desire to understand the distinctive characteristics of the modern economic order as components of a broader sociocultural matrix and to illuminate the process by

55. Parsons, "My Intellectual Development," 5; Parsons, "Building Social Systems," 628; Parsons, "Clarence Ayres," 177.

56. Cited by Wolfgang Schluchter, "Statt einer Einleitung Ansprache zur Eroffnung des wissenschaftlichen Kolloquiums zu Ehren von Talcott Parsons," in *Verhalten, Handeln, und System: Talcott Parsons' Beitrag zur der Sozialwissenschaften*, ed. Wolfgang Schluchter (Frankfurt am Main: Schurkamp Verlag, 1980), 15.

which that order developed. For reasons outlined in the following sections, Parsons avoided identifying these concerns with institutionalism per se. To the contrary: what appears, whenever his early writings speak of "institutional economics," is not an approving mention of the ideas of his Amherst mentors, but a critical attack upon the psychologism and biologism of the best-known forerunners of institutionalism, Thorstein Veblen and the quantitative economist Wesley Mitchell. But Parsons's rejection of these positions (which extends back to his college term papers) was for several years accompanied by a sustained engagement with the problems posed by the "institutionalists" whom he encountered in America and Europe.

This is most evident in his first solo publication, "'Capitalism' in Recent German Literature" (chapter 1 of this volume), which appeared in late 1928 and early 1929 in two installments in one of America's top economics journals, *The Journal of Political Economy*. It has long been assumed that this essay was published "out of" Parsons's dissertation, though it would now seem that the article itself is what fulfilled the Heidelberg thesis requirement.[57] Apparently when Parsons returned to Heidelberg in the summer of 1927 to complete the third chapter of his dissertation, his first two chapters could no longer be located. However, since Parsons was not responsible for their disappearance, Salin allowed his thesis defense to take place with only the third chapter—entitled "Der Geist des Kapitalismus bei Sombart und Max Weber"—in hand. At this point formal award of the doctor of philosophy certificate was still contingent upon publication of the thesis; but when Parsons subsequently published *The Journal of Political Economy* article, which was substantially equivalent with the third thesis chapter, the Heidelberg faculty accepted this as the definitive dissertation, resulting in the award of the degree in April 1929.[58]

The primary purpose of the article is, as Parsons says, "to put . . . before American readers . . . two great theories of capitalism" recently developed in Germany, those of Sombart and Weber. Apparently accepting the advice of Manthey-Zorn and others about the value of importing this body of work, Parsons hoped, as he later recalled, to take "the leadership in the introduction of German sociology into this country."[59] Why the German theories merited consideration is a question the article addresses by contrasting their approach with that of

57. Parsons, *Evolution of Action Theory*, 273 n. 3.
58. Schluchter, "Einleitung," 14.
59. Parsons to Jeffrey Alexander, 19 January 1979. Letter in possession of Jeffrey C. Alexander, Department of Sociology, University of California–Los Angeles.

the "liberal, orthodox" tradition of Anglo-American thought. The hallmark of the latter tradition—Parsons asserts, along the lines of those like Hamilton and Salin—is an "individualistic and rationalistic" outlook which, in the field of economics proper, has produced theories of "abstract generality" that purport to have "universal applicability" and, in the broader field of social theory, has spawned "the hypothesis of continuous evolution as held by most Western sociologists," whose linear suppositions yield an "overhasty optimism" about "progress and freedom" under capitalist conditions.

Parsons blames this pervasive outlook for neglect both on "the economic problems connected with the growth and development of types of economic society, [and on] the differences between . . . different cultural epochs." In his assessment, the great virtue of the work of Sombart and Weber is that it squarely confronts such issues, especially in relation to "the problem of modern capitalism." Particularly important here are Sombart's and Weber's concept of an economic "spirit"—a term that captures "the *differences* between mental attitudes at different times and places"—and the efforts of the two thinkers to identify the characteristic "spirit of modern capitalism," to relate it to modern civilization as a whole, and to use it to explain capitalism's historical development, until its atrophy into "a dead, mechanized [system] in which there is no room left for . . . creative [human] forces." Discussing the last issue, Parsons broaches the subject of Marxism, commending some of Marx's ideas, but objecting to a purely "economic interpretation of history." No less critical of Sombart's swing in the opposite direction, however, Parsons already makes clear his preference for Weber's campaign against "one-sided" interpretations. It is interesting, though, that except on this point, the article tends to favor Sombart over Weber. While uncritically presenting Sombart's "genetic treatment of the development" of capitalism as a "theoretical" approach to history that "marks a great advance over the . . . disconnected studies of historical facts" by the " 'mere' historian," Parsons expresses considerable skepticism about Weber's ideal-type method, which he attacks for confusing general concepts with historically specific ones, thus illegitimately "break[ing] up . . . organically connected historical individuals."

Such difficulties notwithstanding, Parsons concludes that the German theorists' approach to capitalism remains a "very fruitful" one and one that requires no sacrifice of the achievements of orthodox economic theory. With his coursework at Harvard now underway, Parsons seeks to balance his critical observations on the orthodox tradition with some appreciative comments about "the many important developments in [modern] economic theory"—from which point he confidently predicts (in the language of Jaspers and Meiklejohn) the development of a "higher synthesis" that would incorporate both the Anglo-American and the German contributions.

As to what such a synthesis might look like, Parsons as of yet gives little clue. It bears notice, though, that he sees both of these intellectual traditions as deficient in their understanding of socialism: orthodox liberal thought because of its naive glorification of the capitalist era, Sombart and Weber because of their inability to envisage genuine alternatives to the mechanized forces which they associate with this era. Taking issue both with the "determinism" of Sombart (and Marx), which renders the individual "powerless to change" historical tendencies, and with Weber's assumption that socialism too would succumb to bureaucratic domination, Parsons observes that "the present-day power of the bureaucratic mechanism [may be] due to a very special set of circumstances which do not involve the necessity for its continued dominance" and, further, that "there seems to be little reason to believe that it is not possible on the basis which we now have to build by a continuous process something more nearly approaching an ideal society. . . . This is precisely what socialism wishes to do."

Since Sombart and Weber are the focus of the article, Parsons does not elaborate his own position on socialism, and rarely does the topic come up again in his early published work. *The Structure of Social Action* reiterates his approving 1931 remark about "a collectivist state where the whole process of production and allocation of resources was in the hands of a single centralized body working in the general interests,"[60] but this is fairly atypical. With the American electoral realignment of the 1930s and the replacement of the Republican regime by a Democratic administration, Parsons became a staunch New Deal liberal.[61] By this time, questions about fundamental social reorganization ceased to figure significantly in his thinking about the emerging intellectual synthesis. That this is so does not mean, however, that larger sociopolitical conditions and events ceased to attract Parsons's attention. As his view of the social world took shape, he remained deeply conscious of the role in his own society of inequality,

60. Parsons, "Wants and Activities in Marshall," *Quarterly Journal of Economics* 46 (1931): 126; Parsons, *The Structure of Social Action*, 2d ed. (1949; reprint, New York: Free Press, 1968 [original date 1937]), 152–53.

61. Parsons, "The Point of View of the Author," in *The Social Theories of Talcott Parsons*, ed. Max Black (1961; reprint, Carbondale: Southern Illinois University Press, 1976), 350.

force, and fraud, of the realities of the Depression and the rise of Nazism, and of the fragility of "the era of the great war, of communist and fascist revolutions, of oil scandals and Kruger debacles," and on occasion some of these concerns surface directly in his writings.[62]

Before pressing on with his own work, however, Parsons took further steps to awaken American audiences to the writings of his great Heidelberg discovery, Max Weber. The most important of these was his translation of *Die protestantische Ethik*, a project he conceived of during the Heidelberg summer of 1927 in consultation with Marianne Weber. Parsons apparently worked on this translation immediately after finishing his thesis, securing a major publisher for it (via help from some Heidelberg associates and Harvard faculty members) after addressing the manuscript reviewers' objections to some of the specifics of the translation. The work appeared (along with his translation of Weber's "Einleitung" to the *Gesammelte Aufsätze zur Religionssoziologie*) in the summer of 1930, accompanied by a brief preface by Parsons and a more substantial foreword by his professor at the LSE, R. H. Tawney.[63]

Around the same time, Parsons published a review of Henri Sée's *Modern Capitalism*, which had recently been translated by two colleagues from the Harvard Business School (chapter 2).[64] A short work of popularization by France's premier comparative economic historian, Sée's book had already been enthusiastically received in the Harvard-based *Quarterly Journal of Economics*, which presented it as a "valuable complement" to the work of Weber.[65] But, writing again in *The Journal of Political Economy*, Parsons ventured a less positive assessment. A striking characteristic of all Parsons's early book reviews, starting with this first one, is that they are far less concerned

62. The quotation is from Parsons as cited by William Buxton, *Talcott Parsons and the Capitalist Nation-State* (Toronto: University of Toronto Press, 1985), 282. For discussion of the early Parsons in relation to the contemporary socio-political situation, see also Jeffrey C. Alexander, *Twenty Lectures: Sociological Theory Since World War II* (New York: Columbia University Press, 1987), 22–23; Charles Camic, "*Structure* after 50 Years: The Anatomy of a Charter," *American Journal of Sociology* 95 (1989): 40–42; and Alvin W. Gouldner, *The Coming Crisis of Western Sociology* (1970; reprint New York: Avon, 1971). See also chapter 19 of this volume.

63. Max Weber, *The Protestant Ethic and the Spirit of Capitalism,* trans. and with a preface by Talcott Parsons (1930; reprint, New York: Scribner's, 1958), ix–xi.

64. Henri Sée, *Modern Capitalism: Its Origin and Evolution,* trans. Homer B. Vanderblue and Georges F. Doriot (1928; reprint, New York: Kelley, 1968 [original date 1926]).

65. M. M. Knight, "Review: Recent Literature on the Origins of Modern Capitalism," *Quarterly Journal of Economics* 41 (1927): 521.

with describing and evaluating books in terms of their authors' objectives than they are with judging them by their proximity to Parsons's own position; it is this characteristic that makes these reviews valuable for understanding his ideas. Thus, in the instance of Sée's book, one sees that while Parsons allows its usefulness, he says virtually nothing about what others, both then and since, have recognized as Sée's main argument, viz., that the rise of modern capitalism was caused significantly by a configuration of commercial and financial factors.[66] For all his interest in the development of capitalism, Parsons passes over Sée's theory of its emergence only then to write Sée off as a historian engaged merely in the "recital of bald facts," uninformed by an interpretive viewpoint. What attracts Parsons's attention instead are Sée's comments on Sombart and Weber, for while respectful, these comments diverged from the more favorable judgment the two thinkers reached in his own previous work. Confronted with the discrepancy, the review simply declares that it is not Sée but Sombart and Weber who raise "the really important" problems, those concerning "the attitude of men to their economic life" and "the cultural significance of capitalism."

This same point of view is evident in four little-known articles that Parsons was commissioned to write for volumes of the *Encyclopaedia of the Social Sciences* that appeared between 1930 and 1934. The details surrounding these commissions are obscure. Possibly Parsons was recommended for the articles by Edwin Gay, the Harvard economic historian who was also one of the *Encyclopaedia*'s advisory editors in economics. Trained in German historical economics, Gay was sympathetic to Parsons's scholarly interests and was one of his principal supporters during his initial years at Harvard.[67] Be that as it may, the *Encyclopaedia* articles bring to light the neglected empirical dimension of Parsons's early work; two of them examine actual historical figures, John Calvin (chapter 3) and Samuel Smiles (chapter 4), while the other two analyze a pair of concrete phenomena that had been discussed by economists, service (chapter 5) and thrift (chapter 6). Throughout the four pieces, Parsons retains the institutionalist concern with the nature and origins of the distinctive features of the mod-

66. Sée, *Modern Capitalism,* 177–86. For discussion of his argument, see M. M. Knight, "Origins of Modern Capitalism"; M. M. Knight, "Henri Sée," in *Architects and Craftsmen in History: Festschrift für Abbott Payson Usher* (Tübingen: J. C. B. Mohr [Siebeck], 1956); Harold T. Parker, "Henri Sée (1864–1936)," in *Some Historians of Modern Europe,* ed. Bernadette E. Schmitt (1942; reprint, Port Washington, N.Y.: Kennikat Press, 1966).
67. Parsons, "Building Social Systems," 827,832.

ern economic order—the "new economic society," as he calls it in the article on Calvin—and then applies to his subject an interpretation that is a direct extension of Weber's ideas in *The Protestant Ethic*.

In good institutionalist fashion, the articles on service and thrift, for example, object to explaining the two phenomena in individualistic, utilitarian terms, rather than by reference to developments in the larger sociocultural order. According to Parsons, both thrift (acts of saving, or resource accumulation) and service (acts that promote the ends of others) acquired their modern forms only gradually with the breakdown of age-old traditionalistic arrangements. Students of Parsons's later writings will be struck with the anticipations here of the pattern-variable scheme, particularly in the contrast between "diffuse," "personal" service provision and "specific," "impersonal" service. To account for the emergence of the modern forms, Parsons generally lays great stress on changes in ultimate ends and values, changes he links (following his understanding of Weber) to the development of religious attitudes due to the rise of Calvinism and to the subsequent "widespread secularization" and atrophy of ethical motivations. On the whole, there is an idealist tendency in the *Encyclopaedia* articles toward crediting religious factors more heavily than political and economic conditions, though this is less so in "Thrift," arguably the tour de force of this phase of Parsons's work. Here Parsons explores the interplay between religious motives and the concrete circumstances that affect the development of thrift, among them the degree of individual embeddedness in primary groups and the extent to which individuals have confidence that the future will allow them to reap the fruits of their current savings. Focusing on such factors, he examines (in a manner reminiscent of Weber's treatment of the religious propensities of different social strata) the ways in which "attitudes toward thrift have varied . . . in different cultures and on the part of different classes," a topic that leads to the observation that "laissez-faire capitalism" has imposed on the "propertyless laboring class . . . conditions [that] are highly unfavorable to thrift."

The last of Parsons's early publications with capitalist society and its origins as the main theme is an essay that bears the marks of several changes underway in his thinking by the mid-1930s. The essay (chapter 7) is a long review, invited in late 1934 by the economist Frank Knight for *The Journal of Political Economy*,[68] of H. M. Robertson's *Aspects of the Rise of Economic Individualism*. This was a book by a young British-trained economic historian critical of *The Protestant*

68. Frank Knight to Parsons, 25 October 1934, Parsons Papers.

Ethic and of the "sociological method" of ideal-type construction and eager to show that "material conditions" (especially commercial conditions), rather than religious attitudes, influenced the rise of capitalism.[69] By this date, however, Parsons had become, as he says, "a sociologist by profession." Despite his own objections elsewhere to the ideal-type method, therefore, he could no more abide this assault upon the sociological method than he could pass lightly over Robertson's weak criticisms of the very aspects of Weber's work that he had been popularizing. Thus, setting aside much of Robertson's historical analysis, Parsons's review launches an aggressive but astute attack upon the book's critical thesis, combining this with a defense of Weber's multifactor explanation of the emergence of modern capitalism. In the process, the review reveals two important shifts in Parsons's own thinking: first, his movement away from a genetic method that would trace the antecedents of modern civilization as a whole, and toward a method aiming to "break . . . a given phenomenon . . . down into the various causal elements which go to make it up"; second, the conversion of his earlier belief that secularization erodes the ethical factors in economic life into the idea that, secularization notwithstanding, "the element of positive ethical value . . . still remains as a basic element in the modern economic order." These shifts point to new developments that brought to an end the institutionalist phase of Parsons's work.

The Early Years at Harvard

Parsons arrived at Harvard during the final years of the presidency of A. Lawrence Lowell. This was a time, according to historians of the university, of Harvard's retreat "into its golden shell," a time of gradual decline (evident to contemporaries within and without the institution) in faculty research quality and of increased emphasis on educating a generally apolitical, complacent, and homogeneous undergraduate population.[70]

In the face of these trends, Harvard's Department of Economics

---

69. H. M. Robertson, *Aspects of the Rise of Economic Individualism: A Criticism of Max Weber and His School* (1933; reprint, Clifton, N.J.: Kelley, 1973), ix–xiv, 205–6.

70. The quotation is from Richard Norton Smith, *The Harvard Century* (New York: Simon and Schuster, 1986), 86. See this book, along with Lipset, "Political Controversies," 1–278; and David Riesman, "Educational Reform at Harvard College," in *Education and Politics at Harvard*, by Lipset and Riesman, 279–401, for general introductions to this period in Harvard's history.

held out with some success, preserving its long-standing reputation as America's front-ranking center of research and graduate training in classical and neoclassical economics.[71] Just prior to Parsons's arrival, the department lost Allyn Young, a prominent theorist with whom Parsons planned to study; but its faculty still consisted of "an outstanding group of value theorists," economists whose interest lay generally in the development and refinement of the marginal utility theory of value, as originally formulated by Jevons, Menger, and Walras and worked out more fully by Alfred Marshall, Vilfredo Pareto, J. B. Clark and others.[72] These Harvard economists constituted Parsons's main reference group in his first years at the institution. During the 1927/28 year and much of the year following, he "spent the great bulk of [his] time attending courses and seminars" offered by members of the group and made contact with the majority of its senior figures (Gay, Frank W. Taussig, Thomas Nixon Carver, W. Z. Ripley, Joseph Schumpeter), as well as with some of its younger members (Overton Taylor, Edward Mason, Karl Bigelow, Edward Chamberlin, Seymour Harris).[73]

From this list of distinguished names, two were especially important, Taussig and Schumpeter. Taussig, then the dean of American economists, was at once "the staunchest of orthodox thinkers"[74] and a firm believer, as he put it, in "the imperative need of bearing in mind the complexities of real life," and incorporating into economic research the insights of the other social sciences.[75] Taussig was also the leading American exponent of the ideas of Marshall and conducted the courses on economic theory where Parsons "acquired a really thorough acquaintance with the work of Marshall."[76] Schumpeter, the wide-ranging Austrian theorist, was a visiting member of the Harvard faculty during the 1927/28 year (as he was again in 1931, before accepting a permanent appointment in 1932). In that year, Parsons sat in on his course "General Economics," where he gained further ex-

71. Edward S. Mason, "The Harvard Department of Economics from the Beginning to World War II," *Quarterly Journal of Economics* 97 (1982): 383–433.

72. Joseph Dorfman, *The Economic Mind in American Civilization* (New York: Viking, 1959), 4–5: 236.

73. Parsons, "My Intellectual Development," 5; Parsons, "Building Social Systems," 827, 833; Parsons, "Clarence Ayres," 277.

74. Dorfman, *Economic Mind*, 600.

75. Cited by Robert L. Church, "The Economists Study Society: Sociology at Harvard, 1891–1902," in *Social Sciences at Harvard, 1860–1920*, ed. Paul Buck (Cambridge, Mass.: Harvard University Press, 1965), 87.

76. Parsons, "My Intellectual Development," 6.

posure to Marshallian economics and was deeply impressed by Schumpeter's case for economic theory as a bounded analytical system abstracted from concrete reality.[77]

Parsons's coursework at Harvard was more, however, than a bridge carrying him out to thinkers like Marshall. It was also the forum in which, as he later wrote, "I really learned my orientation to economics. This was a very different orientation from that which I had absorbed from Hamilton and . . . Ayres." [78] The difference was apparent in two related areas. The first was the subject matter of economics. Where his Amherst teachers had made economics the study of the problems of the modern industrial order, understood in terms of a larger matrix of cultural developments and social institutions, Parsons's training in economics at Harvard put him in full touch with the orthodox view that economics can neither encompass the whole of social life nor adequately treat the specific constellation of institutions found in particular times. The discipline of history may attempt the latter task, but "economic science" itself is necessarily abstractive or "selective," confining theoretical attention to the formulation of uniform or universal laws pertaining to certain "analytical" factors, "aspects," or "elements" in human action, particularly the rational satisfaction of human wants under conditions of "scarcity." [79] The second area of divergence concerned the relative place allotted in economic analysis to theory and to facts. For the institutionalists, priority belonged to the latter. Thought not opposed to theory, Parsons's Amherst mentors sought to replace the deductive formalism of orthodox theory with a greater "reliance . . . upon a scientific study of fact," the idea being that by "impartially gather[ing] the facts," economics could "formulate principles [for the] intelligent handling of [social] problems." [80] This was an idea echoed in Parsons's student papers, which hold that "about the only thing we can do is to get down and get all the facts we can possibly dig out and make such generalizations as we

77. Ibid.; Parsons, "Building Social Systems," 828–30; Parsons, "Higher Education as a Theoretical Focus," in *Institutions and Social Exchange,* ed. Herman Turk and Richard L. Simpson (Indianapolis: Bobbs-Merrill, 1971), 234.

78. Parsons, "Clarence Ayres," 177.

79. Thomas Nixon Carver, *Essays in Social Justice* (Cambridge, Mass.: Harvard University Press, 1932), 35–38; Schumpeter, *Economic Analysis,* 14, 34; F. W. Taussig, *Principles of Economics,* 2 vols. (New York: Macmillan, 1911), 1:5; Allyn A. Young, "Economics as a Field of Research," *Quarterly Journal of Economics* 42 (1927): 3–7. For a fuller discussion, see Charles Camic, "The Making of a Method," *American Sociological Review* 52 (1987): 421–39.

80. Hamilton, *Industrial Policy,* no pagination.

can piece out of them."[81] In contrast, the economists at Harvard assigned a much larger role to theory, not to the exclusion of facts, but in continual interaction with them. Taussig, for instance, maintained that what was "most needed for the advancement of economic science" was "a hunger for facts" combined with "strict and severe . . . deductive reasoning" from theoretical principles,[82] while Schumpeter argued that "factual work and 'theoretical' work [exist] in an endless relation of give and take, naturally testing one another and setting new tasks for each other": "there is not and there cannot be any fundamental opposition between 'theory' and 'fact finding,' let alone between deduction and induction."[83]

Parsons soon realized, as he came into increased contact with the contemporary economics literature, that these opposed viewpoints were of more than local significance. Not only did institutionalism and neoclassicism both have important spokesmen and followings outside of Amherst and Harvard, but the two groups were embroiled in such rancorous controversy that American economic thought of the interwar period was widely perceived to be in a state of "impasse" and "tangled confusion" over "the purpose, scope, and method of economics."[84] As Parsons was drawn into the issues of this controversy, he was in the privileged position of having studied with leaders from both camps and (all the more unusual) encountering the institutionalist dissent from orthodoxy *before* gaining systematic exposure to the orthodox position itself. When his Harvard training led him to accept the latter as his own "orientation to economics"—a move he regarded as "apostasy" against institutionalism[85]—it was with continuing awareness of the institutionalist criticisms of the neoclassical approach.

Contributing to this turnabout in Parsons's thinking was a related set of experiences that occurred during these years: his encounter with Harvard's reigning authorities on the nature and method of (natural) science, the philosopher Alfred North Whitehead and the biochemist Lawrence J. Henderson. Prior to this point the philosophy of science occupied relatively little of Parsons's attention. As a result of White-

81. Parsons, "Nature of Morals," 21.
82. F. W. Taussig, "Alfred Marshall," *Quarterly Journal of Economics* 39 (1924): 13–14.
83. Schumpeter, *Economic Analysis,* 42, 45.
84. Paul T. Homan, *Contemporary Economic Thought* (New York: Harper, 1928), 439, 465. For a more extended treatment, see Camic, "Making of a Method."
85. Parsons, "Clarence Ayres," 177, 179.

head's teachings, however, especially as represented in *Science and the Modern World,* he came to appreciate the importance not only of distinguishing in scientific work between "an *abstract* analytical scheme" and "concrete reality," but also of delineating the relationship of these two factors.[86] The fundamental lesson of the history of the natural sciences, according to Whitehead, was "that the utmost abstractions are the true weapons with which to control our thought of concrete fact." This was so because, even though science rests on "the supremacy of fact over thought" and the observation of "irreducible and stubborn facts," inevitably "observation is selection"—selection in terms of "a scheme of abstraction," whose ideal form is that of a "theory ... of an ideally isolated system" operating according to "general laws." But, even as he emphasized the importance of theory, Whitehead warned scientists of "the 'Fallacy of Misplaced Concreteness.' " This was an expression that Parsons would borrow throughout his life, and by it Whitehead meant the error of mistaking the abstract for the concrete, or the theoretical for the factual, since this mistake was what thwarted scientific progress toward "a more concrete analysis, which [is] nearer to the complete concreteness of our intuitive experience."[87]

If such ideas diverged from those of the institutionalists, they fit closely with the Harvard economists' own (less philosophically stated) methodological teachings on abstraction, selection, theory, facts, general laws, and so on. And these ideas were then strongly reinforced as Parsons read the writings of Vilfredo Pareto, a thinker who had been presented to him chiefly as an orthodox economist, but who he came to study, around the time of exposure to Whitehead, out of his new concern with "the general nature of scientific theory" and his continuing interest in "the relations between economic and sociological theory."[88] This choice was in line with contemporary tastes at Harvard, where Pareto had come into considerable vogue, primarily through the efforts of the distinguished local influential, L. J. Henderson.[89] Through their common interest in Pareto, Parsons also came into contact with Henderson himself, on an occasional basis in Par-

86. Parsons, "Dialogues with Parsons," 5.

87. Alfred North Whitehead, *Science and the Modern World* (1925; reprint, New York: Free Press, 1967), 16, 18, 32, 44–46, 66–67. For Parsons's own view of his debt to Whitehead, see Parsons, "Approach to Psychological Theory," 624–25; Parsons, "My Intellectual Development," 6; Parsons, "Dialogues with Parsons," 5.

88. Parsons, "My Intellectual Development," 7; Parsons, "Dialogues with Parsons," 6.

89. Parsons, "Dialogues with Parsons," 6.

sons's first years at Harvard, more frequently when he became a regular participant in Henderson's famous 1932–34 faculty seminar on Pareto, and intensively during the 1935–36 period, when the two met twice weekly for several months to go over the first draft of *The Structure of Social Action*. What especially struck Parsons through all this were Henderson's views on the philosophy of science, particularly his enormous emphasis on the concept of system and his teachings on scientific method, ideas that added further support to what Parsons had elsewhere learned since arriving at Harvard.[90] For Henderson too maintained that the objective of science is the formulation of uniform laws (of "the simultaneous variations of mutually dependent variables" in a system) and that attaining this objective entails "abstraction and analysis" and "selection" of different "aspects" of phenomena by scientists guided by the "conceptual scheme" of their particular fields. As Henderson often emphasized, human thought itself is "impossible" without some conceptual scheme, though it is the hallmark of the conceptual schemes of science that they are tempered by the "hard facts of observation," since science is necessarily an "organic whole" in which theory and observation interweave, even as the latter retains "a certain primacy."[91]

Parsons's early years at Harvard are seen too narrowly, however, if they are viewed simply as a period when he became aware of certain ideas that he would subsequently use in his work. Of at least equal importance was the institutional topography of the university, especially with regard to the field of sociology. At the time of his arrival, there was no department of sociology at Harvard, and Parsons did not know of "any plans to do anything with sociology there."[92] From the turn of the century onward, the question of institutionalizing the new discipline had occasionally surfaced, but with little positive effect. Throughout this period, the "debate at Harvard centered largely on . . . whether sociology had the right to be considered a social science at all." Instruction in the field was limited to a few offerings in the Department of Social Ethics and a course, "Principles of Sociology,"

---

90. On Parsons's relationship with Henderson, see Bernard Barber, "Introduction," in *L. J. Henderson on the Social System,* ed. Bernard Barber (Chicago: University of Chicago Press), 46–50; Barbara S. Heyl, "The Harvard 'Pareto Circle,'" *Journal of the History of the Behavioral Sciences* 4 (1968): 316–34; Parsons, "Building Social Systems," 832–33.

91. Lawrence J. Henderson, *Pareto's General Sociology: A Physiologist's Interpretation* (Cambridge, Mass.: Harvard University Press, 1935), 13, 81–86; Henderson, "Sociology 23 Lectures," in *L. J. Henderson on the Social System,* 59–60, 67, 78, 86–89.

92. Parsons, "Dialogues with Parsons," 5.

taught (from 1900 to 1930) out of the economics department by T. N. Carver, a staunch Social Darwinist who denied the autonomy of sociology and held that there is hardly "any question in . . . the social sciences . . . which does not grow out of the initial fact of economic scarcity" as studied by the economist.[93]

Parsons's very first semester at Harvard, however, coincided with the start of the Committee on Sociology and Social Ethics, a special organizational structure created to administer an undergraduate concentration in this composite field. The committee was made up of faculty from already-established Harvard departments, such as economics, history, and government, the administration's theory being "that both social ethics and sociology, lacking unique methods of their own, should be supervised by representatives of those social sciences from which methods were borrowed."[94] Within a short time, Parsons, who soon made known his own interests in sociology, was appointed secretary to the committee and given tutorial responsibilities within the concentration. In this connection, he first met Pitirim Sorokin, who was invited from the Department of Sociology at the University of Minnesota to lecture at Harvard in the spring of 1929 and then returned in August 1930 to become the university's first professor of sociology, as well as the new chairman of the Committee on Sociology and Social Ethics.

From his early negotiations with Lowell, Sorokin successfully extracted a commitment to turn this committee into a department under his own chairmanship; and after further wrangling among committee members over the nature of sociology, a department of sociology was established in the fall of 1931, absorbing the previous Department of Social Ethics.[95] In the course of the committee's deliberations, Parsons himself took an active role (in the view of some of the senior faculty, a *too* active role) in laying out the field of sociology and planning organizational arrangements to "guarantee. . . . its independence." For example, in opposition to local skeptics, his memos from the period insist that "sociology is to be considered a subject of rather unusual difficulty [and] should not let itself be compared unfavorably

    93. Carver, *Essays in Social Justice,* 49–50. For discussion of Carver's ideas, see Church, "Economists Study Society," 18–90; Arthur F. Vidich and Stanford M. Lyman, *American Sociology: Worldly Rejections of Religion and Their Directions* (New Haven: Yale University Press, 1985), 76–82.

    94. David B. Potts, "Social Ethics at Harvard, 1881–1931: A Study in Academic Activism," in *Social Sciences at Harvard, 1860–1920,* 124.

    95. Pitirim A. Sorokin, *A Long Journey* (New Haven: College and University Press, 1963), 240–44.

with Economics, [although] plenty of its ill-wishers would be only too glad of a chance." [96] When the new department was finally launched, Parsons's junior position was transferred into it, though Sorokin was required to build the majority of his senior staff by extending joint appointments to tenured faculty in other Harvard departments. Such a setup meant that sociologists were outnumbered in decision-making votes in their own department, at the same time that many of the required "sociology" courses were actually courses in other departments.[97] Not surprisingly, this arrangement did little to unify the fledgling discipline, which continued to face an uphill struggle for respectability and scientific legitimacy.

Of this Parsons was acutely aware. His principal teaching assignments, for instance, were two courses, "Contemporary Sociological Theories" and "Social Institutions"; but in the latter his main responsibility was to coordinate appearances by Harvard's nonsociologists—an economist on economic institutions, a political scientist on political institutions, an anthropologist on familial institutions, area specialists on Hindu, ancient Greek, modern European, and American institutions, and so on—confining his own contribution to introductory and concluding lectures intended to tie the congeries together. To him, this was never a very satisfactory arrangement, and by the mid-1930s he drafted a proposal to "reorganiz[e] the course . . . in the direction of a more thorough treatment of a small number of subjects," better "integrated" in terms of "a *sociological* theory of institutions." [98] Around the same time, he floated a detailed plan to strengthen the organizational autonomy of the sociology department and curb the influence of its numerous "interdepartmental members," prefacing the plan with the wishful thought that "the question, 'Why a Department of

96. Memo headed "Sociology Department—Comments by T. Parsons," Parsons Papers.

97. Memo entitled "Final Report of the Committee on Sociology and Social Ethics to the Administration on the Organization of a Department of Sociology at Harvard University," Parsons Papers. The results of this situation were clear to contemporaries. John Riley, for example, recalls that when he entered the Harvard sociology department as a graduate student in 1931, its program was without integrity, since there was no real sociology curriculum and graduate students had to "shop around" for themselves. According to Riley, it was the young Parsons who offered the graduate students what their program lacked. Personal communication with John Riley, 1990.

98. Parsons, "Memorandum on the Theory of Social Institutions in Its Bearing on the Organization of Sociology 6," Parsons Papers. See also Parsons's posthumously published 1934 paper, "Prolegomena to a Theory of Social Institutions," *American Sociological Review* 55 (1990):319–33; and Charles Camic "An Historical Prologue," *American Sociological Review* 55 (1990):313–19.

Sociology?' answers itself. It is in no more need of special justification than a department of physics, of psychology or of economics. Surely a modern university considers it an obligation to . . . represent all the main systematic theoretical sciences." [99] But this view of the new field did not yet appear nearly so sure to the Harvard establishment. Indeed, as late as 1939, the Harvard historian Crane Brinton was still willing publicly to ridicule sociology as the "pariah subject," mired in "trivial content" and more akin to "alchemy" than to the natural sciences or economics; and when Parsons protested this to L. J. Henderson, he learned that Henderson agreed with Brinton's dismal assessment. [100]

Nor were these voices of doubt restricted to Harvard. To the contrary: the disciplinary pecking order found at the university closely followed the one present on the national academic scene. Here the differences were striking: the natural sciences, particularly the biological fields (among which psychology then belonged), had wide institutional support and high prestige; economics was securely established as the leading social science; and sociology still lagged well behind, as shown by the limited extent to which it was recognized as a legitimate science and institutionalized in independent university departments. Tremendously exacerbating the problem, as Parsons realized, was the aggressive assault then being waged by some of the biological sciences upon the presumed terrain of the social sciences—the realm of human culture, ideals, values, subjective wants and purposes, choices, attitudes, and so on. Leading this assault were contemporary behaviorist psychologists, newly risen to high prominence by backing John B. Watson's program to transform psychology into the objectivist study of biophysiological stimuli and responses, thereby reducing virtually the whole domain of human conduct and social institutions to the determinism of psychological forces so understood. [101] Parsons first encountered this program during his Amherst days and quickly rejected it to affirm the role of culture over that of biology and psychology. But then, as he has put it, "returning to [America from Germany] I found behaviorism so rampant that anyone who believed in the

99. Untitled memo by Parsons beginning with the words "A systematic classification of all the sciences . . . ," Parsons Papers.

100. Crane Brinton, "What's the Matter with Sociology," *Saturday Review of Literature* 20, no. 2 (1939): 3–4, 14; Buxton, *Talcott Parsons*, 284–85.

101. The summary account of the American academic scene that appears in this and the preceding two sentences draws upon a large literature reviewed by Camic, "*Structure* after 50 Years," 41–45.

scientific validity of the interpretation of subjective states of mind was often held to be fatuously naive." [102]

Concurrently, however, a significant counterattack was underway in the work of anthropologists, sociologists, Gestalt psychologists, and neoclassical economists alarmed at the threat posed by behaviorism to the integrity of their fields. Beyond what he may have recalled from his college years, it is uncertain how extensively Parsons knew this body of work. At least with regard to contemporary American sociology, his knowledge appears to have been spotty. During his early Harvard years, he read some of the work of Robert MacIver and Florian Znaniecki, but otherwise seemed content to write off "American Sociology [as] either glorified economics [or] glorified behaviorism" [103] and to associate "sociology" mainly with what he had encountered in Europe via Hobhouse and Weber and then, at Harvard, in writings of Pareto and Durkheim.[104] What Parsons did become acquainted with and impressed by in this period was the work of the Gestalt psychologists Wolfgang Köhler and Kurt Koffka and the research of Edward Tolman, in all of which he found a vigorous defense of human purposiveness and voluntarism counterposed to the deterministic approach of the behaviorists.[105] Likewise in the writings of certain economists, especially those of his friend Frank Knight, the University of Chicago neoclassicist whom he had come to know through their mutual interest in translating the work of Max Weber. In essays familiar to Parsons, Knight forcefully developed the view that " 'behavior' . . . consists in the concrete of 'voluntary acts' "—which embody "striving," "will," "social ends," "meanings and values"—and that "the aim or purpose of action, [though] not perceptible to sense organs or laboratory instruments, . . . is as real as the action itself." Opposing "the vogue of behaviorism," Knight denied that human wants are ex-

102. Parsons, "Building Social Systems," 830.

103. Parsons to Frank Knight, 13 October 1932, Parsons Papers.

104. It was pointed out above that Parsons first read Durkheim in connection with his coursework at Amherst. Thereafter, he encountered him again via Ginsberg and Malinowski at the LSE and Jaspers at Heidelberg (with the former two portraying Durkheim in a more negative light than did Jaspers). During his second or third year at Harvard, Parsons resumed his reading of Durkheim, who about the same period also attracted the interest of Parsons's colleague from the Harvard Business School, Elton Mayo, and of some other members of the Pareto circle. Parsons, "My Intellectual Development," 7–8; Parsons, "Building Social Systems," 828; Parsons, "Dialogues with Parsons," n. 6; Heyl, "Pareto Circle" 330.

105. Parsons, "Comment on: Current Folklore in the Criticisms of Parsonian Action Theory," *Sociological Inquiry* 44 (1974): 55–58.

clusively "objective" and argued that to conceive them as such is inevitably to reduce " 'higher' wants to a secondary position compared
with 'lower,' and [to] interpret . . . human life in biological terms,"
thereby eliminating "all distinctively human data . . . from consideration." [106] Appreciating the relevance of such ideas for legitimating the
field of sociology, Parsons enlisted eagerly at this point in what he
described as "the 'war of independence' of the social sciences vis-à-vis
the biological." [107]

He did so, however, under circumstances exceptionally trying even
in comparison to those of other contemporary sociologists. For com-
pounding Harvard's wary attitude toward sociology as a discipline
was Parsons's own uncertain position at the university. Here lies the
striking incongruity of Parsons's early career: that, equipped with a
world-class education—from his father, Meiklejohn, Hamilton,
Ayres, Malinowski, Hobhouse, the Weber circle in Heidelberg, Taussig, Schumpeter, Whitehead, and Henderson—he spent the entire period from the fall of 1927 to the fall of 1936 lower in rank than an
untenured assistant professor.[108] Further, this incongruity had more to
do with conditions at Harvard than with Parsons himself. The most
important of these conditions was the Lowell administration's emphasis on undergraduate teaching, which had spurred the development of
the tutorial system and markedly increased the university's demand
for instructors. By the time of Parsons's arrival, "the number of . . .
faculty on annual or three-year appointments had grown considerably
relative to the tenured staff," and "it was conceivable for a man to
spend his entire Harvard career [on renewable short-term appointments and] retire as an instructor emeritus. The junior faculty was
clogged with candidates" of this type.[109] The problem was most severe
in popular undergraduate fields, so that the highly popular Depart-

106. Frank H. Knight, "Ethics and the Economic Interpretation," *Quarterly Journal
of Economics* 36 (1922): 454–81; F. H. Knight, "The Ethics of Competition," *Quarterly Journal of Economics* 37 (1923):579–80; F. H. Knight, "The Limitations of Scientific Method in Economics," in *The Trend of Economics,* ed. Rexford Guy Tugwell
(New York: Croffs, 1935 [original date 1924]), 242–43; F. H. Knight, "Relation of
Utility Theory to Economic Method in the Work of William Stanley Jevons and Others,"
in *Methods in Social Science: A Case Book,* ed. Stuart A. Rice (Chicago: University of
Chicago Press, 1931), 64–67; F. H. Knight, "The Newer Economics and the Control of
Economic Activity," *Journal of Political Economy* 40 (1932): 440, 457.
    107. Parsons, "Approach to Psychological Theory," 625–26.
    108. It is difficult, for this reason, to accept Gouldner's characterization of Parsons's
early years as an "experience of success." Gouldner, *The Coming Crisis,* 148.
    109. Lipset, "Political Controversies," 164; Smith, *Harvard Century,* 133.

ment of Economics experienced a mounting "accumulation of un-promoted younger staff" due to the practice of allowing "a man [to] stay on as an instructor almost indefinitely"—a practice that "choked [the department] with young and not-so-young instructors for whom [a] position could be found as tutor or 'section hand.'"[110]

When he went to Harvard in 1927 as a nonfaculty instructor and tutor in economics, this was the situation that Parsons confronted— "with extremely uncertain expectations for the future."[111] Nor were improvements readily forthcoming, at least in regard to his prospects for a permanent position. In terms of the economics department itself, Parsons's interest in importing a German literature that challenged neoclassicism and lay at the intersection of economics and sociology put him out of sync with his colleagues' intellectual orientation. His chairman, H. H. Burbank, was "unsympathetic" to his work and—as Parsons later put it—"in spite of the friendliness of Taussig, Gay, and Schumpeter, I am quite sure I could not have counted on a future in economics at Harvard."[112] Scarcely better were the circumstances of his tutorial appointment in the Committee on Sociology and Social Ethics: the committee itself was a makeshift arrangement, and in January 1930 its chairman, Ralph Perry, wrote to Gay to express serious doubt about Parsons's future due mainly to the indifferent quality of his undergraduate teaching.[113]

Nevertheless, as plans crystallized to transform the committee into the Department of Sociology, Gay and a few of Parsons's other backers "supported his candidacy in the new department, . . . knowing that [he] was not likely to receive a continuing appointment in Economics and knowing of his deep interest in sociology."[114] In this Sorokin concurred; finding that Parsons "displayed a good analytical mind and a discriminating knowledge of the theories of Durkheim, Pareto, Weber, and other sociologists," he "strongly recommended" his appointment—only to watch the request become the sole initial Sorokin recommendation denied by the administration.[115] Only after consider-

110. Mason, "Harvard Department of Economics," 413.
111. Parsons, "Revisiting the Classics throughout a Long Career," in *The Future of the Sociological Classics*, ed. Buford Rhea (London: Allen and Unwin, 1981), 184.
112. Parsons, "Building Social Systems," 832, 834.
113. Ralph B. Perry to Edwin F. Gay, 14 January 1930, File of the Committee on the Concentration in Sociology and Social Ethics, Harvard University Archives.
114. Barry Johnston, reporting an interview with Robert K. Merton, "Sorokin and Parsons at Harvard: Institutional Conflict and the Origin of a Hegemonic Tradition," *Journal of the History of the Behavioral Sciences* 22 (1986): 111.
115. Sorokin, *Long Journey*, 243–44.

able intervention by Parsons's supporters did Lowell overturn this decision, clearing the way for Parsons to receive a three-year appointment as a faculty instructor and tutor in sociology.

But the period that followed was clouded by additional uncertainties. As his title changed from "nonfaculty" to "faculty" instructor, Parsons's appointment became an official period of probation. He thus felt, as he told Frank Knight in October 1932, that "there is considerable pressure on me to get some things published fairly soon if I want promotion"—pressure made heavier by the recognition that his undergraduate teaching was sometimes "over the heads of the students." [116] Then, too, there was the matter of his salary, which grew at an unusually slow pace even for the period and fell below that of other Harvard instructors, a circumstance that, coinciding as it did with the birth of his three children between 1930 and 1936, drove him to take on additional teaching at Columbia University summer school and at Radcliffe. [117] More galling still was life with Sorokin, who as a theorist chose to break up European social thought into several distinct schools, in contrast to Parsons's strong and defiant emphasis on the development of a unifying "higher synthesis"; [118] and who, as department chairman, appeared "unsympathetic," intrusive, and a powerful barrier to promotion. [119] Perhaps the clearest instance of the latter, in Parsons's eyes, occurred at the end of his three-year appointment as a faculty instructor, when Sorokin decided to retain him in the same rank instead of arranging to advance him to an assistant professor position—a turn of events bitterly denounced by Parsons at the time as a "real injustice" in view of the "enormous . . . scientific development" he had accomplished, while also making major contributions

116. Parsons to Knight, 13 October 1932. Parsons to Pitirim Sorokin, draft letter October/November 1935, Parsons Papers. It was in this context, too, that Parsons decided to undertake his first empirical research project, "The Control of Social Institutions over the Medical Professions," funded by the Harvard Committee on Research in the Social Sciences. Charles J. Bullock to Parsons, 20 February 1934, Parsons Papers. For discussion of Parsons's early empirical work, see Bernard Barber, "Beyond Parsons's Theory of the Professions," in *Neofunctionism,* ed. Jeffrey C. Alexander (Beverly Hills: Sage, 1985), 211–24; Barber, "Theory and Fact in the Work of Talcott Parsons," in *The Nationalization of the Social Sciences,* ed. Samuel Z. Klausner and Victor M. Lidz (Philadelphia: University of Pennsylvania Press, 1986), 123–30; Barber, "Introductory Remarks by Bernard Barber for 1987 ASA Session on 50th Anniversary of Parsons' *The Structure of Social Action*" (paper presented at the American Sociological Association meetings, Chicago, 1987).

117. Parsons to Sorokin, draft letter, October/November 1935.

118. Donald N. Levine, "Simmel and Parsons Reconsidered," *American Journal of Sociology* 96 (1991).

119. Parsons, "Building Social Systems," 832.

to the training of graduate students.[120] Nor can Parsons's career concerns amid these circumstances have been allayed by his awareness of the treatment previously meted out to Edward Parsons and Alexander Meiklejohn—for all *their* contributions—by the higher university authorities who controlled their positions.

Complicating all of this was one further institutional development. In 1933 Lowell retired from the presidency of Harvard and was succeeded by James Conant, a distinguished chemist, generally popular with the faculty (if not with the alumni and students) for his liberal politics, but controversial for his stern measures to arrest the decline in faculty research quality. "Convinced [that Harvard was] filling up the younger ranks with mediocre men whose merit consisted largely in their willingness to be tutors, [and that] standards for promotion were not high enough," Conant imposed a policy, by the mid-1930s, that set a low ceiling on the number of tenured positions in academic departments. The policy disallowed the renewal of the initial three-year contracts of junior faculty who could not be retained for tenured slots and recommended that instructors whose appointments had already been renewed, but for whom a tenured position was unavailable, be given a last terminal appointment.[121] Left unclear, however, was the exact way in which this policy was to apply to individual departments, and this unclarity all the more heightened the junior faculty's alarm over Conant's plan. Parsons felt this very strongly, going so far as to draft a letter to Conant advising him of the "uncertainties [that are] peculiarly prominent in [the Sociology] Department [over] the question of criteria for promotion"; of how the rigid application of his policy for calculating the number of tenure slots would mean that "there will be only three [sociology] vacancies in the permanent

120. Parsons to Sorokin, draft letter October/November 1935, Parsons Papers. The list of men who, as graduate students, studied closely with Parsons during this period is a distinguished one that includes Robert Merton, Kingsley Davis, John Riley, Edward Devereux, and Robert Bierstedt. Parsons, "Building Social Systems," 833. Calling themselves "the Parsons Sociological Group," these men met regularly in Parsons's tutorial quarters in Adams House, keeping minutes that range over many of the major sociological topics of the day. On this group, see Robert Merton, "Remembering the Young Talcott Parsons," *American Sociologist* 15 (1980): 70. Copies of the minutes are held in the Parsons Papers. Riley has drawn attention to the critical role of this interested group in the development of Parsons's ideas in the 1930s, especially given Parsons's comparative loneliness among the sociology faculty. Riley also sees the group as Parsons's way of perpetuating the spirit he had encountered in the salons of Heidelberg. Riley, personal communications.

121. The quotation is from Conant, as cited by Lipset, "Political Controversies," 154. On the policy itself, see ibid., 164; Smith, *Harvard Century*, 133.

staff in the next twenty-five years or more, [the first not for] more than ten years"; and of the fact that the entire situation was causing a "disturbing . . . kind of psychological uncertainty" among the department's junior members.[122]

By late 1935, however, Parsons had finished a large portion of the manuscript that would become *The Structure of Social Action*. Hoping for promotion, he circulated it to Sorokin and later to several members of the Harvard Committee on Research in the Social Sciences. Sorokin's verdict was mixed, as were some of the other reviews; but the general impression of Parsons was by then sufficiently favorable that Gay and Henderson secured his advance to an assistant professor position as of the fall of 1936.[123] In 1937, when Parsons received an attractive academic offer from outside of Harvard, Henderson went to Conant and arranged for Parsons's retention with "definite promise of permanency as associate professor two years later." [124] That promise had been very long in coming, and by the time that it materialized, Parsons's early essays and *The Structure of Social Action* were both essentially completed. These belong still to the period of his "disturbing uncertainty" about his future as a sociologist at Harvard.

Phase II. Studies in the Development of the Theory of Action

Of the two remaining clusters into which Parsons's early writings may be grouped, both are intimately linked to his experiences during the late 1920s and early to mid-1930s. Both lines of work reveal an increasing shift in Parsons's central object of analysis away from capitalist society in particular and toward the topic of human action in general, the same topic that had long been the express focus of orthodox economics. In developing the two lines of work, Parsons accepted the teachings of his Harvard contemporaries on the scientific importance of conceptual schemes; he thus sought a systematic conceptualization of the domain of human action that would enable him to legitimate sociology, as well as economics, while defending both fields against the psychobiological onslaught of the behaviorists. But, in pursuing this new project, Parsons remained cognizant of what he had previously learned, and he continually sought to encompass a number of those ideas within the bounds of his emerging frame of reference.

122. Parsons to James Conant, draft letter, undated, Parsons Papers.
123. Johnson, "Sorokin and Parsons at Harvard," 112–15; Parsons, "Building Social Systems," 832.
124. Parsons, "Building Social Systems," 832.

Carried along in the process were his long-standing reservations about deterministic, unilinear evolutionary laws; his emphasis on the significance of religious ritual, belief, and the religious motives for human conduct; his concern with the social regulation of the individual impulses that can produce conflict; his critique of individualistic, rationalistic social theory; his vision of society as a system of interrelated elements; and his staunch conviction that divergent theories of society emanated from different European intellectual traditions that could eventually be synthesized.

   The way in which Parsons actually conceptualized the domain of human action, and defined sociology's claims upon it, did not, though, spring forth ready made. By the third "phase" of the early work, his approach to these issues more or less stabilized, thus making way for *The Structure of Social Action*. During the second phase, however, Parsons was still working haltingly toward this approach—working toward it through what he described, looking back in early 1935, as "a series of critical studies in European sociological theory." [125] Why Parsons undertook these studies and devoted so much of this period to analyzing the work of earlier social theorists is not difficult to understand. From Hamilton and Cannan to Salin and Taussig, he had been presented with the example of distinguished economists who had given great weight to the writings of earlier economic theorists. And, moving outside the bounds of economics narrowly conceived, he had done likewise himself in his dissertation and immediately afterward— to what he saw as his considerable intellectual benefit. Accordingly, as his concerns over promotion pressed in, he felt these "studies in sociological theory [to be] the most promising" in terms of "get[ting] some things published fairly soon." [126]

   Parsons's first effort in this new direction was an investigation of the ideas of Alfred Marshall, a thinker whom he viewed, following his Harvard teachers, as "overwhelmingly the most eminent representative in his generation of the orthodox school" of neoclassical economists—so much so that "their case may almost be said to stand or fall with his work." [127] Within a few years of his arrival at Harvard, Parsons completed a ninety-some-page manuscript, "Marshall and Laissez-Faire," [128] which then formed the basis for two well-received articles published, in the early thirties, in the *Quarterly Journal of Economics*, of which Taussig was then the editor. Because the first of

125. The quotation is from chapter 18 of this volume.
126. Parsons to Knight, 13 October 1932.
127. Parsons, "Wants and Activities in Marshall," 101.
128. The manuscript is held in the Parsons Papers.

these, "Wants and Activities in Marshall," was subsequently reprinted (with comparatively minor changes) as the fourth chapter of *The Structure of Social Action,* it is not included in the present volume. The objective in this paper had been to delineate the assumptions of Marshall's famous utility theory (viz., that action is an effort to attain ends or to satisfy wants using rational or efficient means, that wants are given independently of want-satisfaction processes, and so on), and to establish that this utility theory is, on Marshall's own testimony, "only part of economics, and the less important part. The more important is the influence of economic conditions [and activities] on human character," particularly on the "progressive development" of a type of human character animated not by selfish wants, but by virtuous activities that are "ends in themselves," at least under conditions of free enterprise, seen not as "a Hobbesian state of nature, [but an age] closely bound by ethical norms." Or, in other words, "Marshall's economic teaching . . . is made up mainly of two strands . . . which he fuses together in his economics. . . . One of the strands is [the] 'utility theory,' the center of which is a study of the rational process of the satisfaction of given wants. . . . The other is the 'study of man,' of the formation of his character through economic activities, [especially those] associated with the system of free enterprise." [129]

The upshot of this analysis was saved for its sequel, "Economics and Sociology: Marshall in Relation to the Thought of His Time" (chapter 8). Written during the months of Parsons's transfer from the Department of Economics to the Department of Sociology, the article presents his first systematic justification for the field of sociology. To build this justification, Parsons first steps back from Marshall to examine his predecessors in the English tradition of social thought, Hobbes, Locke, Malthus, Godwin, and the Darwinians. Like Hamilton and Salin, he again identifies "individualism" (the tendency to conceive "social phenomena . . . in terms of the essentially independent actions and properties of individuals pursuing ends") as the premise of all strands of the tradition, which he then faults for overlooking questions of "social cohesion." He emphasizes how adoption of this premise forced the English tradition alternatively to take "individual wants as given without attempting to . . . explain them," or to explain them by appealing to "objective scientific factors . . . imposed upon man by the external environment"—a move that tended toward a "radical anti-intellectualism" which gave explanatory weight to "biological or psychological factors." In this circumstance,

---

129. Parsons, "Wants and Activities in Marshall," 102, 104, 107, 124, 139.

"sociology," as "the science of society," could be nothing other than "either applied biology or psychology, or . . . economics in the sense of utility theory": precisely the three unsatisfactory options immediately confronting Parsons himself at the time that he wrote.[130]

In his view, however, the "two-strand" nature of Marshall's social theory represented a decisive "improvement on that of his predecessors." While avoiding recourse to psychology or biology, his work subordinated utility theory to the broader study of "the relation of economic activities to human character." But, Parsons continues, although this was all to the good, Marshall too was a product of his tradition. He remained content to subsume this broader field of study "under the rubric of economics," and in so doing imparted a "lack of perspective to his treatment of the activities," a deficiency most apparent in his linear conception of social evolution. In this respect, his work falls short of the achievement of two of his contemporaries, Weber, whom Parsons introduces once again, and Pareto, whom he treats for the first time.

In the article, Parsons calls the positions of Marshall, Pareto, and Weber "alternatives." But what he evidently felt and is trying to suggest—following up on the teachings of his father, Meiklejohn, and Jaspers, and his own previous forecast of a "higher synthesis"—is that there is a kind of "Marshall-Pareto-Weber 'convergence.'" This is the first of several early variants of the Marshall-Pareto-Durkheim-Weber convergence thesis of The Structure of Social Action.[131] In this installment, it takes form in the argument that, like Marshall, Pareto and Weber both accepted utility theory and went beyond it, Pareto to make way for "non-logical action," inspired by values, ideals, and religious traditions, Weber to encompass various "non-rational factors," as well as "ultimate values," the "non-economic category" so central to German thought. Parsons finds such additions essential for counterbalancing the individualism and linear evolutionism of the English tradition by placing emphasis on supraindividual "epochs and cultures, [each seen as] sharply differentiated from others, rather than as a transitory stage in a continuous process." Even more important is that in embracing such factors Pareto and Weber were led, as Mar-

---

130. Here Parsons's argument anticipates the grounds for his rejection of Herbert Spencer and the utilitarians in The Structure of Social Action. See Charles Camic, "The Utilitarians Revisited," American Journal of Sociology 85 (1979):516–50.

131. The quotation is from Parsons, "Building Social Systems," 828. On the several variants of the convergence thesis, see Camic, "Structure after 50 Years"; Bruce Wearne, "Parsons' Sociological Ethic and the Spirit of American Internationalism: A Bibliographic Essay," (paper presented at SAANZ Conference, August 1982).

shall was not, "to develop a science of sociology"—the very thing that
Parsons himself was then laboring to promote. It will be noticed, however, that although Parsons's appeal here is to Weber and Pareto, the
conception of sociology that emerges at this point strongly resembles
that put forth by Hobhouse. Characterizing sociology as the "independent science [which has as its] subject matter . . . the *social* (or
'cultural') factor" and "stud[ies] phenomena specifically social, [i.e.,]
arising out of the *interaction* of human beings," Parsons holds "economics [to] be a part of sociology dealing with one aspect of social
phenomena." This is exactly the position that Hobhouse had taken.

The line of argument worked out in the two articles on Marshall
partly reappears in four of Parsons's briefer writings from the period,
his short pieces on Hankins, Tönnies, Malthus, and Pareto (chapters
9–12). The 1933 essays on Malthus and Pareto for example, expand
remarks from "Economics and Sociology" into fuller accounts of the
two thinkers (each seen as an "economist and sociologist") and their
place in the development of European thought about human action.
The commentaries on Hankins and Tönnies are little-known book reviews that reveal Parsons's attitude toward types of sociological
theory to which he otherwise devoted little consideration.

Especially interesting is his analysis of Hankins's book, which he
apparently reviewed shortly after its publication in 1928.[132] The piece
represents Parsons's only published reaction, in his early Harvard
years, to *American* sociology as it was then practiced. A one-time student of Franklin Giddings, Frank Hankins was a professor of sociology at Smith College of sufficient reputation that he became president
of the American Sociological Society in the mid-thirties. His *Introduction to the Study of Society* [133] was a popular college textbook of the
period. Like many other books of this type, it took a wide sweep and
combined a treatment of "society and its institutions" with a lengthy
examination of "the physiographic, the biological, and the psychological bases of social life" and of the determining role of race and heredity in human affairs.[134] His position on these matters did not prevent

132. An exact date cannot, at this time, be assigned to Parsons's review because it
has not been possible to locate the issue of the *Springfield Republican* in which it appeared. The typescript of the review, held in the Parsons Papers, bears the notation in
Parsons's hand "for Springfield Republican." Although this was a newspaper that
tended to review books shortly after their publication, I have not succeeded in tracing
if or when the paper actually printed Parsons's review. However, since it remains likely
that the review did appear there at some point, and since Parsons clearly wrote it for
publication as is, the piece is included here among his early "publications."

133. Frank Hamilton Hankins, *An Introduction to the Study of Society* (New York:
Macmillan, 1928).

134. Ibid., xi–xii.

Hankins from recognizing the importance both of "the cultural factor in social life" and of the "moral rules . . . which a group sets up to control the behavior of its members in the interest of internal peace and order." [135] But Parsons's review takes no notice of these latter points. Following the model of his other early reviews, it concentrates instead on the objectionable features in Hankins's work and counterposes this work to approaches already favored by Parsons himself, namely, those of Weber, Pareto, Whitehead, and, by this time, Durkheim as well. For Parsons, the decisive thing is that "in attempting to deal with all the factors having the remotest bearing on society," Hankins overemphasizes "the presocial *conditions* of social life," which are the subject matter of disciplines like biology and psychology; he thus effaces the necessary "division of labor between the sciences" and carries sociology off into a miscellany of facts rather than toward "a thorough and consistent social theory of its own."

Parsons's verdict on Ferdinand Tönnies's 1931 *Einführung in die Soziologie*[136] is less severe but also negative. In this case the criticism centers not on a lack of a consistent theory—Parsons says that Tönnies comes near to "a general system of sociological theory"—but on several more incidental objections, such as the book's tendency to present its "system of concepts . . . in abstraction from the concrete use to which it is to be put" (the same complaint that Parsons would later hear from his own critics). What is apparently behind these objections is that Tönnies was then regarded—along with Georg Simmel, Alfred Vierkandt, and Leopold von Wiese—as representing what Sorokin[137] and others called the "formal school" of German sociology, a camp widely seen as opposed to the school of thought represented by Max Weber. For American audiences a compendium of the ideas of the formal school was provided in 1932, when von Wiese's *Systematic Sociology* was translated and adapted by Howard Becker, whom Parsons seems to have regarded as his "rival . . . for the leadership of the introduction of German sociology into this country." [138] In the review, it is thus interesting to find Parsons more occupied with protesting Tönnies's formal concepts than with acknowledging his contribution in areas one would expect Parsons to have noticed—concerning, for in-

135. Ibid., 376–79, 448–49.

136. Ferdinand Tönnies, *Einführung in die Soziologie* (Stuttgart: Enke, 1931). This has been partially translated by Carola Atkinson and Rudolf Heberle, in *Ferdinand Tönnies: On Sociology, Pure, Applied, and Empirical,* ed. Werner Cahnman and Rudolf Heberle (Chicago: University of Chicago Press, 1971).

137. Pitirim Sorokin, *Contemporary Sociological Theories* (New York: Harper and Brothers, 1928), 488–95.

138. Parsons to Alexander, 19 January 1979.

stance, the "oughtness" of norms, or the "attitude of respect and reverence" with which values are upheld.[139] It is also interesting to see Parsons baffling over Tönnies's central trichotomy of the economic, political, and moral "factors" in social life when, by the third phase of his early thinking, he embraced similar distinctions himself.[140]

The first indication of his move in this direction is his 1934 *Encyclopaedia* article "Society" (chapter 13). The essay captures Parsons in transition between the idea (dating back to his second Marshall article) that society is the "complex of relations of man to his fellow man" and the idea (decisive from 1934 onward) that it is "common . . . values [that are] the essential basis of social reality." At one level, the article is an attempt to trace conceptions of society from antiquity to the twentieth century; this was the focus stipulated by the *Encyclopaedia*'s editors when they commissioned the piece. But Parsons is quick to bring the analysis around to thinkers and issues already familiar from his earlier work, with two differences. The first of these is that political thought, rather than economic/sociological thought alone, here finds a significant place in the historical account (though Parsons will lose sight of this again within a few years); the second is that Parsons now adopts the (Jasperian) terminology of "idealism" and "positivism" to describe the contrasting European traditions that gave rise to the "most modern conception of society"—equating "positivism" with efforts to go beyond "utilitarianism" to the "purely scientific," objective "conditions" of social life, that is, "the external environment and man's inherited nature." In addition to these exten-

139. Cahnman and Heberle, *Tönnies: On Sociology,* 170, 188.

140. Note should also be taken of Parsons's subsequent treatment of Tönnies. In Parsons's 1935 article "Ultimate Values" (chapter 18), Tönnies is favorably mentioned as one of the thinkers whose work documents the recent convergence of idealism and positivism, while by the time of *The Structure of Social Action* Tönnies is subtracted from the convergence thesis and relegated to a long end-of-chapter "Note." Parsons, *Structure of Social Action,* 686–94. This shifting view of Tönnies bears comparison with Parsons's treatment of Simmel, who is mentioned briefly in two of the early articles (see chapters 16 and 17); embraced, right along with Tönnies, in the 1935 suggestion of the convergence thesis; included in a chapter ("Georg Simmel and Ferdinand Toennies: Social Relationships and the Elements of Action," Parsons Papers) drafted around the same time for *The Structure of Social Action;* but then deleted from the convergence argument of the book, where the draft chapter is reduced simply to the note on Tönnies. For a thorough discussion on these points and the larger question of Parsons's relationship with Simmel, see Donald N. Levine, "Introduction to the Arno Press Edition," in *Simmel and Parsons: Two Approaches to the Study of Society* (New York: Arno, 1980), iii–lxix. For another view, see Gary Dean Jaworski, "Simmel's Contribution to Parsons's Action Theory and Its Fate," in *Georg Simmel and Contemporary Sociology,* ed. Michael Kaern et al. (Dordrecht: Kluwer Academic, 1990), 109–30.

sions of his intellectual-historical views, "Society" reveals some no-
ticeable development in Parsons's own thinking about human action,
especially in his treatment of "ultimate ends of action" as rooted in
"the element of culture" and integrated (in varying degrees) "into a
harmonious system"; his distinction between ultimate ends and "immediate ends [that] fall into three sections . . . the technological, the
economic and the political"; and his association of ultimate ends with
"symbolic" action and religious ritual, with the "regulatory norms"
or "institutions" of a community, *and* with the workings of the state
and the "social structure" more generally.[141]

As these substantive views took shape, Parsons also developed his
methodological ideas more systematically. Having recently been sen-
sitized to philosophy-of-science questions, he was now convinced that
part of the task of building a science of action was to specify the logic
and objectives of that science. Methodological issues thus became integral to his studies of the development of the theory of action. The
position at which he eventually arrived is seen in his 1936 review of
Alexander von Schelting's *Max Webers Wissenschaftslehre* (chapter
14). Though nominally about von Schelting, the review is actually a
critical reassessment of the methodological teachings of Weber himself. The linchpin of the piece is Parsons's distinction between "empiricism," which holds "scientific knowledge [to be] a complete 'reflection' of the living concrete reality"—that is (to quote the definition
given in chapter 17), a "full explanation of a body of concrete
facts"—and an "analytical" methodological orientation. Arguing
strongly in favor of the latter, he makes clear how fully he has by this
time accepted the methodological opinions then current at Harvard
among the economists and the resident authorities on the natural sciences (Whitehead, Henderson). For Parsons equates the "analytical"
view with the idea that scientific "knowledge . . . is never a complete
reflection of the concrete, [but] always a selective abstraction, [focused
on] those *aspects* of concrete reality which are significant to the investigator." Moreover: entirely abandoning his earlier institutionalist emphasis on the *differences* between historical epochs, the value of the
genetic method, and the limitations of abstract theories with universal
applicability, Parsons now—in a fateful step that will inhibit his treatment of historical diversity hereafter—champions the search for uniform "general laws," minimizes the genetic approach, and proposes

141. Parsons offers a more extended statement of his position on phenomena such
as "institutions" and "social structure" in three other early publications (see chapters
16, 17, and 18) as well as in his "Prolegomena to a Theory of Social Institutions."

that "different historical individuals [are] capable of analysis into different combinations of the *same* elements." To the extent that Weber can be enlisted in support of these methodological beliefs, Parsons praises his work, only to back off where Weber falls short, as when he insufficiently recognizes that "there is a methodological core common to all empirical science, no matter what its concrete subject matter"— a point vital to Parsons's immediate efforts to legitimize sociology.[142] Along the same lines, Parsons inverts a major theme of his earlier writings on Weber; instead of further objecting to Weber's use of "generalizing" rather than "individualizing" concepts, he commends Weber for this move and for his "analytical breakdown of . . . 'society' into its elements."

How this "analytical" orientation relates specifically to the study of human action is the subject of "Pareto's Central Analytical Scheme" (chapter 15). This densely packed essay comes fairly late in Parsons's early career, at a point when his third developmental phase is already underway; a number of the ideas developed here are, for this reason, treated below in the next section. The paper is at the same time, however, the capstone of a line of work on Vilfredo Pareto which occupied Parsons before this last phase began and which was actually instrumental in bringing it about.

As noted above, Parsons formed an interest in Pareto during his first years at Harvard when Pareto was a thinker of growing local popularity. That interest persisted, spurred by Parsons's mounting concern "to distinguish between the economic and the sociological," [143] and, by the end of his project on Marshall, he voiced a decided preference for the approach to action offered by Pareto (along with Weber), a judgment reiterated in his *Encyclopaedia* entry on Pareto. What happened next is recounted by Parsons in a letter to Knight dated October 1932:

> The Marshall study [showed] that Marshall grew out of a tradition of thought which only left him very limited possibilities of dealing with the kind of questions which forced themselves on him. The real fault lay not in the limitations of any single thinker, but in those of a set of 'fundamental' categories they had inherited. The conclusion was . . . mainly negative. The next step might have been to enter directly into a basic general criticism [of those categories]. Instead I left it at what seemed to me a fairly clear formulation of what they were . . . and set off on another tack. I took a man who, on a superficial view (which was all my sketch in the second Marshall

142. For further discussion of this, see Camic, "Making of a Method."
143. Parsons, "Building Social Systems," 828.

article gave) represented a definite departure from Marshall's tradition, and tried to find out what it really consisted in. Instead of criticizing the already formulated categories to the bottom, I chose to hunt for another alternative set, to relate to the first. This I found in Pareto, but with better results than I had hoped for.[144]

Parsons wrote this to explain the 135-page manuscript that he had just finished and sent to Knight under the title "Pareto and the Problems of Positivistic Sociology." [145] Concentrating on Pareto's categories of "logical" and "non-logical action," the short monograph argued for "the logical independence of sociology as a science" by demonstrating "the emergence [in Pareto's thought] of a social factor . . . , the role of values, which is totally incompatible with the positivistic tradition out of which he grew, and . . . represents the breakdown of the main structure of positivistic social theory, essentially from a process of internal self-criticism, quite analogous to that which has taken place in the physical sciences in the last generation." [146] In late 1932, Parsons tried to interest various publishers in bringing out this study; but with a number of other books on Pareto then appearing, no publisher came forth. After it was somewhat reworked, however, material from the study made its way into several of Parsons's publications during the following five-year period (*The Structure of Social Action* included),[147] and in "Pareto's Central Analytical Scheme" one sees what continually drew Parsons to Pareto. The attraction was a body of theoretical work where the well-regarded analytical method of the economists and philosophers of the natural sciences was used, but used to go beyond economics, without at the same time lapsing into a natural-scientific (or "positivistic") reductionism like the behaviorists who gave exclusive weight to the objective "conditions" of environment and heredity. "Pareto," writes Parsons, "was one of the first to transcend . . . the dilemma of accepting the theories of economic individualism as literally and concretely true, or insofar as this position was rejected to fall back on psychological anti-intellectualism."

At the root of this accomplishment, according to Parsons, was the

144. Parsons to Knight, 13 October 1932.

145. The manuscript is held in the Parsons Papers.

146. Table of contents for "Pareto and the Problems of Positivistic Sociology"; Parsons to Stanley Unwin, 22 September 1932—both in Parsons Papers.

147. Included among these are two book reviews not reprinted in this volume: Parsons, review of *The Mind and Society* by Vilfredo Pareto and *Pareto's General Sociology* by Lawrence J. Henderson, *American Economic Review* 25 (1935): 502–8; Parsons, review of *The Mind and Society* by Vilfredo Pareto, *American Sociological Review* 1 (1936): 139–48.

analytical method itself, which he describes here much as in his later
review of von Schelting, and with an interesting consequence. In his
first writings on Pareto, Parsons tended to view the categories of logical and non-logical action as a classification of *types* of human action
(see especially chapter 12). Now, however, with his analytical approach further worked out, what he argues is that these categories are
"not a classification of concrete actions but of *elements* in concrete
action"—elements necessarily abstracted from something larger, the
"total action-system of a society" conceived as "a complicated web of
means-end chains instead of a mere aggregation of isolated acts." Presumably because they did not utilize the analytical method as thoroughly as did Pareto, this cardinal point was one most economists
failed to perceive, as suited their atomistic cast of thought. But, by
making way for "action systems," not only did Pareto "finally break
[from] 'atomistic individualism,'" he also came to recognize (at least
implicitly) that means-ends chains are nested within two broader, independent categories of "non-logical" elements: on the one hand,
conditions of heredity and environment, on the other, "the value element"—that is, "common ethical [rules], ideals and ends." In Parsons's assessment, this idea represented a very promising advance beyond the "two-strand" formulations that he had found in Marshall's
works. To an academic audience that had no doubt about the need for
sciences of the conditional elements, it indicated clearly an analogous
need for a science of the value element. This was a point that Parsons
was prepared to carry much further.

Phase III. The Fundaments of Analytical Sociology

Shortly after completing his monograph on Pareto, Parsons settled on
some ideas which he outlined for Knight in a letter of 23 January
1933. Here he writes that he has come to

> differentiate four levels [in the "hierarchy of explanation"]: 1) the mecha-
> nistic-atomistic, if that exists at all; 2) the "organic"-vital. The difference
> between them lies essentially in the part-whole relations, the first laying
> emphasis on the priority of the parts, the second on the whole. I tend to
> think of this distinction as highly relative. Both would belong in a sphere
> of that which is "external" to us, or "objective" in the sense that it exists
> only as an object of knowledge by means of action. . . .
>   On coming to the third sphere, that of "action" or "conduct," a defi-
> nitely new element crops up, the "subjective" dealing with ends, purposes,
> values, motives. The means-end schema is indispensable and some of the
> central problems have to do with "rationality." . . . Here the problems are

enormously complicated by the problem of understanding the "subjective" aspect of others' action. . . . This sphere is, I think, the one which is central for the social sciences.

Finally 4) there is, I think, what is often called the sphere of "objective mind," of pure *Geist*[?] as the Germans have it. In it belong the complicated *products* of "action," works of art, systems of thought, etc.

Now I should like to lay down three propositions about these levels or spheres:

1) In spite of whatever shading off into each other there may be there is no reason to regard any one of them as "more fundamental" than the others. . . . "Action" and "value" are as ultimate as any other ultimates.

2) I fully accept your view that these spheres do not exactly correspond to separate categories of concrete phenomena—they are rather "aspects" of a single indivisible whole. At least in human life, thought and action, all are involved. A fallacy of "misplaced concreteness" may easily describe it all in terms of any one.

3) The real problems of the sciences dealing with man are concerned with all of them in interrelation—und zwar: a) the first two, the "external" sphere come in either as means or as "conditions"—I don't know how far the two are distinguishable in the last analysis; b) the level at which only means are problematical is one where relations 1 & 2 & 3 are involved; c) the problems of values in conduct concern the place of 4 in relation to the others.

As distinct from the sciences dealing with "external nature," the social sciences cannot evade as all behaviorists try to a) the problem of the "subjective"; . . . b) the problem of the relations of ends and purposes both to the "ideal" sphere of "objective mind," hence its role in conduct. In [this] the social sciences have a claim to be dealing with realities at least as ultimate as, at least as well attested as any "physical world." [148]

The passage is a kind of master key to Parsons's thinking from this point onward. It marks off the underlying grid he will build upon and shows the relationship between the foundation stones that will be used: the premise that action (conceptualized, all at once, as a means-ends affair, infused subjective meaning, animated by motives and purposes, and oriented toward values originating in the realm of *Geist* or culture) constitutes the subject matter of the social sciences; the idea that this subject matter is not a concrete phenomenon but an analytical aspect of an indivisible whole; the rejection of behaviorist theories for overlooking this idea and presuming that the study of objective conditions invalidates the analysis of the subjective element; and the connection of these theoretical and methodological principles with the

148. Parsons to Frank Knight, 23 January 1933, Frank H. Knight Papers, Special Collections Department, Joseph Regenstein Library, University of Chicago.

immediate practical task of defining a legitimate domain for the social sciences, as against the natural sciences.

Yet, having embraced this package of ideas as the outcome of his studies in the development of the theory of action and of his background and local experiences to that point, Parsons still needed to work out its implications—both with regard to his campaign on behalf of the science of sociology itself and with regard to his previous substantive and intellectual-historical concerns (with the emerging synthesis of idealist and positivist social theory, the role of religious motivation and ritual, the problem of order, and so on). This is what he does during the "third phase" of his early work, with results already evident in the first publication belonging to this cluster, his May 1934 article for the *Quarterly Journal of Economics,* "Some Reflections on 'The Nature and Significance of Economics'" (chapter 16).

The stimulus for this article was the 1932 publication of Lionel Robbins's *An Essay on the Nature and Significance of Economic Science* followed by Ralph W. Souter's attack on the book in the May 1933 issue of the *Quarterly Journal of Economics.*[149] The "debate" between the two men immediately attracted Parsons as an opportunity to elaborate to economists (still his primary reference group) his newly developed perspective and show its ability to resolve the debate's main issues. Robbins was a young British neoclassicist who had sought to defend—and with considerably more subtlety than either Souter or Parsons allow—an "analytical economics" that would study "human behavior as a relationship between ends and scarce means [with] alternative uses" and formulate "laws" of this "particular *aspect* of behavior." [150] Souter was a lecturer in economics at Columbia University who wanted to carry forth the ideas of Alfred Marshall as well as the "healthy instincts" of the American institutionalists.[151] Presenting Robbins as a spokesman for "abstract exclusionist positivism," Souter criticized his book for basing the science of economics on an "analytical partitioning" of the common subject matter of all the social sciences, thereby removing a complex array of concrete phenomena from the domain of economics and fostering an "atomistic, mechanical, individualistic" approach to economic theory. To rout such an ap-

---

149. Lionel Robbins, *An Essay on the Nature and Significance of Economic Science* (London: Macmillan, 1932); Ralph Souter, " 'The Nature and Significance of Economic Science' in Recent Discussion," *Quarterly Journal of Economics* 47 (1933): 377–413. Parsons's discussion also made use of Souter's recently published dissertation, *Prolegomena to Relativity Economics* (New York: Columbia University Press, 1933).

150. Robbins, *Essay,* 15, 16, 74, 77.

151. Souter, "Nature and Significance," 395; Souter, *Prolegomena,* ix, 101–30.

proach, Souter proposed to suspend all "*a priori* methodological limits" on economics and to adopt a policy of "economic imperialism," or "the progressive invasion by economic science of the territories of social psychology, sociology, industrial technology, etc."[152]

As one might expect, Parsons's article takes issue with both thinkers, albeit on different grounds. With regard to Robbins, he sympathizes with much of Souter's critique and attempts to push this further by reverting to ideas suggested in his previous work. According to Parsons, Robbins's orthodox conception of ends "lean[s] toward radical positivism," which reduces ends to objective conditions and (like behaviorism) sacrifices the active, "creative element" of action. By its neglect of the way in which the ends of individuals and groups of individuals are integrated through "ultimate ends held in common," this conception also gives rise to an "atomism" that dissolves "society [into] a mere chaos of conflicting individuals." Conversely, though, Parsons continues, Souter avoids the inadequacies of positivism only by lapsing into an "empiricism" that refuses to proceed analytically— as Robbins, to his credit, had sought to do—"in terms of an abstract 'aspect' of concrete life," but strives instead for "the complete explanation of the concrete functioning 'economy' as a concrete whole." Pursuit of this goal is what causes Souter "to abandon the attempt to draw ... methodological boundaries between economics and its neighboring sciences" and to advocate the practice of "economic imperialism," "a tendency against which," Parsons warns, "the sociologist ... must stand up and fight for his scientific life."

Parsons proposes to break this impasse between Robbins and Souter—or, in other words, between positivism and empiricism—by using insights he developed in the course of his work on Pareto. Appealing to the idea of means-ends chains nested between the value element ("ultimate ends") and conditions of heredity and environment ("ultimate means"), Parsons turns attention to the "intermediate means-end relationships" that lie between these two ultimates. He argues for the breakdown of this intermediate sector "into three quite well-defined subdivisions": a "technological" factor, which concerns "the selection, on the basis of scientific knowledge ... of the best adapted means [to attain] a single ... definite end"; an "economic" factor, which pertains "insofar as [action] may be viewed as a rational process of the acquisition and allocation, as between alternative uses [or ends], of scarce means to the satisfaction of wants" (a conception

152. Souter, "Nature and Significance," 378–79; Souter, *Prolegomena*, 61, 93–94 n. 91.

of "economic" much like Robbins's neoclassical definition); and a "political" factor, which involves "action insofar as it may be viewed as a rational process of the attainment of ends through the acquisition and exercise of coercive power over other individuals and groups." Further, Parsons insists on the necessity here of an analytical rather than an empiricist method. The distinctions between ultimate means and ultimate ends, and between the technological, economic, and political factors, "must be considered an analysis of the elements in all action, or the aspects of it, not a classification of concrete actions [or concrete] spheres of real life."

This line of argument brings Parsons to a decisive point. With psychology, biology, and geography already in place to study the element of ultimate conditions, technology to study the technological factor, economics the economic factor, and politics the political factor, sociology emerges as the science necessary for the analysis of "the one so far unoccupied sector" of the means-end chain. This is the sector of the independent "creative element" that is "not capable of complete determination by . . . 'conditions' and is hence 'hanging in the air' ": namely, "ultimate common ends and the attitudes associated with and underlying them, considered in their various modes of expression in human social life," such as in the form of ultimate moral values put "directly into practice," or in the form of the "obligatory normative rules" that guarantee social order. This conceptualization is noteworthy in a number of ways. It indicates an ambitious expansion of Parsons's interdisciplinary horizon and his abandonment of the (Hobhousian) emphasis on social interaction present in his initial definition of sociology in the 1932 Marshall article. It also establishes a significant point of contact between, on the one hand, Parsons's religious background and corresponding interest in the moral values and religious motives underlying human conduct, and, on the other hand, the subject matter of sociology.[153] Of more immediate concern in the article, the conceptualization enables Parsons to meet Souter's objections to Robbins (it is not exclusionist), without following Souter's imperialist move toward an encyclopedic economics (the move becomes superfluous by the assignment of the elements neglected in neo-

153. For discussion of Parsons's shift from an interaction-based definition of the subject matter of sociology to a conception centered on ultimate values, see Levine, "Introduction," xliv-li. For varying views of the bearing of Parsons's Protestant upbringing on his approach to sociology, see Buxton, *Talcott Parsons;* Jaworski, "Simmel's Contribution"; Vidich and Lyman, *American Sociology;* and Bruce C. Wearne, "Parsons' Theory as a Secularized Post-Calvinist Humanism: A Biographical Essay" (paper presented at SAANZ Conference, August 1983).

classical theory to disciplines bordering economics). By extending rather than relinquishing the analytical method, Parsons manages at once to divide the arena of human action equitably among the various social sciences; to foreclose tendencies toward disciplinary separatism (because "concrete reality [is a] synthesis of all the different groups of forces" analyzed in the different sciences); and to establish, at last, that sociology is fully in the same scientific league as the distinguished field of economics—the main difference between the two being that sociology deals with the more ultimate aspect of the means-ends chain.

In Parsons's eyes, this was precisely the vindication of sociology that he had been seeking, and he retains it essentially unchanged for the rest of his early career, returning to it in each of the remaining four essays that belong to this period. Indeed, three of these items are efforts mainly to generalize the contrast between empiricism and analytical sociology beyond the Robbins-Souter debate and apply it to other economists, past and present.

The most substantial of these items is "Sociological Elements in Economic Thought" (chapter 17), which originally appeared in two parts in the *Quarterly Journal of Economics* in 1935. Though this was a year after the Robbins-Souter article, "Sociological Elements" is the older of the two pieces; apparently it was first drafted between the spring of 1932 and the spring of 1933 in response to a request, which Parsons had received in early 1931, for a paper on "sociological tendencies in historical, institutional and welfare economics," to be included in an edited volume on social theory by Harry Elmer Barnes.[154] Characteristically, though, Parsons took his assignment as an opportunity to put forth a more ambitious thesis of his own, a thesis that finally gave substance to his previous prediction of the coming intellectual synthesis.

Following up his earlier hint of a Marshall-Pareto-Weber correspondence, what he argues in this article is that there was a "remarkable convergence of thought" on the part of Weber, Pareto, and Emile Durkheim (the last of whom he here examines for the first time). Although they started from opposite poles—Pareto and Durkheim in the positivist camp, Weber from idealism or, as it is called in the paper, "the 'romantic' tradition of thought"—all three thinkers were led, according to Parsons, to the "analytical" view that economics is an

---

154. Quoting a memo from Barnes to Parsons [1931], Parsons Papers. On the date of the paper's composition, see Parsons to Frank Knight, 25 November 1934, Parsons Papers.

abstract science required for understanding the economic factor or aspect of human action, while the science of sociology is needed for the analysis of the value element or factor, which is of such independent importance in social life. It is Parsons's belief that, because this view had been slow to emerge, the history of economic thought was necessarily a record of vain empiricist attempts to provide a full explanation of the facts of economic life. Now looking back upon this history, and reconsidering the place within it of thinkers discussed in his previous work (Marx, Sombart, Malthus, Marshall,[155] etc.), Parsons expands the boundaries of "empiricism" to encompass both "orthodox empiricists" (economists who regarded economic theory as essentially true of concrete reality) and their various critics, the "positivistic empiricists" (those who either supplemented economic theory with, or abandoned it in favor of, factors like heredity and environment) and the "romantic empiricists" (those who supplemented economic theory with, or relinquished it for, the factor of common ethical values and ideals). Parsons's evaluation of these contending factions is clear: "empirically [the critics] are undoubtedly right"—orthodox economic theory is incapable of supplying a full account of economic life—"but that does not make them any the less disastrously wrong theoretically. Their view has quite definitely resulted in 'throwing out the baby with the bath.'" In seeking to broaden the scope of economics, the critics have come close to "sacrificing . . . the theoretical work of generations of economists"—a sacrifice that ceases to be necessary when the "analytical" orientation is finally adopted and factors outside the purview of economic theory are allotted to other abstract theoretical fields, chief among them, of course, the science of sociology.[156]

One of the reasons this point of view was attractive to Parsons was that it enabled him to claim that he had found a unique way out of the raging controversy in American economics between the neoclassicists and the institutionalists. As the "Sociological Elements" article makes clear, even more than the papers on Marshall and Robbins and Souter, this controversy was one that heavily occupied Parsons's atten-

155. On Parsons's off-again, on-again incorporation of Marshall, see Bruce Wearne, "Talcott Parsons's Appraisal and Critique of Alfred Marshall," *Social Research* 48 (1981): 816–51; Wearne, "Parsons's Sociological Ethic"; Wearne, "Parsons's Theory as a Secularized Post-Calvinist Humanism."

156. For further discussion of Parsons's position here, see Thomas Burger, "Talcott Parsons, the Problem of Order in Society, and the Program of an Analytical Sociology," *American Journal of Sociology* 83 (1977): 320–34; Edward Devereux, "Parsons' Sociological Theory," in *The Social Theories of Talcott Parsons;* Levine, "Introduction"; Levine, *The Flight from Ambiguity* (Chicago: University of Chicago Press, 1985).

tion. Indeed, before he was required to cut "Sociological Elements" for publication, it contained a section explicitly on "institutionalism and the role of institutions." [157] According to Parsons, institutionalism, as developed by its originators Veblen and Mitchell, was a species of "positivistic empiricism" and thus flawed in two respects: because of its tendency to explain conduct in terms of "institutions" conceived in psychological or biological terms, and because of its assumption that economic science could theorize "the whole of concrete 'economic' reality." The first of these ideas tilted the analysis of action toward some of sociology's major disciplinary rivals, while the second vitiated the new science's methodological rationale. This is what was at the root of Parsons's polemicizing during the 1930s against the institutionalist approach that had not only drawn him into the social sciences originally, but which contained ideas that continued to inform his thinking. Appealing to Durkheim against Veblen, "Sociological Elements" argues that "institutions" be conceptualized as "normative rules ultimately dependent on common ethical values." By extension, as Parsons emphasizes in the deleted portion of the article, "economic institutions can mean only the set of normative rules which control economic activities," so that "the theoretical treatment of economic institutions [becomes] the task of sociology, not of economics." [158] To Parsons, this was the great *via media* overlooked by the warring camps of economists: that orthodox economic theory could remain intact (satisfying the neoclassicists) at the same time that economic institutions received systematic examination (as the institutionalists wanted), if analytical sociology were only established to treat the institutional factor.

Variations on this theme appear in "On Certain Sociological Elements in Professor Taussig's Thought" (chapter 19), Parsons's contribution to a 1936 festschrift for his former mentor in the Harvard economics department. For the occasion, Parsons identifies one more subvariety of empiricism. This is "middle-ground" or "commonsense empiricism," an approach that steers between dogmatic orthodoxy and (institutionalist) "negativism" toward orthodoxy by various ad hoc means; it ranges beyond the boundaries of economic theory and brings back to economic science "any conceptual aid"—whether positivistic or nonpositivistic—"which seems useful in the immediate

---

157. The section was later restored when Parsons's article reappeared as "Sociological Elements in Economic Thought," in *Contemporary Social Theory*, ed. Harry Elmer Barnes, Howard Becker, and Frances Bennett Becker (New York: Appleton-Century, 1940), 601–46.

158. Ibid., 645.

context without too much regard for the remoter logical implications of the procedures involved." This was Taussig's strategy, according to Parsons, and for the purposes of the festschrift he goes easy on it, admitting that it has several advantages—albeit fewer than would obtain were the "analytical" road taken and ad hocery "superseded by the explicit relation of economic theory to other . . . comparable *theoretical* systems," such as that of sociology. Especially striking in the paper is Parsons's discussion of the close tie between dogmatic orthodoxy in economic theory and "capitalist apologetics," or the political conviction that practical affairs *should* correspond to neoclassical premises and that "to modify the social order away from this pattern [is] not only foolish but vicious as well." Amplifying the assessment of capitalism suggested in his earliest articles and in brief comments elsewhere (see chapters 8, 16, and 17), Parsons praises Taussig for eschewing such apologetics, upholding "the best traditions of a tolerant liberalism [attuned] to the cry for social justice" and exposing the "grave defects in the individualistic competitive order." Here, certainly, is the least-known feature of Parsons's thinking during the 1930s. For rather than questioning Taussig's position, or qualifying it by invoking the palliative of shared values, Parsons himself elaborates at length on the economic and political processes that prevent capitalism from delivering on the promise of "maximum benefit [for] all."

   This last is not a matter that surfaces again in his early work. More apparent in his 1937 review of Adolf Löwe's *Economics and Sociology*[159] (chapter 20) are the themes of his other writings on empiricism, though with a revealing variation. Löwe was a Manchester University research fellow with interesting resemblances to Parsons himself during his pre-Harvard years, having come to his position from a background in German economics and involvement in the sociological circle at the LSE. Like the institutionalists, Löwe insisted that "forms and tendencies differ widely in the various economic systems of history" and that capitalism is only one among several "individual constellations [with its own] historical structure and historical laws." In contrast to the institutionalists, however, Löwe's goal was to preserve the "pure theory" of the neoclassicists and to supplement it with a sociology that would furnish "middle principles" to connect pure theory with the "structure and regularities of motion of particular 'economic systems.' "[160] Parsons's reaction to this is a measure of the distance that he had travelled beyond his institutionalist begin-

   159. Adolf Löwe, *Economics and Sociology: A Plea for Cooperation in the Social Sciences* (London: Allen and Unwin, 1935).
   160. Ibid., 136, 137, 146.

nings, for his review concentrates almost exclusively on Löwe's proposal to link economics and sociology. This he at once praises for moving beyond ad hoc empiricism and into sociology, but then faults for creating "a fundamental logical lack of symmetry between the two sciences," something inimical to the disciplinary parity Parsons himself hoped to establish. But the review barely notices the abiding interest in understanding historical variety that underlay Löwe's plan. Parsons presumably remained of the belief, stated in the paper on Robbins and Souter and elsewhere, that the analytical elements studied by the sociologist encompass such variety, since "the factor of ultimate common ends is one which is peculiarly open to much qualitative variation." Yet all that he now offers is the assertion that Löwe's historically specific "'middle principles' can be derived from [the] general analytical theory of action [via] certain additional assumptions"—the slightest of concessions to the historicist concerns that he too had once embraced.

What had replaced them, now to a very large degree, is given full space in "The Place of Ultimate Values in Sociological Theory" (chapter 18). To date this is the only one of Parsons's early essays to have received more than passing scholarly attention,[161] too little of it directed, however, toward situating the essay in the interpretive context of his early work as a whole. The paper was written, following a solicitation from the editor of the *International Journal of Ethics* (who had heard of Parsons from Knight), in the fall of 1934, shortly after the Robbins-Souter article.[162] Not surprisingly, therefore, it directly takes off from this piece, expanding its critique of positivism, much as its view of empiricism is developed in the essays on Löwe, Taussig, and "Sociological Elements." As before, "positivism" is a code word for various "objectivist" approaches that reach their extreme in behaviorism's displacement of "the subjective aspect of human beings" by the "determinism" of heredity and environment. Against such approaches, Parsons—appealing this time to a Pareto-Durkheim-Weber-Simmel-Tönnies convergence—sets the "voluntaristic" perspective, so named to emphasize the "active, creative, evaluating" dimension of conduct that was mentioned in some of his previous work and is now given more extensive treatment.

Integral to this fuller treatment is the argument (adumbrated in his

161. See especially Robert Bierstedt, *American Sociological Theory* (New York: Academic, 1981), 395–98; Ian Procter, "Parsons's Early Voluntarism," *Sociological Inquiry* 48 (1978): 37–48; John Finley Scott, "The Changing Foundations of the Parsonian Action Scheme," *American Sociological Review* 28 (1963): 716–35.

162. Frank Knight to Parsons, 4 October 1934; Parsons to Frank Knight, 25 November 1934—both in Parsons Papers.

January 1933 letter to Knight) that, although actors are affected by heredity and environment, they also "stand in significant relations to aspects of reality other than those revealed by science." These relations—to this "nonempirical reality"—are mediated by vague "common ultimate value-attitudes" that find embodiment in "metaphysical theories, theologies," and other cultural products. Such attitudes may also attain manifestation as the ends of the means-ends process—ends independent of positivistic factors and capable, as such, of arousing human "energy," "will," and "effort" to overcome those factors in the pursuit of ends. In Parsons's hands, this becomes a high-yield formulation, and one that accommodates the different dimensions of human conduct associated with his Protestant heritage and with his training in economics. Using the formulation, Parsons can draw an analytical distinction between two types of ends (empirical and transcendental, depending on whether the attainment of an end is or is not verifiable by empirical observation) and two modes by which means may be related to ends (the intrinsic and the symbolic, depending on whether means can or cannot produce the ends by "scientifically understandable" processes), thereby bringing economic activities (a case of empirical ends and intrinsic means) as well as religious action and ritual (an instance of transcendental ends and symbolic means) both within the framework of the means-ends schema which he had adopted from the neoclassicists. In addition, Parsons can make way for the issue he had so often faulted economists for overlooking, the problem of social cohesion. Reintroducing the concept of an "action system" comprised of long means-ends chains, Parsons observes that many actors seek ends that are "removed by a very large number of intermediate links from any system of ultimate ends." This circumstance gives rise to the "problem of control," which "tends to be met by the subjection of [such] action . . . to normative rules" (or "institutions") that—either by the sanctions attached to them or by the "moral authority" that emanates from their basis in obligatory ultimate ends—regulate conduct in conformity with common values, thus promoting "social stability" over "a state of chaos."

In tying all these threads together, however, Parsons is careful to acknowledge the limits of the synthesis he proposes. Warning against the "arbitrary assumption that [the means-end] schema can exhaust the subjective aspect" of action, he offers the examples of art and of *gemeinschaftlich* social relationships as categories of social phenomena that, while still "hav[ing] a great deal to do with [the] value-attitudes" studied by the sociologist, are "very difficult, if not impossible, to fit into the means-end schema." For Parsons, the latter had yet to become the sine qua non of analytical sociology.

Lines Forward

It has long been conventional to regard the publication in 1937 of *The Structure of Social Action* as the beginning, or at least the beginning of a significant new phase, of Parsons's social theory.[163] What the preceding discussion of his early writings should make clear, however, is that, rather than marking a major change in his thinking, *The Structure of Social Action* is very much a part of the third phase of Parsons's early development. This is a view consistent with the historical chronology, for there is no break in time—or in experience—between this third phase and the period during which *The Structure of Social Action* was written. To the contrary, the book was begun in 1934 (with the chapter on Durkheim's early empirical work), completed in first draft by late 1935, and revised in the year that followed—an interval that exactly coincides with the last phase of the early essays.[164]

But beyond mere chronological correspondence lies the fundamental matter of thematic and conceptual continuity. The attack upon positivistic theories and empiricist methods, the argument for human voluntarism and for the independence of the value factor from conditional elements, the concern with the problem of social order, the conceptualization of action as a means-ends process embedded in lengthy means-ends chains, the division of these chains into different sectors allotted to different analytical disciplines, the claim that the value factor defines an autonomous domain for the science of sociology, and the presentation of these beliefs as vindicated by a recent convergence of the long-opposed European intellectual traditions of positivism and idealism—these ideas, which are generally understood as the core of *The Structure of Social Action,* are all of them dominant motifs of the early essays.[165] To say this is not to suggest, of course, that the great book is a redundancy. Just as some of the last essays that Parsons wrote in his third phase extend and develop arguments found in earlier papers from the same phase, so *The Structure of Social Action*

163. The convention is widely followed. For a clear illustration, see François Bourricaud, *The Sociology of Talcott Parsons* (Chicago: University of Chicago Press, 1977), whose chapter on "the starting point" of Parsons's work is an analysis of *The Structure of Social Action,* where no mention is made of the early essays. For a statement of the view that the book marks a new phase in Parsons's work, see Peter Hamilton, *Talcott Parsons* (London: Tavistock, 1983), 62; P. Hamilton, "Introduction," in *Readings from Talcott Parsons* (London: Tavistock, 1985), 65. See also Jeffrey Alexander, *The Modern Reconstruction of Classical Thought: Talcott Parsons,* vol. 4 of *Theoretical Logic in Sociology* (Berkeley and Los Angeles: University of California Press, 1983), 9–16, 335 n. 135; Gouldner, *The Coming Crisis,* 188.

164. On the dating here, see Parsons, "Building Social Systems," 829.

165. On the centrality of these themes in *The Structure of Social Action,* and in the literature surrounding the book, see Camic, "*Structure* after 50 Years."

significantly develops ideas worked out in the essays. In the book, for instance, Parsons engages philosophy-of-science issues more comprehensively than before and systematizes his concept of action by specifying the components of the "unit act" in terms of the "action frame of reference." He also transforms the notion of convergence finally into the Marshall-Pareto-Durkheim-Weber convergence thesis and envelops the thesis at once in a fuller treatment of the history of the positivistic and idealistic traditions, a more complex conceptual apparatus (an apparatus that puts in place all the terms used in the early articles: utilitarianism, individualism, the forms of radical positivism, etc.), and a more elaborate and acute analysis both of the writings of Pareto, Durkheim, and Weber, and of some of the specific topics that surface when examining these writings (social change, social control, religion, charisma, ideal types).

Yet, through nearly all of this, Parsons remains well within the bounds of the substantive and methodological problems, claims, and assumptions that characterize his other writings from the mid-1930s. What is distinctive about *The Structure of Social Action,* as a result, lies less in the areas of method and substance than in the extraordinary package that takes shape as Parsons consolidates in one text (and in conjunction with the various elaborations just described) his previously stated views on voluntaristic conduct, norms and values, means-ends chains, the analytical method as applied to sociology, the convergence of positivism and idealism, and so on. The package, to be sure, comes at a higher price than the essays; in the book, the clarity of expression and reasoning that one tends to see in the essays evaporates under the pressure produced by the combination of many diverse elements. The achievement of this combination nevertheless emboldens Parsons to assume throughout the book a more confident and assertive stance. This is evident when he abandons a number of the important nuances and qualifiers contained in the early essays (regarding, e.g., the complexity of the history of economic theory); and it is evident when he presents his theory of action not only as the "permanently valid precipitate" of the main currents of modern thought, but now also as an approach of such comprehensive scope as to end the conflict among the "many [competing] systems of sociological theory" (those dealing, for example, with relationships, groups, and personality), all of which can be "translat[ed] into terms of the theory of action." [166] To what extent this self-confident rhetoric and the particular consolidation of ideas that accompanied it enabled *The Structure*

166. Parsons, *Structure of Social Action,* 719–24, 744–47, 757, 774–75.

of Social Action eventually to achieve the great impact that was never attained by the early essays is difficult to assess. In any event, it would seem apparent that the book's argument stands in a line of direct continuity with the last phase of Parsons's early essays, as this emerged from his previous writings and from his sociointellectual experiences in the 1920s and 30s and before.

And Parsons's early period left a legacy of a different sort as well. It established as one characteristic feature of his theorizing a self-referential orientation that might be termed "cosmopolitan localism," meaning by this an outlook that gives general—if not, indeed, world-historical—significance to questions and issues growing out of one's immediate intellectual context.[167] The localism of Parsons's early work is apparent. The problems that the work addresses (the origins of capitalist society, the limitations of utilitarian theory, the problem of order, the nature of action, the status of sociology, the inadequacies of "positivism" and "empiricism," the emerging intellectual synthesis) and the tools that it uses to confront these problems (the genetic method, the analytical method, the appeal to the traditions of European thought, the work of Weber, Marshall, Pareto, and even Durkheim) are both in large measure, though obviously not without exception, supplied by local establishments: by Amherst institutionalism and LSE-Heidelberg social science, by Harvard economics and philosophy of science, by contemporary academic controversies over behaviorism and the role of the social sciences, and by the struggles to institutionalize the science of sociology, particularly at Harvard. As a young man, Parsons is a thinker with his ear close to the ground, alert to the big issues under discussion in the different disciplines he makes contact with in the settings where he finds himself, brilliant at seeing relationships between ideas expressed in one place and then another. Even in the face of obstacles, he also displays a singular dedication to making good on contemporary forecasts about a coming intellectual synthesis, as well as great ingenuity in utilizing the tools available to him to construct an original approach to existing intellectual problems.

Yet, possibly because of his international schooling at what *were* some of the principal intellectual centers of the interwar period, Parsons is quick to endow the local with cosmopolitan importance: to view the ideas around him not just as some significant contemporary

167. This conceptualization draws upon Robert K. Merton's 1949 article, "Patterns of Influence: Local and Cosmopolitan Influentials," reprinted in his *Social Theory and Social Structure* (New York: Free Press, 1968).

ideas that could profitably be drawn together, but as ideas that embodied *the* fundamental positions in an ongoing debate over *the* most basic issues of modern thought, issues that themselves grew out of long traditions of social thought which were soon to culminate—and through his own work—in the synthesis that would end the contemporary debate and lay the groundwork for future social science. As to the specifics of this synthesis, the young Parsons does not lock himself in; as the early essays make clear, what he proposes in one place he willingly modifies at another (witness his changing definitions of sociology, the move from the genetic to the analytical method, the shifting makeup of the convergence thesis). But his striking flexibility in this respect is not matched by an inclination to question his world-historical stance. To the contrary, this appears to become more confirmed as the early period advances and Parsons grows more embattled, in part because of his increasingly uncertain situation at Harvard. Certainly by the mid-30s, he simply takes for granted the legitimacy of vaulting from parochial contemporary controversies onto the universal plane: of proceeding, for example, from "the methodological battle between 'orthodox' . . . and 'institutional'" economics straight to the antinomies of the whole "history of [European] economic thought"; or of moving directly from "the objectivist trend [in] behaviorism" to a generalized attack upon "positivism." [168] In *The Structure of Social Action,* this is all carried further until the local referents still visible in the early essays are more completely effaced by the cosmopolitan argot. But the argot does not make Parsons's mode of theorizing in this famous instance any less that of the cosmopolitan local. And thereafter, as his career proceeds, as he engages other controversies and again proves willing to modify and extend his synthesis, it is this precipitate of the early years outlasts nearly all others.

Note on the Selections and on the Editing

At the present time, there is no complete bibliography of Talcott Parsons's published work. In the last two decades of his life, Parsons appended a bibliography of his writings to several of his books, but his listing is incomplete, especially for the period prior to *The Structure of Social Action.* For the current volume, efforts have been made to locate as many of Parsons's early publications as possible and to bring the majority of these together. Only five known items are excluded:

168. The first pair of quotations is taken from chapter 17 of this volume, the second pair from chapter 18.

two reviews of Pareto's *The Mind and Society*,[169] which overlap considerably with chapters 12 and 15 of this volume; the article "Want and Activities in Marshall," discussed above and widely available as a chapter of *The Structure of Social Action;* the brief and also readily available "Translator's Preface" to Max Weber's *The Protestant Ethic and the Spirit of Capitalism;*[170] and the short discussion paper, "Remarks on Education and the Professions."[171] It is not unlikely that other early pieces (e.g., items that Parsons may have written for local newspapers) will, in time, also come to light.

All the articles and book reviews in the present collection appear here essentially as they did when they were originally published. None of the pieces has been shortened, and editorial changes have been kept to a minimum. Trivial spelling mistakes and word omissions have been silently corrected; two-part articles have been combined into one; footnotes have been renumbered where necessary; and slight modifications have been made to establish consistency of format across the items, particularly in the references. With two exceptions (on pp. 29 and 39 below, where the bracketed additions to the quotation from Weber and Sée are Parsons's), words appearing in square brackets are those of the editor.

169. See note 147 above.
170. See note 63 above.
171. *International Journal of Ethics* 47 (1937): 365–69.

I

CAPITALIST SOCIETY AND ITS ORIGINS

1

"Capitalism" in Recent German Literature: Sombart and Weber

Part 1

Anglo-American economic thought, at least in its predominant trend, is a child of the individualistic and rationalistic philosophy of the seventeenth and eighteenth centuries. One of the salient characteristics of this whole trend of thought has been its rather abstract generality; its formulation in terms implying, or at least not denying, universal applicability wherever human economic life is lived. With the general attitude thus assumed it has perforce tended to neglect the economic problems connected with the growth and development of types of economic society, and in particular with the working out of the differences between, and the specific characteristics of, the different cultural epochs.

There has been, however, another major strain in modern thought, which has laid its main emphasis on this aspect of the problems of society, and in particular of economic life. Its principal, though by no means exclusive, field of influence has been Germany, and its intellectual soil more than anything else the romantic movement in its many different phases. It has been preeminently occupied with the problems of history, and among its most important accomplishments is the formulation of various philosophies of history, in Germany notably those of Hegel and Karl Marx. It forms the background of the theories which this paper is to discuss.

The more immediate background is formed by two main influences: first, the historical school in economics, with its attack on orthodox theory, and, much more important, its emphasis on the relativity of economic systems and epochs, and the necessity of analyzing each on its own merits with a view to working out its own particular characteristics rather than getting at general economic laws. Secondly, Karl Marx and the discussion after Marx in Germany of the problems of

Originally published in the *Journal of Political Economy* 36 (1928): 641–44; 37 (1929): 31–51.

3

socialism. And here two main aspects are of importance: First, the economic interpretation of history, the problems connected with which play a major part in the thought of Sombart and Weber. Secondly, Marx is the special forerunner of the particular theory with which I am here concerned: that of capitalism as a great epoch in social and economic development.[1]

In both Sombart and Weber there are views of history which are largely to be understood as answers to the questions raised by the economic interpretation, and in each there is a further development of the idea of capitalism as an epoch of history, tinged with the views of Marx, but at the same time showing important divergences from him and from each other.

The purpose of this paper is not primarily to subject these theories to a critical examination, but to put them before American readers in a more condensed and systematic form than that in which they are available in German, and to project them onto the background of their relations to the general development of social thought. What there is of criticism will be largely incidental to these main tasks.

In the works of Werner Sombart is to be found the first of the two great theories of capitalism with which we have to deal.[2] The aim of his work as he lays it down in the introduction to the *Modern Capitalism,* is to present a systematic, genetic treatment of the development of European and American economic life as a whole. His view of economic science is, one may say, historical, but at the same time theoretical. It is historical in that he goes so far as to deny the existence of

1. This view of capitalism is, of course, to be sharply distinguished from the "capitalistic" round-about process of Boehm-Bawerk. Boehm-Bawerk uses the concept of capitalism entirely analytically and has, for the purposes of his analysis, the theory of interest, no concern with the broader historical and cultural problems with which Sombart and Weber deal.

2. The first edition of Sombart's great work, *Der moderne Kapitalismus,* appeared in 1902. It met much adverse criticism and in the years following he undertook practically to rewrite the whole. Several special studies were published from time to time (*Der Bourgeois* [1913], *Die Juden und das Wirtschaftsleben, Krieg und Kapitalismus, Luxus und Kapitalismus*) and in 1916–17 the first two volumes of the new edition of the *Kapitalismus* appeared. They dealt with the precapitalistic systems and the early capitalistic period, from the breakdown of the Middle Ages to approximately the end of the eighteenth century. The third and last volume, dealing with "mature capitalism" (*Hochkapitalismus*) down to the World War, appeared in two installments, 1926–27. Other works of Sombart bearing on the problems of capitalism are *Die deutsche Volkswirtschaft im 19ten Jakrhundert, Der proletarische Sozialismus* (1924, 2 vols.), the article "Die prinzipielle Eigenart des modernen Kapitalismus," *Grundriss der Sozialökonomik,* vol. 4; and various articles in periodicals, especially the *Archiv für Sozialwissenschaft and Sozialpolitik.*

economic laws transcending history, at any rate beyond what might be considered physical and technical conditions of economic activity (for instance, physical diminishing returns). But aside from this negative attitude to orthodox economic theory, which I do not share, he sees the positive task of economic science in the historical presentation and analysis of concrete economic systems and modes of life.

In this sense he digs out and reduces to order an enormous mass of historical material, filling for *Modern Capitalism* alone, six large volumes. He is certainly not alone concerned or satisfied with working out an ideal type of capitalism which has for him only abstract interest, but his theory is a means of illuminating and understanding the concrete historical development. But he is not a "mere" historian. He is interested, not in working out the particular circumstances of the economic history of any single country for its own sake, but in presenting European economic life as a whole, in its great common trend, and in getting at the laws of its development. His aim is thus definitely theoretical, and his work should be judged as a whole from that point of view. The term "theory," however, is here used in a different and more general sense than that common in economic science, to mean, not merely a system of equilibrium, but any consistent and unified system of concepts to be used in the analysis of social phenomena.[3]

In conformity with this general view of economics stands the leading concept of his work, that of the economic system. He defines it as follows: "Under this term I understand a peculiarly ordered form of economic activity, a particular organization of economic life within which a particular mental attitude predominates and a particular technique is applied."[4] This economic system is to be constructed in the purity of an "ideal type"[5] to be used for the analysis of concrete reality, and will be found to correspond more or less closely to the historical facts. The empirical equivalent of the economic system is for Sombart the economic epoch, a period of time in history within which a particular economic system or form of economic life has predominated.

Every economic system has, he maintains, three aspects: a form of organization, a technique, and a mental attitude or spirit.[6] Of these

---

3. See E. Salin, *Weltwirtschaftliches Archiv,* 1927. It will be impossible to present here any large proportion of Sombart's particular historical interpretations. But they should be included in any complete view of his work.

4. *Kapitalismus* 1:21–22.

5. See second half of this article for a fuller discussion of the "ideal type."

6. The two German terms which Sombart uses are *Wirtschaftsgesinnung* and *Wirtschaftsgeist.* Both are difficult to translate. I shall in general use "spirit" and hope its exact meaning will become clear in the course of the discussion.

three, the side which he most strongly emphasizes is that of the spirit. In Sombart's own words: "It is a fundamental contention of this work that at different times different attitudes toward economic life have prevailed, and that it is the spirit which has created a suitable form for itself and has thus created economic organization."[7] Each spirit is for him a thoroughly unique phenomenon, occurring only once in history. There is no line of development leading from spirit to spirit, and thus from system to system, and each is, therefore, to be considered by and for itself.

He uses the conception of the spirit as the means to bring order and unity into the historical material. It is one of the most striking features of Sombart's work that he is able to interpret a whole epoch of history in such an illuminating and convincing way in terms of one great leading idea. It gives a unity to his presentation which marks a great advance over the entirely disconnected studies of historical facts presented by the historical school proper. It does not give the impression that he is "philosophizing" independently of the facts. On the contrary, he is able to achieve an amazing degree of concreteness in his picture.

The emphasis on the spirit as the moving force of economic and social development is that part of the theories with which this paper deals, which is most distinctively German, and which brings out most clearly the relations they bear to the main currents of European thought. At bottom it goes back to German idealism and the conception there developed of the "life of the spirit." It may be said that Kant's great synthesis saved this whole line of thought from the inundation which threatened to submerge it by reconciling it with mechanistic science. The synthesis, however, was not without its difficulties; and since Kant there has been a pendulum-like movement in German thought, tending to exaggerate first one and then the other of the two great elements of the compromise. In Hegel the pendulum swung far over to the "spiritual" side; then with Feuerbach and some of the young Hegelians it swung just as far the other way. At this point began the application to the analysis of capitalism, starting at the left, so to speak, with the historical materialism of Marx.[8] It was in terms of the

7. *Kapitalismus* 1:25.
8. There has been considerable controversy in the literature on historical materialism as to just what Marx and Engels meant by it. Some interpreters (for instance B. Croce, *Historical Materialism and the Economics of Karl Marx*) maintain that it is to be considered, not a theory of the forces in social evolution, but rather a heuristic principle. Whether that be the correct interpretation of Marx or not, the sense in which I am taking him has certainly had the greatest influence on Sombart (see *Der proletarische Sozialismus*) and also on that aspect of Weber in which I am primarily interested.

Marxian view that the problem was presented to Sombart, and in a sense he represents the extreme of the swing back again toward Hegel. There is, however, the important difference that while retaining in essentials the matter-spirit alternative, Sombart has discarded the peculiar evolutionary form, the dialectic, in which the doctrine appeared in both Hegel and Marx (though in different senses), and has substituted his own type of "cultural morphology." This he derived from conceptions long existing in various forms of historical thought, especially its more romantic aspects.

Sombart proceeds immediately to the application of his idea of the spirit of economic life when he begins to lay the scene for modern capitalism by sketching precapitalistic economy. He distinguishes two precapitalistic systems in Europe: self-sufficient economy (*Eigenwirtschaft*) and the handicraft system. But for his purposes they are much the same and are treated as such because in spirit they are almost identical. The principal characteristic common to them is that economic life was regarded purely as a means for the satisfaction of human needs. Moreover, these needs were neither unlimited nor fluctuating, but were traditionally fixed for each person according to the social station into which he was born. He was expected to receive the support necessary for a given status (what Sombart calls the *Bedarfsdeckungsprinzip* and sharply distinguishes from the principle of unlimited acquisition or *Erwerbsprinzip*). With this traditional character of precapitalistic economic life he contrasts the rationality of capitalism.

Starting as he does from the postulate that economic systems are separate and unique, Sombart is bound to make the most of the differences between them and to minimize the elements of continuity. It is thus the logical necessity of his whole viewpoint which leads him to his well-known and highly controversial thesis that medieval commerce was essentially a handicraft and thus sharply distinguished from that of modern times.[9] Economic historians of liberal leanings would strongly disagree with him, and there is a prima facie case for the accusation of at least serious one-sidedness.[10]

Sombart's most precise formulation of the essence of capitalism is as follows:

> It is an economic system, as above defined, which is distinguished by the following characteristics: (1) Form, organization. (*a*) It is a system based

9. *Kapitalismus* 1:279ff.

10. On Sombart's own ground it seems somewhat incomprehensible that he is able to speak of *two* precapitalistic systems, since the most characteristic criterion of any system is the spirit, and in this case both are dominated by practically the same spirit.

upon private initiative and exchange; (*b*) there is a regular co-operation of two groups of the population, the owners of the means of production and the propertyless workers, all of whom (*c*) are brought into relation through the market. (2) Spirit, mental attitude. It is dominated by the principles of acquisition, of competition, and of economic rationality. (3) The corresponding technique is the revolutionary technique of modern times, emancipated from the limitations of the organic world.[11]

Each of these three aspects may now be dealt with in turn. The basic units of the system are the capitalistic enterprises. In function these are, in contrast to the medieval manor, almost indefinitely varied, but in structure and manner of working they show important similarities.

First of all there is division of labor within the enterprise, especially as between the functions of ownership and management on the one hand, and those of carrying out orders on the other. This cleft forms the starting point of the modern labor movement and of modern socialism, phenomena which are peculiar to the modern era and only to be understood in relation to their capitalistic origin. Only in modern times has there been, according to Sombart, an industrial proletariat as we know it, although there have often been relatively propertyless classes. Further in the course of development comes a more and more complex subdivision of functions, particularly in the first set, through progressive divorce of ownership from management.

Now the interconnection of all these independent units through the market and the price mechanism has most important consequences. All the qualitative differences of the most diverse economic goods are reduced to a single common denominator, money. This quantitative measure gives a means of comparison of diverse goods on the one hand. On the other hand it gives an objective purpose for all economic activity, which is primarily the making of profit in terms of money, and only indirectly the securing of the goods for which money can be exchanged. Thus a wedge is driven between the "natural" end of economic action, the satisfaction of needs, and the means to that satisfaction. Every capitalistic enterprise is forced by its very nature to pursue a given end common to all enterprises, in the pursuit of which there is no stopping place.

From this viewpoint Sombart defines capital as "the sum of exchange value which serves as the working basis of a capitalistic enterprise."[12] He thus gives it substantially the same meaning which it has in accounting practice, and defines it in terms of its function, and not

11. "Die Prinzipielle Eigenart."
12. *Kapitalismus* 3:129.

as a category of goods. Secondly, he makes it a historical concept which has no meaning apart from the capitalistic system. It is Sombart's solution of the difficulty of bringing capital and capitalism into a satisfactory relation. Its great merit is that it avoids the confusion which Weber brings into his idea of capitalism as a historical epoch by basing his concept on a general and abstract definition of capital.[13] Thus it appears that Sombart sees capitalism as an objective system the end of which comes to be the acquisition of profit. It is the compulsion on the individual business man to seek this end which Sombart, following Marx, calls the "necessity of capital to reproduce itself" (*Verwertungsstreben des Kapitals*).

The existence of such an objective and acquisitive system is the dominant fact which Sombart wishes to explain in terms of his theory of the spirit of capitalism, in accordance with his general position regarding the relation of spirit and form of organization. This is not to be taken to mean that Sombart's theory is dependent upon any particular psychology. Both Sombart and Weber would strongly repudiate that suggestion. In the first place they are interested in the action of the individual *as a whole* and hold that any further analysis of him lies beyond the province of social science. The whole individual is the "atom" from which they start. Secondly, they are interested in the *differences* between mental attitudes at different times and places, not in the universal elements which form the subject matter of psychology. That is the essence of the historical nature of their work. In this respect there is an important difference between them and the American "institutional" economists. The results of psychology, say Sombart and Weber, may be useful to supplement the economist's knowledge, but psychology is no part of the proper study of economics or sociology, and its relevance to their problems is on essentially the same plane as that of the other nonsocial sciences which supply data to economics.

The spirit of the entrepreneur or the capitalistic spirit is in Sombart's view made up of two main components: the bourgeois[14] spirit

13. See below, with reference to Weber. That Sombart's way of looking at capital is not necessarily to be considered as inconsistent with a general analytical system of economic theory is attested by the case of Schumpeter (*Theorie der wirtschaftlichen Entwicklung*, 2d ed., Munich, 1926), whose view in this regard is very similar to that of Sombart. Yet Schumpeter is one of the staunchest supporters of those claims of economic theory which Sombart denies.

14. Sombart himself uses the French word *bourgeois* to designate the whole capitalistic man, not one aspect of him. For the single rational aspect he uses the German *Bürger*. It seems best, however, since there is not proper English equivalent of the latter, to translate *Bürger* by *bourgeois,* ignoring Sombart's distinction.

and the spirit of enterprise. The spirit of enterprise is a general phenomenon, by no means peculiar to capitalism, but common to most phases of the social world which came into being with the Renaissance. It is the same spirit that created the modern state, the new religion, science and technique. It is a spirit of worldly character, restless, roving, and adventurous. It finds an especially favorable field of action in capitalistic acquisition. The endlessness of competitive activity in a race without a fixed goal is well suited to its striving toward infinite aims (*Unendlichkeitsstreben*). Capital is used as an instrument of conquest and domination.

The principles of the spirit of enterprise are two: that of acquisition and that of competition. In the pursuit of gain all the many motives of the many different types of men are objectified, are made to express themselves in one set of terms, the pecuniary success of the enterprise, quite oblivious whether the original motive might be desire for power, mere venality, the love of activity for its own sake, or what not. The making of profit becomes an end which dominates the whole system.

The acquisitive principle is strengthened in its effect by that of competition. This it is which makes gain a measure of success, and because of it acquisition comes to be without limit. It occurs in two ways: negatively, in that acquisition loses all relation to the personal needs of the entrepreneur; positively, in that not acquisition alone is the aim but acquisition in competition with others. Therein lies the dynamic force of capitalism in increasing the intensity of economic life. As a result acquisition finally becomes generalized so that the whole world is seen from the point of view of business interests; nature and other men are looked upon as means of production. Economic activity, which is originally purely a means to an end, becomes an absolute end in itself, the expression of a religion.[15]

Organically bound up with the spirit of enterprise is the other main component of the capitalistic spirit, the *bourgeois* spirit. Its leading principle is that of rationality. Its task is to make life systematic, disciplined, secure; to subject the plans of the entrepreneur to careful scrutiny and meticulous calculations of profit and loss. It appears largely in the form of a business ethics whose typical virtues are reliability, temperance, frugality, industry, thrift.

It can easily be seen in what relation the two components of the capitalistic spirit stand to each other. The creative impulse is without question to be attributed to the spirit of enterprise. It is responsible

15. For this viewpoint see T. N. Carver, *The Religion Worth Having.* For Sombart's explanation, "Die prinzipielle Eigenart."

for the destruction of the old order and for the creation of the new. On the other hand, the *bourgeois* spirit has created the framework within which the spirit of enterprise has been able to develop itself. Rationality is a necessary condition of the development of modern large-scale industry.

There is, however, for Sombart a process of development within the capitalistic spirit. The earlier period is one of the predominance of the spirit of enterprise, with on the whole a defective development of rationality. Later, on the other hand, the *bourgeois* spirit gains the upper hand, and the spirit of enterprise, while it does not disappear, is so to speak tamed and brought into the service of the rational pursuit of purely capitalistic aims. Thus the spirit of enterprise becomes objectified and harnessed to the capitalistic system; it becomes divorced from the pursuit of personal aims and comes to serve an entirely abstract one.

Finally, however, the same fate befalls the *bourgeois* spirit also. While capitalism takes on more and more *bourgeois* characteristics, the entrepreneurs as such need not do so. On the contrary, the *bourgeois* virtues are transferred from the person of the entrepreneur to the enterprise. It becomes industrious and thrifty; it possesses the necessary solidity to enjoy good credit, quite independently of the possession of such qualities by the individual entrepreneur. Even saving tends to become divorced from the will of the individual and to be carried on by the enterprise. This is what he calls the process of "objectification" of the capitalistic spirit.

Thus Sombart sees at the end of capitalistic development the creation of a "monster," the capitalistic enterprise, possessed of a purpose, an understanding, and a set of virtues all its own, going its own way independently of human will. Not that it is independent of human activity in itself. That is just where it is most objectionable to Sombart. It calls for more intensive intellectual activity and absorbs a greater proportion of human energy than any other form of economic organization. But this intellectual activity has come to be in the service of abstract nonhuman ends. It is no longer free, but is forced to follow paths marked out in advance by the "system." It forms a treadmill in which everyone is caught, unable to escape.

The spirit of capitalism is the leading concept of Sombart's work. In terms of this everything else is to be understood. Its origins in the history of thought lie in the "conservative" [16] wing of the romantic

---

16. In the sense of identification with an "organic" view of society and more or less feudal ideals, not of defense of the status quo.

movement. From that point of view capitalism appears chiefly as a destructive force tearing down the social ties of an older and more "organic" civilization. Here is the origin of Sombart's adverse ethical judgment of capitalism. It is interesting to note that, in common with almost all social thinkers who for so many centuries have been radically opposed to the existing order, he invokes a "state of nature," namely, the precapitalistic era, by which to measure the shortcomings of capitalism. But while the state of nature of the radical philosophies of the eighteenth century was a state of extreme individual freedom, i.e., freedom from social ties, Sombart takes to a large extent the very society which they were fighting against as his natural state. With it goes an interpretation of the institutions of those times as natural "growths," which is the opposite pole from that of a Voltaire or a Godwin.

Sombart's work in general shows large traces of polemical emphasis, and he shares the common polemical tendency to overstatement. Hence in order to understand him it will be useful to contrast his views with those against which he was struggling. The emphasis on the spirit grows, of course, out of the conflict with historical materialism, giving perhaps an equally one-sided view, but one growing directly out of the alternatives presented by Marx. Most of the other fundamental views he holds are to be explained as a reaction to the optimistic social philosophy of the Enlightenment and its heirs. To the contention that there is one single line of progressive cultural evolution, starting in barbarism and ending with the age of modern science and machine technique, Sombart replies that there is no such thing as progress, but only a succession of mutually independent cultures, which are born, grow to maturity, and die. He holds the position so radically as to include all of social life within these closed systems. In so doing he certainly goes too far and substitutes another equally metaphysical entity, the "spirit," for that of progress. Where such a spirit of economic life should come from and why it should produce a given economic system at a given time and place remains as much a mystery as why we should be so obviously progressing toward a millennium. It may be possible purely empirically to prove the presence of such systems of economic organization, but not to explain them in terms of their spirit. And surely there is some continuity in social evolution, even though it is not so plain as has been thought, and even though its ethical interpretation in terms of pogress is unwarranted. It may very well be that both Sombart and the disciples of progress are mistaking the part for the whole, that there is room for both interpretations applying to different aspects of social life.

The discontinuity of economic systems, which is such a prominent feature of Sombart's work, is not, however, meant to be a concrete historical discontinuity, but only to apply "in principle." The systems shade off into each other almost imperceptibly in actual historical fact; there is no sharp break in the line of development. This shading off he works out in great detail in his presentation of the transition from precapitalistic economy to capitalism. Nonetheless, Sombart's method is radically opposed to the hypothesis of continuous evolution as held by most Western sociologists.

Another salient characteristic of Sombart's thought, his emphasis on the unity of a culture, may well be thought of as a protest against the overoptimistic view that, in order to cure all social ills, it is only necessary to tinker here and there, and thus change some parts independently of others. Up to a certain point he is undoubtedly right. Our social fabric does hang together, but again—like Marx in the opposite sense—he overshoots the mark and attributes an undue rigidity to the system. There seems to be little reason to believe that it is not possible on the basis which we now have to build by a continuous process something more nearly approaching an ideal society. In any case the process of social change is certainly neither so radically discontinuous nor so radically determined by any "principles" as Sombart would have us believe. In the transition from capitalism to a different social system surely many elements of the present would be built into the new order. This is precisely what socialism wishes to do, retaining all the technical progress of capitalism for its utopia. But, Sombart replies, it is just the trouble with socialism that, being a child of capitalism, it could not but share its cultural shortcomings. In this sense he is much more radically opposed to capitalism than any socialist.

Finally, as a part of the general philosophy of progress, we hear a great deal about the conquest of nature. Many have gone so far as to call that the greatest achievement of modern civilization. Sombart does not deny this; on the contrary, he makes a great deal of capitalistic emancipation from the rhythm of natural processes. But he would deny that it meant any increase of true freedom. Quite the contrary, man in emancipating himself from slavery to nature has subordinated himself to a system of his own making whose tyranny over his life is worse. Again, one may point out that Sombart's belief in the beneficence of his "state of nature" is naive romanticism. But it does seem that the apostles of progress and freedom had been somewhat overhasty in their optimism, and it is by no means certain that the conquest of nature is alone sufficient cause to boast of the glory of our civilization. Nonetheless, something it is, and to deny all value to it, as Sombart very nearly does, is going too far. Yet he is perfectly right in maintaining that our tendency to glorify it is evidence of a lack of a proper sense of cultural balance.

Taken all in all, making allowances for polemical overstatement, it does seem that Sombart has presented a view of capitalistic society which is a formidable alternative to the orthodox liberal one. It is seldom that such extremes are either wholly true or wholly false. As Hegel said, important new ideas tend to be presented as extreme antitheses to prevailing ones. When the higher synthesis is achieved, is it not probable that Sombart's train of thought will be incorporated into it?

One of the most typical of Sombart's applications of the spirit of capitalism is the case of technique, the third principal aspect of the capitalistic system. He starts by denying that the explanation of the great inventive activity of capitalistic times is to be found either in a general "instinct of contrivance" or in a special inventive genius of any race, the English or Yankees, for instance. On the contrary, it is a distinctly historical phenomenon, an integral part of capitalism.

The precapitalistic era was, he says, very poor in inventions, because the spirit of the times was against it, not merely because the process of evolution had not yet proceeded far enough. Precapitalistic technique, he says, is not an earlier stage in a direct line of development leading to modern technique, but is something quite different in principle. The big men of the time disdained any interest in economic matters; the thinkers were mainly theologians, while the mass of the people were tightly bound by tradition. And modern science had not yet come into being. Thus medieval technique was on the one hand traditional, as received from a master and handed down; on the other hand it was empirical, relying upon experience for instruction and not on objective scientific reasoning.

In the early capitalistic era a considerable change took place. Where technique had been held down by tradition, those bonds were broken and a great wave of inventive activity swept Europe, a part of the spirit of enterprise which characterized the new times. The traditional principle gave way to the rational, that of casting about for the most suitable means to reach the ends in question. But with the exception of a few men like Leonardo da Vinci, there was no scientific technique. While the same age saw the birth of modern science, the two streams did not converge until later.

It is just that which characterizes modern technique: it is scientific. Science and technique are so closely related as to represent the theoretical and practical sides of the same movement. Discoveries and inventions go hand in hand and in some cases (organic dyes) are identical. The same fundamental conception, that of a mechanistic system of relations, underlies both. "To the elimination of God from the conception of nature corresponds an elimination of man from technique." "While natural science *thinks* of the world as a mechanism or 'chemism,' modern technique artificially *creates* a world which runs according to the formulae set up by natural science." [17] Thus modern technique is both rational and scientific.

The practical consequences of this attitude are most important. (1) All technical knowledge is objectified. It is no longer handed down personally from master to apprentice, but may be learned from books, accessible to all who have the necessary mental equipment. (2) Technical methods are made to follow, not the empirical "rules" learned from the master, but scientific "laws" which are known. (A rule applies only to the particular cases actually experienced; a law applies generally.) (3) All processes are, so far as possible, mechanized, reduced to routine operations and made to a very large extent automatic. And the circumstances have been especially favorable to invention under capitalism.

Could anything bring out more strikingly the peculiarities of Sombart's line of thought? At just the point where the hypothesis of unilinear evolution has been thought to be most secure, and where the results of progress can be most easily measured, he denies them both completely. Once more it seems evident that he overstates his case; but again, can we say there is nothing in it? [18]

At several points it has been evident that Sombart deals with capitalism, not as a static thing, but as a process. And in this process there are two main stages: that of early capitalism, and that of "mature" capitalism (*Hochkapitalismus*). This process is given a conspicuous place not only in his treatment of the capitalistic spirit, and in that of technique, but also in the relation of the state to the economic world, and finally in the nature of the economic thought of the two periods, of which he takes the mercantilists and the classical school as types. [19]

The question would naturally arise whether two such fundamentally different things could reasonably be considered as successive stages of the same economic system. Sombart does regard them so. The differences he ascribes to the continued presence of precapitalistic elements in the early capitalistic society, and the development he sees

17. *Kapitalismus* 3:81.
18. See ibid., vol. 1, chaps. 29, 30; vol. 3, chaps. 7–9.
19. Ibid., vol. 2, chap. 60.

from one side as a process of progressive elimination of those elements. Hence there is in his view no third system in between, which is
entitled to consideration on its own merits. And it may be said that
although Sombart devotes two-thirds of his great work to the precapitalistic and early capitalistic stages, he is primarily interested in the
phenomenon of "mature" capitalism and consistently focuses attention on it. The most important theoretical content of his work, the
objectivation of acquisition, the compulsion of the individual to conform to the system, the process of rationalization, all pertain to it. It
is the center of gravity of the whole work.

Nonetheless, there is serious reason to question this position. The
general cultural differences between the seventeenth and the nineteenth centuries are certainly enormous, as much in the economic field
as any other. And Sombart's attempt to present them both as parts of
the same great system leads him into some serious difficulties—in
dealing, for instance, with the role of the state in modern capitalism.
As regards the early capitalistic era, he greatly emphasizes the positive
functions of the state in developing capitalistic enterprise through
mercantilist policies. But at the height of capitalism in the nineteenth
century he finds a totally different situation, the function of the state
having become wholly negative, limited to external defense, the maintenance of internal order, and the enforcement of contracts. The real
center of gravity lies in the competitive activities of private enterprises.

But at the end of the period he finds again a decided change. The
rise of imperialism in external policy and various tendencies to modify
competition within have greatly complicated the relation of the state
to industry. This cannot be accounted for wholly as due to the growth
of noncapitalistic elements within capitalism, and Sombart's explanation is that the modern state is governed by two ultimately irreconcilable principles: that of power and that of liberty, or sovereignty and
individualism. In general he says that the former is characteristic of
external relations, the latter of internal, but that free trade represented
an "episodic" attempt to apply the later to both spheres, an attempt
which has broken down in a return to the "normal course" of capitalism. This, however, contradicts his earlier sharp distinction between a mercantilist and a liberal state. The confusion seems to be due
to the attempt to fit a very complicated set of facts into an all-too-
simple general scheme of thought.

In general he seems to waver between the unity of capitalism, and
the differences which he has emphasized between early and mature
capitalism, finally deciding in favor of the former viewpoint. But
would it not be equally possible to construct a scheme in which there

were two economic systems in Europe since the Middle Ages instead of one? There seems to be danger that in using a method like Sombart's the unit which is to be called a "culture" may be arbitrarily selected, without sufficient regard for the facts. That all who use the same method do not choose the same units is attested by Spengler's theory,[20] which follows a third possibility, taking his unit of "Western civilization" to include the Middle Ages, i.e., everything since the decline of the Roman Empire. It is even possible that the same unit could not be applied to all phases of a culture, and still more likely that there are some aspects in regard to which the conception is of little value.

The most important forerunner of Sombart in the theory of capitalism was Karl Marx. It is worthwhile in closing [Part I] to say a few words about their relation. It has changed radically in the course of Sombart's scientific development, but I am concerned here only with its final form. The main thing is that Sombart has been influenced by a side of Marxian thought which has received relatively little attention in the West, that in which he is a true representative of *Historismus,* not his abstract economic theory.[21]

The really important elements common to Marx and Sombart are the views of capitalism as unique in historical development, and as a system embracing the whole of social life. It was one of Marx's most important contributions to socialist thought that the fault of capitalistic exploitation lay, not with the capitalist as an individual, but with the system to which he as well as everyone else was forced to conform. Thus abuses could only be remedied by changes in the fundamental basis of class interests within the system. This was a great advance on the utopian socialist view, that the remedy was rational persuasion of the leaders of society. Thus both greatly emphasize the objective sys-

20. Oswald Spengler, *Der Untergang des Abendlandes,* Munich, 1920.

21. As in so many cases of the interpretation of Marx, there is difference of opinion as to whether he ever intended to develop a "general" economic theory. That he did is evidently the view of Schumpeter ("Dogmengeschichte der Volkswirtschaftslehre," *Grundriss der Sozialökonomik,* vol. 1), who treats him as a member of the classical school. The criticism of Boehm-Bawerk (*Gesammelte Schriften,* vol. 2) is based on the same interpretation. There is, however, another interpretation, first suggested by Sombart himself (*Jahrbuch für soziale Gesetzgebung,* 1894) and developed by Sorel and notably Croce (*Historical Materialism and the Economics of Karl Marx*), according to which the Marxian theory of value is meant to be an "ideal type" of a hypothetical capitalist society to be used for purposes of comparison with the real capitalistic and other economic systems. The latter view is much the more favorable to Marx and the unity of his system, and brings him into much closer relations with Sombart and the general currents of thought dealt with in this paper. Of course this interpretation would admit that the content of Marx's theory was largely taken over from Ricardo, but would maintain that the logical use to which it was put was quite different.

tem and both sum up its peculiarities as due to the "necessity of capital to reproduce itself." But in the interpretation of that phrase an essential difference comes to light. Marx understands it, in terms of the economic interpretation of history, as an internal necessity imposed by the conditions of production. Moreover, this philosophy of history is applied, not only to capitalism, but to the whole of history, in which, as the direct opposite of Hegel, Marx attributes the causal effect to an immanent law of the material conditions of production. But Marx further differs from Sombart in that he attempts a complete theory of social evolution as a single unitary movement. He does it, however, in such a way as to preserve unimpaired the conception of the "economic system" as a unique historical epoch. By means of the dialectic he uses these systems as units in the process according to the formula: Thesis (Feudalism)—Antithesis (Capitalism)—Synthesis (Communism). Such is the essential difference between Hegelian evolution and the Western conception of continuous unilinear evolution.

Now Sombart takes over the system as a historical epoch, but discards the dialectic evolutionary connection between systems, leaving them in principle quite discrete. In doing this Sombart follows a well-marked tradition of the more romantic elements of German thought. On the other hand, he denies the economic interpretation of history. If a spirit of capitalism could exist at all for Marx, it would be in the nature of a "superstructure" dependent in the last analysis on the economic conditions underlying it. Sombart takes the precisely opposite view that the economic conditions are themselves the creation of a spirit which, having once appeared, develops according to its own organic law, but is itself ultimate, having nothing further to explain it. His view results in fully as rigid a determinism as that of Marx. All that the individual can do is to "express" this spirit in his thoughts and actions. He is powerless to change it.

This peculiar determinism makes possible another highly interesting point of agreement. In spite of his definite rejection of the economic interpretation as a general philosophy of history, Sombart does not entirely forget it. On the contrary, he maintains it as a characteristic of capitalism. "The period of the predominance of capitalism is thus a period of culture which is characterized by the predominance of economic factors; but not because this is in general the primary factor in cultural life, as a one-sided and false philosophy of history maintains, but because it is the destiny of our time, that in it—and perhaps for all eternity only in it—there is a predominance of the economic." [22] That is why capitalism is its most suitable designation. Not only is the

22. *Kapitalismus* 3:317.

modern *economic* system different from any other, but our whole culture is characterized by the predominance of its economic over all its other aspects. In this sense Sombart thinks modern life lacks "proportion," a view which would be quite foreign to Marx.

The general divergence of their views leads also to an interesting difference in their ethical judgment of capitalism. To Marx it is the mother destined to give birth to the future ideal society which is developing within her. And since this future communism is the final end of all social development and the most perfect conceivable form of society, Marx may be called in Sombart's words a cultural optimist, thus showing perhaps a remnant of the heritage of the eighteenth century. But more especially he accepts capitalism because of its possibilities. Sombart, while in general neither optimist nor pessimist, leaves no doubt of his attitude with respect to capitalism. "We can no longer believe in the creative power of capitalism as Marx did. . . . We know that in spite of all the noise nothing of any cultural importance has come of it, and nothing ever will. . . . Salvation can only be sought in turning away from it."[23]

A further great difference between them is of course that a large part of the economic theory of Marx has been dropped by Sombart (if, to be sure, it can be said at all that Marx had any general economic theory). Sombart substitutes some theory of his own, a good deal of which is unsatisfactory. In general it may be said that it is a decided weakness of Sombart's work that he fails to appreciate and make use of the many important developments in economic theory since Marx's day on lines totally different from his own. His failure in this regard is not, however, a valid reason for minimizing or losing sight of the value of his own unique contribution.

Sombart freely acknowledges his debt to Marx. He says, "This work is meant to be nothing other than a continuation and in a certain sense a completion of that of Marx." Thus on Sombart's authority Marx may be called the originator of this whole theory of capitalism. I have only failed to deal with him separately because the most important elements of this aspect of Marx's thought have been taken up by Sombart and incorporated into his work.

Part 2

Max Weber has none of Sombart's concentration of attention upon a single line of development. His researches extend over the whole of human history. He investigates the classic world, China, India, ancient

23. Ibid. 3:xxi.

Judea, and others. But it always remains his purpose to throw light upon the problems of modern society, and especially upon modern capitalism.[24] Thus in spite of methodological differences between the two scholars, the one working genetically, the other by the comparative method, with the aid of "ideal types," the final object in view is the same, to understand the peculiarities of our modern economic and social situation. Nonetheless the difference of method is, as I shall hope to show, responsible for some of the most important differences between the two authors.

The "ideal type" (*Idealtypus*) is Weber's special instrument of sociological analysis. He asserts that the historical social sciences are faced with an infinite variety of facts from which a selection for purposes of analysis must be made. The objective of these sciences is the knowledge and understanding of specific individual cultural phenomena in their uniqueness, as different from all others even of similar character. These "historical individuals"[25] he seeks to "understand" in terms of the human motives which have given rise to the social action summed up in them. The standard under which a group of actions is to be brought together as a historical individual is the "significance" (*Bedeutung*) of those actions for human ends and values. Hence the discovery of uniform relations and their formulation in terms of "laws" cannot be the objective of such a science.

That "understanding" Weber attempts to attain by means of the ideal type. It is a special *construction* in the mind of the investigator of what social action would be if it were directed with perfect rationality[26] toward a given end. It is not a reflection of actual behav-

24. See Karl Jaspers, *Max Weber: Gedächtnisrede*, Tübingen, 1921.

25. The German term is *historisches Individuum*. It refers to a cultural phenomenon in which many men may be involved.

26. The "perfect rationality" meant by Weber may not always be perfect, but rather a relative, rationality, the degree of which depends on the purpose for which the ideal type is constructed. It is always used to separate the relatively rational from the relatively irrational elements of the situation to be analyzed. However, the ideal type based upon the perfectly rational adaptation of means to given ends (what he calls *zweckrational*) is the most important class for Weber. As he says (*Wirtschaft und Gesellschaft*, 2, 3): "For scientific analysis working with ideal types, all irrational, emotionally determined complexes of behavior, which influence action, are most easily investigated and presented as 'deviations' from a construction of the purely rational (with regard to means) order of occurrence in them." And again: "The construction of a strictly rational course of action serves the sociologist in these cases, on account of its evident understandability and lack of ambiguity, . . . as an ideal type for the purpose of understanding real action which is influenced by irrationalities of all kinds, in terms of their 'departure' from what the action would be if it were purely rational." Only in this sense is Weber's sociology to be considered rational. It makes no assumption as to the actual relative importance of the rational elements in social life.

ior, since it is purposely a "fictitious" construction, which can never occur in reality. Nor is it an abstraction in the ordinary sense which operates under the assumption "other things being equal," for even with respect to the elements with which it specifically deals it makes assumptions contrary to fact. Nor can it be a hypothesis to be "verified," nor a general concept of a class (*Gattungsbegriff*) under which many "cases" may be included. It is a picture of what things would be under "ideal," not actual, conditions.

Given this instrument of analysis the investigator may compare with it the actual record of events in many different instances and thus attempt to "understand" them, each in its individual uniqueness, by seeing how far they conform to action rationally directed toward the given ends, and to distinguish such elements as are not "understandable" in these terms. Furthermore, the single ideal type is directed toward understanding, not the whole of the "historical individual," but only one side or aspect of it. A whole would thus be analyzed in terms of several ideal types. Finally, this ideal type is never the end of the scientific investigation, but always a *means* to understanding. It has no "reality" in itself; it does not "reproduce" reality, but is a fiction, always involving assumptions purposely contrary to fact. Its function is to form a standard for the systematic selection, arrangement, and analysis of the historical facts.

In this process Weber does not exclude "values" from his consideration, but the whole point of his method is to analyze social action in terms of them, and to include in his analysis only what can be understood in such terms. But nonetheless he claims objectivity for his method, since it takes the values as given and attempts no ultimate judgment or criticism of them. He does, however, deal with them in attempting to refine the values he finds in history into ideal types of themselves.[27]

Investigation of Weber's work,[28] however, has shown that while all this is true of one class of ideal type, there is another group of concepts which Weber calls ideal types, but which are of a quite different nature. They are directed toward *one particular* historical individual and

27. This question of the objectivity of his type of social science is one of the most difficult aspects of Weber's position. It unfortunately cannot be discussed here. For his viewpoint see "Die Objectivität sozialwissenschaftlicher Erkenntnis, *Gesammelte Aufsätze zur Wissenschaftslehre*, 146ff.

28. For the best analysis of Weber's methodology see A. von Schelting, "Die logische Theorie der historischen Kulturwissenschaften von Max Weber usw.," *Archiv für Sozialwissenschaft und Sozialpolitik*, Bd. 49. Parts of Weber's own writings which deal with the problem of the ideal type are: several of the essays in the volume *Gesammelte Aufsätze zur Wissenschaftslehre* and the first part of *Wirtschaft und Gesellschaft, Grundriss der Sozialökonomik*, vol. 3.

are applicable only to it, are thus *historical* and not general concepts like the others. Secondly, they attempt to work out the *whole* "essence" of the thing, not just one side of it. Such a concept cannot be purely a means, but its construction must be in some measure the end of the investigation in question. That Weber calls both ideal types without distinguishing them leads to serious confusion, a confusion which is especially marked in his analysis of capitalism, as I shall show at the end of the discussion.

The propositions of abstract economic theory were thought by Weber to be ideal types in the first sense, a view perhaps not very different from its conception as an "engine of analysis" which has become common in English theory in recent times. In the latter of the two senses the "theory" of Sombart may be said to consist of ideal types, of which that of capitalism was the most interesting for this paper. It is a picture of the rationalized and distilled "essence" of the epoch, free from all the irrationalities of the actual historical material. But it is definitely historical, not general.

Unlike Sombart, Weber never developed a unified theory of capitalism. In spite of the fact that a very large proportion of his sociological work was devoted to this problem, he left only a number of fragments which from our point of view are to be regarded as special investigations.[29] It is thus unavoidable that in piecing these together a certain element of construction should enter in.

At the outset there is the difficulty that Weber seems to have used the term "capitalism" in two different senses without clearly distinguishing them. It is necessary to analyze them both and to keep them distinct from one another. They may be called "capitalism in general" and "modern capitalism."

The first is, one may say, an ideal type in the former of the foregoing senses. It is a general concept in terms of which many different sorts of capitalism, such as, for example, colonial, finance, and political, may be analyzed. It is thus not a historical concept in the same sense as Sombart's capitalism, but stands above and beyond all historical periods, serving in the analysis and comparison of one aspect of many of them. It is built upon a general economic concept of capital which

---

29. Those of Weber's works which bear upon this problem are above all the three volumes of the *Gesammelte Aufsätze zur Religionssoziologie*, especially the first essay, "Die protestantische Ethik und der Geist des Kapitalismus"; various parts of his great general work on sociology, *Wirtschaft und Gesellschaft*, the essay "Agrarverhältnisse im Altertum" in the *Gesammelte Aufsätze zur Sozial- und Wirtschaftsgeschichte;* and the *General Economic History* (English translation of *Wirtschaftsgeschichte* by Professor F. H. Knight).

Weber defines as "goods which are devoted to securing a profit in exchange,"[30] i.e., having about the same connotation as Boehm-Bawerk's "private capital." Thus capitalism is a system in which such goods are used, or play a prominent part, and may be defined most generally as a system of (rationally conducted) exchange for profit. It is a purely economic category, and Weber explicitly excludes all social components, such as a factory system using free labor, etc., from it.

It is unnecessary to point out that this is not a solution of the problem of modern capitalism which has absorbed Sombart's attention and which is the subject of this paper. And Weber is quite clear about that. In spite of his continual references to capitalism in antiquity and other times, he is very careful to point out the vital differences between all those and modern society.

There is, however, some relation to modern conditions in that all capitalism is classed as essentially acquisitive. "A capitalistic action is one which is oriented to the exploitation of opportunities for profit in exchange, that is (formally) peaceful opportunities."[31] Thus it is directed toward acquisition and not toward the satisfaction of need, driving the same "wedge" between the immediate and the ultimate end of economic action, as Sombart pointed out. But although capitalistic activity is directed toward acquisition, Weber refuses to identify capitalism or the spirit of it with a psychological instinct or impulse of acquisition. He says, "Capitalism may even be identical with the suppression, or at least the tempering, of this irrational impulse. But that does not mean that capitalism has nothing to do with acquisition. On the contrary, it is identical with the struggle for gain in a *continuous, rationally conducted capitalistic enterprise,* a struggle for ever renewed profit, for rentability. And it must be. In a capitalistic order of society as a whole an enterprise which did not strive for gain would be condemned to destruction."[32]

Thus Weber emphasizes the same thing as Sombart: that capitalism forces the individual business man into the race for profit, not because he is venal by nature, not because it represents the highest values in life for him, but because his enterprise must earn profit or go under. It is the objective system to which the individual must conform if he wants to do business at all. The remarkable thing is that this objectivity appears at a point where Weber is obviously speaking of capitalism in general, whereas Sombart makes it a characteristic of modern cap-

30. "Agrarverhältnisse im Altertum," 13.
31. *Wirtschaft und Gesellschaft,* 48.
32. *Religionssoziologie,* 1:4.

italism. The key may perhaps be found in the words "in a capitalistic order of society as a whole." Weber says there were capitalistic enterprises at many times and places, and hence, in a broad sense, capitalism; but he would maintain that only in the modern occident has there been a sufficient number of them to dominate society as a whole. Hence the difference between the different sorts of capitalism would be for him one of degree. But that is not the whole story, as will be shown presently.

In the foregoing quotation a further element has appeared which was not contained in his original definition of capitalism, but evidently applies to "capitalism in general." That is, the struggle for gain is a *"continuous, rationally conducted capitalistic enterprise."* This rationality, by which he means neither "reasonableness" nor a high degree of theoretical scientific development, but a thoroughgoing systematization and adaptation of practical life to a particular set of ideals, indicates what features of modern society are of importance for his theory of capitalism. That it appears in his discussion of general capitalism indicates that he did not clearly distinguish in his own mind the two separate concepts of capitalism to be found in his work.

But even with this hint it cannot be capitalism in this simple form to which Weber refers as "the most fateful force in our modern life." [33] When one comes to inquire what he did mean by that statement one finds him analyzing a highly complex "constellation" of factors which together form a unique and unified whole, what he has called a historical individual.

His first contribution is a negative one, the definite exclusion of the "capitalistic adventurers" from any essential place in modern capitalism. Such people are, he says, found at all times, and are in no way peculiar to ours. The particular basis of their exclusion is the irrational character of their activity which is directly opposed to the systematic and rational spirit of modern capitalism. This indicates the most essential substantive difference between the theories of Weber and Sombart. Sombart's spirit of enterprise is not for Weber harnessed to the chariot of capitalism, but remains outside it, even though it may appear prominently in capitalistic times.

The common characteristic of all the principal features of modern society, noneconomic as well as economic, Weber sees in their peculiar type of rationality. Its principal institutions belong to his general type of "rational organization," or what he calls in a special sense "bu-

33. Ibid. 1:4.

reaucracy."[34] Its main characteristics are: rationality, resting on a complex, hierarchically organized division of tasks, each with a sharply marked-off sphere of "competence"; specialization of functions, whereby a special premium is placed upon expert knowledge of whatever kind it may be; and impersonality, in the sense that the ends which the organization serves are impersonal (acquisition, political domination, etc.) and that commands are given and obeyed by virtue of a "legal" authority vested in the position of the individual who gives them, not his personal qualities.

The two most important noneconomic institutions for Weber are the modern state and modern science, both of which are organized on definitely bureaucratic principles. He particularly emphasizes this aspect of science, which was originally based far more on the purely individual accomplishment of genius.

The specific characteristic of modern capitalism on the economic side is what Weber calls the rational organization of free labor. "Only the occident has known rational capitalistic enterprise with fixed capital, free labor, and rational division and integration of labor, with a division of functions through exchange on the basis of capitalistic acquisition."[35] This is in turn the key to some other economic features of modern society. Of course modern capitalistic acquisition is achieved by at least formally peaceful means, and Weber emphasizes the aspect of stability as a condition of accurate calculation. This is largely carried out by another typical feature of modern times, a rational system of bookkeeping.[36]

The development of bookkeeping makes possible still another highly important phenomenon, the rigid separation of the private interest of the business man from those of the business unit; not necessarily a spatial separation, though this comes to be usual, but in thought and for purposes of calculation the individual is split into two. One is a producer who as such is part of a great mechanistic system with no individuality of his own. The other is a consumer who has still a part of his life left to devote to his family, recreation, cultural interests, etc. But the relations between the two tend to weaken, and

34. "Bureaucracy" is here used in a more general sense than that of common speech. It refers to any large-scale organization of the sort indicated, and does not carry any of the implications of cumbersomeness, red tape, etc., which are so often associated with it. See *Wirtschaft und Gesellschaft*, 125–30, 650–78.

35. Ibid., 96.

36. Sombart also makes a great deal of this point, going very thoroughly into the history of bookkeeping methods. *Kapitalismus*, 2:1, 10ff., 159–62.

the business side of life to run on its own tracks without regard to the private side.

It is Weber's peculiar view that this all-important bureaucracy is essentially the same phenomenon whether it appears in a great corporation, a government department, or a political party machine. Its spread rests primarily upon its purely technical superiority to all other forms of large-scale organization of human activity. Capitalism is, one may say, simply bureaucratic organization placed in the service of pecuniary profit.

Weber's view of the relation of bureaucracy to capitalism stands in close relation to the socialistic contention that in the transition from capitalism to socialism the state will tend to disappear. Weber would not put it quite that way, but would say that the sharp distinction between economic and political organization tended with the bureaucratization of economic life to fade out, and that the line of development was in the direction of a fusion of the two. The fusion is, moreover, characterized for Weber by the fact that the economic element comes to predominate over the political. The acquisitive nature of capitalism permeates all modern bureaucracy as distinguished from that of other times, and thus justifies the name "capitalism" as the most apt designation of modern society. The element of competition, which is of primary importance for Sombart, recedes quite into the background for Weber. In fact all the specific elements of capitalism which we think of as contrasting it with socialism—competition, private property, production for exchange, class antagonism between *bourgeois* and proletariat, although a part of Weber's theory—are of secondary importance as compared with the great central fact of bureaucracy. The final result of the development, a great unified organization in the service of economic production, would not be far from socialism as ordinarily conceived.

Bureaucracy is for Weber so fundamental as to dominate *all* aspects of modern society where large-scale administration is necessary. "Without it existence, for everyone who was not in possession of the necessities of life, would be impossible in any society with separation of workers from the means of their work and with the necessity for discipline and specialized knowledge." [37] Thus any conceivable society which retains the modern technical basis must inevitably tolerate it. Socialism, as already indicated, would not be an escape, but would mean an immense increase in the importance of bureaucratic organization. So in the aspect which is for Weber by far the most important,

37. *Wirtschaft und Gesellschaft*, 128.

socialism is not fundamentally different from capitalism, but a further stage in the same line of development. It is on this basis, not on the ground of their difference, that he rejects socialism. This attitude toward socialism brings out perhaps more strikingly than anything else the fundamental difference between Weber's view of capitalism and the picture of "free enterprise" common in Anglo-Saxon countries. It is interesting to note that for all three, Marx, Sombart, and Weber, capitalism and socialism are intimately connected in the line of social evolution, but that only for the last two does the difference become very much less important than the common elements. That was not true of Marx.[38]

The second principal element of Weber's theory, the spirit of capitalism, takes its departure from the dominant fact of rational bureaucratic organization. In terms of it he wishes to explain its peculiar type of rationality. As already noted, that does not mean its "reasonableness." Whether it is so or not is for Weber's sociological treatment strictly irrelevant. What he means by the rationality of capitalism, then, is its nice adaptation of the whole way of life of the modern man to a particular set of values. The next task is concerned with the analysis of the nature and origin of that particular set of values, in order to show how economic life is to be understood in terms of them. These values, which for Weber are in the last analysis of religious origin, having done their work have disappeared and have left only the rationalized way of life, which Weber calls capitalism, behind them.

Weber's attempt to explain capitalism in terms of a particular set of ethical values at once brings out his attitude to the problems of the economic interpretation of history. The essay in which his view is presented[39] was intended to be a refutation of the Marxian thesis in a particular historical case by proving that capitalism could only be understood in terms of an ethics which preceded it in time. The interesting thing is that Weber puts the question in this way: that either a materialistic or a spiritualistic interpretation or a compromise between them must be accepted. There is no other way of looking at the problem. Here he is again on common ground with Sombart.[40]

38. There is in this view of Weber's a striking resemblance to Professor Schumpeter's view of "trustified society" as expressed in lectures at Harvard University. He states that Western society is developing toward a state to which the application of the term "socialism" would be a matter of taste.

39. "Die protestantische Ethik," *Religionssoziologie,* vol. 1.

40. See below. In another sense Weber accepted the economic interpretation of history, namely, as a working principle. Outside the realm of pure economic theory he sees the principal task of economics as a historical discipline in the investigation of social

The first characteristic of the spirit of capitalism he finds in the entire absence of any connection with hedonism or utilitarianism. In fact from any hedonistic standpoint it is completely irrational. Its central point is the ethical obligation to earn more and more money, at the same time avoiding all spontaneous enjoyment of life as positively wicked. It involves a highly rationalized disciplining of one's whole life in the interests of this economic activity, which is thought of as an end in itself. Thus waste of time is on the same level with that of money as a sin against the discipline and self-control of a capitalistic existence. It is not, however, acquisition alone which is at the bottom of the thing, but acquisition is in turn the particular expression of another ideal, that of virtue and proficiency in one's "calling" or profession. It is the idea of duty in a calling which is the real kernel of capitalistic ethics.

It is evident that this is not simply an ideal of cleverness in business, but it is a truly ethical conception. It also has nothing to do with an impulse or instinct of acquisition, as has been pointed out before. Such an impulse has often been closely associated with a traditional manner of administering economic affairs, and traditionalism is the most deadly enemy of capitalism. The impulse was also never ethically justified, but rather was looked upon as having nothing to do with ethics, or as something undesirable, but unfortunately "human nature."

The only possible source of capitalistic ethics Weber finds in Protestantism, particularly in the "ascetic" branches of the movement. It

------

phenomena on the assumption that the sole moving force is economic, leaving the restoration of balance to a wider synthetic view. On the other hand, the "sociology" of economic life has the opposite task of analyzing the influence of noneconomic factors, religion, legal institutions, etc., on economic activity. Sociology and economics are thus for him correlative points of view rather than disciplines with separate subject matters. See "Objektivität sozialwissenschaftlicher Erkenntnis," and [von] Schelting, "Der logische Theorie," 705.

In other parts of his work (the *Religionssoziologie* taken as a whole) Weber backs up the thesis that capitalism is to be understood in terms of an ethics by asking the equally fruitful question: Why did capitalism *not* appear at any other time or place than in modern Western society? His general conclusion is that in several other cultures (for instance, China and India) the strictly economic conditions were at least as favorable to capitalistic development as they were in Europe, but that the economic spirit was in both cases, though in each for totally different reasons, so radically opposed to it as to account for its failure to appear. It is interesting to note that Weber particularly emphasizes the high degree of rationality of both the Chinese social morality and the ascetic discipline of India. But the original ethical values being so different, the outcome also was entirely different from capitalism. It may thus be seen that Weber's view, while based on his analysis of the Protestant ethics, is reinforced by a comprehensive study of other societies.

shares both the otherworldly interest in salvation and the doctrine of the sinfulness of this world with the Catholic faith. To both the "natural man" is sinful and both are thus fundamentally ascetic. But while Catholic asceticism took the form of outdoing worldly morality by complete withdrawal from the world, the Protestant considered it his duty to work in the world and to transform its order into rational activity in the service of God.

How the Protestant was led to this is best explained in Weber's own words:

> Both the rationalization of the world [from a practical ethical, not a theoretical, standpoint] and the transfer of the road to salvation from the contemplative renunciation of the world to the active ascetic conquest of it . . . were attained only in the great churches and sects of ascetic Protestantism in the West. [It was due partly to the social environment, but] just as much to their genuine religious character: their God, definitely separated from the world, and the . . . peculiarities of their means to salvation. . . . Where the religious believer was sent into the world as an "instrument" of God's will and thus cut off from all magical means to salvation, with the task of "proving" himself through the ethical quality of his actions within its order and *only* in that way, as chosen for eternal blessedness . . . , the world might appear religiously to any extent sinful, might be deprived of value and rejected: psychologically it was accepted all the more as the scene of activity in a "calling" willed by God. For this worldly asceticism was to be sure unworldly in the sense that it condemned and fought against the good things of this world like beauty and dignity, intoxication and dreams, worldly power and heroism, as competitors of the Kingdom of God. But precisely for that reason it did not flee from the world as contemplative religion did, but sought to carry out the commands of God by rationalizing the world in the sense of its ethics, and thus remained in a peculiar sense even more "worldly" than the naïve acceptance of the world of unspoiled antique humanism or of lay Catholicism. Precisely in everyday life was the state of grace to be proved. To be sure, not in everyday life, as the believer found it, but in routine action as it had been methodically *rationalized* in the service of God. Everyday activity rationally turned into a calling was the proof of salvation. The sects of religious believers in the occident were the ferment for the rationalization of the whole of life, including economic activity, not like the Asiatic communities of contemplative, orgiastic, or apathetic mystics, outlets for the longing to escape from the senselessness of worldly activity.[41]

In its practical effects this view of life could not help fostering capitalistic (in Weber's sense) development. It did not object to the acqui-

---

41. *Religionssoziologie* 1:263–64. [The words in brackets are Parsons's.]

sition of wealth in itself, and recommended a way of life extremely favorable to it. And in the course of time the pressure of the question of individual salvation led people to look upon success in business enterprise as a sign of grace. It was argued that God would surely be good to his chosen ones in this world as well as the next. This attitude meant a great incentive to the acquisition of wealth, and is also, perhaps, one source of the rather smug self-righteousness often thought typical of the *bourgeois*.

On the other hand, Protestantism long retained its ascetic character. It favored discipline, orderliness, frugality, temperance, and condemned everything spontaneous and unsystematic. It thus favored the development of those uniformly regimented forms of life which are an ideal basis for the standardization of production and consumption so important for capitalism. Furthermore, it looked upon the individual, not as the owner of wealth, but as its trustee, which was a force greatly inhibiting spending and extravagance, and extraordinarily favorable to the accumulation of capital. It released acquisition from the bonds of traditional ethics and it looked upon it, not only as permissible, but as directly willed by God.

Finally, says Weber, "While the Puritan wanted to lead this rational, ascetic life, we are forced to do it." [42] The religious values which gave it meaning have for the most part disappeared. They have left behind them an automatic, mechanistic system where the place of work in the service of the glory of God has been taken by the fetish of "production." The result has been that "the material goods of this world have gained an increasing and finally inexorable power over the lives of men, as at no previous period in history." [43] Here again is the objective system of capitalism to which the individual must conform whether he will or no. And we have a statement, applying not to history in general, but to modern capitalism, which looks very much like the Marxian economic interpretation of history. On both these highly important points Weber and Sombart are agreed.

Now, of what significance is this theory of the spirit of capitalism for Weber's view of capitalism as a whole? He repeatedly states that he is not to be thought to mean that Protestantism is the sole historical cause of capitalism. [44] In other places he discusses many other factors to which he ascribes great importance. But it is not the historical ques-

42. Ibid. 1:203.
43. Ibid., 203–4.
44. There has been a great deal of discussion on this point. Many historians, and some economists, especially Brentano (*Anfänge des modernen Kapitalismus*), in their

tion with which I am concerned. And for the other question, that of the nature of capitalism as a system of economic life, there is no doubt that Weber considered the spirit of capitalism as decisive, as expressing the essence of the system, the core around which everything else is built and as the creative force of capitalism.

Thus the first important characteristic of the system as a whole is its objectivity. The individual member of it does not need to will it, but is forced by the circumstances in which he is placed to abide by its rules. And secondly it is a rational system, all activity being adjusted to the values expressed by the capitalistic spirit in a relatively exact adaptation of means to ends. It is only in relation to the ultimate validity of those values that there is room for doubt. This rationality is expressed in the extreme discipline and self-control of the whole life of every individual in it. Thirdly, this rational, objective system is ascetic, which means fundamentally that the individual's own good is not taken as a norm of action, but rather something beyond him. Originally it was the glory of God, but through the fading out of the religious background it becomes economic activity for its own sake, "productivity" and "service." At one end of the scale man is an instrument of God's will. At the other, man, entrepreneur and workman alike, is an instrument for the production of economic goods.

Fourthly, the system is mechanistic. Man becomes a specialist to such an extent that he is only one tiny cog in a great machine, and a cog for which any other similarly trained one might be substituted. Human relations become more and more matter-of-fact, impersonal, contractual. It is a society in which the element of *Gesellschaft* in the sense of Tönnies and Weber definitely predominates over that of *Gemeinschaft*,[45] or, to put it into English terms, the element of "society," in the sense of relationships deliberately entered into, for a specific purpose, prevails over "community," or those relationships in which man finds himself placed by his natural environment, his psychological nature and tradition.

Finally, the system further resembles a mechanism in that it follows its own laws independently of human will. This reversal of the "nat-

---

anxiety to point out faults in Weber's historical analysis, have on the one hand overestimated the *historical* importance of the Protestant ethics for Weber himself, but on the other have overlooked its great *theoretical* significance for his view of capitalism. It is important to keep these two aspects distinct.

45. See F. Tönnies, *Gemeinschaft und Gesellschaft*. Also Weber, *Wirtschaft und Gesellschaft*, 21–23. It is a distinction which has come to be of primary importance in German social thought. It is of course implicit in Sombart's work.

ural" relationship between men and things is one of Weber's versions of the economic interpretation of history.[46] He definitely rejects the doctrine as a general theory of historical causation and in particular as an explanation of the genesis of capitalism. But he does accept economic determinism as a characteristic of capitalism, and thus gives it a relative validity.

The development of capitalism is not, in Weber's theory, an event unique in history and unconnected with other things; but it forms a logical end of the process dominating the whole of history: what he calls the process of rationalization. The process does not appear only in the development which leads to modern capitalism, but in all other lines of cultural development as well. His picture is not that of a single line of evolution leading from the earliest known human culture to modern capitalism, but rather of a number of different ones, branching off from a common trunk but developing in different directions. Each, however, is undergoing a process of rationalization in terms of the particular set of values by which it is dominated. The rationality of capitalism represents the final stage of the development in one direction, namely, toward the realization of the spirit of capitalism. It is in this form of separate lines of development each dominated by a set of values of its own that the "morphological" conception of a separate and distinct culture plays its most important part in Weber's view of history.[47]

This process of evolution is very clearly seen in Weber's treatment of the relation between "charisma"[48] and routine (*Alltag*). Charisma he defines as "a quality of a personality generally considered out of the ordinary . . . , on account of which its bearer is looked upon as possessed of supernatural or superhuman, or at least specifically unusual, powers or qualities, which are not accessible to the ordinary person; or as appointed of God, or a model to be imitated, and thus looked up to as a "leader." [49] It is the type of leadership which appeals to the specifically nonrational elements of human nature, whose claims to obedience rest upon the purely personal authority of the leader, not on his ability to "convince" by rational argument. On the other hand it is, because of its out-of-the-ordinary nature, the specific

46. For the other see above, footnote 40.

47. This is most strikingly brought out by the *Religionssoziologie* taken as a whole.

48. Charisma is a term and conception introduced by Weber himself into sociology. It is taken from the Greek χάρισμα meaning a "mission." It has been introduced to American readers by Robert Michels in his book on *Political Parties*, and recently in an article in the *American Political Science Review*, 1927.

49. *Wirtschaft und Gesellschaft*, 140.

enemy of tradition. It is, says Weber, "the specifically revolutionary force in history."[50]

Weber analyzes routine organization in terms of two main types: the traditional, of which the main subtype is the patriarchal, and the rational, legalized, or bureaucratic. All social movements start from charismatic sources, but there is always a tendency to reduce them in the course of time to some form of routine. The final result will be a tradition-bound or a mechanized bureaucratic society, with a general tendency for the former to be an earlier stage leading to the latter, as Weber thinks has happened in Western society.[51]

Charisma has been by no means foreign to economic affairs. The whole "romantic" side of capitalism, the spirit of enterprise on which Sombart lays such emphasis, is thoroughly saturated with it. Weber also admits that it has played an important part in the historical development of capitalism, but emphasizes strongly that it must be sharply distinguished from the rational, systematic *bourgeois* spirit which is for him the essence of capitalism. Capitalistic development has meant by and large the destruction of the charismatic elements of social life. The whole of it has come to be dominated by settled routine, and predominantly of the rational, bureaucratic, rather than the traditional, type. It is this which is the ground of Weber's pessimism. He holds that the really vital human forces appear only in charismatic forms, and that the very nature of social development progressively eliminates the possibility of the further appearance of such forms. Capitalism presents a dead, mechanized condition of society in which there is no room left for these truly creative forces because all human activity is forced to follow the "system."

But is Weber entirely right in this pessimism? That such a process of rationalization has taken place in many phases of human culture is beyond doubt, and that it has been in some degree continuous throughout history is true in spite of Sombart. In projecting this process beyond the limits of modern capitalism Weber has certainly gone an important step beyond Sombart. It may, however, be doubted whether Sombart is not nearer the truth in emphasizing the discontinuity and uniqueness of some elements. Surely Weber puts the question in a false form when he denies any possibilities other than that either the spiritual forces (charisma) or the material conditions (in this case the rational bureaucratic machine) must dominate society. This is a too ready acceptance of the alternatives of the economic interpretation

50. Ibid., 759.
51. See *Religionssoziologie* 1:267–73; *Wirtschaft und Gesellschaft*, 122–76.

of history, of which Weber's version is that there is a process of evolution from the predominance of the spiritual forces to that of the conditions of production, or more accurately the mechanism of social control, which for him would be of a predominantly economic nature only in the case of capitalism. But is it not possible that all manner of combinations between them are possible, and that the present-day power of the bureaucratic mechanism is due to a very special set of circumstances which do not involve the necessity for its continued dominance over life, but leave the possibility open that it may again be made to serve "spiritual" aims? Weber does not admit this possibility, but to him it would be the only hope for Western society, for no one was more insistent than he on the impossibility of returning to precapitalistic conditions.

Moreover, is it certain that these two are the ultimate factors in social development? It seems that Weber's difficulties come in part from assuming that they are. Assuming the reality of the process of rationalization, it may well be that it applies, not to the human spirit as a whole, but only to certain elements of it. Perhaps also the "material" side is composed of various elements only one of which is subject to the tendency to develop "bureaucratic" forms. Weber's own conception of traditional forms would indicate this possibility. It may be, not as he tends to make it, a transitional stage in development, but an independent and permanent element in social life.[52] Certainly in this direction are great possibilities of further scientific progress.

Finally, another cause of Weber's difficulties lies in his method. He wishes to work in terms of a comparative sociology by means of ideal types. He thus takes sections and aspects of all sorts of societies away from their context and tries to compare them, but in so doing he loses the very thing he is looking for, the very individuality which they can have only in that context. Thus he speaks of the various sorts of capitalism, of bureaucracy, and so forth. On the other hand, in his treatment of the spirit of capitalism he follows an entirely different procedure. Here he works out as an organic whole, as a "historical individual," a set of ethical ideals, and tries to understand contemporary civilization in terms of them. This sort of capitalism is unique, existing only in modern times in Western society. But on trying to develop this concept he comes into conflict with his other conception

52. A notable attempt at further analysis of the factors, prompted largely by the problem of Max Weber's process of rationalization, has been made by Alfred Weber, "Prinzipielles zur Kultursoziologie," *Archiv für Sozialwissenschaft und Sozialpolitik*, vol. 47 (1920–21).

of "capitalism in general" and is unable to reconcile them. He does, however, try, and in the attempt he is forced to characterize modern capitalism in terms of one feature, the rational organization of labor, superimposed upon his capitalism in general. But this feature loses its original nature as a "fictitious" ideal type and becomes identified with historical reality. Because it originates as an ideal type it is impossible to establish an organic connection between it, on the one hand, and the spirit of enterprise and several other features of modern society on the other, because they belong for him in quite different and distinct sociological categories. And the tendencies of development which he works out for this isolated element of society he tends to hypostatize as true for society as a whole. In doing so he does violence to the facts and presents a picture different from what it would have been had he not been forced by his method to break up the organically connected historical individuals with which he started.

The real trouble is that Weber treats as "ideal types" two fundamentally different sorts of concepts. The one deals with generalized "aspects" of phenomena for comparative purposes, the other with unique historical epochs, cultures, etc., as wholes and by and for themselves. Because he does not clearly distinguish these two types of concepts he constantly wavers between them. Because the second class of ideal type does have a historical significance he does not strictly adhere to his methodological principle that a *general* ideal type is purely a fiction, a means to further analysis, and has no reality in itself. In fact his "capitalism in general," and more especially his "bureaucracy," which start off as such ideal types, come in the end to have this definite historical reality from which he deduces very important consequences. In thus attempting to apply a method suitable only for comparative purposes to the analysis of a culture as a whole he seriously confuses the picture which he gives. I think there is no doubt that the logical basis of Weber's ironbound process of rationalization lies in the isolation of one aspect of social development and the attribution of historical reality to an ideal type which was never meant to represent it. If this error is corrected the absolute domination of the process of rationalization over the whole social process falls to the ground.

In conclusion, the significance for social science in general of the work of Sombart and Weber is to be sought in four principal directions:

1. As far as general social theory is concerned, it bears most directly upon a set of problems which are not primarily economic, but are

certainly, in a broad sense, sociological, namely, those growing out of the economic interpretation of history. I have attempted to show the great importance of the influence exercised by the Marxian thesis in shaping the views of these men. In fact, German sociology, insofar as it aims at an appraisal of the moving forces in social life, has its starting point to a very large extent in Marx. Here is a set of problems which sociology cannot afford to neglect.

2. It bears upon some important methodological questions concerning this peculiar type of "historical theory." Its aim is to throw light on the individuality of "historical individuals," periods, epochs, cultures, institutions. Sombart attempts it by a "genetic," Weber ostensibly by a comparative, method, but really by a combination of both. Are the two methods supplementary to each other, or mutually contradictory? We have seen the confusing results of Weber's failure to distinguish them.

3. With regard to the positive problem of capitalism itself, Western analysis of modern economic society has been largely concerned with the application of general economic theory to it. This, no matter what its value for other purposes, has tended to blur over its distinctive features as compared with other historical or theoretically possible types of economic order. Even historical analysis has operated largely from the viewpoint of unilinear evolution. So it seems to me that the totally different approach of these investigators merits serious attention and should prove very fruitful.[53] Furthermore, the positive results which are common to both authors, the objectivity of the capitalistic system, its connection with ethical values, and the peculiar predominance of economic influences under capitalism, have received a wide acceptance in Germany and merit much more discussion than they have had in this country.

4. However exaggerated Weber's view of the dominating importance of "bureaucracy" may be, it certainly calls attention in a most striking way to an aspect of our modern society which we have all felt to be there, but which has received far less attention from the econo-

53. Professor Allyn Young ("Economics as a Field of Research," *Quarterly Journal of Economics*, November 1927) recognizes the validity of this type of "historical" economics, but gravely questions its claim to objectivity, because the problem of selection and evaluation of facts involves an element of "aesthetic construction" which is certain to be influenced by the personal equation of the investigator. It is, perhaps, significant that the three men here discussed, Marx, Sombart, and Weber, were, although from different points of view, all strong antagonists of capitalism. No doubt that suggests some connection between their interest in the problem of capitalism and their dislike of the fact. The problems here raised cannot be briefly dismissed, and I do not think it can be said that they have been satisfactorily worked out.

mists than it deserves. Orthodox economic theory does not furnish the technique or set of concepts necessary for its study. Weber, with his sociology of ideal types, has made an attempt to grapple with the problem which deserves recognition and which should lead to much further investigation.

2

Review of *Modern Capitalism: Its Origin and Development,* by Henri Sée

Professor Sée has given us what is probably the best short historical account of the development of modern capitalism. It is extraordinarily compact, and the style is admirably clear and lucid.

Professor Sée fails to give any clear-cut definition of modern capitalism, and refuses to tie himself down to any single criterion. It includes not only international commerce on a large scale, but also "the flowering of large-scale industry, the triumph of machinery, and the growing power of the great financial houses." In other words, one might say, the present economic order. In this combination of elements, with their present-day importance, capitalism is peculiar to the modern era.

When he comes to tie capitalism up with capital, Professor Sée has some difficulty. In the first place he quite rightly remarks that from the historical point of view capital must be conceived as narrower than in the usage of economic theory—otherwise there would be no means of distinguishing capitalism from any other economic system in terms of it, and then why the name? But he himself fails to state precisely how much narrower it should be or what should be included. In particular he fails to distinguish carefully between capital as a monetary concept and as a material factor in production. He lays most of his stress on the former concept, but the other is always there, and his failure to distinguish them leads him into one or two rather bad errors of analysis. For instance: "But was it [the rise of agricultural prices] not mainly the result of an increase of capital, such as generally leads to a fall in the value of money?" This question certainly has no meaning unless capital is conceived as nothing more than money. But in the general discussion it means very much more, and it is quite obvious that Professor Sée does not intend his capitalism to be understood simply as "money economy." His denial of any great importance to capitalism in ancient times is sufficient proof of that. The only conclu-

Originally published in *The Journal of Political Economy* 38 (1930): 364–66.

sion seems to be that he has not very clearly worked out his fundamental concepts.

Professor Sée mentions Sombart more than any other general writer on capitalism, and seems to agree with him on many general points. He also mentions Max Weber's theory of Protestantism and capitalism, conceding to it some validity. But in general his interpretation is very different from that of these writers. His subtypes of commercial, financial, and industrial capitalism are conceived in terms of the fields of activity which capitalism has taken over. But while both Sombart's distinction between the "spirit of enterprise" and the "bourgeois spirit" and Weber's between "adventurers' capitalism" and "modern rational capitalism" have some relation to Professor Sée's types, they are by no means the same thing but cut very largely across them. They refer primarily to the attitude of people toward their economic activity, whatever its content may be. Starting as he does from such a different position, it is not surprising that Professor Sée should find comparatively little in Weber's theory. But are not problems like those raised by Weber the really important ones? It seems to the reviewer that his close attention to forms of organization for their own sake, and his failure to make use of the German analysis in terms of the attitude of men to their economic life, has shut Professor Sée out from making any contribution to the understanding of the cultural significance of capitalism at all comparable to those of Sombart and Weber. Things with which they have dealt, but which he entirely neglects, are especially a consideration of the nature and significance of economic rationalism, and the problems growing out of the economic interpretation of history in the sense in which Sombart and Weber have understood it. Professor Sée's account comes to be very largely a recital of bald facts, not illuminated by any very large viewpoint of interpretation. As such it is very well done, and very useful. But after all such work is only a means to something more important. Perhaps Professor Sée will reply that such further contribution is not in the province of the historian but rather of the philosopher. But have not most great historians been philosophers in this sense?

The translation by Professors Vanderblue and Doriot is thoroughly satisfactory and helps greatly to make the book the pleasure to read that it is.

3

Jean Calvin

Jean Calvin (1509–64), leader of the Protestant Reformation in Geneva. He was primarily a theologian and his social thought is in the main a by-product of his religious ideas. Calvin's Protestantism, although thoroughgoing, was differentiated from that of Luther both by his conception of God as the absolute sovereign who while infinitely removed from a wholly sinful world had yet created its every detail for the increase of His glory and by the doctrine of predestination in its most drastic form of the double decree. This theology, while it insisted on salvation by grace not works, shut out mystical contemplation and drove the believer into an active, strenuous life directed toward the realization of Christian ideals of conduct. Calvin's objective conception of religious truth precluded toleration and caused him to retain the ideal of the universal church to which even the unregenerate must be made to conform. The combination of these elements led to the church discipline of Geneva.

From his hypothesis of the immediate dependence of all worldly events on God's will Calvin derived his doctrine of the divine ordination of the principal institutions of society—church, state, property, family. He was thus a strong upholder of authority. The state is coordinate with the church in promoting God's kingdom on earth; the two have a common purpose but different spheres of influence. Underneath his conservative authoritarianism, however, lay a revolutionary principle which after his death was to become of great importance: although a strong defender of passive resistance he conceded that in extreme cases obedience to God's will was an obligation transcending all other duties and abrogating all other allegiances.

The general tenor of Calvin's own system in Geneva was an authoritarian Christian socialism strictly subordinating individuals to the one great aim of increasing the glory of God. But later developments of Calvinism, by bringing out its latent anti-authoritarian tenden-

Originally published in the *Encyclopaedia of the Social Sciences,* Edwin R. A. Seligman (editor in chief), 3: 151–53. Copyright 1930, renewed 1958 by Macmillan Publishing Company. Reprinted by permission of the publisher.

cies, favored a democratic individualism, tinged, however, as a consequence of the doctrine of predestination, with a conservative anti-equalitarianism. During Calvin's lifetime the civil government in the city-state of Geneva, as represented by the Civil Council, was nothing more than a subordinate body, a coercive agency, for enforcing on the community the strict church discipline promulgated by Calvin and the ecclesiastical committee known as the Consistory. The policy of complete separation of church and state which was later forced upon Calvinism was the result not of any recognition on its part of relativity in religious truth but of the fear of political interference by a more powerful civil authority.

Calvinism, which at the outset found its greatest support in urban centers, was the first of the Reformation movements to recognize the existence of a new economic society characterized by the commercial rather than the medieval agrarian viewpoint. Calvin's justification of moderate interest, which hitherto church moralists had condemned, reveals him as among the first to understand the productive functions of capital. Rejecting monasticism Calvin dignified ordinary economic activities by designating them as "callings," as tasks set directly by God. For hedonistic motives to labor he substituted the glory of God and the general good; the economic virtues of thrift and industry he identified with the moral virtues. In no sense did he encourage moral laxity in economic relations. On the contrary, he tried to moralize as never before all phases of social life.

The very rigor of its standards made Calvinism a constructive rather than a hindering force in modern economic development. The idea of "calling" reinforced by the psychological effect of the doctrine of predestination gave a religious sanction to the most strenuous, rational, systematic labor for impersonal ends. Labor thus became a means of serving God and of proving one's own state of grace through ascetic self-discipline. Slothfulness became the deadliest of sins and fear of self-indulgence made the Calvinist a small consumer and a large saver. In Geneva this resulted in an extraordinary system of church discipline, but with the change of emphasis from church to self-discipline it later powerfully furthered the development of individual capitalistic acquisition, especially after worldly success came to be recognized as a token of grace.

WORKS: *Christianae religionis institutio* (Basel, 1536), trans. by John Allen, 2 vols. (6th American ed., Philadelphia, 1928). His *Opera quae supersunt,* ed. J. W. Baum and others, 59 vols. (Brunswick and Berlin, 1863–1900), have been partly translated by the Calvin Translation Society, 48 vols. (Edinburgh, 1843–55).

CONSULT: Doumergue, E., *Jean Calvin: Les hommes et les choses de son temps*, 7 vols. (Lausanne, 1899–1927); Choisy, Eugène, *La théocratie à Genève au temps de Calvin* (Geneva, 1897), and *L'état chrétien calviniste à Genève au temps de Théodore de Bèze* (Geneva, 1902); Allen, J. W., *A History of Political Thought in the Sixteenth Century* (London, 1928), chaps. 4 and 5; Troeltsch, E. D., *Die Soziallehren der christlichen Kirchen und Gruppen*, in his *Gesammelte Schriften*, vol. 1 (3d ed., Tübingen, 1923), 509–12, 605–794; Weber, Max, *Die protestantische Ethik und der Geist des Kapitalismus*, in his *Gesammelte Aufsätze zur Religionssoziologie*, 3 vols. (2d ed., Tübingen, 1922–23), vol. 1, trans. by T. Parsons (London, 1930); Tawney, R. H., *Religion and the Rise of Capitalism* (London, 1926), 102–32; Hunt, R. N. C., "Calvin's Theory of Church and State," *Church Quarterly Review* 108 (1929): 56–71; Hauser, Henri, "A propos des idées économiques de Calvin," in *Mélanges d'histoire offerts à Henri Pirenne*, 2 vols. (Brussels, 1926), vol. 1, 211–24.

4

Samuel Smiles

Samuel Smiles (1812–1904), English popular author. Smiles was editor of the Leeds *Times* and later a railway official. As a journalist active in radical politics in the north of England Smiles was an exponent of middle-class, individualistic radicalism and, although an ardent supporter of many measures in the interest of the working classes, he energetically opposed chartism and later socialism. After the initial success of his *Life of George Stephenson* (London 1857, rev. ed. 1864) he wrote biographies of many of the inventors and business men of early English industrialism, in which he emphasized the personal qualities that had led to their attainments. His works of popular edification were very widely read, notably *Self Help* (London 1859, new ed. 1860), which sold about 300,000 copies and was translated into many languages.

Smiles's immediate forebears were of the radical wing of Scotch Calvinism, and his own views were largely the secularized expression of this religious background. Despite their facile optimism his teachings reflect the moral rigor that lay behind Victorian economic individualism. With all shades of radicalism he shared a general hostility to privilege of birth or inherited wealth, but his primary emphasis was on individualistic economic virtues as ends in themselves. His writings comprise not merely a series of precepts for success but a definite ethical doctrine. The necessity of labor is no longer portrayed as the curse of Adam but as a positive blessing; knowledge and education are valuable but only when combined with a worthy and generally practical purpose. Smiles held that the careful utilization of time is of paramount importance; that honesty and uprightness, industry and perseverance, always triumph over difficult external circumstances; and that for the most part people have only their own neglect, mismanagement, and improvidence to blame for their misfortunes. Smiles thus saw in individual economy and providence the only salvation of the

Originally published in the *Encyclopaedia of the Social Sciences*, Edwin R. A. Seligman (editor in chief), 14: 111–12. Copyright 1934, renewed 1962 by Macmillan Publishing Company. Reprinted by permission of the publisher.

working classes. Although he praised the same ethical qualities in all walks of life, he regarded business as by far the most favorable calling for the exercise of virtue and the development of character.

OTHER IMPORTANT WORKS: *Lives of the Engineers,* 3 vols. (London, 1861–62; new ed., 5 vols., 1874); *Life and Labour* (London, 1887); *Autobiography,* ed. Thomas Mackay (London, 1905).

5

Service

Service may be defined most generally as any act of an individual insofar as it contributes to the realization of the ends of other individuals. The universal existence of differentiation of the social functions of individuals makes mutual service an inexorable necessity of all life in society. Starting with the elementary biological differences of sex and age it becomes more important with the increasing complexities of social differentiation.

The theories of pure individualism attempted to account for the performance of these mutual services entirely as by-products of the pursuit of their enlightened self-interest by individuals to whom the needs and desires of others are only means to their own ends. But, however important this interlocking of interests may be, attempts to interpret society in terms of it alone have definitely broken down. No such society has ever existed. On the contrary, all societies depend to a greater or less degree on the disinterested performance of service and maintain specific ethical sanctions of it, either as an end in itself or as contributory to some higher end even farther removed from self-interest.

Sociologically the principal kinds of service may be reduced to two main types. The one, limited in obligation to a particular group of persons, whether determined in extent by the objective situation, as by birth, or by personal choice, is yet undefined as to the limits of its actual content but rather left to the exigencies of need as manifested in changing situations. Its prototype in almost all societies is the family, with its sharing of the common vicissitudes of life, its distribution of its resources according to the needs of the members and of its burdens according to their respective ability to bear them. This is a type of relationship where the formula of altruism in the usual sense is scarcely applicable. It is not a sacrifice of the interests of some to those of others but rather a fusion of all into a single unit, a common inter-

Originally published in the *Encyclopaedia of the Social Sciences,* Edwin R. A. Seligman (editor in chief), 13: 672–74. Copyright 1934, renewed 1962 by Macmillan Publishing Company. Reprinted by permission of the publisher.

est in the maintenance and prosperity of the whole which forbids the segregation of individual interests even for purposes of their sacrifice. But while the extent of mutual obligation remains unspecified, it is still not necessarily unlimited but subject always to being superseded in a scale of values. And although not itself an explicit realization of specific ultimate values, it must be in relative conformity with them; otherwise deep-seated conflicts will arise.

From the family as a nucleus this type of mutual service extends to all groups the members of which have a general and relatively undefined obligation of solidarity to one another, groups of friends, wider kinship groups, neighborhood groups, and, on the largest scale, nations.

Contrasted with this type is that where the object of the service tends to be impersonal and indefinite, any one of a large, undefined category of persons, such as "consumers," while the content of the obligation becomes specific and limited to definite functions. It is this type which comes to dominate when differentiation proceeds so far that those benefiting from services and those performing them are no longer united in a close community of general interest and life but are to a high degree separated from one another. Here service tends to be thought of as the function of an office held on behalf of the larger impersonal whole including both parties or as a profession or calling which, although not an office in an organization, has in fact a functional role on behalf of the whole.

In Western society, at least until relatively recent times, the principal ethical sanctions of service have come from the social implications of Christianity in its various historical forms. The content of the Gospels was essentially religious and transcendental and by no means immediately the basis of a movement for social reform. But the peculiar combination of religious individualism, the absolute and equal valuation of every human soul in relation to God, and the universalism of brotherly love gave a basis for subsequent social teachings. In the early Christian communities men lived apart from the rest of the sinful world in communistic societies. It was a communism of consumption alone, not of production; its motives were indifference to worldly things on the one hand, brotherly love on the other. But such a simple state of affairs was not possible when hope of an immediate coming of the kingdom faded and Christianity spread to include all classes of society and finally became the state religion of the Roman Empire. Paul himself, through the doctrine of the role of the inscrutable will of God, opened the way for a purely otherworldly interpretation of religious equality and hence a recognition of the inequalities of this world as inevitable and even positively ordained. Society came to be thought of as an organic unity in which every task is a service to the whole and to God. But while the social system was accepted and submitted to, this was only at best as an opportunity for Christian service. The world itself remained wholly sinful and corrupt. The early church never developed a conception of a really Christian society.

This idea did not come into being until the Middle Ages, where it found its classic medieval formulation in Thomas Aquinas. Here the social world was thought of again as an organic unity, each status having a part in the whole and contributing, although unequally, to the religious end of the whole. The highest life was of course the purely religious one in the monastery, where a segregated class acquired merit for the rest of the society as well as themselves. But worldly occupations had their positive if relative and inferior religious merit in their own right, not merely, as in the early church, as an opportunity for brotherly love. Taken together they were thought of as service of God and one's fellows in a system of the division of labor. The relatively personal and traditional character of most of the relationships of medieval society made it possible to conceive the whole in Christian terms as a system of mutual service, with a patriarchal element, for example, as between lord and serf and an egalitarian element as in the case of the relationship of craftsman and customer. The violence of feudal warfare was the most difficult thing to fit in; but, while in general interpreted merely as sin, in chivalry even it was brought within the Christian conception of service, to God above all, as in the crusades, and to other men (and of course women). Thus the medieval conception sanctioned primarily the first of the above types of service, that involving a personal relationship but without specific limits of content.

The Reformation brought another step in the secularization of the Christian idea of service, in that by abolishing monasticism it left only worldly callings as the fields of service and emphasized their conscientious performance as a religious duty. In the Lutheran branch the traditional and patriarchal elements remained uppermost and led to a conservative acceptance of things as they were and submission to authority, paralleled by the development of a conscientious devotion to duty, which bore fruits in the Prussian concept of duty in the service of the state.

It remained for Calvinism and the Protestant sects to emancipate the religious idea of service from patriarchalism and from traditionalism, by removing its indifference to the world, and to give its special sanction to rational work on individual responsibility for impersonal ends. This fitted in admirably with the individualistic economic developments of early modern times and has given an even stronger religious sanction to individual economic enterprise than the Thomist ethics gave to medieval traditionalism. By a process of secularization the original religious motivation has faded away and has tended to give place to a self-righteousness in the pursuit of self-interest often shading over into the hypocritical. What was originally conceived as disinterested service of God and one's fellows has become at best an end in itself, at worst sheer egoism covered by a thin veil of rationalization. Thus Lutheranism has provided a religious sanction to service of the impersonal and specific content type in the authoritarian state, while only Calvinism and the sects have given it for the voluntary and individualistic contractual type of relationship.

Since the eighteenth century various purely secular doctrines of service have arisen to fill the gap left by the fading religious sanction. Rationalistic humanitarianism and social utilitarianism are perhaps the most widespread. They seem to lack the power of justifying to the individual a real submergence of his self-interest, which the transcendental basis has given to the ideals of service arising out of Christianity.

CONSULT: Tönnies, F., *Gemeinschaft und Gesellschaft* (7th ed., Berlin, 1926); Durkheim, E., *De la division du travail social* (5th ed., Paris, 1926), trans. by G. Simpson (New York, 1933); MacIver, R. M., *Community: A Sociological Study* (3d ed., London, 1924); Ross, E. A., *Social Control* (New York, 1901); Clark, J. M., *The Social Control of Business* (Chicago, 1926); Troeltsch, E. D., *Die Soziallehren der christlichen Kirchen und Gruppen*, in his *Gesammelte Schriften*, vol. 1 (3d ed., Tübingen, 1923), trans. by Olive Wyon, 2 vols. (London, 1931); Weber, Max, *Die protestantische Ethik und der Geist des Kapitalismus*, in his *Gesammelte Aufsätze zur Religionssoziologie*, vol. 1 (2d ed., Tübingen, 1922), trans. by T. Parsons (London, 1930); Tawney, R. H., *Religion and the Rise of Capitalism* (London, 1926).

6

Thrift

Although it originally connotes saving, the term thrift has a tendency both in technical economic and in popular discussions to become identified with economic rationality in general, with the "wise" and "efficient" use and disposal of all resources, time, labor, and material things as well as money. In harmony, however, with its original connotation the emphasis tends to be put on the long as against the short-run point of view. The thrifty person is he who resists the temptation to satisfy momentary whims, but husbands his resources for the satisfaction of his "true" needs and desires.

But the ultimate ends of concrete economic activities are never given on economic terms alone. Hence it is not surprising that there should be a variety of different interpretations of what thrift really means. For at the basis of every doctrine of what is economical and rational must lie some view of the chief end of man. Two main tendencies may be distinguished. All doctrines of thrift go beyond the immediate interests of an "eat, drink, and be merry, for tomorrow we die" philosophy and most go beyond a rational distribution of the resources of an individual over his probable expectancy of life. But there is a whole class of doctrines which preach thrift as a means of attaining and maintaining, generally for a family over a period of generations, a standard of consumption that is fixed mainly in terms of noneconomic considerations. Thrift being thought of as a means, there is inherent in this type of thought a limit to its practice—when the end is attained there is no further need for the means. In the modern world this type is perhaps best exemplified by the thrift of the French lower middle class; a significant index is retirement and cessation of earning when enough has been laid by.

The second type is characterized by the absence of such a limit. It elevates thrift into an end in itself, a virtue, good for its own sake. It then becomes an ethical obligation to devote one's whole power to the

Originally published in the *Encyclopaedia of the Social Sciences*, Edwin R. A. Seligman (editor in chief), 14: 623–26. Copyright 1934, renewed 1962 by Macmillan Publishing Company. Reprinted by permission of the publisher.

largest possible accumulation without any clear conception of what the means are to be used for. The pure type is relatively rare but nonetheless important. There is almost always some rationalization of why inordinate thrift should be practiced, if only the assumption that the more wealth one has the better off one is. Perhaps the most important connecting link in the concrete shading off of the two attitudes is the role of wealth as a mark of social prestige, not merely in the Veblenian sense of conspicuous consumption but also through mere possession and accumulation: above all the objective not only of individual but of family social advancement over a series of generations. "Getting ahead in the world" is perhaps the most ubiquitous motive given for the practice of thrift.

A further classification of doctrines of thrift cutting across the others should be made. The primary connotation of the term lays its emphasis on the allocation of given resources. Just as the "means" concept of thrift noted above tends to be associated with a general traditionalism in standards of consumption, this type is associated with traditionalism in the means of earning a living and, more generally, of the productive processes as a whole. The principal problem of allocation of course is that of time, but the term thrift is often used to cover the avoidance of waste in general.

On the other hand, by something of a twist in the meaning the emphasis may be placed not on the thrifty use of given resources but rather on the continual increase of one's resources—on enterprise and initiative in earning and production. This interpretation occurs particularly when it appears desirable to retain the pleasant overtones of the term thrift and at the same time to avoid the connotation of niggardliness often connected with it. It is clear that this type along with the valuation of thrift as an end in itself is generally associated with a breaking through of traditionalism, often in both production and consumption. It is in fact an attitude very likely to appear with a weakening of the sentiment for unlimited thrift.

Historically attitudes toward thrift have varied greatly in different cultures and on the part of different classes within them. Hostility to thrift in almost any form tends to spring from two main sources: the *carpe diem* attitude and an attitude of indifference either to the good things of this world as such or to the thrifty ways of acquiring or safeguarding them. The attitude of *carpe diem* tends to become widespread above all in the well-to-do classes in relatively opulent and highly individualized and secularized periods. The Hellenistic age in Greece, the late republic and early empire in Rome, Renaissance Italy, and eighteenth-century France are examples. On a smaller scale and with less duration the same thing tends to happen in the reaction following a period of tense crisis, as in the "cocktail" era of the decade after the World War.

Of the attitude of indifference one of the main types is that arising from religious motives. The "take no thought for the morrow" of the Christian Gospels is primarily an expression of the sense of the utter unimportance of worldly things in comparison with the religious life. In more extreme forms this indifference may develop into active hostility with an ascetic prohibition of all worldly possessions, as in monasticism. The other type of indifference which does not affect worldly goods as such but thrift as a means to them is to be found above all in the attitude of aristocracies, which have almost universally looked down upon peaceful economic production and saving as beneath their dignity. The main exception in this group is that of commercial aristocracies. Above all a military aristocracy, which has booty as a source of acquisition, cannot but disdain the meanness of thrift. But even apart from resources obtained through war an aristocracy will almost always have a source of income from the labor and thrift of others.

By far the most common form of thrift historically has been the means type, and it has very generally been associated with traditionalism in both production and consumption. It exemplifies the kind of economic rationalism Aristotle had in mind in his discussions of the "management of a household." It is not incompatible even with aristocratic ways of life so long as it is limited to the thrifty management of the estates of nobles or the properties of monarchs as well as of the small tradesman, the artisan, or the peasant. The principle is very generally the same.

The valuation of unlimited thrift as a virtue for its own sake is far less common and has appeared on a large scale only in the modern Western bourgeois class. It is one of the most important aspects of the peculiar cultural constellation which has produced modern industrialism. Before its crystallization into a system of more or less automatic social pressures it is difficult to account for it except as a product of the religious motivations of ascetic Protestantism, especially Calvinism. For from purely religious motives these movements enjoined a rational participation in the affairs of this world, including disinterested devotion to economic production as a calling, combined with great frugality in consumption as the only means of avoiding the cardinal sin of self-indulgence.

The influences affecting thrift may be divided into two great classes: those operating on people's motives relatively independently of external conditions, and the conditions themselves, relatively independently of specific motives. Pure rational calculation of advantage and hence the rate of interest as a factor can account for a certain amount of thrift—the tendency to adapt uneven income over a lifetime to the uneven needs of the individual. But the great bulk of thrift must be explained differently. Everything which transcends the lifetime and personal interests of a single individual must be motivated by ultimate values. The most potent force here is religion but, as has been pointed out, its influence is by no means simple. The only attitude which no major religion sanctions is the *carpe diem* type of thriftlessness. But aside from that, according to the specific character of the religious attitude involved, everything else is possible. Within the Christian tradition alone there is the indifference of the Gospels; the ascetic hostility of monasticism and the mendicant orders; the traditional means thrift of lay Catholicism, which is still typical of countries like France with a predominantly Catholic background; and, finally, the "worldly ascetic" sanction of unlimited accumulation in some branches of Protestantism.

We may call attention to three important conditions for the development of thrift. One is the extent to which the individual is identified with groups in which his own interest is merged with that of the larger whole, above all the family. In general a strongly integrated family organization will be favorable to thrift of the traditional means type. The Chinese, for instance, practice an extraordinary frugality. Breakdown of family solidarity and individualization, on the other hand, will tend to be unfavorable to thrift, unless other positive influences, like the Protestant worldly asceticism, are present to counteract it.

A second important influence is what may be called the "security of careers," the extent to which the individual may look forward with reasonable certainty to a settled course of the development of his life and may expect in the relatively distant future to enjoy the fruits of present thrift for himself and his family. Not only is this a matter of settled conditions but also of the existence of tangible uses for savings which are close to the interests and sentiments of the individual. The conditions of the modern industrial laboring class are highly unfavorable to thrift in this respect as compared to those of an owner-peasant class, a skilled independent artisan class, or an independent small business class. Those of the early phases of economic individualism which had the combination of relatively settled conditions, wide diffusion and personal control and operation of productive property, and a relatively open opportunity for substantial but gradual rise in social status were much more favorable than the later phases of large-scale industry, a propertyless laboring class, and concentration of industrial control.

Thirdly, insofar as the prestige of wealth is a powerful social force, it makes a great difference to thrift if the standard is primarily one of scale of consumption, the aspect which Veblen brought out, or one of the possession and control of wealth, as farms and factories. The latter type may favor thrift while the other favors extravagance. Recently there has been a shift from the latter to the former, which is largely explained by the increasing intangibility of the sources of income.

The classical economists of the early nineteenth century laid enormous emphasis on individual thrift as the cornerstone of the stability of laissez-faire capitalism. In their invectives against the demoralizing poor law they failed to see that the very conditions which had made possible the freedom and mobility they prized so highly were also largely responsible for the thriftlessness they deplored. The gospel of thrift as preached by them and their successors was not sufficient to counteract the influence of these conditions. In fact the very vehemence with which the gospel has been preached may be regarded as an index of the failure of thrift to be a natural result of the social situation of recent times.

The modern economic order has created two important substitutes for individual thrift as a source of capital accumulation. One is the accumulation of corporate surpluses and their direct reinvestment in industry. The other is the operation of the banking mechanism to extend credit to business enterprise and through the resulting inflation, as it were, to tax the rest of the community. But it is highly questionable how far these mechanisms can take the place of individual thrift.

Individualistic ascetic Protestantism was one of the prime agencies in destroying the framework of solidarities which largely lay behind the practice of thrift of the means type. It supplied for a time a far more powerful motive of accumulation but one which rested on a highly precarious basis. Widespread secularization has already rendered it largely ineffective, while there seems to be little sign of a revival of the family and small-property conditions which might restore the previous situation.

CONSULT: Johnson, Alvin, "Influences Affecting the Development of Thrift," *Political Science Quarterly* 22 (1907): 224–44; Smiles, Samuel, *Thrift* (London, 1875); American Academy of Political and Social Science, "The New American Thrift," in *Annals*, vol. 87 (1920); Straus, S. W., *History of the Thrift Movement in America* (Philadelphia, 1920); MacGregor, T. D., *The Book of Thrift* (New York, 1915); Weber, Max, *Die protestantische Ethik und der Geist des Kapitalismus* (2d ed., Tübingen, 1922), trans. by T. Parsons (London, 1930); Troeltsch, E. D., *Die Soziallehren der christlichen Kirchen und Gruppen,* in his *Gesammelte Schriften,* vol. 1 (3d ed., Tübingen, 1923), trans. by Olive Wyon, 2 vols. (London, 1931); Tawney, R. H., *Religion and the Rise of Capitalism* (London, 1926); Veblen, Thorstein, *The Theory of the Leisure Class* (new ed., New York, 1918); Sombart, Werner, *Der moderne Kapitalismus,* 3 vols. (new ed., Munich, 1921–27). For a selected bibliography, see Russell Sage Foundation Library, *Thrift and Savings* (New York, 1919).

7

H. M. Robertson on Max Weber
and His School

The present note will not be concerned with a general critical evaluation of Dr. Robertson's book on *Aspects of the Rise of Economic Individualism.*[1] For that, in the absence of a sufficient knowledge of economic history, I, a sociologist by profession, am not competent. I shall rather take my departure from the subtitle of the book—"A Criticism of Max Weber and His School."[2] It will, I think, be generally agreed that a scholar who undertakes an adverse criticism of another's work can only hope to succeed when he has fully understood the work he has criticized and his either refuted the position he is criticizing on its own ground or has satisfactorily demonstrated that the mode of attack which the author has taken is so altogether out of touch with the facts of the situation that it can be thrown out without detailed refutation. It is my contention that Dr. Robertson's criticism fails to succeed in any one of these three directions and that Weber's work survives his onslaught without essential damage.

In the first place it is necessary to state quite specifically what the object of the attack, Weber's essay, *The Protestant Ethic and the Spirit of Capitalism*, was meant to be by its author. It was not a general theory of the "cause" of modern capitalism in the least. It was rather a specialized monograph maintaining the thesis that the Protestant ethic, in ways which Weber analyzed in great detail, could reasonably be assigned an important role along with several other factors in the great historical process which has resulted among other things in producing the modern economic order.[3] In the introduction to his series

Originally published in *The Journal of Political Economy* 43 (1935): 688–96.

1. H. M. Robertson, *Aspects of the Rise of Economic Individualism: A Criticism of Max Weber and His School,* Cambridge: Cambridge University Press; New York: Macmillan Co., 1933.

2. The concentration of this note on Weber himself rather than the "school" is justified by the fact that Dr. Robertson scarcely mentions any other authors.

3. Weber, *The Protestant Ethic and the Spirit of Capitalism*, New York and London, 1930, 29. (Translated from *Gesammelte Aufsätze zur Religionssoziologie*, vol. 1.)

on the "Sociology of Religion," Weber specifically mentions three of these others—modern science, itself partly influenced by capitalistic interests, and the rational structures of law and administration, again partly influenced by capitalistic interests. Thus these last two elements he thinks of as quite separate from the Protestant ethic, but each in its concrete development is partly independent of, partly influenced by, the third, "capitalistic interests." [4] But with respect to the Protestant ethic alone he quite specifically states "we are dealing with the connection of the spirit of modern economic life with the rational ethics of ascetic Protestantism. Thus we treat here only one side of the causal chain." [5] At the end of the essay he again reiterates this qualification: "It would further be necessary to investigate how Protestant Asceticism was in turn influenced in its development and its character by the totality of social conditions, especially economic. . . . It is of course not my aim to substitute for a one-sided materialistic an equally one-sided spiritualistic causal interpretation of culture and of history." [6]

Though Dr. Robertson does not explicitly deny that Weber introduced qualifications into his thesis, he continually writes in a vein which allows the reader to think that Weber was putting forward a "monistic" view of capitalistic development such that the demonstration of the importance of any factors other than the Protestant ethic was quite sufficient to refute Weber's position. Obviously such is not the case. Even the demonstration of the importance of the influence of capitalistic interests on the Protestant ethic itself is not in the least conclusive unless it goes so far as a proof that this influence completely accounts for it. Though he sometimes seems to claim this, I am sure a disinterested reader will agree with me that Dr. Robertson has furnished no such proof. For Weber the *concrete* Protestant ethic was not a wholly independent entity, and he advanced no specific claim as to the quantitative importance of the purely religious element in it. He merely claimed it was "important."

But we can be much more specific than this. Dr. Robertson claims to refute Weber further by taking up religious doctrines relating to economic life and attempting to show that these doctrines do not bear out Weber's claims of an influence on capitalistic development. The argument runs in terms of three main propositions: first, that Puritan teaching was not, particularly in its early phases, nearly so favorable to capitalism as Weber maintained; second, that where it was relatively favorable, especially in later phases, Catholic doctrine was just

4. Ibid., 25.
5. Ibid., 27.
6. Ibid., 183; see also 91.

as favorable or in many cases more so; third, that in both cases the discernible process of change is due to the influence on the policy of religious bodies of an independently rising capitalistic class which forced concessions which were in both cases essentially inimical to the principles of religious ethics.

I find two main difficulties with this central argument of Dr. Robertson insofar as it claims to be a valid criticism of Weber's position. The first concerns the point at which he chooses to seek his evidence. Dr. Robertson, that is, concentrates entirely on the concrete maxims of conduct put forward by religious writers and completely neglects to consider the religious derivation of these maxims. That is, he is concerned with what true believers were exhorted to do, not with the motivation of the typical believer in doing it. He entirely neglects the possibility that very similar maxims will work out quite differently in practice according to differences in the motivational background. But it is the latter with which Weber is primarily concerned. As he put it, ascetic Protestantism placed peculiarly powerful "psychological sanctions"[7] on certain types of conduct and the source of these sanctions lies in the way in which Protestant dogma, above all the doctrine of predestination, canalized the individual's attitudes and conduct in a certain peculiar direction—that of systematic, rational mastery over the external environment, and lent these attitudes a very special ethical intensity. This argument Dr. Robertson entirely ignores, but it is the central core of Weber's thesis.

A specific case which brings out the difficulty with especial clarity is Dr. Robertson's treatment of the doctrine of the "calling."[8] He first points out that the doctrine in the works of the *early* Puritans did not work in the direction of encouragement of acquisition but rather in that of a check on personal ambition and covetousness.[9] It is rather an affirmation of conservatism in a world of economic change. Moreover, there is no essential difference from the Catholic doctrine. Then Dr. Robertson proceeds to note that there was a marked change in Puritan teaching by the seventeenth century and that the doctrine of the later period as represented by Richard Baxter was much more favorable to capitalism than the earlier doctrine. Then he accuses Weber of paying attention only to the later doctrine and projecting it into the past—his "unhistorical" method made him incapable of perceiving the change.[10] Finally, Dr. Robertson asserts roundly and without qualification that the change was due primarily to the influence of

7. Ibid., 94.
8. Robertson, chap. 1.
9. Ibid., 6–8.
10. Ibid., 15.

capitalistic interests on religion without even entering into the question whether on the religious side itself there might not be causes of change also.[11]

A more inconclusive "criticism" than this would be difficult to imagine. In the first place it simply is not true that Weber failed to notice the change in the doctrine of the "calling." Weber says, "But it is not to be understood that we expect to find any of the founders or representatives of these religious movements considering the promotion of what we have called the spirit of capitalism in any sense the end of his life-work. We cannot well maintain that the pursuit of worldly goods, conceived as an end in itself, was to any of these of positive ethical value." [12] Then having made this definite misstatement of Weber's position, Dr. Robertson proceeds to ignore the central theme of Weber's argument, that precisely through the processes of its own internal dynamic development the Protestant ethic, in a manner quite unforeseen by its founders, had the practical effect of creating attitudes which could not but powerfully further types of activity of the greatest importance to economic life. Reduced to its lowest terms then, Dr. Robertson's argument is as follows: (1) There are two main forms of the concrete doctrine of the "calling," early and late (a true statement). (2) Weber did not perceive this difference and assumed the doctrine to be constant (a bald misstatement of Weber's position, inexcusable in anyone who claims to be a careful scholar). (3) An unspoken premise that the religious element in this doctrine must be constant (which is without justification, either in Weber or in the facts, and which in any case could not be established without careful analysis of the religious ideas underlying the doctrine of the "calling" and their development, which Dr. Robertson omits entirely to provide). Only on the basis of such analysis, if at all, could Dr. Robertson's conclusion (4) that the change is due to the influence of "capitalistic interests" be substantiated.

But underlying all this discussion is my second difficulty which concerns a still deeper misunderstanding of Weber's position. Dr. Robertson, at various points in his book, makes much of what he regards as the fallacies involved in Weber's "sociological" method and proposes to rectify them by using a sound "historical" method. There is naturally no space in such a brief note to enter adequately into the complex methodological issues involved. But it seems to me that this attitude

11. I purposely do not enter into any consideration of Dr. Robertson's attempted refutation of Weber's philological arguments about the idea of the "calling" as I do not feel myself competent in that field.

12. Weber, 89.

of Dr. Robertson is closely associated with the misunderstanding just referred to since the latter is shared by a number of historians who have essayed to criticize Weber's work.

Whatever else it may be, I should think of a sociological theory as concerned with the discrimination and analysis of certain causal factors in concrete situations. It consists not merely in working out the genetic antecedents of a given phenomenon, but also of analysis of the phenomenon itself, breaking it down into the various causal elements which go to make it up. Whether it be true of historians in general I shall not attempt to judge, but in this particular case the tendency has been for Dr. Robertson and others to take "capitalism" as an integral concrete phenomenon. For purposes of their discussion its "nature" is not in question but only its antecedents or "causes" in *that* sense.

But it is seldom possible for a "historical" method in this sense to operate without "sociological" preconceptions, and in fact there is clearly discernible in Dr. Robertson's and others' discussions a quite definite thesis as to what constitutes the essential element of capitalism. In this particular case it is evidenced by its equation with what Dr. Robertson calls "economic individualism." [13] What is meant here by economic individualism?

It is a version of something which has played a very great part indeed in modern social and economic thought—perhaps more generally described as the "rational pursuit of individual self-interest." The tendency is to think of the economic order as consisting of a plurality of individuals motivated primarily by the pursuit of their own economic interests, and of the total picture of the order as a resultant of these multifarious activities of the numerous individuals.

Now such a concept can, in turn, be applied in two essentially different ways which are often confused. It may, in the first place, be used to describe a concrete state of affairs—that of the "modern economic order" or "capitalism." Such a use implies a factual thesis that the modern order constitutes an "individualistic" order in this sense. Dr. Robertson's equation of capitalism with economic individualism certainly involves this thesis. In the second place such a concept may be used historically to help explain the genesis of the order. Then it becomes a question of the relation of the rational pursuit of self-interest as a causal factor to others in the situation.

The point of departure for understanding Weber's position seems to me to be the realization that his first difference from the position just sketched lies in his interpretation of the elements involved in the con-

13. Robertson, 15.

crete phenomenon he calls "capitalism." It is most emphatically not adequately described as Dr. Robertson's economic individualism, though that is one of the elements involved in it. It is true that Weber concurs in many of the conventional descriptive terms applied to the "capitalistic system." It is "individualistic" in the sense opposed to governmental control. It is "competitive," and above all it is "acquisitive"—the earning of profit becomes the immediate end of "business" activities.

But Weber sees what Dr. Robertson does not, that these descriptive terms do not immediately justify the explanation of these features by the element of "economic individualism." On the contrary, his deeper, sociological analysis of the concrete phenomenon resulted in the discovery of another element of a totally different order but manifested on the same, or almost[14] the same, concrete aspects of the system which Dr. Robertson calls "individualistic" and "acquisitive." This is not the pursuit of self-interest, that is, of means to personal satisfactions, but is rather a case of "objective," "selfless" devotion to worldly tasks, which is "disinterested" as opposed to the "interest" of the other element.[15] Under certain peculiar circumstances which Weber outlines, this disinterested attitude may become devoted to the task of profit making—*not* for the sake of enjoying the expenditure of the profits, but of earning as an ethical duty in itself. This is what Weber calls the element of "rational bourgeois capitalism" as distinguished from the "capitalistic adventurers." It is this element, not the total concrete phenomenon of capitalism, which is the theme of the essay on *The Protestant Ethic*. Dr. Robertson's complete failure to understand this background is vividly indicated by his cavalier dismissal of this element in his initial definition of terms.[16]

14. There is no space here to go into the concrete reasons for suspecting the presence of such an element. Weber gives a number. One important one is the lack of limitation on the extent of approved acquisition; another, the disapproval of self-indulgent and ostentatious consumption.

15. Two independent descriptions of the same phenomena from totally different theoretical points of view from Weber's are Veblen's "Instinct of Workmanship" and Professor Carver's "Work Bench Philosophy."

16. "What was this capitalist spirit? To Weber it was hardly more than bilateral. It consisted first in a rationalist as opposed to a traditionalist outlook. It consisted also in the desire to seek profit continuously (by means of the rational organization of free labor) for its own sake—even as a duty—and not for the purpose of enjoying the fruits. . . . But Weber's second criterion of the capitalist spirit is too narrow. It leads inevitably to the defect which I feel vitiates his whole argument: he hardly considers any capitalist other than the Puritan capitalist who seeks wealth for the fulfilment of his 'calling.'" Robertson, xii.

Only with this in mind is it possible to see the basis of the difference over the role of religion in "capitalistic" development. Christianity has certainly been in all its phases in one sense "otherworldly." It has always held the ultimate ends of human life to lie in a transcendental sphere. Hence it has always given only a relative sanction to the "world and the flesh" as necessary evils. Economic acquisition has received its blessing mainly as a necessary evil, and has been approved only in proportion as it was closely related to "function" as an indispensable means of securing the necessities of life or social status. On the other hand, capitalistic acquisition with its tendency to become detached from such relatively approved functions, to degenerate into a competitive game, to promote avarice or, with great wealth, un-Christian self-indulgence has pretty generally been under suspicion. This suspicion has been the more acute the more closely acquisition has approached the type of "economic individualism."

Protestantism has been no exception to this general rule. Disapproval of avarice, of covetousness, of self-indulgence is as strong as in any other branch of Christianity. Indeed, in some respects, Protestant "asceticism" has been more rigorous and uncompromising than Catholic lay ethics, a fact upon which Weber lays great stress. Thus, so long as "capitalism" is identified with "economic individualism" the gulf between it and Christian ethics cannot be bridged. The only possible alternative to acute hostility and attempted suppression of capitalistic tendencies is "accommodation" and "concession." From this point of view the relation of the development of "capitalism" to Christianity in all its forms has necessarily been one of "emancipation" from religious control, partly by out-and-out defiance of religious authority, partly by compromise on the part of the latter with the evil necessities of the world. There can be no doubt of the existence and importance of this process, which is the sole concern of Dr. Robertson's argument.

It is not, however, Weber's main concern. He is not in this essay interested in the problem of the development of "economic individualism" in Dr. Robertson's sense at all, but with that of the other element. But the question of the relation of this to Protestantism is an entirely different matter. The Protestant repudiation of monasticism, without in the least affecting the otherworldly orientation of its ethics, threw the ascetic element into everyday life—"every man became a monk." Especially in the Calvinistic form this resulted in a positive religious sanction of mundane activities, but at the same time under a strict ethico-religious discipline in certain respects. This *combination* is what Weber calls "worldly asceticism" (*innerweltliche Askese*).

The doctrine underwent, for religious reasons, a process of change. It was not at the beginning but at a later stage in the process that the "individualistic" aspect of it became sufficiently prominent for it to become an important element in the promotion of "individualistic economic enterprise"—roughly the seventeenth century. At that time the connection with the religious background was still evident. Later it became progressively secularized and this connection largely disappeared. But the element of positive ethical value remained and still remains as a basic element in the modern economic order. Thus according to Weber the peculiarities of Protestantism had two kinds of effects which differentiate it from that of Catholicism. In the first place, its sanction of "capitalism," that is, of individualistic, acquisitive activities, was positive and not merely permissive. But at the same time this positive sanction was accompanied by a stringent ethical control totally lacking in the concept of "economic individualism," but which served because of its peculiar character to promote rather than to retard the development of modern "industrialism."

All this is totally outside of Dr. Robertson's horizon—it is dismissed as the unsound "sociological" method. As previously noted, he makes capitalism virtually interchangeable with "economic individualism." With the exception of the chapter on the doctrine of the "calling," which has already been commented on, and a short discussion of Calvinist theocracy, which is open to much the same criticism, the whole of the book is concerned with the aspects of the economic order which are distinguished by an individualistic resistance to outside control— and religion is thought of as such an outside agency imposing an essentially foreign control which gradually breaks down under the pressure of capitalistic interests.

It is typical in this connection that Dr. Robertson thinks of the religious influence throughout in terms of church discipline imposed upon the individual by an authoritarian agency, entirely ignoring Weber's insistence that he was not concerned with church discipline but with the working of religious motives and their secularized derivatives on the individual directly. The most typical instance of this bias is the large amount of space Dr. Robertson gives to the question of usury which, he claims, is of central importance, for "free trade in capital is the essence of capitalism." [17] Weber, on the other hand, states, "For, as has been said, the prohibition of usury and its fate can have at most a symptomatic significance for us, and that only to a limited degree." [18]

17. Ibid., 111.
18. Weber, 202.

Dr. Robertson does not even refer to this statement of Weber's, to say nothing of raising the question why Weber ignored the usury question (there was only one quite incidental reference to it in Weber's text). Yet in a "criticism" of Weber, Dr. Robertson devotes two and a half chapters to this question without ever even attempting to prove that it has anything to do with Weber's problem.

Thus throughout, Dr. Robertson has "refuted" Weber by persistently ignoring the problems Weber was concerned with and talking about something else. There is no evidence that Weber was in the least unaware of that something else—he discussed it quite fully on a number of occasions under the heading of "speculative capitalism" and the "capitalistic adventurers." He just didn't happen to be concerned with it in this particular study. On the other hand, neither he nor, as far as I know, anyone else is concerned to deny either the existence or the importance of capitalistic interests as a factor. But neither can I see that Dr. Robertson has brought the slightest evidence of any sort to refute Weber's contention of the importance of disinterested ethical discipline in modern economic life, or Weber's explanation of its origin. Considered by its subtitle as a "Criticism of Max Weber and His School," this book quite definitely fails to live up to its promise. I am not concerned to deny either that there are defects in Weber's analysis or that Dr. Robertson has, in his book, made genuine contributions aside from his criticism of Weber. But the former Dr. Robertson has entirely failed to find, and the latter fall outside the scope of this note with the limits deliberately set to it.[19]

19. Of course Weber was in this essay concerned with the Protestant ethic particularly in contradistinction to the Catholic. But it is again only fair, in reaching a final judgment of it, to take account of the fact that for Weber himself this fell into a much wider perspective. In these terms he thought of the "rationalism" of the Protestant ethic as a peculiarly advanced phase of a "process of rationalization" which to him was the dominant trait of Western culture as a whole. As distinct from the cultures of China and India, for instance, the whole of Christianity, along with Western science, law, administration, and other elements, has a place in this process. So in the wider perspective the difference between the Protestant and the Catholic ethics is somewhat less prominent. Of course, it is too much to expect that Dr. Robertson should have gone beyond the one essay to try to see its significance in terms of Weber's sociological thought as a whole—that would be resorting to the "sociological" method and be unworthy of a historian. But nevertheless, a final assessment of Weber's work cannot omit this.

One other evidence of bias on Dr. Robertson's part calls for comment. On several occasions he quotes Troeltsch—*Social Teachings of the Christian Churches*—on particular points against Weber, but never mentions the fact that on the central point Troeltsch strongly endorsed Weber's position.

II

STUDIES IN THE DEVELOPMENT OF
THE THEORY OF ACTION

8

Economics and Sociology: Marshall in Relation to the Thought of His Time

In the last issue of this journal[1] I undertook to analyze Marshall's writings with a view to culling out certain vital elements to be found there which were logically separable from his "organon" of economic theory strictly defined. The outcome of that investigation was the thesis that running throughout Marshall's work is a line of thought which is almost everywhere coordinate in importance with what I have called his "utility theory," namely, his belief in the importance, both ethically and for explanatory purposes, of certain types of activities pursued largely as ends in themselves, and of certain types of character of which these activities are partly the expression, partly the formative agent. Marshall's attitude toward and interest in these activities and qualities of character play a decisive part in determining his position on a number of important problems, both of technical economic theory and of broader scope. Such considerations are among the things involved in his attitude toward Ricardo, his doctrines of the supplies of the agents of production, his views of real cost, his attitude toward laissez-faire, social evolution, and human nature.

The present paper will broaden the scope of the discussion by inquiring into the relations of Marshall's ideas to those of other writers. Moreover, having in mind two alternatives to Marshall's own approach to the problems he was interested in, it will discuss his position critically.

I

The issues with which this discussion is to be concerned can perhaps best be raised by pointing out a striking relationship which Marshall's idea of "free enterprise" bears to the doctrines of another recent

Originally published in the *Quarterly Journal of Economics* 46 (1932): 316–47.

1. [This is a reference to Parsons's article, "Wants and Activities in Marshall," *Quarterly Journal of Economics* 46 (1931): 101–40.]

69

writer on modern capitalism, Max Weber, who is the representative of a totally different school of thought.[2]

Weber finds the dominant characteristic of modern capitalism in a certain peculiar rationality of the conduct of life, a rationality sharply opposed to the irrationalities both of "traditionalism" and of undisciplined instinct, whim, impulse, or sentiment. It is characterized on the part of the individual by a careful systematic planning of his life as a whole and the elimination of all activities inconsistent with such a comprehensive plan. In actual economic life it results in the far-reaching application of science to industrial technique and business organization, the longtime planning of operations, the vivid realization of the future—all serving to make the whole economic organization predominantly into what Weber calls a "bureaucratic" type. This rational bureaucratic organization of modern society is most conspicuous in the economic sphere, in enterprises producing goods for a competitive market. The making of profit and the increase of capital being the common aim of all such enterprises, the system as a whole is most appropriately called capitalism.

But the very impersonality of profit as an aim raises the question of motivation. Is such activity carried on to satisfy individual desires by the expenditure of the profits? Is the rationality of capitalism peculiar only in the perfection with which it adapts means to *universal* human ends? Weber definitely rejects such views. There is nothing natural and universal about the capitalistic way of life such that, given favorable external conditions, it will become established of itself. On the contrary it is an entirely unique phenomenon, which has appeared only once in history in an equally unique constellation of circumstances. It is not explicable in terms of the wants which are expressed in consumers' demand, assumed to be given from the point of view of the productive process. Nor is it explicable in terms of wants in the sense of instincts, such as acquisition or workmanship.

Then what does account for it? In its fully developed form the competitive discipline is enough, the system is self-sustaining. Any individual who failed to conform to its rules and ways would be eliminated from the struggle. But selection alone cannot account for the *origin*. The standards of this particular selective process themselves are not universal; they had to originate somewhere. Their origin Weber finds

2. See Max Weber, *The Protestant Ethic and the Spirit of Capitalism*, London and New York, 1930. This essay, while containing the core of Weber's theory of capitalism, is only a fragment of the whole, which he unfortunately never formulated in one place. For a fuller analysis of it see the present writer's article, "'Capitalism' in Recent German Literature: Sombart and Weber" [chapter 1 of this volume].

above all[3] in the Protestant ethic which created a state of mind favorable to such a way of life. Through the idea of a "calling," a task to which every man felt himself to be assigned by divine Providence, economic activities came to be pursued not as means to other worldly ends, but from the mundane point of view as ends in themselves— justified to the individual by their relation to his eternal salvation.

Weber's main emphasis throughout is on the importance of this "ascetic" element in modern economic life, as against the more orthodox view that it is merely the result of "natural" tendencies of behavior, instinctive or hedonistic. His explanation of modern capitalism is in a sense in terms of wants, but not in the same sense as that of utility theory. The "ascetic" aspect means on the whole an inhibition of wants in the latter sense, which, however, greatly favored capitalism because it promoted accumulation. On the other hand the "wants," or perhaps rather values, behind the system are expressed directly in economic activities, not in demand; in the system and rationality of conduct, in industry and frugality, in short the "economic virtues."

This suggests some interesting points of correspondence between Weber and Marshall. In the first place, both are agreed that modern capitalism, or "free enterprise," is characterized by a peculiarly high degree of rationality; it is in fact the result of a long "process of rationalization." They are also agreed that, in so far as rationality is a mark of "economic" conduct, the development of capitalism is characterized by an increasing importance of economic factors in social life. Moreover, both emphasize the importance of the economic in another way. Economic development leads to a greater and greater spread of the competitive price system, so that an increasing proportion of men's lives is determined by their relations to it. Weber greatly emphasizes the compulsive nature of competition, while Marshall does so only by implication; it is for him an important agent in keeping up the springs of energy and enterprise. This makes it possible to say that, in a sense, both hold an "economic interpretation of capitalism" though not of history as a whole.

But in both cases, and this is the most significant agreement, these first two elements, rationality and dependence on the competitive price system, derive their meaning largely from a third factor, Weber's "callings," pursued first for the glory of God, later, with the dying out of the religious motives, as ends in themselves; and Marshall's "activ-

3. Of course other conditions had to be favorable. Weber has often been unjustly accused of holding that capitalism was "created" by Protestantism, out of a vacuum as it were. Such is by no means his position.

ities." For both, especially, the rationality in question is relative to these activities, centering around them as a nucleus. Weber makes the relativity highly explicit, contrasting this form of rationality with many others that are possible. Marshall's conception of rationality is much more absolute, but his ruling out the rational satisfaction of those wants which he calls "artificial" from a role in social progress, clearly shows the relation of rationality to activities in his doctrine. With Marshall as with Weber this same element is the basis of the denial that civilization can be understood either in terms of biological instinct, the "wants" which rule the lower animals, or of "artificial wants" which would be either primarily hedonistic or random.

Moreover Marshall agrees with Weber, and on similar grounds, that the concept of selection is inadequate as a general explanatory principle. Weber's position, cited above, is that while selection[4] can sometimes explain the maintenance of a given social organization once established, it can never explain the origin of the standards of selection themselves. Marshall, in more directly ethical terms, says survival power is the power "to *thrive in* the environment, not necessarily to *benefit* the environment."[5] Given the fact that the development of free enterprise has in Marshall's view meant specifically moral advance, it is quite clear that a process of "benefiting the environment" must have gone on continuously, i.e., that the competitive process has been supplemented by another source of standards.

As will be shown later, Weber's general sociological position is fundamentally different from Marshall's. Hence Weber's scientific motives for studying modern capitalism in the terms in which he did are completely foreign to Marshall.[6] Then whence the remarkable correspondence? The explanation seems to be that Marshall was a living example of the "spirit of capitalism" of which Weber was talking. While he happened to be right about the role of certain ethical qualities in modern life, the reason for his ability to see them was not, as with Weber, an extraordinarily wide perspective, but his own deep-rooted belief in them. It was here that Marshall, the seer and reformer,[7] made

4. Combined of course with the formative effect of a social environment upon individuals.

5. *Principles* [*of Economics,* 8th ed., London, 1925], 596; also *Industry and Trade,* [London, 1919], 175.

6. Moreover, any important reciprocal influence is out of the question. It is practically certain that Marshall never read Weber's essay and even had he done so he could not have been greatly influenced by it—the point of view is too different. The main lines of Marshall's views were certainly fixed before Weber's essay was written (1904).

7. See Keynes, ["Alfred Marshall, 1842–1924," in *Memorials of Alfred Marshall,* ed. A. C. Pigou, London, 1925], 11, 12.

his contact with Marshall, the scientist. This reforming zeal was at least as important an influence in his life as a whole as his purely "positive" scientific interest.

Marshall's own ethic was also certainly a derivative of the Protestant ethic of which Weber speaks. As Keynes tells us, "The Marshalls were a clerical family of the West of England" and his father though not himself a clergyman was "cast in the mould of the strictest Evangelicals."[8] While Marshall himself was a free thinker in his adult life, he retained all the more tenaciously the ethical fruits of his strict religious bringing up. Moreover, he himself ascribed considerable importance to religious factors of the Reformation in "strengthening the English character."[9]

Before going into the difference of sociological views lying back of this remarkable though unconscious agreement of the two thinkers, it will be best to place Marshall somewhat more accurately in the tradition which formed his intellectual background.

II

In sketching the history of the main currents of English social thought relevant here, I shall confine myself to the period since the seventeenth century; Hobbes and Locke may be regarded as initiating the trends which are of primary interest. A striking feature of the whole tradition in this period has been its predominant individualism, and this in two senses. It has always conceived society to exist for the benefit of independent individuals, and has been profoundly suspicious of any suggestions that the whole was, in almost any sense, superior to the parts.[10] While recent versions of English individualism have gone quite a distance in toning down the more extreme "atomism" of writers even as late as Spencer, they certainly have not abandoned the central position.[11]

8. *Memorials*, 1.

9. "The isolation of each person's religious responsibility . . . is a necessary condition of the highest spiritual progress." "The natural gravity and intrepidity of the stern races that settled on the shores of England inclined them to embrace the doctrines of the Reformation; and these reacted on their habits of life." *Principles*, 742.

10. Two of the most prominent English representatives of the theory that "society is an organism," Hobbes and Spencer, have balked at interpreting it in this sense.

11. See especially the works of the late Professor Hobhouse. His *Metaphysical Theory of the State* remains the classical English refutation of idealist social theory. The latter cannot be said ever to have gained a real ascendancy in English social thought, though perhaps it has come nearer to that in official philosophy.

More important for present purposes than this ethical sense of individualism, though generally associated with it, is the more definitely sociological sense. It may be defined as the conception that social phenomena are to be *understood* primarily in terms of the essentially independent actions and properties of individuals pursuing ends in the last analysis private to themselves, so that the "social" is conceived as a resultant of the various forces of individual activity.

The great controversies of English social thought have not been concerned with the validity of this general individualistic position but with differences which have arisen within it. In order to show this it will suffice briefly to state the issues at a few main stages.

The first stage is the conflict between Hobbes and Locke. Both are social contract theorists, thinking of social bonds as existing for the satisfaction of individual desires alone. In particular the state and its authority is only a means, a necessary evil. The main difference lies in their interpretation of the role of reason. For Hobbes it is the servant of the "passions" which are thought of as essentially unlimited and independent of each other.[12] The full satisfaction of the passions of any one individual is hence incompatible with an equal satisfaction for others; they must be forcibly restrained or the result is the war of all against all, the reign of force and fraud. Locke reverses the relationship; reason rules the passions. Man is not only rational, but "reasonable"[13] and there is no essential disharmony of the desires of individuals and life in society. Authority is not so necessary and can be challenged without such great risks to security. Force and fraud are suppressed primarily by the reasonableness of the individual, not by external authority.

In rather different terms similar issues reappear in the controversy between the Malthusians and classical economists on the one hand and the optimistic radicals like Godwin and Owen on the other. Malthus emphasizes, not the plurality of warring passions that Hobbes does, but one specific passion, the "tendency to reproduce." This change shifted the scene of the major disharmony from the conflicting passions of individuals to the relation of man to natural resources. This really involves a radical difference from Hobbes; the classical economists hold that the pursuit of self-interest does not lead to a war

12. Hobbes can hardly be made out to be a modern "survivalist." The desire for self-preservation dominates the others merely because it is inconceivable to Hobbes's "practical" mind that anyone should set other values above life itself.

13. For Locke this was because men were reasonable. The position was, however, open to another interpretation in terms of a moral instinct implanted by nature, so that it was nature, not man, which was reasonable.

of all against all, but is the principal agency in mitigating the evil consequences of the principle of population. This position assumes that force and fraud are ruled out of individual competition by improved morality rather than by the strengthening of authority, and is insofar like that of Locke, and again Marshall.[14] At this stage it is hardly possible to speak of radical anti-intellectualism in spite of the difference of opinion on the scope of reason. The Malthusian objection to Godwin is that reason cannot easily control the sexual appetite, but no one denied at least an important "instrumental" role to reason, especially in the economic sphere.

So far English individualism had had a predominantly static character. It thought in terms of an equilibrium adjustment to fixed factors; the external environment, human passions, the standard of living. When the idea of evolution came into English thought with Darwinism, the particular form it took involved a minimum of modification of the existing tradition. Darwin himself was of course influenced by social thought, particularly by Malthus, but at least indirectly by Hobbes also. Indeed the resemblance of the Darwinian conception of nature to the conception of society of the classical economists was so close that Keynes has remarked "the principle of the Survival of the Fittest could be regarded as a vast generalization of the Ricardian economics." [15]

But there was a new element in Darwinism, the conception of random variation. Instead of the selective process merely keeping numbers down to protect a static standard, the process is dynamic. Indeed it is only this element which makes Darwinism an evolutionary doctrine. One of its principal applications to the social sphere lay in permitting a synthesis of the old pessimistic individualism of Hobbes and Malthus with a new optimistic philosophy. The war of all against all, the process of elimination, is not to be regretted, since after all only the unfit are eliminated and the whole movement is one of progress. On the other hand the "reasonable" tradition, when it adopted the

14. The utilitarians still further modified Hobbes's position by their doctrine of sympathy, which is in turn associated with a general leaning to biological environmentalism. Through association the good of others may come to give pleasure to any given individual and hence altruism is not inconsistent with hedonism. Furthermore sympathy may help to account for social cohesion under conditions of laissez-faire, while Hobbes could only derive it from the coercive authority of the sovereign. The scope of doctrine, however, was strictly limited by the individualism of the utilitarians. The "good of the whole" of social utilitarianism is a very different thing from the analogous conception of Rousseau or Hegel. The other factor of social cohesion at this stage was economic interdependence through the division of labor.

15. *The End of Laissez-Faire*, New Republic edition, 17.

doctrine of evolution in a biological sense, tended to Lamarckian environmentalism, and in a social sense to the conception of active adaptation through collective mastery of the external environment. Indeed if men are really "reasonable" why should there be any necessity for a struggle; if environment forms human beings directly why should there be any unfit to eliminate?[16]

It is noteworthy that where the doctrine of evolution was applied to society by this kind of thought it has been in terms of a continuous unilinear process. The result is by no means arbitrary; it is a natural result of the whole structure of these theories. Why?

The social theories under discussion have been characterized by the attempt to explain human society in terms of objective scientific factors, which are stable and easily verified. In this regard the most obvious are the conditions imposed upon man by the external environment. If its influence can be pushed far enough almost all the highly complex problems of human motivation can be pushed to one side. Only one "motive" need be postulated: survival. Given this one "motive" all human actions can be explained as resulting from the necessity of meeting the inexorable conditions of survival. This view may be called "survivalism." Suggestions of it may be found in Hobbes, in the dominant role he assigns to the passion for self-preservation. It is much farther developed in Malthusianism, at least of the more drastic variety. One dominant urge, the tendency to increase, being postulated, the hard necessities of the subsistence problem account for everything else.[17] To be sure the doctrine was modified by elements summed up in the conception of the standard of living; and the interpretation of the effects of competition as relatively beneficent in maintaining a standard also involves other elements. But such disturbing elements may be found in almost any body of thought and do not alter the main outline.

This becomes a truly evolutionary doctrine only by introducing the Darwinian conception of variation as underlying that of selection. In its social application the new element assumes social variations also to be random and to be submitted equally to the selective exigencies

16. Spencer represents a curious mixture of these lines of thought. On one hand he was the original coiner of the phrase "survival of the fittest," on the other, a believer in the inheritance of acquired characters.

17. An excellent illustration of the way in which conviction of the importance of a biological factor can divert attention from other problems is Mill's treatment of wages. The population problem so dominated his mind that he never even attempted a thorough analysis of the demand for labor, since it made no difference after all. (I am indebted to Professor Taussig for this suggestion.)

of the external environment.[18] The leading idea is that of adaptation, becoming progressively better by virtue of the element of variations. Another version of the same concept, associated with Lamarckian environmentalism in biology, is the idea of rational adaptation in society, often repudiating competition in favor of spontaneous cooperation. The two versions differ only as to the process of adaptation; since the really decisive factor, the environment, is the same in both cases, the end result is also the same.[19]

A certain broadening of the point of view takes place when, on the "human" side of the equation, not one all-pervading aim—survival— is assumed, but a multiplicity of wants. Then the external environment retreats into the role of a limiting condition and the center of the sociological problem becomes that of the choice of means to satisfy as large a quantity[20] of these wants as possible within the limitations imposed on the one hand by the environment, on the other by the potential conflicts of individuals with each other. This is the view which seems to be dominant in Hobbes, in spite of the role he assigns to self-preservation, and certainly is so in Locke. The principal difference between them lies within these limitations—in their estimation of the seriousness of the possibilities of conflict, and hence of the role of the principal agency in the prevention of conflict, the state. This doctrine may be called sociological "liberalism."[21] Its essential feature is that it simply assumes individual wants as given without attempting to justify or explain them. It remains strictly scientific insofar as it follows this course. In this sense Bentham was quite correct and con-

18. The whole line of thought uppermost in this "social Darwinism" is closely identified with the "scientific" aspects of the doctrines of Natural Law. Its emphasis is on the inexorability of social determinism. The other line of thought derived from Locke is tied up with normative conceptions of Natural Law. See the two articles by O. H. Taylor, *Quarterly Journal of Economics*, February and May 1930. I am much indebted to Dr. Taylor, both his articles and his conversation, for clarification of many points both in the history of English social thought and in Marshall.

19. This emphasis on the "objective conditions" is a perfect example of what W. Köhler (*Gestalt Psychology*) calls "mechanistic theory." It avoids all "dynamic" problems by explaining phenomena exclusively in terms of what Köhler calls "topographical conditions."

20. Such a theory necessarily requires a quantitative standard of want-satisfaction. Since "utility" is the only satisfactory one ever discovered, this "sociology" has always been closely associated with economics.

21. This is of course not to be confused with political liberalism, though it is one of the doctrines underlying it. It and the view called "survivalism" above may be united to form what may be designated sociological "individualism." I use the term "liberalism" only in default of a better. It is more liberal than survivalism because it leaves an important margin of variation to individual wants.

sistent in his insistence that from the viewpoint of utilitarianism "push-pin is as good as poetry," if the individual happens to think so. The most consistent form of the doctrine, utilitarianism, so long as it sticks to this position, is a scientific account of human action, and, so far as it claims to be a complete account of it in society, a sociology.

So far as "liberalism" has simply assumed the wants of the moment as given[22] it has remained a strictly "social" doctrine. But there have frequently been attempts to search further for *universal* tendencies of action underlying momentary wants which have naturally ended in a psychological interpretation of social phenomena, in "psychologism." In this sense the passions of Hobbes and the pleasure[23] of utilitarianism are psychological conceptions. Finally a still further reduction of "wants" to those fundamental biological urges related to survival tends to reduce the doctrine to a biological one.[24] Between these steps there are of course all conceivable gradations.

Both "survivalism" and "liberalism," if taken to be the final and ultimate accounts of human life, may be considered as ethical doctrines; if they are the ultimate *scientific* accounts of man in society they are sociologies, though they may be systems of ethics as well. If they accept a doctrine of evolution at all, it is necessarily continuous and unilinear, as in both cases there is a single goal toward which the process tends,[25] and no logical break in the process. In both cases also a scientific doctrine of "progress" is possible, for the goals are objectively fixed and the process of social change, whether by selective or rational adaptation, or want-satisfaction, moves inevitably[26] toward them.

There is one other ground on which a unilinear theory of social evolution is possible. If, namely, survivalism is rejected and human

22. This naturally does not exclude the use of relatively general types.

23. The economic conception of utility can scarcely be called psychological as it refers at most only to the immediate, not the ultimate, motive of an act of choice. It is important to distinguish it from "pleasure."

24. F. H. Knight, "Ethics and the Economic Interpretation," *Quarterly Journal of Economics* 36 (1921–22): 469, remarks that "modern Pragmatism (and some versions of Utilitarianism) runs in terms of the twofold assumption that the Good is identical with both the biologically beneficial and the actually desired." It may do so, but the two assumptions need not go together. Both tend to make of sociology as well as ethics a "glorified economics." I am much indebted to this article by Professor Knight and the sequel to it, "The Ethics of Competition," for many stimulating ideas which have influenced the present study at too many points for separate reference.

25. In the one case adaptation to environment, in the other, satisfaction of desires.

26. Since there is no possible motive for human beings to make choices which would lead away from the goal, except as "errors" which would be random and not predominate in any one direction.

desires are not simply taken as ultimate, but qualitative distinctions are made between them, if poetry is held to be better than push-pin, the process of evolution may be thought of as leading to the development and realization of the "higher" at the expense of the "lower" desires or values. But for the unilinear direction to be given there can be only one set of "higher" desires, or a fixed scale from lower to higher. On the other hand the introduction of this element brings with it the possibility of a struggle of man with himself, of "temptation" which had no place in the other two frameworks, and which lends an aspect of uncertainty to the whole process.

There has been one other movement in English thought which needs a brief word here: anti-intellectualism. The way to it may be said to have been opened by the Darwinian movement. The activities (resulting from variations) which it supposes to form the raw material of selection need not be rationally directed to given ends, they might be wholly random or instinctive.[27] There has since been a widespread questioning of even Hobbes's limited conception of the role of rationality, the two most conspicuous forms of which are behaviorism and the instinct psychology. But the conspicuous fact about anti-intellectualism in England and America has been that the repudiation of reason has taken place in favor of biological or psychological factors, and has thus served merely to strengthen the already powerful tendency to bio-psychological interpretations. The anti-intellectualist has turned to the reflexes and conditioned reflexes of the behaviorists, to the instincts of McDougall, or to some related factors. We have never produced an important *sociological* anti-intellectualism such as has appeared on the continent of Europe with the work of Pareto.

Let it be stressed again that the strong tendency to biological or psychological interpretations of social life is a natural result of the sociological individualism of English social thought; it tries to get down to the fundamental nature of that individual who is the basic unit of society, and of the external environment he lives in. Insofar as it has not done so, the main emphasis has been thrown on economics. For "orthodox" economic theory has been concerned with a rational process of individual want-satisfaction, the wants being considered as given.[28] If that assumption was made not merely for the limited methodological purposes of economic theory, but as a basic postulate of social theory as a whole, and combined with the general belief in ra-

27. For strict Darwinism even instincts must originate in random movements.

28. They need not be in fact absolutely constant, but must be considered as data from the viewpoint of economic science. It is the relative independence, not the fixity of wants, which matters.

tionality, the inevitable result was to make economic theory the central element of social thought. This position was still further reinforced by the incorporation in a great part of the tradition of the egoism of Hobbes's natural man, which put strong props under the competitive aspect of classical economics. To be sure there were elements which did not readily find a place in this structure, such as the standard of living, but they tended to be simply taken for granted, without further inquiry into their origin.[29] With the double advent of the doctrine of evolution and the emphasis on elements which did not fit into this general scheme such as "custom" and the role of irrational instinct and impulse, it was easy to project such elements back into the past as characteristic of the primitive stages of development, and look upon the evolutionary process as one of emancipation from them through the development of reason.

III

What has all this to do with Marshall? He fits admirably into certain elements of the tradition. He is, in some respects, as thoroughgoing an individualist in the sociological sense as any of them. He certainly accepts the general postulate of rationality of human action, though in accordance with his evolutionary doctrine he makes it a growing rationality at the expense of the dominion both of custom and of irrational impulse. He was not appreciably influenced by the anti-intellectualist movement, which is but natural since that movement has only grown to large proportions since his formative period. Nevertheless there is one striking point where Marshall does not fit into the tradition, his treatment of wants.

It is quite clear that he did not think primarily in terms of biological "survivalism." That would be entirely inconsistent with his categorical denial that civilized men were the creatures of "wants" in the same sense in which he considered the lower animals were. His general refusal to ascribe very great importance to the influence of external environment is further evidence.

Nor was he mainly an adherent of a psychological interpretation. To have been one in the anti-intellectualist sense would have contradicted his belief in reason. He was certainly not a consistent adherent of the natural egoism of Hobbes. The most current psychological theory of his formative years was utilitarian hedonism. In spite of the fact that, as Keynes points out, he never explicitly rejected it, it has been shown in my first paper that he could not have been primarily a

---

29. Which is the same as saying they are outside the scope of the science in question.

hedonist.[30] Nor, finally, could he have been a strict "liberal" in the above sense. His very refusal to take man's wants for granted as data is sufficient proof. But further his category of "artificial" wants would be quite illegitimate from that point of view. He refused to recognize that push-pin was as good as poetry. What then was his position?

It is clear that what differentiates him from any of the doctrines just outlined is his insistence on the importance of activities and the development of faculties, in connection with the wants "adjusted to" or created by them. It is their adjustment to activities which distinguishes this kind of wants from either "artificial" wants or biological needs. They and the activities adjusted to them refuse to fit into any of the above categories. Given the role of activities, it is Marshall's belief in their absolute nature which makes him an adherent of the doctrine of unilinear social evolution. He does not even consider the possibility that evolution might lead in any other direction than the development of his particular set of activities and qualities of character. All phenomena differing from his free enterprise are interpreted as stages in its development. If they exist contemporaneously they are arrested stages, their adherents are "backward" peoples.[31] Even socialism is

30. The evidence for this statement need not be repeated here. It is true that Marshall not only did not explicitly repudiate hedonism, but retained a sufficient hold on it to give plausibility to the view that this was the keynote of his whole thought. It is easy enough to quote hedonistic statements from his works. The only way of refuting such a view is by considering the structure of his thought as a whole. With that in mind I have no hesitation in saying that hedonism was a subsidiary rather than a major current in his thought. When hedonism and the role of activities are brought face to face, as in the attitude toward Jevons and toward "artificial" wants, it is always hedonism that gives way.

31. One of the best examples of Marshall's attempts to fit difficult cases into his scheme is to be found in what seems to be the solution of a puzzling problem of interpretation. I have already pointed out (in the first paper) [see note 1 above] that, while Marshall does not in general greatly emphasize the role of external environment, there is one striking exception: he repeatedly insists on the debilitating effects of hot climates; they sap the springs of energy and make for sluggishness. Why does he make the exception? I think he had primarily the case of India in mind. Because of his absolute belief in his activities, he was blind to the possibility that Indian civilization might be simply *different* from European, guided by different ideals. He tried rather to find a place for it in his evolutionary scheme. The Indians are obviously an intelligent people; so their failure to develop free enterprise cannot be due to innate stupidity. It must be ascribed to some arresting agency which he thinks to find in the climate. India is not essentially different from Europe, but an arrested stage in the same process of development. The Indians belong to the "more ignorant and phlegmatic of races." (He also had a certain tendency to minimize the differences: see his continual statements that there is more operation of "economic forces" in India than is generally supposed.)

It is interesting to compare this with Max Weber's view, expressed in his study of the social implications of Hindu religion (*Religionssoziologie* 2: 133). "The belief that the

not a step *away* from his line of progress, but one *backward* along it, into sluggishness and stagnation.

But does Marshall really depart radically from the intellectual tradition in which he grew up? He has been said to have been influenced largely, so far as I know, by only two other traditions than that sketched here: by Hegel[32] and by the German historical school.[33] It is true that certain elements of Hegel were congenial to him, but even where there is a superficial likeness it covers up a deeper difference. Moreover, what is still more important, the elements of Hegel which have been most decisive in influencing subsequent German thought, have left scarcely a trace in Marshall. His idea of evolution is *continuous*, not dialectic. Both the (logical) discontinuity and the element of conflict, the two primary elements of Hegelian evolution, are missing from Marshall. Instead of emphasizing the historical uniqueness and discontinuity of past economics systems, Marshall systematically minimizes them.[34] This separates him sharply from Hegel, Marx, and their successors. Marshall's low opinion of Marx is in itself sufficient proof of his lack of touch with the essence of the Hegelian tradition. He took from Hegel only what suited his own preconceptions, and used it only to round off the sharp edges of his own tradition—as in his idea of the "organic" nature of social change.[35]

Essentially the same is true of his relation to the historical school, which was in turn closely related to Hegel. He used that school primarily to emphasize explicitly the importance of the historical relativ-

---

Indians are characterized by a 'sluggishness' which is the result of the climate, and that this explains their supposed aversion to activity, is wholly without foundation. No country in the world has ever known such continual and savage warfare, such ruthless conquests, subject to so few limitations, as India." In view of Weber's totally different sociological approach it is not surprising he should come to the diametrically opposite conclusion from Marshall. That makes their agreement on capitalism all the more significant.

32. See Keynes, *Memorials*, 11, and Marshall himself, *Principles*, ix.

33. For his attitude to this school see "The Present Position of Economics," *Memorials*, 152ff. Right as Marshall is in his criticism of them in terms of economic theory, he misses some of their broader aims. By the same token they were wrong in trying to bring those aims into economic theory as such.

34. As in his treatment of mercantilism.

35. See "Mechanical and Biological Analogies in Economics," *Memorials*, 312–18. "Progress or evolution, industrial and social is not mere increase and decrease. It is organic growth." *Memorials*, 317. "Economic problems are imperfectly treated, as problems of statical equilibrium and not of organic growth." *Principles*, 461. It is evident that he linked this "organic" idea with his activities. "Organic" growth is the simultaneous development of wants adjusted to activities, of the "standard of life"; a rise in the "standard of comfort" on the other hand is not organic growth.

ity of institutions and customs, and hence of the study of economic history. This did indeed mark a change from some of his predecessors, but he interpreted this relativity in terms of his own doctrine of social evolution. His doctrine was no by means the radical relativity or the absolute logical independence of historical epochs toward which the historical school was tending, *Historismus*. Marshall's differences from the leading legitimate heir of the historical school today, Sombart, bring that out clearly. The influences which shaped Sombart's thought cannot possibly have been decisive for that of Marshall.

The fact of the matter is that Marshall accepted the fundamentals of English thought, with one exception: he made room for the element of activities by widening the scope of economics to include it. That widening was not arbitrary, but was the only way to deal with it without splitting open the whole conceptual framework of his inherited tradition. For this tradition included, as has been shown, three main elements, or alternative explanatory principles. There was the "survival" principle, acceptance of which would reduce social science to applied biology. Marshall rejected that view decisively. The alternative was the "liberal" view. One interpretation of it, the "psychologistic," Marshall also decisively rejected. It would have meant assuming a constancy of human nature which was inconsistent with his view of the progressive development of character. The only thing left was the "liberal" view shorn of psychological implications; the simple assumption that men acted rationally in the satisfaction of their wants, whatever they might be. Marshall's course was to fuse his doctrine of activities with this element, with utility theory, to form a broader economics. The element of rationality caused no difficulty in effecting the fusion, since for a narrow rationality of action in the service of any wants which happened to exist he could substitute a broader conception which included the element of activities. Moreover the particular activities Marshall was interested in happened in themselves to be highly rational. The most radical alteration his position did involve was in abandoning the constancy, or the purely random nature, of wants, and discriminating between those which were "adjusted to activities" and those which were merely "artificial." The latter category was virtually left out of consideration, or pushed back into the earlier stages of social evolution and doomed to be progressively eliminated, while the former formed an indissoluble unity with the activities, obeying a particular evolutionary law.

At the same time factors in the social equilibrium other than this broadened economic factor became distinctly subordinate. Geographical and bio-psychological factors become limiting conditions, while other specifically social factors, such as custom, force and fraud, religious and other ideals, so far as they cannot be incorporated into the economic factor as Marshall understands it, are relegated to that vague generally background the gradual emancipation from which is the essence of the process of social evolution. They are obstacles which must be overcome in the forward march and play less and less of an independent role. Thus, as I have already remarked, Marshall has what may be called an economic interpretation of free enterprise, though not of history as a whole. One aspect of evolution is the increasing predominance of the economic factor; it enlarges to such an extent that the others recede eventually into a very dim background.

The most important result of Marshall's attempt to fit his interest in activities into his intellectual tradition is the implicit thesis that the development of his activities is the central element in the process of social evolution as a whole. Englishmen have often ridiculed Hegel for supposing that the evolution of the *Weltgeist* had taken place solely for the purpose of producing the Prussian state of the early nineteenth century. And yet Marshall, good Englishman that he was, supposes that the whole process leads to the production of the English business man and artisan of the latter part of the same century. With all due respect to those worthy gentlemen, does anyone really suppose that they alone will inherit the earth? I am not here concerned with disputing the validity or propriety of Marshall's ethical conviction of the supreme value of one type of character. What is important is whether such subjective ethical convictions should be allowed to color the whole perspective of the past and present tendencies of social development as it undoubtedly does in the case of Marshall. The complete disregard of most other things which it entails is a narrow-mindedness hardly compatible with the ideal of scientific objectivity.

Furthermore, Marshall must be held open to the charge of treating such highly controversial views as if they were mere commonplaces. It takes considerable effort to discover merely what he means to say and much more to grasp the implications. As I have remarked several times before, Marshall explicitly refuses to consider those implications himself. But this study will have served its purpose if it has shown that he cannot be interpreted otherwise than as taking a position of the highest importance on the fundamental questions he professes to ignore. I am tempted to regard his reluctance to recognize that fact as a symptom of a certain evasiveness in Marshall's scientific character.[36]

36. See Professor Taussig's obituary note of Marshall, *Quarterly Journal of Economics,* November 1924. The same evasiveness which Professor Taussig here finds characteristic of Marshall's attitude toward social problems can, I think, be extended to fundamental scientific questions.

The truth is these basic ideas of his are very far from being common-places; they are in need of the most explicit justification, if indeed they are tenable at all.

IV

I now come to what is, from a scientific point of view, the most im-portant stage of the argument. Marshall puts forward the views which have been under discussion in these two papers under the rubric of economics. They involve, however, implications for his conception of the whole social process so broad that it is justifiable, even though Marshall himself would have repudiated the suggestion, to regard his body of "economic" thought taken as a whole as a sociology. While he thought he was avoiding anything beyond legitimate economic analysis, and even held that, at least in his day, a science of society as a whole was not attainable,[37] he did not succeed in avoiding the wider problems. The only trouble is that his treatment of them is unsatisfac-tory.

It has been shown, I think, that his position follows not unnaturally from that of his predecessors. They really left only the alternative that sociology was either applied biology or psychology, or that it was simply economics in the sense of utility theory. Insofar as utilitarian-ism represented the "liberalism" sketched above, freed from hedon-ism, it was a sociology which consisted solely of a universal applica-tion of economic theory in the "utility" sense. As compared with any of these, Marshall's position, regarded as a sociology, is a distinct ad-vance. He is able to account for a group of phenomena which are of great importance, but have no place in any of the above frameworks.[38] So much must be said for him in spite of the difficulties of his position. But is his widening of the boundaries of economics to include the study of activities and character a service to economics? To be sure it places the phenomena studied by utility theory in a wider perspective and hence gives a more correct total view of them. But this may not be the best way of gaining such a perspective. Is not the perspective which Marshall gains on the process of want-satisfaction more than counterbalanced by his conspicuous lack of perspective on the activi-ties themselves? From the above analysis it must be concluded that the main lines of Marshall's treatment of activities, insofar as it is more

37. *Principles,* Appendix C, 770.
38. By virtue of their principles, of course. As "human beings" the holders of such theories may have insight into such things. Fortunately we do not always live up to our principles.

than a bare recognition of their importance, results from its assimilation to the tradition of English economics. Only a separation can avoid Marshall's difficulties.

But how can this separation be brought about without losing sight of the importance of the activities? Marshall is quite right in holding that they cannot adequately be dealt with in terms either of a biological struggle for survival or of a study of human nature. The character in which he is interested is not an inborn trait of man's biological or psychological nature; it is socially conditioned. In part no doubt it is economically conditioned. But Marshall is committed from the start to the view that it is best studied as part of the system of economic[39] equilibrium. The only remaining alternative seems to be to turn its explanation over to a still wider science: sociology. But there is a sense in which it can be said that the whole English intellectual tradition of which Marshall was a part had no place for sociology.[40] Within the scope of that tradition the only phenomena not specifically explicable in terms of the principles of nonsocial sciences, biology and psychology, are those ordinarily understood as economic—the rational pursuit of individual want-satisfaction. But by sociology I should mean a science which studies phenomena specifically social, those arising out of the *interaction* of human beings as such, which would hence not be reducible to the "nature" of those human beings. The biological and psychological factors would assume the position of limiting conditions, knowledge of which might be of great importance in understanding any *particular* concrete problem but which would not be a part of the specific logical subject matter of sociology.[41] Economics, on the other hand, would be a part of sociology dealing with one aspect of social phenomena, which would need to be supplemented by

39. In his wide sense, of course.

40. Of course if sociology means simply the science of society as a whole, comprising a study of all the factors bearing on society in whatever manner in its specific subject matter, it is out of the question that there should be no place for it; but that does not make it an independent science. On the other hand, if the central subject matter of sociology be limited to the *social* (or "cultural") factor, as I prefer to do, it is quite possible to dispute its independent existence on the ground that its alleged subject matter does not exist except as a resultant of factors already adequately treated by other sciences. The quarrel here is analogous to that over the question whether biological phenomena are reducible to applications of the laws of physics and chemistry. I am quite aware that the similar denial that social phenomena are reducible to applications of biological and psychological principles involves a philosophical stand. It is ultimately the character of English philosophy which is at the basis of the whole position which shuts out sociology in this sense.

41. That is, would form data, not problems, for sociology.

other sociological factors before it could give adequate solutions of concrete[42] problems. Does such a science exist at all? What would be the position of economics within it? Above all how would it deal with problems such as those Marshall tried to solve by his treatment of activities and character within the framework of economics? Is it capable of dealing with types of "activities" which cannot be so easily assimilated to the conceptions of a narrower economics as those of Marshall? The starting point of this final stage of the inquiry is the recognition that the universal importance which Marshall attaches to *his* activities cannot be founded in the facts alone; it is at least partly a matter of the perspective imposed by his sociological framework and can only be escaped by altering that framework.

V

It is fortunately not necessary to venture into entirely unexplored territory in order to show that a way out of Marshall's impasse is possible. Let us here consider two[43] general conceptions of the scope and problems of social science, and of the relation of economics to sociology which offer an escape from his difficulties. I choose these two, Pareto and Max Weber, not because I wish to hail them as the only possible alternatives to the "Anglo-American" tradition of which Marshall forms a part—whether they are cannot be decided within

42. Concrete again only in a relative sense. The understanding of completely concrete phenomena, so far as they are accessible to science at all, would involve application of the principles of *all* the basic sciences.

43. In many respects the American "institutionalist" movement is deserving of a place in this discussion. As is quite evident from the way in which the problems with which the present study deals were put, the controversy between the orthodox and the institutionalists has played a decisive part in the development of the position presented here. I do not include an explicit discussion of it for two reasons: because it is impossible to do justice to the complexity of the issues in the space available, and because I do not consider institutionalism a genuine solution of Marshall's predicament, while I do so regard the positions both of Pareto and of Weber. On account of limitations of space the close of the present discussion must be concerned with pointing to satisfactory ways out rather than warning against false paths. It must suffice to say here that the institutionalists are even more open than Marshall to the charge of failing to consider the basic implications of their position. Insofar as they do not repudiate theory altogether, which is fatal, they tend to fall back into the "psychologism" and "survivalism" which Marshall successfully avoided. It is clear that a *sine qua non* of a position satisfactory from the present viewpoint is immunity from such tendencies. This does not mean, of course, that many of the institutionalists' criticisms of the orthodox, especially the more dogmatic of the latter, are not well taken.

the scope of the present study—but because they both have a peculiar relevance to Marshall's problems.

The anti-intellectualist movement and its relation to Anglo-American social thought has already been touched upon. Pareto is the most eminent sociological representative of the movement in continental Europe; the revolt against exaggerating the role of reason may be considered his starting point. He, however, has escaped the predominant tendency of Anglo-American anti-intellectualism to psychologism and survivalism; hence for present purposes his doctrine is to be differentiated sharply from the latter.

Pareto, as the leading representative of the "mathematical school" of economics, made important contributions to economic theory.[44] It is interesting to note that, however much his theoretical system differs from that of Marshall in form, in substance it is very similar to what I have called the latter's utility theory. It was, on the other hand, a keen realization of the inadequacy of economics in this sense for the understanding of concrete social phenomena which led Pareto finally, in his old age, to formulate a whole system of sociology.[45] Its beginnings are to be found in his work on socialism,[46] and it is to be remarked that though he did not devote a special work to the problem of protectionism this occupied a large place in the development of his thought.[47]

Pareto defined economics as the science of "logical" action—what I have called "rational"—as opposed to "nonlogical." He is insistent that "nonlogical" is not necessarily "illogical" from the point of view of the outside observer. His criterion of "logical" is the correspondence of the subjective with the objective end of a given act. By thus tying logical or economic action up with the existence of a subjective end, a "want," Pareto cuts himself off sharply from any economic "behaviorism"; for the behaviorist by categorically denying the relevance of the "subjective" to his scientific problems, has no possible means of distinguishing the logical from the nonlogical when the latter is not illogical. Thus, for Pareto, economics is the study essentially of the logical—or rational—process of the satisfaction of "wants" (*goûts*)

44. In his *Cours d'économie politique,* 2 vols., 1896, and *Manuel d'économie politique,* 1906.

45. *Traité de sociologie générale,* 2 vols., 1917–19.

46. *Les systèmes socialistes,* 2 vols., 1902.

47. In both cases his problem was to explain why men acted counter to the deductions of pure economic theory, which sees in harmonious cooperation of the factors of production the way to maximum satisfaction, and in protection a necessary destruction of wealth.

insofar as that is permitted by the "obstacles," the cost factors, whether they be scarcity of natural resources, disinclination to work, or to save, or anything else.[48] Pareto studies the economic process in terms of a general equilibrium theory. The "wants" are definitely taken for granted as ultimate for economic purposes. At the same time force and fraud are ruled out, partly because of the dominant part played by deliberate choice on the part of consumers. But since consumers, and sellers, choose between the alternatives actually open to them, the exercise of economic "power" is not excluded.

But, as Pareto insists throughout, this economic theory is abstract. It deals only with certain selected elements of social life, and before being applied to any concrete problem needs to be corrected by the reintroduction of the elements from which abstraction was made. A systematic study of the more important of those other elements forms the principal content of his sociology. In formulating it he takes his departure from a study of nonlogical action. He distinguishes two fundamental elements which are involved; the professed motives of action (values, ideals, and the like) which he classifies as "derivations," and which he finds to vary enormously; and, more constant than they, certain more or less universal tendencies of action which he calls "residues." It is important to note the great caution with which Pareto defines the "residues." They are simply the relatively constant factors in nonlogical action. He is particularly careful not to identify them with instincts. The residue is not a psychological but a sociological conception. They are not constant attributes of an abstract human nature but relatively constant tendencies of the behavior of human beings *in society*. It is change in the residues and their combinations which primarily accounts for social change, though of course that change may be due to the changing composition of a population with respect to hereditary type, as well as to change within the same hereditary type[49] due to social influences. It is this position which marks Pareto off from "psychologism." [50]

His anti-intellectualism appears in the general contention that the

48. By thinking in terms of "obstacles" Pareto intentionally avoids the morass into which Marshall fell on the question of real cost. In effect he limits it to opportunity cost.

49. Moreover the standards of the selective processes by which the biological composition of a population changes are partly social, not biological-environmental alone. Pareto, like Marshall and Weber, sharply repudiates what he calls "social Darwinism."

50. In this sense he is an "environmentalist." But biological environmentalism simply opens the door for sociology. It is the positive solution of sociological problems within that leeway which is his real contribution.

residues far outweigh the derivations in importance, though he is careful not to exclude the latter from some role in the social equilibrium. Finally besides these two factors, and the economic, Pareto lays great stress on the fact of social stratification and the processes of selection by which the composition of the higher layers, the elite, and their relation to that of the lower are determined.

Had he discussed Marshall's activities and character Pareto would probably have ascribed them primarily to a particular combination of residues, partly perhaps influenced by past derivations of a religious nature. This would be a combination which gave a specially large importance to economic, or logical action. Its rise to predominance Pareto would explain in terms of a particular process of circulation of the elite which favored this type. But these phenomena would be placed in a very different general framework from that of Marshall. Instead of being the one combination favored by the historical process as a whole, it would be only one of a large number of possible combinations. Pareto is not committed by his methodological position, as Marshall is, to one special type of unilinear evolutionary process leading to the progressive elimination of certain factors of social causation. On the contrary he brings about a very convincing reinstatement of some of those factors, notably force and fraud. Moreover, so far as he has any theory of the historical process as a whole, it is not Marshall's unilinear evolution but a succession of never-ending cycles of change. That doctrine, receiving as it does a notable revival in Pareto's work, is a measure of the radicality of his departure from the tradition which has been under discussion here. Thus Pareto, while he would be able to find a place in his scientific scheme for Marshall's problems, commands an immensely widened perspective which enables him to escape the provincial narrow-mindedness of which Marshall is guilty.

The other alternative conception to that of Marshall which I wish to consider is Max Weber's. Weber is a true representative of the main currents of German social thought, which never has been very closely related to that of the Anglo-Saxon world. The central interest of Weber, as of Pareto, was in "economic" problems, the explanation of the phenomenon of modern capitalism. But as he soon realized that economics alone is incapable of solving his problems, he pushed further on to develop a science of sociology. The motivation of the two men in undertaking this task was strikingly similar.

Their conception of economics is also very similar. Weber makes it the science which studies human actions insofar as they are directed toward the acquisition of utilities (*Nutzleistungen*).[51] So far, like the British and Pareto, by defining economic action in terms of its subjective aim, he radically repudiates economic "behaviorism." But, in accord with Pareto, he denies that this means basing economics on psychology. Utility here refers only to the actual end of action, the motive of concrete choices, not to the ultimate psychological "drives." Economic action is moreover in principle rational, though it may in practice be tinged with traditionalism or other nonrational factors. But it is not the whole of the rational. It does not at all include one of the fundamental types of rational action, that concerned with putting ultimate values directly into practice (*wertrational*). It concerns only action in the service of limited finite ends, and not even all of that. The use of force, even though it be rational, is excluded, as is "technique." [52] On the other hand the ends which are compared are taken as data. The explanation of their origin is not the task of economics. Nonrational action is understood largely in terms of its deviation from rational types.

For present purposes the most important noneconomic category of Weber's sociology is that of action in direct pursuit of ultimate values (*wertrationales Handeln*). The conception is a leading one in the whole line of thought of which he is representative. It implies that not merely individuals, as the sociological "liberal" might admit, but historical epochs and cultures are characterized by the predominance of sets of ultimate values which form an essential element in the understanding of the social phenomena connected with them. Besides this category he adduces others of a noneconomic nature; emotional determination, force, tradition, which do not necessarily involve recourse to bio-psychological explanations. Nevertheless it is the specific role of "values" which is characteristic of German sociology. They may be wholly independent and logically unconnected, as for Sombart and Spengler, or connected in a dialectic process as for Hegel, or Marx, or they may form the main differentiating elements in a branching-tree conception of social development, as for Weber. In any case they introduce a highly important element of relativism into sociology. They encourage the conception of a society dominated by

51. See *Wirtschaft und Gesellschaft*, 31.

52. Technique is concerned solely with choice of means for unmistakable ends, while economic action is concerned with comparison of and choice between immediate, though not ultimate, ends since the latter cannot be "weighed." Weber's conception of economics clearly includes the use of power, though not that of force. See *Wirtschaft und Gesellschaft*, 32.

such a system of values as a closed, complete whole, sharply differentiated from others, rather than as a transitory stage in a continuous
process.

It is in these terms that Weber approaches the problem of capitalism. He considers it as a system sharply differentiated from others
which have existed in history. The "activities" involved in it are specific products of highly specific influences, among which the ethic of
Protestantism occupies the central place. There is no reason to suppose that without the presence of such a specific constellation of factors any such way of life would ever have come into existence. It is
emphatically not the sole result of the whole evolutionary process;
Weber is immune from such surreptitious teleology. Similarly the civilization of India is to be understood to a large extent in terms of the
peculiar values it embodies—again mainly religious—and not as
merely a "retarded" stage of social development as a whole. Thus
Weber, like Pareto, achieves a wide perspective on the characteristics
of modern capitalism, which was closed to Marshall. In his case also
it is the totally different sociological framework which enables him to
do this. Nothing would be further from the truth than to suppose it
was *more knowledge,* in any quantitative sense, that gave Weber and
Pareto their advantage over Marshall. On the contrary, it is their
strictly theoretical insight; in other words, clarity of thought on fundamental problems. That is the point of this whole analysis.

To conclude. These two papers[53] have been concerned with supporting
the following line of argument. Marshall in his economic writings
does not confine himself to the narrow range of problems of value and
distribution which are ordinarily thought to have constituted the field
of orthodox economics. On the contrary, parallel with, and inextric-
ably bound up with, his "pure theory" runs a second line of doctrine
concerning the relation of economic activities to human character. In
his own estimation this second line is at least as important as the first.
It must be considered as a theory and not as the "application" of his
real theory.

The peculiar way in which Marshall deals with these problems and
the way he fuses his thought concerning them with his pure economic
theory implies a position on the broadest questions of social theory so
definite that it must be held to constitute a system of sociology. The
characteristic features of this sociology are not a matter of Marshall's
more or less random observations on things lying outside his field, but

53. [A reference to the current paper and the paper cited in note 1 above.]

grow out of the logical exigencies of fitting his own central doctrines into the framework of sociological theory dominant in the England of his time. This is the real reason why Marshall's doctrines are of more than historical interest. They throw a bright light on the whole structure of English social thought.

Considered as a sociology, his work represents in some respects an improvement on that of his predecessors. But both his own strong belief in the importance of the activities which form his central theme, and the narrowness of the tradition into which he had to fit them, combined to lend a certain lack of perspective to his treatment of the activities which closed his eyes to the importance of many other things. His views of their place in social evolution will not stand criticism in terms of the wide sweep of history with which sociology after all must concern itself.

It is possible to escape this lack of perspective, but only by undertaking a thorough reconstruction of the intellectual tradition of which Marshall formed a part. The first essential step in such a reconstruction is the limitation of the field of economics so as to deprive it of the tendency it shows in Marshall's hands to expand into a general sociology with a very particular bias. This demarcation has been the starting point of the two systems of sociology just sketched. Both make room for an important and legitimate science of economics within the framework of a sociological scheme so broad as to counteract any tendency to economic one-sidedness. But both are built on a logical basis radically opposed to that of most previous Anglo-American social thought. This is not a plea for unqualified acceptance of the doctrines either of Pareto or of Weber,[54] indeed in some respects they are incompatible with each other. Other possibilities equally promising may exist, or are likely to be developed in the future. But I think any system of sociology satisfactory from the viewpoint of this paper will necessarily involve departures from the main lines of the Anglo-American tradition as radical as those of Pareto and Weber.

In any case, I make a very serious plea that the theoretical questions here raised be faced. They cannot be evaded either by complacent and unquestioning acceptance of tradition or by flight to the "facts." Marshall himself once said "the most reckless and treacherous of all theorists is he who professes to let facts and figures speak for themselves." [55] In the field of the ultimate questions regarding the basis of

54. I have dealt with some of the difficulties in Weber's position in my article in *The Journal of Political Economy* [chapter 1 of this volume].

55. "Present Position of Economics," *Memorials,* 168. Of course Marshall is perfectly correct, especially as against the historical school at which the remark was aimed.

his science he stands convicted by his own indictment. Let us hope
that others who have his experience to build upon will not turn even
further away from such questions than he did. Science, if it failed to
map out its course, would be as lost in the uncharted seas of "fact" as
a ship without a navigator.

I am merely construing his statement even more widely than he intended in order to
turn it against him.

9

Review of *An Introduction to the Study of Society*, by Frank H. Hankins

Professor Hankins's *Introduction to the Study of Society* is a useful book. It seems to make no very original contribution to the subject, what there is of originality being for the most part in the attitude taken to various theories. But it contains a great deal of information and much good sound observation and criticism. Moreover the book is very readable and the style never becomes heavy.

However, without forgetting its virtues I may permit myself a few remarks on some features of the book.

1. It seems to me that in attempting to deal with all the factors having the remotest bearing on society, Professor Hankins undertakes a task which it is impossible to carry out really well. It leads him to make claims to proficiency in at least four sciences besides economics and sociology proper, namely geography, biology, physical anthropology, and psychology. That seems to me impossible in the present state of the division of labor between the sciences.

Besides the difficulty of the task as such it brings about what seems to the reviewer a bad apportionment of the material. Almost exactly half the book (375 out of 746 pages) is devoted to the presocial *conditions* of social life. The treatment of them seems on the whole good, although he takes a rather strong stand on some points which are distinctly debatable, for instance the decline in the biological quality of the race and the imminent danger of overpopulation. This latter is especially unjustified since Professor Hankins, like so many other writers on the subject, fails to provide a rigorous standard of overpopulation. It is eminently desirable that students of sociology should know these things, but my question is whether they could not get them from other sources without the sociologist devoting fully half his time to them. On the other hand through lack of space the treatment of

Written for publication in *The Springfield Republican*. The typescript copy of the review, currently held in the Parsons Papers, is printed here by permission of the Harvard University Archives.

social problems as such becomes extremely sketchy and consists very largely of a juxtaposition of facts and theories taken from many sources without a thorough and consistent social theory of its own.

2. In his sharp contrast of the "theological" and the "evolutionary" or "naturalistic" viewpoints, and his insistence that one or the other must be adopted, Professor Hankins seems to be dragging a controversy into sociology which complicates matters entirely unnecessarily. He is really espousing a metaphysical view of science and the universe which leads him into interpretations of concrete phenomena which are quite unjustified by the facts alone. In maintaining that objective science involves a general rationalistic philosophy and an essentially mechanistic interpretation of phenomena, Hankins falls distinctly behind the best recent work on the nature of science (Poincaré, Whitehead) and its application to society (Max Weber, Pareto). The most striking point at which this viewpoint colors his theory is of course in the treatment of religion. Thus religion becomes for him essentially a reaction to an unknown which will eventually become known through the progress of science, hence making religion superfluous. It is a view which is certainly widespread. But is it justified on the basis of the facts alone without the addition of metaphysical assumptions?

The same attitude involves a theory of progress from ignorance to enlightenment, with science providing the ultimate solution of all human problems. This view takes no adequate account of the formidable opposing views which have been current elsewhere, especially in Germany, but it simply underlies his work without criticism.

3. In general it may be said that the book lacks coherent unity of viewpoint. This rather barren and antiquated rationalism is the only thing that binds it together into a unified view of society as a whole. There is nothing at all comparable to Marx's economic interpretation of history, or Durkheim's idea of the predominance of the social factor in individual action, or Pareto's highly developed theory of the social equilibrium. It rather leaves sociology in the primitive scientific stage of observing isolated facts, enumerating various opposing theories about them, seeing something in each, but not weaving them into a consistent whole. Hence it falls far behind the great achievements of the science.

Nevertheless, it is certainly distinctly above the general level of American textbooks in sociology. But one wonders whether this is the time for more textbooks, arranging the old material in a slightly different way, or rather for new work on pioneer lines.

10

Review of *Einführung in die Soziologie,* by Ferdinand Tönnies

Professor Tönnies is a man of one dominant idea. His new *Einführung in die Soziologie* may be said to consist of variations of the theme *Gemeinschaft* and *Gesellschaft*. It is a further elaboration of the scheme of social life based on this fundamental distinction. But it is much fuller and more highly developed, and thus comes nearer constituting a general system of sociological theory.

Around the central distinction of *Gemeinschaft* and *Gesellschaft* is grouped a series of other categories. Perhaps the most important is one of social "factors," the economic, the political, and the spiritual-moral (*geistig-moralisch*) which cuts completely across the other, though, like it, it runs through the whole structure. The reviewer has some difficulty in getting a clear picture of the lines of distinction between the three factors.

Book 2, after a discussion of the "Grundbegriffe" in book 1, is devoted to the social "entities or forms" (*Wesenheiten oder Gestalten*). Each of these types of grouping is exemplified by an ideal type at the *Gesellschaft* end of the scale and then contrasted with *Gemeinschaft* types. This gives the following scheme: (1) social "relations" (*Verhältnis*): a) contractual (*Bündnis*), b) subordination (*Herrschaft*), and c) comradeship (*Genossenschaft*); (2) "collectivities" (*Samtschaften*): a) party, and b) people and others; (3) organized bodies (*Körperschaften, Verbände*): a) association (*Verein*), and b) church.

Following this in book 3 is a treatment of social values (*Werte*) which, however, turns out to be rather unsatisfactory since, attempting to hold itself to what is "objective," it treats only of general social institutions which are valued each as property, the state and language. It can hardly be considered an adequate statement of the role of values in social life. Book 4, dealing with social norms, gives a most interesting treatment in terms of three types—order, law, and morality. These

Originally published in *Sociologus* 8 (1932): 124–26. Reprinted with permission of Duncker and Humblot Verlagsbuchhandlung.

are types having a predominance of the *Gesellschaft* element; with them at the other end of the scale are contrasted harmony (*Eintracht*), a "gemeinschaftliches Naturrecht," and religion. The idea of a system of natural law based on *Gemeinschaft* is worked out most interestingly.

In book 5, on "Soziale Bezugsgebilde," the three "factors," economic, political, and spiritual, are taken up explicitly, and under each a series of polar conceptions based on the difference of *Gemeinschaft* and *Gesellschaft*. The attitude is pluralistic, with no overwhelming importance given to any one. Finally, book 6 gives an extremely brief program for applied and empirical sociology.

The value of Professor Tönnies's basic idea of the role of *Gemeinschaft* and *Gesellschaft* is attested by its extremely wide influence, and by the number of other sociologists who have advanced similar ideas. It goes without saying that this further elaboration and attempt to fit the ideas into a wider system of thought is significant and important. On the other hand, there are some criticisms which, I think, can legitimately be made. I will enumerate them briefly:

1. Professor Tönnies's attempt to limit himself to "positive" social relations, which unite, and disregard those influences which divide, is not really successful. He is continually bringing the latter in, and it would be better to make this treatment explicit.

2. There is an interesting discussion of the relation of his ideas to those of Max Weber, which states that the conception of *Gemeinschaft* includes three of Weber's basic categories, *wertrationales, affektuelles,* and *traditionales Handeln*. The failure to distinguish the first from the others is, in my opinion, a source of confusion, especially in the treatment of social values.

3. The title of the book is misleading. It is not an introduction to sociology, but the exposition of a very abstract system of sociological type concepts. This is indeed a very important part of sociology but certainly not the whole of it. Moreover, the beginning student, particularly, is in danger of serious confusion if such a system of concepts is presented to him in abstraction from the concrete use to which it is to be put. It gives too much the impression that it is an end in itself rather than a set of tools of analysis. Professor Tönnies's often very apt and penetrating illustrations can hardly be said to compensate for this defect.

4. Finally it may be asked in what relation this type classification stands to "causal" analysis. The immediate aim seems to be to describe forms, or "anatomy." But is it clear that the aim really goes much further. But Professor Tönnies has introduced a scheme of three

"factors" which seem to stand in no very clear relation to the rest of his theory, which, whether he wills it or not, has definitely causal implications (for instance, the general tendency for *Gemeinschaft* to become *Gesellschaft*). This whole aspect of the case, which is really a central difficulty for "formal" sociology, needs considerably more clarification than Professor Tönnies gives us.

11

Thomas Robert Malthus

Thomas Robert Malthus (1766–1834), English economist, sociologist, and utilitarian moralist. Malthus's entire social and economic thought may be said to center about his theory of population. According to this theory population when unchecked increased at a rate so much more rapid than it is possible to increase food supply that numbers are constantly pressing on means of subsistence; or, as Malthus himself somewhat unfortunately put it, while population increases in geometrical ratio, food supply can increase only arithmetically. The law had been stated previously by a number of writers, and it was only in his analysis of the mechanism of adjustment that Malthus claimed originality. In the first edition of his *Essay on the Principle of Population* (1798) he limited the possible checks on population to misery and vice. The strong tendency of his thought was to consider that at least the bottom of the social pyramid was always at the bare physical minimum of subsistence. In the second edition (1803), which was greatly amplified and modified in the light of his intervening travels and reflections, he introduced a third check, "moral restraint," which he thought had operated in civilized countries to maintain even the laboring classes at a level considerably above the physical minimum. Thus he introduced the doctrine of a "standard of living" determined by "habit" rather than by purely physiological causes as a regulator of population. But in either case his theory stressed the constancy of the standard, however fixed. The fact that a change in economic conditions brought no change of standard but only a decrease or increase of numbers at the same standard placed almost insuperable difficulties in the way of a permanent improvement in the condition of the working classes. In the later phases of his work he also developed greatly his ideas on the subsistence side of the problem, laying less emphasis on the empirical arithmetical ration and more on the conditions underlying it. This led him to discover independently,

Originally published in the *Encyclopaedia of the Social Sciences*, Edwin R. A. Seligman (editor in chief), 10: 68–69. Copyright 1933, renewed 1961 by Macmillan Publishing Company. Reprinted by permission of the publisher.

although he was not the first to do so, the theory now called the Ricardian law of rent and its implication, the law of diminishing returns. The latter law, however, he never formulated explicitly.

Malthus's essay was in part an attack upon the indiscriminate policy of charity, particularly as exemplified by Pitt's poor law bill of 1796, which the conservative government was pursuing in its efforts to cope with the distress resulting from the breakdown of the feudal and mercantile society and the attendant emergence of modern industrialism. It was at the same time a devastating response to the utopian thinkers—represented chiefly by the rationalistic-anarchistic philosophy of Godwin—who under the impulse of the French Revolution had reexpressed in extreme form the optimistic version of English utilitarianism. To Godwin's thesis that a regime of ideal equality both in property and sexual relations could be brought into existence by the mere removal of institutional restraints and the release of the triumphant power of reason, Malthus replied that only the individual pursuit of self-interest working within the framework of the institutions of property, marriage, and class division could save society from the unlimited increase of population and complete disintegration. Malthus's social philosophy represents a recrudescence of the Hobbesian current in utilitarianism, with important differences. He conceived of man as dominated not by a multiplicity of passions but by one, "the passion between the sexes." From this it followed that the Hobbesian conception of the basic disharmony between individuals was transformed by Malthus into the idea of a cleavage between the great classes—landlords, capitalists, and laborers—into which society was divided by the conditions necessary to procure subsistence. Finally, Malthus like the other classical economists considers self-interest not as wholly destructive but as the chief mitigating principle, the *vis mediatrix rei publicae*, enabling man to avert the worst of the evil consequences of the pressure of population. This is the last remnant in Malthus of any idea of a natural harmony of interests.

Some of the most prominent features of the classical system of economics resulted from the modification of the Smithian doctrines necessitated by Ricardo's acceptance of Malthus's ideas. The principle of population and the theory of diminishing returns and of rent were the principal elements which Ricardo worked into a theory of the distribution of wealth marked by the iron law of wages and the tendency of profits to decline. But while on the distribution side of the analysis Malthus and Ricardo were at one in substituting the assumption of class antagonism for the conception of the natural harmony of interests which, although modified by other elements, predominated in

Adam Smith, they differed fundamentally with respect to the theory of value. The labor theory as foreshadowed by Locke and developed by Smith started from a "state of nature" characterized by a natural equality and harmony of interests. While Ricardo fully recognized the difficulties involved in its application to a capitalist society, on the whole he adhered to the same type of thought, although reluctantly. His followers, however, forgot his qualifications and hardened his theory into dogma. Malthus, on the other hand, emphatically denied the postulate of equality implied in the more orthodox form of the labor theory and based his theory of value as well as of distribution squarely on the principle of population. He was therefore more consistent than Ricardo, even though the general tendency of his work was more empirical; this fact and the implications of his basic principle led him at times in his discussion of value to emphasize demand rather than cost of production. It was also because of fidelity to the theory of population that Malthus favored moderate protection for agricultural products and became almost the sole exception among the economists of his time to the predominant free trade sentiment, as applied especially to the corn laws.

In addition to the great impetus he gave to demographic studies Malthus's ideas exerted an influence on social theory subsequent to the classical economics in at least two other important respects. First, the element of disharmony, which he introduced into the economy of competitive individualism, was one factor which paved the way for Marx's use of Ricardian doctrines in his theory of the evolution of capitalist society. Secondly, Darwin drew from Malthus important elements of the theory of natural selection. The tendency for reproduction to outrun subsistence, generalized to include all organic life, gave the surplus of numbers on which selection could operate. In fact Malthus himself made use of the phrase "struggle for existence."

WORKS: *An Essay on the Principle of Population as It Affects the Future Improvement of Society* (London, 1798; 2d ed. enlarged as *An Essay on the Principle of Population; or, A View of Its Past and Present Effects on Human Happiness with an Inquiry into Our Prospects respecting the Future Removal or Mitigation of the Evils Which It Occasions,* London, 1803; 6th ed., 2 vols., London, 1826); "Population," in *Encyclopaedia Britannica,* supplement to 4th, 5th, and 6th eds., vol. 6 (Edinburgh, 1824), 307–33, abridged as *A Summary View of the Principle of Population* (London, 1830); *Principles of Political Economy* (London, 1820; 2d ed., 1836); *Definitions in Political Economy* (London, 1827); *Observations on the Effects of the Corn Laws* (London, 1814; 3d ed., London, 1815); *Inquiry into the Nature and Progress of Rent* (London, 1815); *The Grounds of an Opinion on the Policy of Restricting the*

Importation of Foreign Corn (London, 1815); *The Measure of Value Stated and Illustrated* (London, 1823).

CONSULT: Bonar, James, *Malthus and His Work* (2d ed., London, 1924); Halévy, Elie, *La formation du radicalisme philosophique*, 3 vols. (Paris, 1901–4), trans. by Mary Morris, 1 vol. (London, 1928), especially part 2, chap. 2, and part 3, chap. 1; Stephen, Leslie, *The English Utilitarians*, 3 vols. (London, 1900), especially vol. 2, chaps. 4–6; *Letters of David Ricardo to Thomas Robert Malthus*, ed. James Bonar (Oxford, 1887); Schumpeter, J., "Epochen der Dogmen- und Methodengeschichte," in *Grundriss der Sozialökonomik*, vol. 1 (2d ed., Tübingen, 1924), part 1, chap. 2; Field, J. A., *Essays on Population and Other Papers* (Chicago, 1931), chap. 1; Mombert, P., *Bevölkerungslehre*, Grundrisse zum Studium der Nationalökonomie, vol. 15 (Jena, 1929), especially part 1, chap. 5; Griffith, G. T., *Population Problems of the Age of Malthus* (Cambridge, England, 1926).

12

Vilfredo Pareto

Vilfredo Pareto (Marchese di Parigi) (1848–1923), Italian economist and sociologist. Pareto came into the social sciences late in life after an education mainly in mathematics and physical science and some twenty years' experience as a practicing engineer. He then interested himself both in the economic implications of contemporary political questions and in the applicability of mathematics to the formulation of economic theory. His work in the latter field attracted the attention of Léon Walras and led to Pareto's appointment in 1893 to succeed him as professor of political economy at Lausanne.

The best known of his earlier contributions is the much discussed Pareto's law of income distribution, the statistical basis of which has been so severely criticized that it is not now generally accepted. Pareto's most important contributions to economics, however, lie in the field of general economic theory. Here, although he was an "orthodox" economist, his position differs in important respects from that generally held in Anglo-Saxon countries. He went farther than anyone in his generation to work out a mathematical formulation of the system of economic equilibrium as a whole. In spite of the fact that, as Pareto was well aware, his equations could not be solved, on account both of lack of data and of the great number of variables, his achievement was of the greatest importance from the point of view of logical clarity.

Furthermore Pareto realized and emphasized the abstractness of economic theory. He held that it deals with type actions which are logical with reference to the processes of securing means to satisfy wants. Both the wants themselves and the ultimate obstacles to their satisfaction must be taken as data by economic science. Above all Pareto showed that by the use of indifference curves it was possible to formulate all the equations of economic equilibrium without recourse to the concept of utility, and he thus emancipated economic theory

Originally published in the *Encyclopaedia of the Social Sciences*, Edwin R. A. Seligman (editor in chief), 11: 576–78. Copyright 1933, renewed 1961 by Macmillan Publishing Company. Reprinted by permission of the publisher.

from the last vestiges of dependence on psychological hedonism. He also departed from orthodoxy by working out a complete theoretical framework not only on the usual competitive assumptions but also on those of monopoly and of collectivism, all three being of concrete importance. Clearly he did not hold that economic theory alone is capable of an adequate complete explanation of concrete social events.

Acutely conscious of the concrete problems his economics could not solve, he felt an intense need for a broader science to supplement it and so turned to sociology. For material he depended largely on two sources: first, his encyclopaedic knowledge of the history and literature of classical antiquity, the fruit of a lifelong interest in these subjects; and, second, his detailed knowledge of the inner workings of modern government, acquired from years of study of contemporary politics. Although he was unable here to carry the application of the methods of the physical sciences as far as in economics, their influence was of the greatest importance to his sociology as a model of method as well as for the central position of the problem of the role of scientific knowledge in human action.

In fact his whole sociological theory turns on the concepts of "logical" and "nonlogical" action. The former is formulated with the type of economic action primarily in mind, as action rational with reference to a given subjective end. The main analytical problems of Pareto's sociology, however, concern the other type. Once having abstracted the logical elements he attempts to study nonlogical action inductively and on this basis distinguishes two main elements. One, a highly variable factor, consisting of logical or pseudo-logical reasoning about action, he calls "derivations." The other, the relatively constant element, a "manifestation of sentiments" not rationally based or justified, he calls "residues."

In attempting to interpret these concepts one finds a very serious ambiguity, of which Pareto himself apparently was not aware. When thinking of logical action mainly in economic terms, he conceives action as nonlogical only insofar as it is not determined by the conscious purpose of the acting individual. Here the main factors in nonlogical action become the instincts and drives of anti-intellectualist psychology, and "ideas" play at best a minor part. But intertwined with this is an entirely different strand of thought. Its starting point is a narrower concept of logical action in terms of scientific knowledge alone, where from the point of view of the acting individual only knowledge of empirical external facts and strictly logical deductions from such knowledge enter into action. All subjective ends thus become nonlogical elements. Here Pareto does not question the role of subjective ends, but rather the scientific status of such ends, denying that they are scientific facts. On this line of thought the residues turn out to be precisely these nonscientific subjective ends; in short, ideals or values. His theory of the residues instead of being a means of minimizing the role of values in history is thus an affirmation of it. His attack is on a very different thesis: that the really important ideas for action are those of science.

While the first strand of thought furnishes the usual interpretation of Pareto's concepts, the second may be considered the more important, particularly in its theoretical consequences. Furthermore the ideal ends on which Pareto lays stress, those of religious and ethical systems, are in a sense essentially social, marked off sharply from the essentially individual wants of economics. Thus Pareto may with proper precautions be claimed as an adherent of social "realism," an aspect of his thought which obtrudes most sharply in his discussion of the theory of social utility, where, for instance, he speaks of "the end which a society pursues" as distinct from those of its individual members.

Pareto's most important contribution to the concrete interpretation of social phenomena lies in his cyclical theory of social change. This is conceived of as the alternate predominance in the governing groups of two classes of residues, the "instinct of combinations" and the "persistence of aggregates." The latter describes a type of action in which ideal ends are predominant and is characterized by subordination of individual and immediate interest to them; the former type is that of absorption in immediate and tangible interest.

The cycle has three main aspects, political, economic, and ideological. The political cycle starts with the accession to power of men strong in the persistence of aggregates, the "lions," who because of the very absoluteness of their belief in ideal ends use force to promote them. But the exigencies of maintaining power, especially the inconvenience of force as an instrument, causes them to turn to "ruse," to become "foxes." This in turn favors the rise from below of men skilled in ruse and prevents that of those strong in the persistence of aggregates. The result is a dilution of these residues in the governing classes and finally a state of disequilibrium leading to their overthrow. In the economic field there are the "rentiers," who though savers are timid and have little enterprise, and the "speculators," the economic counterpart of the political foxes, strong and daring but tending to extravagance and instability. Finally, there is a similar alternation of predominant skepticism in the intellectual sphere, accompanying the rule of the foxes and speculators, and of faith at the opposite extreme.

Contemporary society Pareto regarded as nearing the extreme of possible predominance of the residues of combination. The Fascist movement, of which he was sometimes held to be a prophet, may be regarded as one element in the expected reaction toward the opposite phase of the cycle. Pareto's intellectual detachment, however, made it quite impossible for him to be an ardent adherent of any political movement.

In spite of its inconsistencies and incompleteness Pareto's sociology may be considered as one of the first and thus far one of the few most important attempts to rebuild on the ruins of the fallen classical positivism, as represented, for instance, by Spencer. While Pareto was himself too deeply embedded in positivistic thought to achieve complete emancipation, he nevertheless broke through the old shell and took long steps toward the construction of a new edifice of theory.

WORKS: *Cours d'économie politique*, 2 vols. (Lausanne, 1896–97); *Manuale d'economia politica* (Milan, 1906); "Anwendung der Mathematik auf Nationalökonomie," in *Encyklopädie der mathematischen Wissenschaften*, vol. 1, part 2 (Leipzig, 1904), 1094–1120; *La mythe vertuiste et la littérature immorale* (Paris, 1911); *Les systèmes socialistes*, 2 vols. (Paris, 1902–3); *Trattato di sociologia generale*, 2 vols. (Florence, 1916; 2d ed., 3 vols., 1923); *Fatti et teorie* (Florence, 1920). For bibliography of Pareto's works see Rocca, G., and Spinedi, F., in *Giornale degli economisti e rivista di statistica*, 4th ser., 64 (1924): 144–53.

CONSULT: Pantaleoni, Maffeo, and others, in *Giornale degli economisti e rivista di statistica*, 4th ser., 64 (1924): 1–144; Sensini, Guido, "La sociologia generale di Vilfredo Pareto," and "Le equazioni dell' equilibrio economico-finanziario, per un punto dato, nel caso delle imposte e in un regime di libera concorrenza economica," *Rivista italiana de sociologia* 21 (1917): 198–253, and 24 (1920): 420–37; Carli, Filippo, "Paretos soziologisches System und der 'Behaviorismus,'" *Kölner Vierteljahrshefte für Soziologie* 4 (1924–25): 273–85; Spirito, Ugo, in *Nuovi studi di diritto economico e politica* 1 (1927–28): 24–35, 105–21; Bousquet, G. -H., *Vilfredo Pareto: Sa vie et son oeuvre* (Paris, 1928), *The Work of Vilfredo Pareto,* trans. from ms. by McQuilkin DeGrange (Hanover, N.H., 1928), *Précis de sociologie d'après Vilfredo Pareto* (Paris, 1925), and *Introduction à l'étude de Manuel de V. Pareto* (Paris, 1927); Bompaire, François, *Du principe de liberté économique dans l'oeuvre de Cournot et dans celle de l'école de Lausanne (Walras, Pareto)* (Paris, 1931); Michels, Roberto, *Bedeutende Männer* (Leipzig, 1927); Ziegler, H. O., "Ideologienlehre," *Archiv für Sozialwissenschaft und Sozialpolitik* 57 (1927): 657–700; Sorokin, P. A., *Contemporary Sociological Theories* (New York, 1928), especially 37–62; Bongiorno, Andrew, "A Study of Pareto's Treatise on General Sociology," *American Journal of Sociology* 36 (1930–31): 349–70.

13

Society

Society may be regarded as the most general term referring to the whole complex of the relations of man to his fellows. In an attempt to arrive at a more precise definition the present article will discuss the main trends of social thought in the West as they bear on the concept.

In the Greek language there is no actual equivalent of the English word society. Insofar as man was thought of as anything more than a biological organism he was, in Aristotle's phrase, a "political" animal, that is, he was thought of as participating in the life of a *polis;* essentially his membership in the *polis* constituted his humanity. There is no modern institution corresponding exactly to the *polis.* Like the modern state it was a territorial unit and as such it held jurisdiction over all residents within its borders; but its scope was far broader, for it combined state, church, and society. Only the family and the individualistic aspect of economic acquisition were to a certain extent outside its domain. They were regarded by the Greeks as of secondary importance largely because the individual did not in the modern sense constitute a being with his own independent aims and values, apart from and even potentially in opposition to the consensus in which he participated in the *polis.* Plato carried these principles to their fullest logical development.

Later Greek thought, concurrent with the actual breakdown of the *polis,* developed a far more individualistic conception of social life. The individual, especially in the stoic doctrine, had an independent position of his own. On the other hand, the objective law to which he was obliged to conform was no longer that peculiar to his native *polis* but expressed the natural order of the whole universe. With this cosmopolitan conception there became fused the developing doctrines of the Roman law, which, while possessing essentially the same objective and superindividual conception of the *polis* as the Greek theories, from a very early date left room for a jealously guarded sphere of

Originally published in the *Encyclopaedia of the Social Sciences,* Edwin R. A. Seligman (editor in chief), 14: 225–31. Copyright 1934, renewed 1962 by Macmillan Publishing Company. Reprinted by permission of the publisher.

private interest, untouched by public authority, on the part of the individual paterfamilias. The fusion of the two made possible the later Roman stoic conception of the civilized world as constituting a single world empire, the expanded Roman *polis,* comprising a rigid legal framework of order within the limitations of which individuals were free to pursue their private interests without let or hindrance. The final extension of Roman citizenship to all freemen of the empire completed the institutional development corresponding to the theory. The whole conception rested on a rigid dualism of the sphere of public concern, which was conceived as a unit as in the original *polis,* and the private sphere of individuals, in which they were thought of as essentially independent, entering only into contractual relations with one another. Local and functional groups had only secondary place in the Roman conception and were considered strictly subordinate to the state.

Christianity brought into this absolutist-individualistic world of late antiquity a new element. In its social aspect it was at once transcendental, universalistic, and individualistic. Its universalism fitted in admirably with the cosmopolitanism of stoicism and Roman private law. Its transcendentalism, on the other hand, gave men a set of values entirely outside of and, from the Christian point of view, superior to everything in this life. While the predominant early Christian development accepted the existing social order as necessary and enjoined men to "render unto Caesar the things which are Caesar's," it insisted even more strongly that the inner religious life of the individual was to be kept apart from and above all worldly things. It thus gave the individualistic aspect of the social thought of late antiquity a deeper transcendental foundation than had any of the pagan theories. Especially in its more ascetic leanings it could under certain circumstances radically undermine secular authority.

At the same time the fact that the predominant development of Christianity was toward the organization of a sacramental church added a further complication. Not only were individuals religiously independent of the politico-legal order of the Roman state, but that religious independence was organized in and supervised by a highly integrated group structure which could in no case accede to the doctrine of Roman law that corporations derived their right of existence solely from the sanction of the state. Henceforward it was scarcely any longer possible, at least on a Catholic Christian basis, to think in terms of the simple dichotomy of pagan antiquity, between individual and state. The raising of the problem of church and state, which was to dominate social thought for nearly a thousand years, was the first major break in the old identification of man's total social relations with the political unit to which he owed allegiance.

In two fundamental respects medieval social thought differed from that of antiquity, even in its latest Christian phase. The latter remained in its peculiar sense strictly dualistic. Society belonged in the realm of the flesh, with the sole exceptions of the Christian church and the extent to which on a private level the individual utilized his social relations as an opportunity for the practice of Christian charity. But the emphasis was on the non-Christian, sinful aspects, especially coercion in the institutions of slavery, property, and the state. Medieval thought first worked out the conception of human society as essentially an expression of Christian principles. At the same time this was possible, given the original Christian dualism of the worlds of the spirit and of the flesh, only on the basis of a hierarchy of groups, orders, and estates which formed a gradual transition from the purely carnal to the purely spiritual.

With regard to the first aspect it was common ground for all medieval thinkers that the eternal law, both revealed and natural, was the measure of all things, that all authority and all principles of justice came from God. Human society was a single organized unit under these principles, the *respublica christiana*. The controversies were over the question whether there were one or two channels by which that authority was transmitted to human hands. According to the extreme papalists the pope was the sole immediate representative of God on earth, while the secular authorities were in effect merely branches of the church. The most extreme expression of this view was put forward by some of the canon lawyers who, having transferred to the church the unitary conception of authority derived from the Roman law, could think of other authorities only as delegated by this one supreme authority. The imperialist view, on the other hand, was that the emperor and through him all secular authorities were sanctioned directly by God without the church as an intermediary. In neither case was pope or emperor thought of as sovereign in the modern sense, but both were subject to the eternal law, however independent of earthly superiors they might be. The idea of any human authority as empowered to legislate, that is, to lay down the fundamentals of social organization, was not medieval.

In the other main aspect of medieval society and thought, that of its hierarchical group structure, the principal influence appears to have come from Germanic conceptions of group relations. The rigid dualism of individual and unitary single group was foreign to feudal law, which dealt rather in terms of a hierarchy of independent units, each with real personality, extending from the individual at one end, through a whole series of corporate groups—village community, guild, commune, estate, monastic order, ecclesiastical chapter, and kingdom—to the supreme groups of church and empire at the summit. Just as in medieval property law the *dominium* of one person did not exclude that of others in the same thing, so the real personality of the individual human being, an indispensable axiom of Christianity, did not exclude the simultaneous attribution of personality to a plurality of group relations in which he participated.

Moreover the rigid dualism of antiquity was further repudiated in that not only were the individual and the Christian church given positive religious sanction, but this was extended in greater or less degree to all the main groupings of medieval society. To be sure, the principle of its extension was not that of equal merit but of a hierarchical order extending from the mere village community of peasants at the bottom to the rigorous monastic communities at the top, on a religious scale. Furthermore it was extended in such a way as to confirm the general traditionalism of medieval life. But even this relative sanction was possible only because of a great change in actual social relations. The "great society" of Roman imperial times, which had largely broken down, was replaced by a society based in the main on relationships of personal loyalty, even though socially sanctioned, which opened a far wider opportunity for the exercise of the Christian virtues than had hitherto been available. And anything which, like much of feudal warfare, did not exactly fit this religious schema was often attributed to the ever present element of carnal sin.

The medieval synthesis, which reached its highest degree of rationalization in the thought of Thomas Aquinas, contained, however, significant elements of instability. The most important lay in the extent to which from a very early time medieval thinkers had been dependent on the conceptual tools inherited from antiquity, above all in the Roman law and in Aristotle. This was evident first in the conception of the church built up by the canon lawyers. Not only was the church conceived as a power at least independent of if not sovereign over the state, but it came to be regarded as having a structure radically different from that of the secular medieval hierarchy of groups. There was only one source of authority which flowed from the papacy down through the various ranks of the organization, ultimately reaching the parish priest. No other element had independence in its own right. And even when the papal absolutism was challenged, it was generally in Roman fashion in the name of the united body of the church as a whole, as in the conciliar movement, and not of the several organs.

Thus there was a genuine structural disharmony between the bureau-cratic hierarchy of the church and the feudal hierarchy of the secular sphere, both in fact and in theory. This was the more evident the more strenuously the papal claims were pushed.

At the same time the growth of nationalism at the expense of feu-dalism gradually eliminated the relativity of the true medieval hier-archy and brought early modern theories more and more into line with those of antiquity. This movement was accelerated by the extent to which monarchs made use of the revived learning in the Roman law to justify their continual attacks on the powers of the great feudal estates and corporations. The result was an increasing tendency to-ward the conception of an absolute state on the one hand and a soci-ety of independent individuals on the other. Christianity, however, had become far too deeply embedded in European thought for the devel-opment ever to revert completely to the Greek idea of absorption of the individual in the state. On the contrary, an increasingly important place was given to a theory of the natural rights of individuals. The main trend was thus against the kind of absolutism which left no room for the independent rights of individuals and on the whole more and more against any absolutism at all.

The irreducible independence of the Catholic church remained the principal obstacle in the way of the completion of this process of the elimination of the quasi-independent groups between the individual and the state. The Reformation brought a change in the situation in this respect both in fact and in thought by its repudiation of the sacra-mental church. Protestantism did not cast aside the conception of an organized church as such, but it radically altered its sociological sta-tus. Nor did it reject the essentially medieval ideal of a Christian so-ciety; in some respects it carried it even farther. The various branches of the Protestant movement came to essentially different results in these respects. Once the independent sacramental church was elimi-nated, the organized aspect of religion began to fall into line with one or the other of the two elements into which contemporary thought was dividing secular society, the state or the plurality of independent individuals. The Lutheran branch, which laid emphasis on the purely subjective and emotional state of penitence, had little place for a direct Christian influence on daily life even in matters close to religion and tended to place all organization in the hands of the secular prince ruling by divine right. This trend was accentuated by the Lutheran tendency to renew the radical dualism of early Christianity without the complication of the sacramental church. All organization even though divinely sanctioned belongs to the world of sin. The individual's attitude toward it is one of passive acceptance of authority and tradition, since these are ordained of God, but he reserves his inner religious life in a world apart. Only in a modified sense could Lutheranism be said to hold that society could or should be radically Christianized.

At the other extreme stand the radical Protestant sects, Baptists, Quakers, and others, which stem from a long history of sect movements prior to the Reformation. These hold that there is no objective institutional church structure at all, and that such religious organization as exists is entirely in the form of voluntary associations of true believers without coercive authority of any kind. In the literal interpretation of the evangelical ethics this hostility to ecclesiastical authority tended in some cases to be extended to all authority whatever. Thus the radical sects carried the implications of the individualistic side of Christianity to the extreme and were among the most important forerunners of modern anarchism.

Calvinism was in most respects midway between these two wings. Sharing with the sects the attempt to remodel the sinful world into the kingdom of God on earth, it could not subscribe to the Lutherans' passive acceptance of things as they were. Nor could it accept their turning of authority, religious or moral, over to a secular government. In so far as Calvinism was dominant it therefore tended toward a theocratic system of discipline, as in Geneva in Calvin's time, where the secular government was thought of as merely an instrument in the hands of the church in its attempt to realize the kingdom. But when the Calvinistic churches could not control the secular authorities, they tried above all to avoid being controlled by them and were pushed more and more in the direction of the radical sects and of the separation of church and state. The ascetic branches of Protestantism, especially Calvinism, have thus thrown the main weight of their ethical sanction into the activities of the individual in the sphere of his private relations. In particular the concept of the "calling" as a field for proving one's state of grace has served to promote individualism and to emphasize the ethical value of economic activities.

Thus Calvinism and the Protestant sects may be said substantially to have completed a process which had been going on since classical antiquity, the transfer of the locus of religious values in this world, and with them the bulk of culture, from the state to the individual. This process may be divided into three main stages. The later Greco-Roman cosmopolitanism created a sphere for the individual outside the state without giving it a religious content. Early Christianity then removed religious values from the state but largely to embody them in the sacramental church, in which, to be sure, the individual retained a highly important position. Finally, the Protestant repudiation of the church passed these values on to the individual. This accentuated the tendency to look upon the state and every other social grouping as essentially instrumental in the realization of individual values, culminating in the radical individualism of the eighteenth and nineteenth centuries.

After the close of the religious struggles following the Reformation there came a pronounced secularization of social thought. Man in relation to his fellows was no longer thought of in terms of his relations to an eternal law, transcendently ordained by a personal God. The first phase of secularized thought did not, however, depart radically from this fundamental thought form. In place of the law of God was put a law of nature, a conception which had been taken over from later antiquity and incorporated into Christian thought, where it performed the highly important function of supplementing the revealed law. Now it became again an independent standard of human institutions. It still retained the character of changelessness and eternity which it had held from the beginning; there was one law of nature for all times and places.

As it emerged into independence in the seventeenth and eighteenth centuries, however, the conception of an order of nature had a strongly individualistic cast because of the peculiar character of the later phases of Christian thought from which it had emerged. It focused on a doctrine of natural rights, of the liberties of man which should not be interfered with by human institutions or authorities. The standard by which institutions were measured was largely negative; they were criticized insofar as they were held to violate these natural rights.

With the shift of emphasis in the interpretation of the idea of natural order from the normative to the explanatory, which was already strong in the physical science of the seventeenth century and was making itself felt in the social realm in the work of such thinkers as Hobbes, it was easy for this individualism of natural rights to pass over into utilitarianism and thus to introduce a relativism in the realm of individual wants essentially unknown to previous social thought.

From this point of view society became the mechanism whereby individual wants, conceived to vary at random with no common standard, could be satisfied in the greatest possible degree under the existing conditions of human life. Social relations were thus reduced to the level of means to individual satisfactions. All idea of essentially normative control was abandoned; but on the other hand an element of determinism of a different sort was introduced by the analysis of the nature and extent of the limitations imposed on action by the conditions, the external environment and man's inherited nature under which it took place. Pushed to its final logical conclusion this determinism in terms of conditions ended up in the positivism of the later nineteenth century, completely eliminating the relativism of the earlier utilitarianism. This view of society as simply a phase of deterministic nature has, down to quite recent times at least, grown progressively in importance among theorists.

On this secularized, individualistic basis there have been two great phases of social thought. The one, on the whole earlier in time, was concerned primarily with the individual's relation to the organized state, the problem of political obligation. This has tended to end up at two poles. The one tendency, first in terms of natural rights, then of individual utility, has looked upon the state merely as a contracted instrument for the protection or promotion of individual rights or interests. The other, in terms of the modern doctrine of sovereignty in particular, has reaffirmed the Greco-Roman qualitative supremacy of the state over the individual and, especially in its later utilitarian form, has conceived of a state absolved from obedience to any eternal law whatever. While in Hobbes this doctrine was in its relativity narrowly limited by the difficulty of maintaining the conditions of mere order and security, in Rousseau the positive aspect became much more prominent. Each state has its own general will, and whatever it wills is right.

On the other hand, thought was turned more and more to the relations of individual to individual within civil society. The same theorists, like Hobbes and Locke, who were concerned primarily with the relation of the individual to the state, at the same time laid the foundations of the individualistic theory of social relationships. Since previous developments had tended to rob all organized groups and finally even the state of any but an instrumental value, the predominant conception of society came to be that of a plurality of individuals entering into relations of contract for the promotion of their own personal interests.

The most prominent relationship is that of exchange, which results from the division of labor and is entered into for mutual advantage. The earlier laissez-faire individualists pictured a society consisting solely of these independent individual units. Since conditions of peace and substantial equality in exchange were assumed, the center of this society came to lie in economic relations. The peak of influence of this view lay in the classical economics of the first half of the nineteenth century. A further element was the voluntary association entered into by contract. The more radical contract theorists conceived of the state in these terms, and voluntary cooperation on the level of means was besides exchange the other principal mode of carrying out individual aims through the medium of relations to others. On the whole, however, the exchange relationship has predominated in this type of thought.

The most modern development of social thought and with it of the concept of society has been largely in reaction to this individualistic utilitarian tradition. One main alternative has lain in the emphasis on the determining influence of the limiting conditions of individual action. In this direction under the influence of the Darwinian movement and of psychological anti-intellectualism society has come to be thought of as simply the human phase of the organic evolutionary process. In particular, human conflict, especially economic competition, has been interpreted as a special case of the biological struggle for existence. This movement accounts for a large part of the social thought of the later nineteenth and the earlier twentieth century.

This positivistic and in some ways also individualistic trend of thought has, however, been only one of the two important modern movements in reaction against utilitarianism. Men have never ceased to think that in some sense social groupings constitute more than a mere sum of individuals and must be thought of as possessing in some sense independent reality. There have, however, been many different interpretations of the nature of this reality and of its relation to individuals.

Attention was originally concentrated on the state, and the first important version of modern social realism is to be found in the modern doctrine of sovereignty. The aspect on which emphasis is placed here is the phenomenon of coercive authority, which no individual can legitimately exercise over another in ordinary contractual relations. Even the most extreme modern adherents of this line of thought do not necessarily exclude the essentially Christian idea of an inviolable sphere of individual personality. Bodin, generally regarded as the founder of the doctrine, still considered the sovereign as bound by an eternal law of nature in the normative sense. When that limitation was dropped, there was introduced a fundamental element of relativism, which played a very important part in subsequent social thought. Each sovereign unit represented a specific synthesis which did not have to coincide with that of any other. This is the essential type of relativism which, although not necessarily bound to the state, has been maintained down to the present by the anti-individualists.

The next great step may be considered to have been Rousseau's doctrine of the general will. This went behind the question of the fact of sovereign authority over the individual to find its origin in a common will, in values shared by the members of the community. But in harmony with traditional dualism of state and plurality of individuals Rousseau saw his general will as expressed entirely in the state. There was no place for internal social differentiation on the superindividual level. This view, with some modification, was passed on to Hegel as well as to the more recent philosophical theory of the state.

Later social theory, while retaining the element of common will or values as the essential basis of social reality, has tended to divorce it more and more from the state alone and to find a plurality of manifestations for it. Thus in a sense there has been a movement back toward the more instrumental conception of the role of the state, but this time not on an individualistic basis. The state then becomes not so much a contractual instrument for promoting individual interests as an organ of the entire community for the promotion of certain of its common ends.

At the same time the tendency has been to find that the basis of social reality lies deeper than in the state itself in something like a consensus, explicit or implicit, of the members of the community. With Rousseau's conception of will as a point of departure, the coercion of a sovereign authority has come to be seen as only one means of enforcing on the individual the supremacy of common ideals and attitudes. In fact it is moral authority which is held to be fundamental, since without its general backing among the majority the coercion of the state cannot in the long run be effective and interests cannot be made to conform. The secondary importance of state coercion has been illuminated further by the recognition of the relatively effective functioning of social norms in primitive communities which are entirely without any organized state machinery.

The immediate historical background of the development of the most modern conception of society and the main elements in the thought of the late nineteenth and early twentieth century lies in positivism and idealism. The former is of much greater importance for the English-speaking world, and the main process of development of thought there may be said to have been one of emancipation from positivistic conceptions. The first step in this process is the distinction between a scientific theory and a practical art, which is implicitly at issue between utilitarianism and the radical positivistic position that attempts a purely scientific interpretation of human life and action. A scientific theory involves only the coordination of elements in the experience of the scientist, all of them of things "external" to himself. A practical art, on the other hand, involves the adaptation of means, on the basis of scientific knowledge of course, to an end which is not, to the actor, an element of the external world in the same sense. It involves in some sense the admission of the role of ideas in action. The second step is the realization that the ideas involved at least in the ultimate ends of action cannot be scientific theories in the positivistic sense, simply because insofar as they are true ends they cannot be mere reflections of external empirical reality. They are hence in some sense nonscientific or even metaphysical.

It has been observed that these ultimate ends of action cannot be thought of as merely existing at random but must, both in the individual and in any significantly coherent group, be regarded as integrated into a harmonious system of ends, governing in various ways all the actions of the members of the group. Without a system common to the members of a community social order itself cannot be accounted for, as Hobbes's analysis of the state of nature so clearly showed. The recognition of such a common system is a return to Rousseau's general will, but in the more strictly sociological thought growing out of positivism it has been most prominent implicitly in the thought of Pareto and much more explicitly in that of Durkheim.

These considerations apply to the ultimate ends of action, which cannot be considered as means to further specific and tangible ends. But subsidiary to them is an important element of action in the pursuit of ends which are not ultimate. This intermediate element may be said to fall into the three sections: the technological, the economic, and the political. All action of course takes place also under certain ultimate conditions of external environment and human nature which must always be considered as present; they are not, however, properly speaking elements of human action or of society itself. At the same time the intermediate elements of action can never be thought of as taking place in the absence of a system of ultimate ends, an error implicit in a great deal of individualistic thought.

The system of ultimate ends of the community determines what is specifically sought after as wealth and power but also affects action in other fundamental ways. In the first place, ultimate ends may form the immediate ends of specific actions, as in the case of a religious war. Second, they may form the basis of a framework of regulatory norms which guide and control action in the pursuit of immediate ends, maintaining orderly processes and relationships and keeping the vast complex of such utilitarian actions in some kind of harmony with the ultimate value system of the community. This system of regulatory norms, which exists in every community, may be called its institutions. In mode of embodiment, whether in custom or the law of the state, in the type of enforcement and in their structure they may vary enormously from one community to another. They form the backbone of the social structure. Durkheim may perhaps be regarded as the most eminent theorist of institutions in terms of their relation to the individual, and Max Weber in terms of the comparative analysis of their structure. Third, where action becomes a direct expression of ultimate value attitudes outside the sphere of practical techniques, the means is no longer intrinsically related to a tangible end but becomes a symbol. This is illustrated particularly in the case of religious ritual, which is another fundamental constituent of the life of every community.

In this scheme of analysis the state has a triple role. First, it is the principal organ of common action of the community. Second, it is the main guardian of its institutions, especially insofar as their automatic and informal functioning through custom breaks down and the need of deliberate and sometimes coercive enforcement arises. This is brought out particularly in the case of a change in the type of institutional relationship from the communal to the rational-legal or, as Tönnies put it, from *Gemeinschaft* to *Gesellschaft*. Third, the state constitutes one but only one of the principal focuses of the common sentiment and thus plays an important symbolic role.

While it is true that to a greater or less degree the common value attitudes of a community must be regarded as integrated into a single system, there is room for wide variation both in the degree of integration and in the kind of system. In the latter relation there is no reason for excluding a type of social organization involving many different kinds of complex structure of real groups and social classes. Hence modern social theory rejects as far too simple the rigid alternatives of the view that there is on the one hand the state and on the other the unintegrated plurality of separate individuals. It is true, however, that some social structures, as notably the Roman republic in its earlier stages, may approximate this simple type.

In the light of the analysis presented here society may be defined as the total complex of human relationships insofar as they grow out of action in terms of the means-end relationship, intrinsic or symbolic. According to such a definition society is but an element in the concrete whole of human social life, which is also affected by the factors of heredity and environment as well as by the element of culture—scientific knowledge and techniques, religious, metaphysical, and ethical systems of ideas, and forms of artistic expression. Society cannot exist apart from these things; they play a part in all its concrete manifestations, but they are not society, which comprises only the complex of social relationships as such.

CONSULT: Barker, Ernest, *The Political Thought of Plato and Aristotle* (London, 1906); McIlwain, C. H., *The Growth of Political Thought in the West* (New York, 1932); Zeller, Eduard, *Die Philosophie der Griechen,* 3 vols. (5th–7th ed. by W. Nestle and E. Wellmann, Leipzig, 1920–23), vol. 3, part 1, sec. 1, trans. by O. J. Reichel as *The Stoics, Epicureans, and Sceptics* (London, 1870), 293–313, 462–65; Troeltsch, E. D., *Die Soziallehren der christlichen Kirchen und Gruppen,* in his *Gesammelte Schriften,* vol. 1 (3d ed., Tübingen, 1923), trans. by Olive Wyon, 2 vols. (London, 1931); Carlyle, R. W. and A. J., *A History of Mediaeval Political Theory in the West,* 5 vols. (Edinburgh, 1903–28); *The Social and Political Ideas of Some Great Mediaeval Thinkers,* ed. F. J. C. Hearnshaw (London, 1923); *The Social and Political Ideas of Some Great Thinkers of the Renaissance and the Reformation,* ed. F. J. C. Hearnshaw (London, 1925); *The Social and Political Ideas of Some Great Thinkers of the Sixteenth and Seventeenth Centuries,* ed. F. J. C. Hearnshaw (London, 1926); *The Social and Political Ideas of Some Great French Thinkers of the Age of Reason,* ed. F. J. C. Hearnshaw (London, 1930); *The Social and Political Ideas of Some Representative Thinkers of the Revolutionary Era,* ed. F. J. C. Hearnshaw (London, 1931); *The Social and Political Ideas of Some Representative Thinkers of the Age of Reaction and Reconstruction,* ed. F. J. C. Hearnshaw (London, 1932); *The Social and Political Ideas of Some Representative Thinkers of the Victorian Age,* ed. F. J. C. Hearnshaw (London, 1933); Gierke, Otto von, *Das deutsche Genossenschaftsrecht,* 4 vols. (Berlin, 1868–1913), especially vols. 3 and 4; Allen, J. W., *A History of Political Thought in the Sixteenth Century* (London, 1928); Halévy, Elie, *La formation du radicalisme philosophique,* 3 vols. (Paris, 1901–4), trans. by Mary Morris, 1 vol. (London, 1928); Freyer, H., *Soziologie als Wirklichkeitswissenschaft* (Leipzig, 1930); Troeltsch, E. D., *Der Historismus und seine Probleme,* in his *Gesammelte Schriften,* vol. 3 (Tübingen, 1922); Simmel, G., *Soziologie* (Leipzig, 1908); Weber, Max, *Wirtschaft und Gesellschaft* (Tübingen, 1922); Pareto, V., *Trattato di sociologia generale,* 3 vols. (2d ed., Florence, 1923); Durkheim, E., *De la division du travail social* (5th ed., Paris, 1926), *Le suicide* (2d ed., Paris, 1911), *Les règles de la méthode sociologique* (6th ed., Paris, 1912), and *Les formes élémentaires de la vie religieuse* (Paris, 1912), trans. by J. W. Swain (London, 1915); MacIver, R. M., *Community: A Sociological Study* (3d ed., London, 1924), and *Society: Its Structure and Changes* (New York, 1931); Sorokin, P. A., *Contemporary Sociological Theories* (New York, 1928); Hobhouse, L. T., *Social Development* (London, 1924).

14

Review of *Max Webers Wissenschaftslehre,* by Alexander von Schelting

It is a great pleasure to be able to bring to the notice of the American scientific public so distinguished a contribution to the methodological literature of the social sciences as Dr. von Schelting's book. It is at the same time a secondary work of the *first* rank and, like all secondary works which go beyond the level of summary exposition to that of analysis and interpretation, *an important contribution in its own right.* Dr. von Schelting not only tells us what Max Weber's methodological views actually were, but he further develops, clarifies, and deepens the philosophical foundations of Weber's position and throws into clear relief its importance for some of the principal methodological controversies of our own day with which Weber could not himself be directly concerned.

Weber's own methodological writings took the form mainly of scattered, polemical essays bearing on questions currently under discussion. He nowhere brought them together in a comprehensive work—only in very brief summary form. It is rather in fragmentary form than as an integrated whole, therefore, that his views have entered into the subsequent discussion. Hence it is a great service for Schelting, for the first time in a comparably authoritative way, to bring the whole thing together, analyze and systematize it, and place it in its proper setting (both in Weber's own motivation and in its bearing on the current situation).

Weber was a scholar whose main intellectual training lay in the German historical schools of jurisprudence and of economics as they stood toward the end of the last century. He came to feel more and more that the methodological foundations on which these schools of thought were building were unsatisfactory, and hence strove to rebuild a firmer foundation for his own historical-sociological investigations. But Weber's "pure" scientific interests stood by no means alone. Throughout his life he was deeply concerned with political affairs in a

Originally published in the *American Sociological Review* 1 (1936): 675–81.

practical sense. In this connection he took an ethical attitude (which Schelting ably analyzes), according to which it was essential for the actor to be able to have objective knowledge of the probable consequences of alternative lines of action, and of the implications of any decision for the whole system of ultimate values to which it is related.

In both these contexts Weber faced a milieu in which the dominant note was relativism, a relativism which threatened to issue in an attitude of general scepticism. The trend of the historical schools of German social thought had been to lay increasing stress on the relativity of social arrangements and institutions and the underlying value systems which were employed to understand them. On the practical side he was faced with a warring plurality of conflicting political viewpoints. In this situation he sought to determine the logical conditions and criteria of valid objective knowledge as at least one settled and reliable landmark from which some kind of orientation in a relativistic world, where values and historical interpretations were in flux, could be attempted. *That neither science nor rational action can dispense with valid objective knowledge is Weber's central thesis.*

The delineation of the "island" of scientific objectivity in the shifting ocean of conflicting values and policies Weber achieved by granting the relativity of scientific knowledge itself in important respects. The methodological doctrines he attacked, though various, had one thing in common; namely that in conformity with their empiricist tendencies they claimed to make scientific knowledge itself a complete "reflection" of the living concrete reality of human action and society. It was largely on this basis that they advanced the thesis that these sciences cannot build up systems of general laws; for is not history made up for individually unique personalities and cultural systems?

To this Weber replied that knowledge in all the sciences, natural or social, is never a complete reflection of the concrete, it never includes *all* the facts. It is always a selective abstraction from the concrete reality. It is not a simple reflection of it but stands in a "functional relation" to it. Against the "objectivism" of the historical schools Weber set his own neo-Kantian "subjectivism." The selective principles according to which abstraction is carried out cannot lie "in the facts" but rather in the mind of the scientist. They are determined by his direction of interest, which is in turn a function of the values motivating his action. As a responsible actor, he must seek to know the objective conditions of realization and the consequences, direct and indirect, of his actions; what interests him is only what is relevant to this context. More indirectly, as a "pure" scientist, his aim is not merely to "know about" phenomena but to find solutions to *problems*. But the problems are set by relation to his motivating values. Scientific investigation is itself a process of action, not of passive contemplation of the panorama of "given" reality.

Now since Weber held that there have been in history and still are a plurality of possible value systems, ultimate decision between which cannot be attained on objective scientific grounds, the principle of "relevance to value" (*Wertbeziehung*) introduces an element of extra-scientific relativism into science itself. How then does he escape being drawn into a close relativistic circle so that "knowledge" becomes a function only of the subjective values of the scientist, an expression of his valuations (*Wertungen*)?

Weber's way out is the rigorous logical distinction between the *motives* of scientific interest in phenomena and problems and the *logical validity* of the conclusions. The latter is bound to a formal schema of proof which is universal. Without its explicit or implicit employment no empirical proposition involving causal relationships is capable of demonstration. Yet it is *logically* independent of any value system and hence outside the relativistic circle. Anyone who claims for his allegations of fact that validity which we associate with the conception of "objective empirical truth" can justify this claim, can *demonstrate* the truth of his propositions, only by procedures which at least imply this constant formal scheme. To attempt to evade it is always to become involved in circular arguments which destroy the cogency of the position. This is the foundation of the solid island of empirical knowledge—on the solidity of which the possibility both of scientific objectivity and of rational action depend. It is to its elucidation that the major part of Schelting's work is devoted.

The relation between the relative and the nonrelative aspects of scientific knowledge, in Weber's view, can best be illuminated by a somewhat further development of the subject. In the first place, the actual object or phenomenon which the scientist studies is not a "fully concrete" reality but is a "construction" which brings together in a coherent descriptive whole those *aspects* of concrete reality which are significant to the investigator. Such a construction Weber calls a "historical individual." The essence of his view is contained in the common current formulas that observation takes place "in terms of a conceptual scheme," "within a frame of reference." The element of relativity then enters into the "objects" of scientific study themselves, not only into our conclusions about them.

But no causal conclusions can be drawn about factors in the genesis of such objects or the relations between them by mere description, however accurate and verifiable it may be. They must be analyzed.

This involves breaking down the "historical individual" into elements each of which can be subsumed under a "general law." In order to impute causal genetic significance to a factor antecedent to a given "historical individual," it is necessary to be able to construct, at least negatively, the course of events which would have taken place had the factor in question been altered or eliminated, and to compare it with the actual course of events. Only insofar as the two differ can causal significance be attributed to the factor under investigation.

What Dr. von Schelting has given us in his excellent presentation of Weber's position here is essentially the logic of "experiment." Weber's category of "objective possibility," the construction of the hypothetical course of events on the assumption of alteration in a factor, is the *logical* equivalent, for the case where conditions cannot be controlled, of the controlled conditions of experimental observation. Where we cannot, on account of practical obstacles, actually alter the situation and *see* what would happen, we must resort to "mental experiment" and construct what would happen *if* we could alter the conditions. But regardless of the practical possibilities of experimentation the *logic* of the situation is the same. Attention may be called to the fact that one of the most "exact" of the natural sciences, astronomy, is oftentimes in essentially the same situation in this respect as the social sciences. Yet no one questions the validity of astronomical knowledge on this account.

Vis-à-vis the historical-relativistic methodologies which Weber was criticizing, there are two particularly notable features of this logical schema of proof. First, it involves the logical indispensability, for empirical demonstration, of *general* concepts—both the general "elements," into which the "historical individual" may be resolved, and the general laws relative to the behavior of these elements. However important the role of the concept of individuality in the historical-social sciences may be, it cannot be held to eliminate that of generalization—in this case of *abstract* generalization—except at the heavy cost of destroying the logical basis of objective validity.

The corollary of this is that the methodology of the social sciences cannot be confined to the "genetic" tracing of temporal sequences. The logical equivalent of experimentation is "comparative method." Different historical individuals must be capable of analysis into different combinations of the *same* elements, the identification of which in distinction from each other is dependent on comparison. It is essentially the logic of "independent variation."

The German "historical" methodologies, going back as they did to an idealistic philosophical basis, created a deep gulf between the logic of the natural and the historical-social sciences. The net effect of Weber's methodological work has been to go a long way toward bridging this gulf. The principal means of building the bridge has been the insistence, not only on the necessary role of general theoretical conceptualization, but on the abstractness of this theory in the case of both groups of sciences. So long as this is not realized, the obvious concrete differences between their subject matters tend to force the methodologist into maintaining an untenable logical distinction between the sciences. My principal criticism both of Weber and of Schelting, who follows him in this respect, is that they have not completed the process.

The criticism sets in at two main points. First: Weber, following Rickert, tried to maintain an untenable distinction between the relative roles of generalizing and individualizing concepts in the natural and the social sciences respectively. The position is that in the natural sciences the end of scientific endeavor is the building up of systems of general theoretical concepts, while in the social such concepts can serve only as means to the understanding of unique historical individuals. On the contrary, it seems to me that in both fields we have a bifurcation of the direction of scientific interest. One group of sciences, such as theoretical physics and theoretical economics, is primarily concerned with building theoretical systems, while the other, like geology and history, is concerned with understanding unique historical individuals. In the one case general concepts constitute an end in themselves, in the other a means. The distinction of these two bases of classification of the empirical sciences, which do not coincide but cut across each other, lies at a deeper methodological level than that between the natural and the social sciences. The Rickert-Weber-Schelting position constitutes an unwarranted assimilation of the two distinctions to each other.

The other criticism is that both Weber and Schelting failed to see that the "elements" and "general laws" of the schema of proof are not homogeneous categories, but that under each two different types of concepts are included. This raises the question of the status of the "ideal type" concept which forms one of Weber's major methodological contributions. Dr. von Schelting has already shown in a previous study, the results of which are summarized in the present volume, that Weber was not consistent in his treatment of this category, including both "individualizing" and "generalizing" concepts under it. The present point concerns only the status of the "general" ideal type, which I think is in turn ambiguous. Weber laid great stress upon its abstractness. This, however, is open to two interpretations. It may mean either a hypothetical "objectively possible" fictional entity, a "unit" or "part" of a historical individual. This is logically analogous to the fictional "frictionless machine" or "perfect gas" of physics. If this is the "element," then the law is a generalization about the behavior of this hypothetical entity under certain assumed conditions.

On the other hand, the element may be a "general property" of historical individuals, such as "economic rationality," analogous to the "mass" or "velocity" of mechanics. Then a "law" is a uniform mode of relationship between the specific "values" of two or more such elements or properties. Both are abstract, general concepts, but the logical distinction between them is vital. Weber's own theoretical work in fact tended to bifurcate in these two directions, with the former tendency predominating in his explicit formulations.

Of course, even with these corrections, the substantive theoretical propositions of science, both natural and social, are subject to the relativity inherent in their relevance to value. There is, as Weber says, no one ultimate conceptual schema. What then of objectivity? The answer is that, while the form of statement of the facts is relative to the conceptual schema in terms of which they are formulated, the content, so far as it meets the criteria of empirical validity, is capable of restatement in terms of any other schema which also meets the same criteria. That is, in the change of theoretical systems with the advance of science and shifting foci of interest *facts once proved to be true do not cease to be so.* To the extent in which they really have been established, they constitute a "permanently valid precipitate" of science, capable of translation into and restatement in terms of any usable new conceptual scheme which may come into the field.

One of Weber's most important methodological services on which Schelting lays great stress was the careful discrimination of the *substantive* peculiarities of the subject matter of the social sciences from the *logical* grounds of the validity of their propositions. It is in the former not the latter respect that the two groups of sciences differ. There is a methodological core common to all empirical science, no matter what its concrete subject matter.

In the tradition of which Weber forms a part, however, a great deal of stress has rightly been laid on the status of "subjective categories" and the specific modes of "understanding" of the subjective aspect of human action, generally called in the German literature *Verstehen*. It is on this connection that Schelting makes one of his independent contributions. In the last chapter of the book he shows that for Weber the possibility of *Verstehen* of the "subjective" was a simple unanalyzed postulate, and that he failed to make adequately a vitally important distinction between two types of context in which it may be employed. The one, on which he laid the principal stress, was the grasp of meaningful complexes of motivation which served as the causal explanation of real processes in time. The other, which he ignored in his methodological discussions, was the grasp of atemporal complexes of meaning, although he employed them a great deal in his empirical work. This distinction is of great importance, and its clarification on the background of Weber's general methodological position is an important service.

Finally, Schelting has brought Weber's position up to date by employing it as the basis for a thoroughgoing critique of certain aspects of a movement of thought which has risen into prominence since Weber's day. This is the *Wissenssoziologie*, "sociology of ideas," "sociology of knowledge," or "theory of cultural compulsives," which has occupied perhaps the center of the sociological stage in Germany in the past decade. Schelting chooses as the target for his blows the work of its best-known representative, Karl Mannheim. This makes consideration of Schelting's book particularly appropriate in the present situation, as Professor Mannheim's main book *Ideologie und Utopie* is about to appear in English translation (by Louis Wirth and Edward A. Shils). The importance of the issues far transcends the borders of Germany, as this movement is one phase of a much more general tendency to relativize modes of thought in relation to social structure.[1]

There is no space here for a detailed statement of the issues. One distinction, however, is basic. Schelting does not in the least attack the thesis that the explanation of why given theories have arisen and spread at given times and places and in given social classes is to be sought to a large extent in various aspects of the social milieu. He leaves a wide range of usefulness open to what may be called *substantive Wissenssoziologie* as a most fruitful field of sociological investigation.

His attack is directed rather at a much more radical thesis; namely, Mannheim's conclusion that this causal genetic relation to the social situation of their producers is fatal to a theory's claim to objective validity. Theories, especially those of social science, are relative to the social basis not only on this genetic level, but also in their logical and

---

1. In addition to the Marxian line of thought which has influenced Mannheim profoundly, attention may be called to the work of Durkheim, Lévy-Bruhl, and their successors.

methodological foundations. The traditional scientific methodology and epistemology must therefore be abandoned, says Mannheim, in favor of a new, socially relative position.

Apart from his detailed critique of the ambiguities and indeterminacies of the concepts in terms of which Mannheim attempts to prove this thesis and which are too complex to follow through here, his main central theses are two. First, Mannheim ignores, or at least fails to break down, Weber's basic distinction between the motives of the scientist in arriving at a theory and the logical grounds of its validity. His relativizing arguments concern the first problem, but leave the second untouched. Second, the thesis is placed on empirical scientific grounds. It depends on the empirical demonstration of the causal connection between the social situation (*Lagerung*) of the scientist and the character of his theories. But conclusions can be drawn from this only on the assumption that the causal relationship has been demonstrated as valid. This places Mannheim in a dilemma. Either his relativistic conclusions are true, in which case the basis of their empirical demonstration cannot be accepted, or contrariwise, the causal relationship has been demonstrated, in which case his sociological relativism as a *general* epistemological doctrine *cannot* be true. From this dilemma there is no escape. You cannot employ reason to demonstrate that conclusions reached through reason can never be valid.

More generally, it may be said that Mannheim's position rests on an empiricism of the character which it was one of Weber's greatest achievements to have transcended. It is just as easy to demonstrate that his *society* could not exist without valid scientific knowledge as that knowledge is itself a social product. The only escape from the dilemma of either a naive rationalistic positivism or a relativism of Mannheim's variety, is an analytical breakdown of this entity "society" into its elements. Both Weber and Schelting, to name no others, have contributed greatly to the foundations of such an analytical theory. It is a sound foundation on which to build. In view of its close relations to certain currents of thought associated with pragmatism, Mannheim's book is likely to enjoy a considerable popularity in this country. I suggest that before accepting some of its more radical conclusions the reader consider carefully Schelting's thorough and closely reasoned critique.

In short, this volume is a thoroughly able and scholarly discussion of many vital methodological problems of the social sciences (only a few of which could be touched here). It presents, in a form superior to the original, both in accessibility and in systematization, the position of one of the few eminent creative minds which has dealt with

Review of Von Schelting's *Max Webers Wissenschaftslehre* 131

these problems in the recent past. In addition to these merits, it presents both in analysis and in application important contributions of its own. In spite of a few not unimportant reservations it is seldom, particularly in such a field, that a conscientious reviewer is privileged to approve and recommend a work with such wholehearted enthusiasm.

15

Pareto's Central Analytical Scheme

There has recently been much discussion of Pareto's sociology apropos of the appearance of the English translation. A large part of this discussion seems to me to have suffered from being at cross-purposes. Each participant has tended to pick out things which seemed to him particularly praiseworthy or objectionable, as the case might be. If one were to subject this critical literature to an inductive analysis, I for one think it would be exceedingly difficult to arrive at any clear conclusion as to what the common reference to "Pareto's theory" really is.

If this be true, it must be explicable in one of two sets of terms. Either Pareto's treatise is really a hodgepodge and does not contain a coherent theory at all, or the critics have failed to penetrate to the deeper levels of the work. In my opinion the truth is nearer the latter than the former alternative. There is in Pareto's work a definite analytical scheme of which, with few exceptions,[1] one does not get a clear conception from the secondary discussion. At the same time it does not constitute a finished sociological theory, but rather an approach to one.

It is my strong conviction that a clear understanding of the theoretical issues raised by Pareto's work cannot be attained until *this* scheme is clearly worked out. The reasons for Pareto's use of it and the way in which unsolved problems emerge out of it must be grasped before a judgment can be ventured. It is to this task of elucidating Pareto's central analytical scheme, and this alone, that the present paper will be devoted. It is not a general critical evaluation of Pareto's work.

There are two elements in Pareto's personal background which are of decisive importance in understanding his approach to sociology— physical science and economics. He was himself trained in physical science and mathematics, and spent many years as a practicing engi-

Originally published in the *Journal of Social Philosophy* 1 (1936): 244–62.

1. The principal exception is Professor L. J. Henderson's *Pareto's General Sociology,* which, however, is largely confined to the methodological side.

neer. He was also, later, an economic theorist of distinction and a professor of economics at Lausanne.

The first significance of the background of physical science is methodological in a specific sense. Pareto wished to base his work in both economics and sociology on essentially the same methodological foundation which had made the phenomenal success of the physical sciences possible. In this ideal he was, of course, by no means alone, having perhaps the majority of social scientists outside Germany, at least since Comte, with him. But there is an important difference. Most previous social scientists following the natural science ideal have carried over the dogmas connected with an illegitimate "reification" of some elements of the classical physics. This is certainly far less true of Pareto, whose views of scientific methodology are much more skeptical and sophisticated.

As readers have doubtless been told ad nauseam, he reduces the essentials of science to the two elements he indicates in the name "logico-experimental." Science consists essentially of observation of fact (with or without experimental aid) and logical inference from fact. Logic by itself is capable of yielding only tautologies[2]—hence, though logic is an indispensable tool, the central content of science lies in the factual element.

It is noteworthy that in his discussion of fact Pareto is extremely cautious, and nowhere to my knowledge commits himself to a definition which would draw an arbitrary line. Above all, two things are to be noted: First, he does not commit himself to any such formula as "sense data," which is so common among natural science methodologists. Second, he does not exclude data concerning the subjective states of mind of persons other than the observer. In particular his treatment of propositions as observable facts[3] clearly implies that not merely the physical properties of objects but also the meaning of symbols is capable of observation. This is, as we shall see, a matter of far-reaching importance. In fact, one may lay down only two very general criteria of what constitutes fact for Pareto—one that a factual observation must involve a "thing" or "event" or aspects of it, which is "given" in the sense of being independent of the subjective wishes, whims, or sentiments of the observer, and second, as a check on this, that by a combination of "pointing" and rational argument any two

2. *Traité de sociologie générale*, sec. 28. All references are to the French edition. The sections are uniform through the Italian, French, and English editions.
3. Ibid., sec. 7. The general methodological discussion occupies the whole of chapter 1.

"reasonable" men may be brought to agree in the essentials of their description of it.[4]

There is one other highly important point. It is quite clear that Pareto does not mean by "fact" necessarily a *concrete* thing or event; indeed, it is questionable whether a completely concrete description exists at all.[5] But, however that may be, most "facts" of science fall far short of the empirically possible degree of concrete completeness— they state only certain aspects or elements of the concrete situation in hand.

It is only with this in mind that we can appreciate the meaning of Pareto's conception of scientific law as the statement of a uniformity existing in the facts.[6] This is not a repudiation of the role of abstraction in scientific theory. But Pareto does not set concept over against fact—the one abstract, the other concrete. This position, short of the radical empiricism which repudiates abstract concepts altogether, issues in the "fiction" theory that concepts are useful fictions, but somehow not "true." Contrary to this view, the element of abstraction is included in his concept of fact as such.

Then any concrete phenomenon is to be regarded as resulting from a concatenation (an *entrelacement,* as Pareto says[7]) of a number of different laws meeting in a given concrete situation. The failure of any particular law to provide a satisfactory account of the *total* concretely observable facts of the situation is not prima facie evidence that the law is wrong, but rather than the elements formulated in it need to be supplemented by those formulated in other laws.

On this crucial methodological point Pareto's experience with economics was of decisive importance for his view of sociology. For there seems to be no doubt that his principal personal motive for venturing into sociology lay in his dissatisfaction with the concepts of economic theory as adequate tools for the solution of concrete problems, even of what are generally regarded as a predominantly "economic" character, such as that of the effects of protectionist measures. But from this inadequacy, which he realized more and more vividly, he did not conclude (as does, for instance, the "institutionalist" school of economists) that the proper course was to discard the economic theory to which he himself had greatly contributed, but rather to supplement its

4. Pareto himself clearly recognized the relativity of this last criterion. There is no space here to enter into the methodological issues.

5. *Traité,* sec. 106.

6. Sec. 99.

7. Sec. 101.

abstractions with other sociological theories applicable to the same concrete phenomena. It is highly significant that it is just this example which he gave to illustrate the abstractness of scientific theory in his own methodological discussion.[8]

We may, then, take Pareto as, with all his insistence on logico-experimental method, representing an undogmatic, relatively open-minded view of science and its method[9] which, above all, leaves room for the admission to scientific treatment of subjective phenomena, and which avoids the pitfalls of radical empiricism with an explicit vindication of the role of theoretical abstraction in science. Whatever its shortcomings from the point of view of completeness, it is, in my opinion, a sound foundation on which to build.

With these methodological considerations in mind, we may now turn to Pareto's substantive theoretical structure, the distinction between "logical" and "nonlogical" action. This is, as Pareto explicitly says, not a classification of concrete actions but of *elements* in concrete action.[10] Moreover, there can be no doubt that the concept of logical action is framed with the concepts of economic theory primarily in mind, though it is a broader category than the economic, containing other elements.[11]

It is defined as consisting of "operations logically united to their end" from the point of view both of the actor and of an outside observer "with a more extended knowledge of the circumstances."[12] From the context it is made clear that the "more extended knowledge" in question is the best available scientific knowledge. That is, action is logical insofar as it may be thought of as guided by a scientifically verifiable theory of the intrinsic relations of means to the end in question. The standard of "logicality" or rationality is thus derived from science. In another place Pareto says that logical action may be thought of as determined by a "process of reasoning,"[13] that is of scientific reasoning.

Nonlogical action, on the other hand, is not positively defined at all, but is a residual category. It comprises all the elements of action not falling within Pareto's explicit definition of the logical element.

---

8. Sec. 34.

9. In rather marked contrast to the dogmatism of some of his followers.

10. Sec. 148.

11. Sec. 152.

12. Sec. 150. Pareto also gives another definition, where the objective and subjective ends coincide (197). I do not take this up explicitly because it would complicate the discussion without contributing sufficiently to justify it.

13. Sec. 161.

This is a fact of the first importance which must be kept continually in mind if Pareto's thought is to be understood.

The "sociological" theories of which Pareto spoke as constituting the necessary supplement to economic theory in understanding concrete action[14] are predominantly those dealing with the nonlogical elements of action, and these are the only ones which he attempts to develop by an explicit analysis in his own sociological treatise.

Having abstracted the logical elements of action from his immediate concern, Pareto proceeds to develop an analytical scheme for the study of the nonlogical, predominantly on an inductive basis. There are two essential steps in this development which have not generally been clearly understood in relation to each other. The first is the setting up of a scheme the essential purpose of which is to attain a clear statement of the problem and to decide what concrete data to select for intensive study.

It takes the form of a discrimination between three elements of the problem.[15] Two of them are roughly distinguishable sets of concrete data bearing on nonlogical action, those of "overt acts," designated as B, on the one hand, "linguistic expressions" or "theories," called C, concretely associated with them, on the other. Human beings, unlike animals, both "act"—that is, their organisms go through changes which may be interpreted as spatiotemporal events, and also express explanations and justifications of their actions in linguistic, i.e., symbolic, form. Causally connected in a state of mutual interdependence with both these sets of concrete data is a third entity which Pareto designates as A, the "state of mind" of the actor or, more frequently in his later usage, his "sentiments," which is not directly observable in the same sense as B and C. But insofar as B and C, the observed phenomena are not determined by the external situation of the actor, the forces which determine nonlogical action, and hence in the last analysis the state of society,[16] will be found in A.

It should be noted that A is *not* specifically defined, but is rather left as indefinite as possible. Indeed, there is good reason for this, since its investigation is the problem of the study, and to define it rigorously at this stage would be to beg the question. All that can be said about it at the outset are three things: that since the whole scheme is concerned with *non*logical action, it excludes the prime determinant force of logical action, that is, scientific knowledge; that Pareto's phrase a "state

14. Sec. 38.
15. Sec. 162. Pareto illustrates this scheme graphically by means of a triangle with the apexes denominated by A, B, and C, respectively.
16. Only insofar as it is dependent on *non*logical forces, of course.

of mind" (*état psychique*) indicates he intends to approach the problem primarily in "subjective" terms, and that it is roughly distinguishable from the concrete categories of fact, B and C, indeed, it cannot be a concrete category at all, but must be an analytical element—its "factualness" is on the analytical plane like that of logical action.

Now, both B and C, being in a state of mutual interdependence with A, may be regarded as in part "manifestations" of it. But of the two, for *non*logical action C is the more closely tied to A because it is less affected by the external circumstances of action. Hence Pareto decides to confine his analytical attention to the study of C, the "theories" associated with nonlogical action,[17] and leave B aside until he comes to his synthetic treatment in the last three chapters of the work. The essential function of this A B C scheme which, to differentiate it from another introduced presently we may call the triangle scheme, is to state his inductive problem in this way—it is not his final analytical scheme at all. This is the *first* step in the inductive process.

The second step is the substantive study of theories themselves. But since he is concerned with studying nonlogical action only, he is confronted immediately with a problem—it is not concrete theories he wants to study, but only the nonlogical elements in them. But how are these to be identified? The answer to this question takes Pareto back to the original starting point, the concept of logical action. Its principal distinguishing feature, it will be remembered, was that means were intrinsically related to their end in a scientifically verifiable way. Then insofar as logical action is guided by a "theory," it will be a theory which meets the requirements of logico-experimental science. True to the residual character of nonlogical action then, any departure from this standard will suffice to mark the theory in question as relevant to nonlogical action, as a datum for Pareto's problem.

His first concern, then, is an exhaustive critique of theories associated with action according to the scientific standard.[18] His second is an inductive study of the nonscientific elements found. The result of this second procedure is the distinction of two types of nonscientific elements, a fundamental, relatively constant one and a contingent, much more highly variable one. These two are the residues and derivations, respectively.[19] It must never be forgotten, as it generally has

17. Cf. Secs. 798, 851.

18. This is why the criticism of theories from a scientific point of view is so prominent in chapters 4 and 5. It is not a continuation of the methodological discussion of chapter 1 but a part of his *positive* analytical procedure.

19. Defined as the elements (a) and (b) respectively of his *second* analytical scheme which is wholly different from the A B C triangle. Cf. sec. 803.

been, that these much discussed concepts of Pareto *both* designate elements of nonscientific *theories*. Above all, the residues are still not elements of the A of the earlier scheme, but only manifestations of A.

In fact, the theory of the residues as such is not a substantive sociological theory at all, but only a conceptual framework in terms of which the task of developing a theory may be approached. It is rather a method than a theory. It does not even tell us what *order* of forces are predominant in determining the state of society except negatively—it is not those involved in logical action so far as the residues are important, for they are elements of nonlogical action. But nonlogical action is a residual category, and this character is shared by that of residues. It all depends on what they "manifest," and there is no reason whatever why the simple inductive distinction of residues and derivations should exhaust the question.

This is the point at which Pareto's own *explicit* analytical scheme stops. Even it is not, in the terms in which it is put forward, without serious difficulties. Indeed, the scheme as stated contains an embarrassing ambiguity which until the analysis is pushed further threatens to develop into a serious contradiction. It is worth a brief exposition in order to show the importance of the further development which is implicit, as I shall show, in Pareto's later synthetic treatment.

The difficulty reaches back into the concept of logical action. There Pareto's mode of treatment had two outstanding features—his definition was exclusively in terms of the character of the means-end relationships, it was the case of "operations logically united to their end"; but at the same time there is, in the conceptual scheme itself, no reference to *systems* of logical action, but only to a logical element in the particular act. The effect of this is to leave the status of ends indeterminate. For the determination "by a process of reasoning"—that is, by a scientific theory—may be meant with or without the qualification "*given* the end." The importance of this lies in the fact that logical action is thought of as a *causal* element, and hence the whole great question of the causal role of ends is involved.[20]

In these terms two lines of thought tend to open out. In the one case it may be assumed that the logical element includes a given end. Then the latter takes the central role in logical action, and the tendency is to think of nonlogical action as determined by factors other than a subjective end. This leads to the interpretation of the sentiments manifested in the residues as psychological drives to which the subjective

20. That is in one sense the question of teleology. But this slippery concept must be handled with great caution.

aspect of the "theories" is irrelevant except as an index of forces of a different order.

If, on the other hand, a scientific theory be taken as the complete determinant of action (without the end being "given" apart from the theory), the trend of thought is entirely different. Instead of the question at issue between logical and nonlogical action being the role of subjective ends as such, it is the character of the theories in terms of which the subjective aspect of action is expressed. At least the ultimate ends of action do not have a place in a scientific theory, because they do not constitute elements of knowledge of the situation, that is, "facts" to the actor, but are "subjective," are "manifestations of sentiments." [21] Then insofar as action is determined by ultimate ends or values which cannot as such be "justified" by a scientific theory, the action is insofar nonlogical, no matter what the character of the means-end relationship. This clearly brings quite different considerations into the picture from the other trend of thought. If the residues constitute or manifest the ultimate values, the major premises on which systems of action are based,[22] the term must be something quite distinct from a "fancy name for instinct."

Moreover, whatever his original bent may have been, Pareto was strongly pushed in this direction by the procedure he chose for the study of nonlogical action. For, having selected *theories* as the factual material to study, he was, in order to identify his data, forced to lay special stress on the scientific standard in connection with logical action and hence ipso facto to emphasize the nonscientific character of the theories in the nonlogical case, rather than to question the general importance of the subjective elements expressed in them. It is no mere coincidence that the secondary writers who have interpreted Pareto as primarily putting forward a new version of instinct theory have uniformly overlooked the fact that his central analysis, issuing in the concepts of residue and derivation, was concerned with theories and not with total complexes of action.[23]

21. It is to be noted that Pareto speaks of the residue as always the "manifestation of certain sentiments." Cf. sec. 868.

22. As Pareto put it at one point "le principe qui existe dans l'esprit de l'homme." Cf. sec. 798. An instinct is not a principle. To be sure a residue "corresponds to" and "manifests" instincts, but curiously enough *so do all the other major sociological categories.* Cf. sec. 851.

23. Thus for instance Professor Sorokin, perhaps the most eminent sociologist who has written on Pareto, interprets them as elements of the A B C triangle schema: cf. *Contemporary Sociological Theories*, 50. We are here concerned with Pareto's explicit conceptual scheme. His actual usage is often forced by the latent ambiguity just discussed in the direction of an instinct theory.

The effect of this dichotomy is to bring into the foreground a distinction between two entirely different categories of nonlogical elements in action which cuts across the residue-derivation distinction so that both of them are "manifested" in the residues. The combination of the residual way of conceiving nonlogical action, with Pareto's inductive method of its study, made it impossible for him to develop the distinction systematically without going beyond the point to which he pushed his own analytical scheme. The distinction is that between the elements of heredity and environment on the one hand and what may be called "value" elements on the other.

Its significance is best brought out in terms of its relation to the means-end schema which is, after all, Pareto's own starting point and is central to any tradition of thought in which the concept of rationality of action has a place. Analysis[24] will show that if the means-end scheme is to have more than descriptive—that is, causal—analytical meaning, ends as a factor in action must be conceived as containing an element independent of the conditions of the situation of action, including the "given" features of the actor's own hereditary equipment.

If this general proposition be accepted and its implications applied to the understanding of systems of logical action defined as Pareto does it in terms of the character of the means-end relationship, we get somewhat the following picture: Such a system will be found to involve a series of interrelated "chains" of means-end relationships. But the postulate of the causal independence of ends implies that there will at one extreme be elements which constitute "ultimate means and conditions" of action, at the other "ultimate ends" which are, in terms of the chain, "ends in themselves" and not means to any further ends.[25] In between will lie an "intermediate sector" of elements which constitute both means and ends, according to the point of view.[26]

Both the ultimate condition element and the ultimate end element are nonlogical in the sense that they do not constitute or involve means-end *relationships*. In fact, Pareto's definition of logical action will be found to apply quite satisfactorily to the intermediate sector of the intrinsic means-end chain. But this very fact indicates the great importance of the distinction between the two categories of nonlogical

24. For the details of which, unfortunately there is no space in the present paper. See my "Place of Ultimate Values in Sociological Theory" [chapter 18 of this volume].

25. This whole analysis has reference to *elements* and not to concrete entities, acts, or otherwise.

26. Thus money is an end of acquisitive activities but in turn a means of purchasing goods and services.

factors. Objectively, that is from the point of view of an outside observer, the one element is to be attributed to the agency of the actor,
the other not. Subjectively,[27] from the point of view of the actor, the
difference is equally marked. The conditions of action[28] manifest
themselves in the "theories" guiding action in the form of "facts" of
the situation known to the actor. His ultimate ends on the other hand
are not "reflections" of an external reality in the same sense, but are
subjective, are, as Pareto says, "manifestations of sentiments." It follows from this that to conceive concrete action as guided entirely by a
scientific theory is to eliminate the role of ends altogether, in fact to
eliminate action itself, by making its subjective aspect merely a reflection of the facts of the situation.

This dichotomy of nonlogical elements is not, as has been pointed
out, present in Pareto's original explicit analytical scheme. It does,
however, make its appearance in a most interesting manner in the later
synthetic portion of his work. In connection with his discussion of
social utility he formulates two abstract types of society.[29] One is that
where "reason" does not enter in at all but where action is determined
exclusively by the sentiments and the external conditions of the society, or if we add the determination of the sentiments by the external
conditions "the form of the society is determined if the external conditions alone are given."[30] The other is one where action is determined
"exclusively by logico-experimental reasoning."[31] But in this case the
form of the society is "by no means determined when the external
conditions are given. It is necessary to know in addition the end which
is to be pursued by means of logico-experimental reasoning."[32] Pareto
then goes on to say that the essential reason why a society based exclusively on reason "does not and cannot exist"[33] is not that men's
"prejudices" prevent them from acting reasonably; it is not that it is
impossible to know the conditions accurately and to act upon the
knowledge, but that data essential to the solution of the problems
presented by action to reason are lacking. These essential data are the
ultimate ends of action.

Thus Pareto, when he has come to consider action systems as a

27. This is a highly important distinction which Pareto himself makes use of. Cf. sec.
199.
28. At the rational pole. See below for the main qualifications of this proposition.
29. Sec. 2041.
30. Sec. 2142.
31. Sec. 2143.
32. Ibid.
33. Ibid.

whole instead of isolated acts, has clearly seen what is in his terms the "nonlogical" character of ultimate ends, and at the same time the clear distinction of this nonlogical element from the conditions of action. The "sentiments" of the first abstract type of society can clearly not be those manifested in the ultimate ends of action, for Pareto does not hesitate to think of the former as determined by the external conditions while, for ends as a factor in action to be so determined would be a contradiction in terms. Conversely the ends which constitute the missing data equally cannot be mere reflections of the conditions—there is no bar in principle to the latter constituting data of a scientific theory which can serve as a guide to action. Thus we see one essential reason why the theories associated with action always contain nonlogical elements.

I now wish to call attention to two further important features of Pareto's treatment of action which are not explicit in his main analytical scheme but which emerge from a careful study of the synthetic parts of his work.

The first concerns the way in which his thinking finally breaks with the "atomistic individualism" which has been a conspicuous feature of the utilitarian climate of opinion of orthodox economic theory and has constituted an important element in the background of his own thought. We have already seen how the distinction between logical and nonlogical action in the way in which he formulated it involved by implication, in order to avoid otherwise insuperable difficulties, the conception of a complicated web of means-end chains instead of a mere aggregation of isolated acts. Only these considerations give a clear determination of the relation of the logical element to the two orders of nonlogical, heredity and environment and the value element.

There emerges, however, in the theory of social utility, a further differentiation of the modes in which the latter are related to action. In spite of the fact that this treatment is couched in normative terms, it has highly important theoretical implications. Its point of departure is the normative aspect of economic theory in the form of the traditional economic doctrine of maximum satisfaction. This is the proposition that, under certain rigidly defined conditions the most important of which are rationality of action, mobility of resources, freedom of competition, and independence of wants from the processes of their satisfaction, the pursuit by each individual of his own economic self-interest will result in the maximum possible satisfaction of the wants of all the members of the community.

Pareto starts by noting that dropping certain of these conditions pertaining to equality in the terms of exchange, a distinction emerges between the two types of maxima of satisfaction, or utility which he calls maxima *for* and *of* a collectivity respectively.[34] The first is a point in a given process of change up to which the utilities of all the members of the collectivity without exception are affected in the same direction. This is the only type of maximum which can be treated on an economic level of analysis,[35] for the economic level is concerned with means only and precludes the comparative evaluation of the wants, that is of the ultimate ends of different individuals. Going beyond this point involves, because it would benefit some individuals and groups to the detriment of others, no matter what the numbers on each side, extra-economic considerations precisely because it cannot dispense with such extra-economic evaluation.

The economic point of view is inherently distributive, it concerns the allocation as between competing wants of *scarce* resources. But the reason why this allocation when the claims are conflicting cannot be settled on economic grounds alone is that it involves the ethical consideration of relative claims of different individuals. But this is still a distributive question. It becomes meaningful on a sociological level just because the sociological level for Pareto does include the factor of ethical values, or ultimate ends, while the economic does not. But just because this is a distributive question, on the sociological level it becomes one of utility *for* the collectivity, not *of* it.

But on the sociological level this other set of considerations of utility does arise, that involved in defining a maximum *of* a collectivity.[36] Here the question is no longer distributive, a matter of settling relative claims of different individuals and groups within the community. It involves the treatment of the collectivity "if not as a person, at least as a unity."[37] This concerns value elements, at the rationalized pole ultimate ends, *common* to the members of the community, in a phrase which crept into the French edition of the *Traité* "the end which a society should pursue."[38]

What is the significance of this rather curious distinction, as it may seem to many? It concerns the senses in which the ultimate values of

34. Secs. 2128–29.
35. Sec. 2130.
36. Secs. 2133ff.
37. Sec. 2133.
38. Sec. 2143. This phrase does not occur in the original Italian nor in the English translation, which was made from the Italian. Its occurrence in the French cannot, however, be regarded as a mere error of translation since first the translation was itself approved by Pareto, who, himself as much French as Italian linguistically, would surely not have let such a thing slip at so crucial a point had he not meant it. Even more important, it fits very definitely with the line of his thought at this point.

different members of a community are related to each other—the ends of the different means-end chains. The underlying, often implicit, assumption of much individualistic thought has been that they are random and relative to each other. Such has come to be more and more the explicit assumption of certain economic theorists, and is expressed in the theorem of the incomparability of the wants of different individuals.

Pareto's first qualification of this assumption of randomness may be interpreted to mean that the rational pursuit of purely "private" ends unintegrated with those of others, is only possible as an aspect of a social system within the framework of a distributive order, a system of rules and practices which settle the relative claims of different individuals to desirable but scarce "goods." [39] Pareto's statement that a "hypothesis" is necessary to render these claims comparable may in its empirical application be interpreted to mean that every functioning social system actually embodies such a system of rules which more or less effectively settles these claims. And, since such a hypothesis rests, not on judgments of fact but of ethical value, in relation to different traits, achievements, and positions of status, a social order insofar involves a nonlogical element of the value order.

But this distributive aspect does not exhaust the question. There are equally involved in a social order certain common ethical elements which do not involve such a distributive aspect at all. By virtue of these a collectivity is not merely as it were "coerced" into unity in the sense of repressing potential internal conflict, but it constitutes a unity in a more positive sense, it involves the promotion of common ideals and ends—its members share a common "faith" as Pareto frequently says. The place in sociology of a maximum of utility *of* a collectivity indicates the empirical role of this *common* value element which is also nonlogical for the same reasons that the distributive standards are.

This element still further transcends the "atomism" of the predominant strain of individualistic thought, conceiving social unity as conditioned by an integration of values. It completes the elaboration of the total implications of the means-end schema at the intrinsic rational pole indicated by Pareto's initial concept of logical action.

Pareto's use of the phrase "if not as a person, at least as a unity" suggests the theoretical significance of this element. It is unquestionably an important version of what is sometimes called the "organic"

39. Which, for reasons which cannot be gone into here, focus on the two categories of wealth and power.

theory of society, or better the "sociologistic theorem." It is this element which constitutes society, in Durkheim's phrase, a "reality *sui generis*" not reducible to terms of its individual constituent parts, in this case the "private ends" of the individuals which make it up.

We may now turn to the second emergent theoretical element mentioned above. It concerns the significance of a fact which must strike any careful reader of Pareto forcibly—the very great prominence in his empirical examples of the nonlogical of a special type of actions which may roughly be called "ritual." Almost the first case by which he illustrates the distinction of logical and nonlogical is that of the Greek sailors who as a means of getting to port on the one hand row and navigate, on the other make sacrifices to Poseidon—the latter is of course the nonlogical element. Similarly the first large-scale case in terms of which he illustrates his method of arriving at the residues is also a ritual case, that of magical practices aimed at control over the weather.[40]

Since ritual is so very prominent empirically in the work, the question naturally arises as to its theoretical significance in Pareto's scheme. But beyond the mere fact that it is predominantly nonlogical he gives no explicit answer. There is one highly interesting point at which he makes a distinction between ritual and nonritual acts, but curiously enough he drops it and does not develop its implications further.[41] One possible view is that ritual constitutes merely "illogical" action, that it is a manifestation of certain instinctive tendencies of men which simply have nothing to do with whatever modicum of rationality they may possess.

The first objection to this is the curiously close connection between theory and overt act in the case of ritual. In the case of action in pursuit of a specific end by rational means the gap between the rational norm and the actual issue is often too conspicuous to be ignored. And to account for it, factors resistant to the realization of the norm must be posited. But in treating of the "theories" associated with ritual acts Pareto often[42] goes so far as to include the *means* employed in the *derivations* which are ostensibly elements of theories, not of overt acts. In fact in connection with ritual what impresses Pareto is not the difficulty men find in living up to the prescriptions of their theories, not the difficulty of carrying out the sacrifices to Poseidon correctly according to the prescriptions of the ritual tradition. On the contrary

40. Secs. 186ff.
41. Sec. 167.
42. For instance secs. 863, 865.

it seems to be assumed that this is very generally achieved. What impresses him is rather the arbitrariness of the "combinations" of means and end laid down in the prescriptions of the theories themselves. In other words the peculiarities of ritual which make it nonlogical lie in the nature of the whole complex of action, "theories" and overt acts taken together, not in the relations of the theories to the acts.

A second possible interpretation is that the theories are simply erroneous, that with the progress of knowledge they will gradually be transformed into scientific theories and ritual actions will become "logical." There are several things in Pareto which argue against this as the principal interpretation. In the first place he warns in general that "nonlogical is not to be taken to mean illogical,"[43] and error is surely a case of *illogicality*. Second, with reference to nonlogical action in general the main tenor of his argument is definitely against any progressive tendency for the nonlogical elements to be eliminated with the progress of science. He surely does not deny the existence of the latter, but at the same time his general emphasis is strongly on the relative constancy of nonlogical elements—which would argue that the nonlogical basis of ritual is not primarily error but rather something positive. Third, there are a good many specific statements which repudiate this interpretation in particular instances.

A third interpretation is possible. So far the ultimate value element has been dealt with only in its direct relations to "logical" action or, as I prefer to say, the intrinsic means-end schema. In the latter context it appears primarily in the role of ultimate ends. And, considering his starting point from the concept of logical action it is not surprising that it is only this aspect which Pareto brought to explicit formulation at all in his theory of social utility. But there is no reason why this should be the only type of relation of the value element to action.

Perhaps the best starting point is a consideration of the connotations of the term "manifestation" of which Pareto makes such frequent use. Such a proposition as "a residue is the manifestation of certain sentiments" seems to me to be open to two interpretations which fall in with the general dichotomy which has formed the main theme of this discussion. One is suggested by the analogy of the thermometer reading which Pareto himself used.[44] The thermal properties of mercury are such that when some of it is placed in a narrow vacuum tube and the end of the tube placed in a substance, the elevation of the mercury in the tube may be taken as an index of the thermal

43. Sec. 150.
44. Sec. 875.

state of the substance. This is because the mercury in the tube and the substance in question both form part of the same system of physical causation or mutual interdependence—there is a causal interrelation between the two. Similarly, for instance, certain mental symptoms, as financial irresponsibility, may be taken in paresis as evidence of certain syphilitic lesions of the brain. Insofar as residues, which are propositions, are taken to be manifestations of instincts the relation between manifestation and thing manifested is of this character.

On the other hand the relation may be that between a symbol and its meaning. Insofar the causal relation is always "arbitrary" but the symbolic relation is nonetheless important to human life.[45] Thus a residue which, being a proposition, is after all a complex of linguistic symbols, may manifest sentiments in the sense that it is a symbolic expression of a "state of mind." I think it a fair inference that insofar as the nonlogical elements of action are value elements and not those of heredity and environment and manifestation involved is predominantly of this and not the other character. There is of course no reason why the symbolic relation should be confined to such media as language, and altogether excluded from overt action.

What characterizes logical action in this respect is that the systems of symbols involved in it refer to or express systems of intrinsic relationships in the external world. Their "function" is that of intrinsic alteration of the external world in the service of an "end." But there is no reason why there should not equally be systems of symbols, i.e., "theories" whose reference is not "objective" in this sense but "subjective," which manifest sentiments in the sense of forms of expression. Insofar as these theories imply and determine overt action, the action itself also becomes a form of expression, the function of which is not modification of the "real" world but something quite different.[46] In this case the theories, just because of their subjective reference, must necessarily be nonscientific and the action hence nonlogical.

Ritual I should consider as *one*[47] of these modes of expression of values, of value attitudes in overt action. And indeed there are certain types of situations where the urge to such expression is particularly strong because of a combination of a strong interest in the value con-

45. Once a given symbol is accepted it of course comes to form part of a causal system but this depends on the phenomenon of "acceptance" which is foreign to physical systems.

46. The empirical line between these two types may well be quite indistinct with a gradual shading off.

47. The other principal ones I should consider art and play. Limitations of space forbid entering into the distinctions here.

cerned and limitations on doing anything about it by intrinsic means. On the one hand there is the type of situation where we have available certain intrinsic means of attaining an end but their inadequacy is such as to leave an important margin of uncertainty of success even with their most efficient possible employment. This is the situation which typically calls forth magical ritual as in such activities as love and war. On the other hand, there are equally situations which bring us hard up against the absolute boundaries of human comprehension and control but where circumstances are such that we cannot remain indifferent—perhaps the most typical is death. It is this type of situation which occasions religious ritual.

Ritual, however, is not necessarily merely a mode of expression if by that is meant something functionally unimportant to action. The total action system of a society is integrated in a way which makes it extremely unlikely such a prominent part of it could simply be dropped out without repercussions on the rest. And indeed concrete studies of ritual, including Pareto's own, tend strongly to show that it is functionally highly important. Wherein then lies its function since by definition it cannot be intrinsically effective? The answer seems to be largely in relation to "effort." Ritual is largely important as a social mechanism for the maintenance of the tone of effort of a society.[48]

The theoretical scheme we have outlined of course by no means exhausts Pareto's sociological work. In particular he had a great deal to say about many more empirical subjects, highly interesting and important in themselves, but for which there is no space in the present discussion. At the same time this scheme and its ramifications are central to the work. I do not think it possible to get very far in the interpretation of any part of it without these questions becoming involved. Hence it has seemed worthwhile to devote the present article to the lucidation of this scheme and the theoretical problems growing immediately out of it.

In closing I should like to make a very few general remarks. The problem of the rationality of human action undoubtedly forms one of the few main foci of modern social thought. The two aspects of the problem which constitute Pareto's main starting points, the role of scientific knowledge on the one hand, the "economic" problem on the other, constitute with equal certainty vitally important modes in

---

48. The general view of ritual presented here, and admittedly to a considerable extent "read into" Pareto, is closely related to that developed by Durkheim and some of the anthropologists especially of the "functional" school. See *Les formes élémentaires de la vie religieuse;* Malinowski, *Magic, Science, and Religion;* and Radcliffe-Brown, *The Andaman Islanders.*

which the more general problem has been involved in our intellectual tradition. Since these problems are the main focus of Pareto's theoretical scheme, I think there can be no doubt of the interest of his work to general social theory.

Within this general stream of thought his importance seems to me to lie mainly at two points. Outside Germany at least I think it is safe to say that the treatment of the problem of rationality has been in the main "positivistic." More specifically it has been placed in the dilemma of accepting the theories of economic individualism as literally and concretely true, or insofar as this position was rejected to fall back on psychological anti-intellectualism, above all some version of the "instinct" theory.

Pareto was one of the first to transcend this dilemma in a thoroughgoing way. In the first place he treated "logical action" as an element of concrete action, not as a class of acts. He thereby escaped the objectionable "reification" with which so much of orthodox economic theory has been burdened. Secondly, he treated nonlogical action as a *genuine* residual category. The door was open for its content to emerge as a result of empirical study. For both of these results a large share of the credit is due to his sceptical "natural science" methodology.

From this starting point, Pareto did not develop a satisfactory general theory of human action. His residue and derivation analysis is, however, properly understood, a highly useful analytical tool for certain purposes. At the same time we have shown that underlying his empirical work in the later parts of the *Treatise* are to be found emerging several further categories which can be given a place in an analytical theory of human action.

I submit that the aspect of Pareto's sociology to which this discussion has been devoted constitutes in spite of its incompleteness a major contribution to social theory. Both for understanding the rest of Pareto's work, and for the further development of the theory of action, a clear grasp of it is essential.

III

THE FOUNDATIONS OF ANALYTICAL SOCIOLOGY

16

Some Reflections on "The Nature and Significance of Economics"

I

At the outset the reader is asked to bear in mind that the present writer is a sociologist, not an economist. But the interrelations of the social sciences are so close that their basic methodological questions must be treated together. The debate between Professors Robbins and Souter on these questions is the occasion for the present essay.[1] Both in the article printed in this journal and in his book, Souter uses Robbins's recent book as the principal target for his thrusts, and it is hardly possible to discuss the issues involved without considering both writers. My purpose, however, is not to make a detailed analysis of the arguments of either, but rather to use them as the starting point for some general reflections.

The general issues involved center around Souter's perfectly sound emphasis on the proposition that the social sciences form an organically united "society"[2] rather than an atomistic "Nebeneinander." I may remark at once that unfortunately he fails to live up to this doctrine. He does not consider the scope of economics in relation to the current discussion of the scope of the neighboring sciences, but rather attempts to settle the question on the grounds of "economic philosophy" alone. This failure, as we shall see, leads him into an "economic imperialism" (to borrow his own phrase[3]), which results not only in enriching these neighboring "countries," which of course it does, but in putting some of them into a straitjacket of "economic" categories which is ill-suited to their own conditions. The issues involved, however, can best be followed by beginning with Robbins.

Originally published in the *Quarterly Journal of Economics* 48 (1934): 511–45.
1. Lionel Robbins, *An Essay on the Nature and Significance of Economic Science,* London, 1932. Ralph W. Souter, *Prolegomena to Relativity Economics,* New York, 1933, and "The Nature and Significance of Economic Science in Recent Discussions," *Quarterly Journal of Economics,* May 1933.
2. *Quarterly Journal of Economics,* 399.
3. *Prolegomena,* 94, footnote.

The principal terms of opprobrium which Souter freely applies to Robbins and his ilk are "atomism," "exclusionist positivism," and "static formalism." In these are implied five interrelated concepts, all of which are in need of analysis. The one of most general bearing and hence the natural starting point is "positivism." What does it imply in the present context?

Very roughly positivism may be defined as the tendency to emphasize the importance of the methods and general doctrines of the physical sciences, and conversely to depreciate anything thought to be radically different from such methods under such uncomplimentary epithets as "metaphysics" and "mysticism." As applied to such a science as biology it implies in the most general sense the use of the methods of observation, logical reasoning and verification, where possible by experiment, and the strict avoidance of concepts which are not subject to verification by observation. This position, with its tendency to interpret "observation" narrowly as sense impressions of events in the "external" world of physical space and time, when applied to the study of human beings, generally leans heavily in the direction of behaviorism. The latter implies above all repudiation, in the name of scientific rigor, of all evidence derived from "observation" of the "subjective" aspect of other people's minds—their ideas, desires, ends, or "internal" mental states or processes. With it is generally combined a strong "reductive" tendency to think of the physiological or even physicochemical factors as the "real" determinants of behavior.

But as applied to human beings there is another tendency of "positivistic" thought which is perhaps as much historically as logically connected with the first. Since physical science is held to be the only really "sound" achievement of the human mind, the attempt is made to use its methodology as a standard for the measurement of the rationality of human action. This of course involves the admission from the very start of the "subjective" as an object of scientific study. In these terms action is held to be rational insofar as the actor can be conceived as solving a scientific problem. The standard is the situation where all the elements of the problem he solves, except sheer logic, and hence all other elements necessary to understand his action, are "data," that is, facts of the external world to the actor. This view may be called "radical rationalistic positivism."

These two radical positivistic positions have been present in widely varying degrees and combinations in a great deal of actual social thought. The one, laying its emphasis on scientific "objectivism" by eliminating the "subjective aspect" of action from the status of a le-

gitimate object of scientific investigation, tends to reduce the explanation of human behavior to terms of the objective external conditions of its occurrence. The other, while admitting the legitimacy of
studying the subjective aspect, tries to press it into a very narrow and
particular mold, the consequences of which must now be pointed out.

Action, considered from the "subjective" point of view, i.e., that of
the actor, is, apart from the positivistic bias, generally thought of as
understandable only in terms of a relation of means and ends of some
sort. But there is a very fundamental difference between the relation
of means and ends and the elements of a scientist's problem. The "conditions" of the situation in which a person acts, the means to his end,
are to be sure "given" independently of his ends or desires. In this
respect they are strictly analogous to the "observations" of the scientist. But the same cannot be true of "ends." To be sure an "end" may
refer to a state of affairs which can be observed by the actor himself
or someone else, *after* it has been accomplished. But at the time of
inception of the action, that is, when the end is thought of as a *factor*
in the action, such is not the case. Then it is "subjective" to the actor.
A scientific problem is one of bringing into coherent relations data, all
observed *in the past* by the scientist. But an end of action is not to the
actor something observed as having happened. It is the anticipation of
a future state of affairs. While a scientific theory (not necessarily the
phenomena it explains) is timeless, a course of rational action is by its
very essence something spread over time. Hence any theory of action
which squeezes out this time element is fundamentally objectionable.
It can only be done by somehow denaturing the factor of ends. This
is generally done by trying to assimilate them to the category of "given
data," as seen by the actor.

Almost from its inception economic science has been thought of as
concerned with the relations of means and ends. But it has by no
means always been clear what that implied. Robbins makes it the central theme of his treatment, but does not really face the issues just
discussed. In his anxiety to make economics a "positive" science free
from "metaphysics," he is continually being pressed into a radically
positivistic position which really eliminates ends altogether.

This is evident in his definition of ends as "tendencies to conduct
which can be defined or understood."[4] The statement conceals a very
serious ambiguity. For in using the term "tendency" he omits altogether to face the question of the nature of the factors conceived to be
in operation. Insofar as a person's "tendencies" to conduct are merely

4. Robbins, 23.

expressions or results of forces "external" to him (considered from the subjective point of view)—namely, the physiological processes of his body or those of external nature—they can be "defined and understood." But they are not ends in any proper sense. Being carried out to sea by the undertow is a "tendency" which can be defined and understood, but except to one who chooses to commit suicide by this method it is not an "end." Ends are "subjective" not merely in the sense of being "reflected in the consciousness" of the actor but in the more radical sense of being adhered to by him independently of those "conditions" of the situation which are outside his control. Robbins, by defining ends thus ambiguously, has completely erased the fundamental distinction and opened the door wide both to behaviorism and to radical rationalistic positivism. In either case the "subjective aspect" of actions becomes only an "epiphenomenon." For if the subjective aspect of action is a purely scientific theory it is merely a reflection of the external "facts" and cannot itself be a creative element.

These are consequences arrived at by following Robbins's position to its logical conclusion in a certain direction. They can scarcely be said to constitute a statement of his position itself. The just criticism of him is rather that, remaining on the surface, he fails to see and meet the very serious problems lurking underneath, but inevitably gets involved in them by implication. Souter's criticism,[5] which is at these points in the main justified, hits at the implications rather than the letter.

Two fundamental consequences follow from this leaning toward radical positivism. The failure to distinguish true "ends" from mere "tendencies," and the general positivistic bias in favor of emphasis on the "observable" facts in the restricted behavioristic sense result in an elimination of the time element from the conception of economic action. This is essentially what underlies the charge so frequently made by Souter that the neo-Austrian theory is "static." It is not that the theory fails to conceive of *processes* taking place in the observed phenomena, but that from the point of view of the actor all the elements affecting his action are conceived as simultaneously given on the same plane with each other. But ends are not "given data" in the same sense as "conditions." Since they contain a future reference, in the sense of being data of the physical world, they can, unlike the other elements of action, only become "given" after its completion. Hence a set of "equilibrium" curves, that is those analyzing all the fundamental elements of a complex of actions, must refer to a period, not to an in-

5. Souter, *Quarterly Journal of Economics,* 387ff.

stant. Souter's criticism of the conception of a set of "instantaneous" curves in equilibrium is quite sound,[6] but he fails to carry the analysis far enough. Such formulae as "dynamic," "organic," and "biological" do not cover the case. It is fundamentally the failure to realize the true nature of ends and their place in action which is responsible for the "static" character of "static formalism."[7]

Secondly, a matter very closely related to this is that of the "atomism" of Robbins's thought. Examination of this question will lead us into the very center of our methodological problem. It must be considered in two different contexts, that of the individual and that of the economy as a whole.

What Souter calls the "pellet" theory of a "plurality of ends," the idea that the individual's action is the resultant of a set of "conflicting psychological pulls,"[8] is really a strict consequence of the radical positivistic position we have found to be lurking in the background of Robbins's work. It is perhaps better to say "drives," since these psychological forces are most conveniently thought of as "operating upon" the actor. But if action is thought of as a resultant of such drives, whatever organization and coherence is to be found in it is the result of environmental selection, whether thought of as operating through the direct conditioning of the individual, or indirectly through the mechanism of heredity. As Souter quite correctly points out it is not at all a process of rational choice resting on a scale of relative valuation of these different ends. The scale of valuation is not a factor in action, but is merely a resultant, a reflection of the relative strengths of the "psychological pulls."[9]

In other words the role of demand as an effective factor in economic action, the independent reality of the scale of valuations reflected in demand, is dependent on, or is another aspect of, the reality of ends in action. Any positivistic theory which tends to eliminate the latter is really incompatible with the view of economic action as a process of the rational allocation of resources between alternative uses.

This conception has a further consequence which Souter quite clearly sees.[10] A rational process of allocation involves not merely given ends, but a coherent system of ends, a scale of relative valuations. It is not mere plurality, but plurality within a larger unity, an organic whole in which each of the particular ends or wants has its

6. *Prolegomena*, 11ff, especially 23.
7. Souter, *Quarterly Journal of Economics*, 387–89.
8. Robbins, 34.
9. See Souter, *Quarterly Journal of Economics*, 380ff, especially 389–90, 410.
10. Ibid., 381.

place. In other words each individual's actions must be thought of as in the last analysis subordinate to a set of ultimate ends or principles of action. This integrated system of ends is something fundamentally distinct from the coordination of behavior by means of environmental selection. It is active, not passive. Insofar as the categories of means and ends have any meaning at all, human action must be more than a mere resultant of "conflicting psychological pulls."

So much for the individual. But the problem of "atomism" arises again on another plane. It is logically possible to conceive a society composed of a plurality of individuals, each acting in terms of such a system of ultimate ends but each thinking of and related to the others only in the capacity of means to each others' ends or hindrances to them. Such a society is, to be sure, logically conceivable, but there are sound reasons for believing it is not empirically possible. For insofar as ends—in this case the integrated systems of ultimate ends of individuals—are real factors in action, to the same degree they cannot be completely determined in their nature or limited in their accomplishment by the "conditions" of the situation of the society. This degree is of course never unlimited, but precisely insofar as the kind of analysis we are discussing is significant, it is substantial. And of the fact that it is really substantial there is ample empirical evidence. Then there is no reason to believe that the ultimate ends of individuals should be automatically compatible with each other. In the absence of some positive factor bringing them into coherence, such a society would be a mere chaos of conflicting individuals—would in fact be Hobbes's celebrated state of nature. But of course in such a state human life itself would be impossible.

There are three logical possibilities of escape from this dilemma. One is Hobbes's own solution, that the ends are not integrated and brought into harmony at all, but that coercive authority restrains the actions of individuals in terms of them so as to prevent the conflict being fatal to order and security. The second is the assumption that somehow, for some unknown reason, the ends do not conflict—that there is a "natural identity of interests." This is of course a strictly inexplicable preestablished harmony attributed to a metaphysical "nature." It has in fact lurked in the background of much laissez-faire economic theory.

There is the third possibility, that men's ends should be not separate, and either forcibly restrained or miraculously compatible, but in fact, in a given society, held in common. This is a view which has been steadily gaining ground in recent sociological thought, and which seems to form by far the most satisfactory general solution of the problem of the basis of order in society. It would follow from this that while for purposes of analysis of the actions of an individual, his scale of valuations may be taken in abstraction from those of his fellows, it is no more legitimate to conceive the actions of a whole society as a mere resultant of an indefinite plurality of individual systems of ends in given conditions, than it is to conceive individual action as the resultant of a similar plurality of "conflicting psychological pulls." The ultimate ends of the members of a whole society also form to a greater or less degree an integrated system which to be understood must be taken as a whole.[11] This is the essential set of facts underlying Souter's repeated assertions that the subject matter of economics is "organic" and not "atomistic."[12] It follows, however, essentially from the basic conception of action as a process of adaptation of means to ends. As a criticism of the implications of certain of Robbins's trends of thought it is quite valid.

One other difficulty lurking behind the "positivistic" approach of Robbins should be pointed out before we enter on our central question of the scope of economics in relation to other sciences. Most economists with positivistic leanings have set up as the goal of their endeavors the formulation of "laws" of the same logical nature as those of the physical sciences. In the earlier and more naive sense these were ironbound laws, thought to be full concrete descriptions of the course of events in the real world. Robbins quite rightly criticizes this view as involving the fallacy of "misplaced concreteness."

Parallel with the physical sciences, however, economists have reinterpreted their concept of economic law to mean the much more modest statement of what will happen given certain specified conditions. But since the conditions are never fully given in concrete reality independently of other "disturbing" elements, we cannot expect such a "law" to give a fully accurate description of concrete events. It must be thought of as an abstraction, a formulation of only part of the forces at work in concrete reality. Its empirical relevance will be dependent on the context to which the factors formulated in it can be shown empirically to be present and of quantitative importance in relation to others. Thus it has been thought possible to avoid the fal-

11. It follows from this that it is just as legitimate for social science for certain purposes to assume the comparability of the wants of individuals according to a socially accepted scale of valuation, as to assume that the various wants of an individual are comparable. This assumption is, however, to my mind more on the sociological than the economic plane. See below. See also Souter, *Quarterly Journal of Economics,* 409–10.

12. See ibid., 405, 412.

lacy of misplaced concreteness and to retain the character of economics as a "positive" science.

Though this is a step forward it does not go far enough. It fails to take account of the implications of centering the concepts of economics on the relation of means and ends. What is formulated in an "economic law" is not a descriptive generalization in the first instance at all, but a rational type case. It is how action would proceed given the "wants" of the subjects and given the conditions under which they act, insofar as they act rationally. It is, given the data, a *norm* of rational action. Its empirical relevance rests on the circumstance that men do in fact *try* (not merely "tend") to "economize," to "exploit" the conditions of their lives rationally in order to satisfy their wants. This idea of a norm which men can be conceived as striving to attain by *effort* is something entirely foreign to the "positive" physical sciences. Celestial bodies do not "strive" to follow their orbits whether by the Newtonian or Einsteinian formulae, they merely *do*. These considerations make "economic law" something quite different from "positive" law even in the abstract sense.

To be sure all this can be fitted into the formal logic of "positive" scientific theory. These norms can be formulated in terms of equations of equilibrium. They are "abstractions" which must be combined with other elements to give a full explanation of concrete reality. Again Robbins's formulation is not so much positively wrong as superficial, failing to get at the serious difficulties under the surface. But Souter is quite right in insisting that this makes the positivistic doctrine of the "logical gap" between "fact" and "norm," which are interpreted as "positive" and "metaphysical" respectively, quite untenable, at least so far as certain aspects of the sciences of human action are concerned. At the basis of this position is really the old confusion between the points of view of the actor and of the observer. What is to the actor a norm must be to the observer a fact. Otherwise by a logical trick, and not by empirical proof, we must maintain that insofar as it can be scientifically studied human action cannot be guided by norms but only by "psychological pulls." What is wrong with the doctrine of the "logical gap" is not the logical distinction itself, but the idea that a science dealing with "facts" cannot also deal with "norms." [13] That is quite untenable. Insofar as economics refuses to deal with norms it becomes mere behaviorism, that is, not economics at all—the concept of economy becomes quite meaningless. Here also Robbins is not con-

13. Robbins, 123. A normative element has no place in pure science.

sistent.[14] Souter's just criticism strikes implications rather than views. He is of course right in insisting that to say "normative" is not necessarily to say "ethical." [15] That economics is necessarily in one sense a normative science does not imply that it rests on ethical postulates.

II

What has been said thus far has been concerned mainly with the "positivistic" trend in Robbins's thought and its unfortunate tendency to lead to implications fatal to what appears on the surface to be the central theme of his book—the concept of "economy" in terms of the relation of means to ends. The main underlying purpose of the discussion has been to show that it is not really possible to make economics a "positive" science on the analogy of the physical sciences without altogether discarding the essential features of the "subjective" means-end analysis. The failure to realize that this is a genuine dilemma involves Robbins in numerous difficulties of which only a part have been able to find a place in the discussion.

While I have been in essential agreement with Souter's criticism, my analysis has been couched in different terms from his. This is because I wish now to proceed to a further development which will be found to be incompatible with some of the most important implications of Souter's own position. This development concerns mainly the implications of the epithet "exclusionist" which Souter applies as a term of criticism to Robbins's position, and will show some of the reasons why a sociologist should take the trouble to enter so far into what would appear on the surface to be only a family quarrel of economists. The discussion thus far has been almost solely concerned with methodological problems which economics shares with the other sciences

14. This is an excellent illustration of the way in which a "positive" attitude can justify the evasion of basic methodological questions. He speaks (43) of the "materialist" interpretation of history as "a general statement about the causation of human motive which, from the point of view of Economic Science, is sheer metaphysics," implying, I think, that any such general statement is sheer metaphysics. But whether it be metaphysics or not the economist is forced to make the statement that ends form a real independent factor in conduct. Otherwise his whole science becomes completely meaningless. There is no evading this obligation.

15. See Souter, *Quarterly Journal of Economics*, 402. By "normative economics" Souter apparently means more than that economic concepts are norms of economic rationality. He means rather that its concepts must be normative in the full concrete sense and thus involve ethical values. See ibid., 404.

dealing with human action. Let me turn now to what specifically distinguishes economics from these other sciences.

My thesis will be that Souter takes a position which makes a satisfactory set of distinctions impossible. It commits him, like his master Alfred Marshall, to an "economic imperialism" in the bad sense of suppressing the "rights" of neighboring sciences to an "independent" [16] existence in the society of the sciences. To show this it will not suffice to analyze Souter's own remarks about economics in isolation from the other sciences. It will be necessary to consider the place of economics in the whole system of the sciences of action. Such a system can be derived by the further development of the scheme of means-end analysis already begun. Only when its outline is complete can a just critical appreciation of Souter's position be attained. The aim is to test him in terms of his own doctrine that the sciences, forming a true *society*, can only be judged *in relation* to one another. This he unfortunately fails to do.

It is already clear, I hope, that short of the radical positivistic positions we have sketched, ends must be conceived as an independent and effective factor in action and of a fundamentally different order from the "conditions" in which action takes place. These conditions must be held to include not merely the natural environment, but also the facts of his own nature insofar as they must be "taken account of" by the actor.

If this essential independence of ends be conceded it follows that, from the point of view of determination by the "conditions," there must be an element of action which is so to speak left "hanging in the air." But this applies only to the "ultimate" ends of action which must be conceived as a (more or less) integrated system.

This system is the culmination of the whole complicated chain of means-end relationships. Subordinate to it is a class of actions which are both means and ends—means to more ultimate ends, but also ends of the action leading up to them.[17] In this intermediate sector of the means-end chain will belong all elements of action other than the ultimate ends, except the "ultimate means" at the other end of the chain, the fundamental "positivistic" factors of "environment" and "human nature." [18] However complex the interweaving and turning

16. "Independent" here does not mean unrelated to the others. See below.

17. Thus money is the "end" of wage work, but the "means" of acquiring beefsteak.

18. I heartily agree with Souter that philosophy or metaphysics cannot be kept out of discussions of methodology. The position here taken involves the definite repudiation of the metaphysical materialistic monism implied in both the radical positivistic views of "action."

back on itself may be, it is a logical necessity that this whole system of means-end chains should be resolvable in the last analysis into the three great categories of "ultimate means," "ultimate ends," and "intermediate means-end relationships."

Is there any way in which this very simple basic scheme can be made to yield criteria for the separation of the various sciences of action from each other? The simplest case is that of the "ultimate means," the "conditions" of action. Falling as they do into two great categories of nonhuman "environment" and "human nature" it is clear that they are dealt with by the already well-developed sciences of "geography" (in the broadest sense embodying the application of physics, chemistry, and biology to the understanding of man's nonhuman environment), biology, and psychology. Of these, psychology is the nearest to the sciences of action but is not, in my opinion, one of them. Its task is the analysis of the "mechanisms" or "powers" or "faculties" on which human action and thought depend. These form only one aspect of the concrete actions of men, only one element in them. Given the same "faculties" it does not follow that the same concrete actions will always result.

As the history of the great body of thought sometimes called "social Darwinism" amply shows, the radical positivistic position leads directly to the view that these conditions are the decisive factors in social life. It is, as Pareto puts it, the view that maintains the "complete determination of the form of a society by the conditions of its existence." [19] It is only where "positivism" leaves off that the true sciences of action begin.

Leaving aside the "ultimate means," then, we have left the "ultimate ends" and the "intermediate" sector. As a result of the preceding discussion of the integration of ends into a system, we must start from the postulate that neither in the case of the individual nor of the group can we conceive of ultimate ends as an unorganized plurality. No individual exists who does not, to a significant degree, act in terms of such an integrated system. Moreover, the system of each individual must also, to a significant degree, be thought of as integrated with that common to the members of society.

It follows from these considerations that the concept of an "individualistic" economic society, a pure *Tauschgesellschaft,* is a highly unreal abstraction. Action can only be understood as in some way dependent upon and related to such a socially integrated system of ultimate ends. But does not this dispose of the idea that it is possible

19. *Traité de sociologie générale,* 2:1348.

to distinguish an "economic" element of action from rational action in terms of means and ends in general? The whole great utilitarian tradition thought in terms of just such a pure individualistic order. Though nowhere explicitly entering into the question it is quite clear that Robbins's thought is continually slipping into these grooves. But Souter in reacting against this tendency unfortunately is forced to doubt the possibility of such a distinction at all.

While the postulate of action independent of—i.e., *in the absence of*—a framework of socially integrated ultimate ends is unreal and I think very nearly unusable, it does not follow that *within* such a framework certain elements of action cannot usefully be separated out for analytical purposes. The "intermediate" sector of the means-end chain implies the existence of the ultimate ends. But that does not mean that it is not analytically separable from them. In this sense I wish to maintain that economics is logically separable from sociology. A sociology which does not explicitly study the role of ultimate ends in human life is a poor thing indeed. But so long as there is realization of the presence of that factor and of its main characteristics, economics can study certain intermediate phases of action in abstraction from it. It is highly important to realize the fundamental difference of this view from that which postulates as the subject matter of economic theory an abstract "individualistic" society. It involves none of the atomistic assumptions against which Souter rightly protests,[20] but deals with one aspect of an "organic" (if you will) social process.[21]

While the logical subject matter of economics must be held to lie in the "intermediate" sector of the means-end chain, it is not in my opinion expedient for it to attempt to cover the whole of that sector. On the contrary the whole sector seems to fall into three quite well defined subdivisions, each involving progressively wider considerations.

The simplest means-end relationship is that which, given a single unambiguous and definite end, consists in the selection, on the basis of scientific knowledge of the circumstances, of the best adapted means available for its attainment, and the actual process of their application. In a very broad sense this element of action may be called the "technological."[22] At most relations to other persons should be brought in only so far as they do not involve the others' ends,[23] since

---

20. See *Prolegomena*, 5.

21. To be sure one in which the "organic" elements are less conspicuous than elsewhere.

22. This does not imply "physical" or "material" as is so often the case in defining the concept.

23. Thus the relation of a master to his slave is "theoretically" purely technological so long as there is only one purpose for which his use is being considered.

this would necessitate a comparison of ends, which is not technological.

A further complication is introduced when more than one end is thought of as competing for the use of available and scarce means. It is here, of course, that the concept of economy comes in. It is an element additional to that of technological efficiency, which is not concerned with competing uses for the means. It can arise for the individual in isolation: "Crusoe economics" makes sense. But by far the more significant problems arise where the competing ends, or uses for resources, are not merely those of one individual but of a plurality in relation to each other. This introduces the complications of the division of labor and exchange and possibly the organization of the productive units which are naturally fundamental to all economic theory beyond the "Crusoe" stage of analysis.

But before entering upon the implications of these latter facts, it is well to note that the previous discussion excludes the definition of economics as the science of "want-satisfaction" in general. To keep it on the intermediate plane it is necessary to sever it from any direct relation to ultimate ends. Thus a preliminary definition embodying the considerations so far adduced is as follows: "Economics is the science dealing with human action insofar as it may be viewed as a rational process of the acquisition and allocation, as between alternative uses, of scarce means to the satisfaction of wants."

For Crusoe the only means of acquisition is "production," that is, appropriation from nature, change of form and place and distribution in time, by his own initiative and effort. But on the social plane the question arises whether all possible means of acquisition from others, or through the services of others, are to be called "economic." This involves the status of such factors as use or threat of physical violence, some aspects of the use of fraud, and other milder forms of the use of power. All can undoubtedly serve as modes of acquisition of scarce means.

Economists in general have been notably vague on this question, including both Robbins and Souter. But it does seem that a reasonably clear and significant line can be drawn between two great classes of modes of acquisition. In the one case A can acquire what he wants from B by offering in exchange for B's goods or services which he (A) wishes to acquire as a means to his ends, what is from B's point of view a better means of attaining his (B's) ends than would have been available to him without A's action. In other words A's action attains its end by virtue of widening B's otherwise existing range of acceptable choice. This phenomenon may be called, in a strict sense, "economic exchange." It involves in an equally strict sense "mutual advantage."

On the other hand A may get what he wants from B by essentially the opposite method. He may place obstacles in B's way, by attaching to certain of the alternative courses of action otherwise open to B "arbitrary" (that is, not inherent in the action itself apart from what A does) consequences or "sanctions" so unpleasant to B as to outweigh the advantages otherwise existing, and thereby narrow the range of acceptable choice open to B. This may be called the exercise of "coercive power." Its three more important instruments are force, fraud (in certain aspects), and use of strategic position.[24]

The new elements which come into an exchange relationship when coercive power forms an important element, alter the whole situation so profoundly, above all in destroying substantial "equivalence" in exchange, that it does not seem expedient to treat these factors under the same rubric as "economic" exchange. Moreover the use of coercion is by no means confined to exchange relationships. Yet the laws of its operation are essentially the same whether in the (in the commonsense meaning) "economic" field or any other. In my own opinion this should be called a "political" factor. In fact I should define politics, complementary to economics, as "the science dealing with human action insofar as it may be viewed as a rational process of the attainment of ends through the acquisition and exercise of coercive power over other individuals and groups." Thus to the term acquisition in the above definition of economics must be added the qualifying phrases: "by production or economic exchange." [25]

It is a noteworthy fact that, in spite of both the very great intrinsic importance of the question and the large amount of explicit and implicit discussion of it in the literature of economics, neither Robbins nor Souter, when trying to draw the boundary lines of economics, mentions anywhere the question of the role of coercive power. This is surely indicative of a "liberal" bias running through current professional economic discussion. It does so in spite of the glaring facts of the Fascist and Communist movements which, if anything could, ought to be able to awaken people to the importance of coercion in

24. These types both are on the plane of rationality. Nonrational factors such as suggestion fall in still another category.

25. It is to be noted that this differs from Robbins's definition (15) as "the science which studies human behavior as a relationship between ends and scarce means which have alternative uses." This fails to exclude coercive power as a means of acquisition of scarce means. It fails also to distinguish between the "intermediate" and "ultimate" sectors of the means-end chain. It concerns not merely acquisition and allocation of means, but also the processes of "want-satisfaction" themselves, and any other manner in which human ends may be related to scarce means.

social life, and not least in what is popularly called its "economic" sphere. Truly both these writers have failed to consider fully the place of economics in a *society* of the sciences.

Thus the "intermediate means-end relationships" fall into the three subsectors of the "technological," the "economic," and the "political." It remains to discuss briefly the place of sociology before returning to Souter's position in more detail. Three main concepts of the scope of sociology may be said to be current, the "broad encyclopedic," the "narrow encyclopedic," and the "specific." The broad encyclopedic view has been most common in the past. It is that sociology should be a synthesis of all the scientific knowledge we possess concerning man in relation to his fellows. This makes it an *application,* to a particular concrete subject matter, of the theoretical principles of at least all the sciences so far discussed. As a theoretical discipline it would have no principles peculiar to itself.

The "narrow encyclopedic" view differs from the broad one in excluding the factors concerned with the "conditions" of action, but making sociology concern itself with a synthesis of the sciences dealing with "action" proper. The "specific" view, finally, would give to sociology a subject matter essentially its own and not shared by any other systematic theoretical discipline.

Heretofore this last view has been held in methodological self-consciousness only by Simmel and his followers of the so-called formal school. It is impossible here to enter into a critique of their position. While there are certain fundamental objections to it they can be met, and many essential contributions of the school retained, by applying the "specific" view of sociology to the one so far unoccupied sector of our scheme of analysis. Then sociology would become the science of the role of ultimate common ends and the attitudes associated with and underlying them, considered in their various modes of expression in human social life. It is impossible to enter into the implications of this view except in one connection[26] later. But it does, for the present purpose, place sociology, as well as politics and technology, in a definite systematic relation to economics, and completes the general outline of the "society" of the sciences of action.[27]

All this has a series of implications which I shall now proceed to apply to Souter's (and in part Robbins's) views of economics. In the

26. See below for a discussion of its application to the theory of economic institutions.

27. I can merely state here, without attempting to justify it, my view that these exhaust the roster of the systematic, explanatory, theoretical, social sciences. Others such as the "science of law" are of a quite different logical order.

first place what is the kind and degree of abstraction involved in this scheme of the relation of the social sciences? The most cursory glance at concrete reality will show that the complexities of interrelation of the means-end chains are so great, there is so much interweaving with other chains and turning back on themselves, and, moreover, the extent to which the same concrete actions are both ends in themselves and means to other ends is so obvious, that the abstract distinctions we have made cannot possibly delimit *concrete* spheres of real life. However much one element may predominate over others in the concrete facts of any particular action, in principle this must be considered an analysis of the elements in all action, or the aspect[28] of it, not a classification of concrete actions. Economics then must be considered a science concerned with one aspect of all human action—in that sense abstract. It is true that in all societies to some degree and in some, like our own, to a relatively high degree, concrete actions have become differentiated from each other so that there is a large class in which the economic element predominates—such as those roughly designated as "business" today. But even here, as specific studies have shown, it is highly dangerous to assume that the "noneconomic" elements are negligible.

The only alternative to this "aspect" view of the subject matter of economics is that it has for its province just this concrete "department" of social life—men's activities in "business." Souter's opposition to Robbins's in large part inadequate version of the "aspect" view is continually drawing him in this direction, because he succeeds only partially in uncovering the roots of Robbins's difficulties. Perhaps the most striking manifestation of this "empiricist" tendency is his forthright statement that the only precise meaning which can be given to the concept of moving general equilibrium is the actual historical trend.[29] This I take to imply that a theory of moving general economic equilibrium is the complete explanation of the concrete functioning "economy" as a concrete whole. It is, in other words, the complete repudiation of the legitimacy of any abstraction whatever for the purposes of general theory, as against the "one at a time method."

It is only Souter's close adherence to the Marshallian teaching, in sociology as well as in economics, which prevents him from seeing where this position is leading him. I am quite sure he does not see.[30]

28. These may be considered, for present purposes, interchangeable terms.

29. *Prolegomena*, 160.

30. At a good many points Souter vaguely refers to the distinctions between economics and the neighboring sciences, empirically recognizing their existence and justifica-

It leads in fact to something no less terrifying, to an Anglo-Saxon economist, than the radical historical relativism of the more extreme German *Historismus*, represented for instance by Sombart. He is bound to be forced to agree with Sombart that there can be no such thing as a generally applicable economic theory, but only a plurality of theories each applying to a particular historical economic system.

It is characteristic of English and American social thought that, being predominantly positivistic or utilitarian, it has failed to observe or adequately allow for elements of social life which manifest qualitative differences in different times and places. Hence its addiction to the more naive form of the theory of linear social evolution. But it is clear that the factor of ultimate common ends is one which is peculiarly open to much qualitative variation. For it is not capable of complete determination by essentially uniform "conditions" and is hence "hanging in the air." The only escape from such qualitative variation, except on a positivistic or utilitarian basis which eliminates this factor altogether on a priori grounds, is to postulate a metaphysical tendency toward *one* such system of ends to the exclusion of all possible alternatives. This is in essence what Marshall does. The values embodied in his "activities" are for him the absolute goal of the process of social evolution as a whole.[31]

They also happen to be a type of values which fuse readily with certain aspects of the "economic" element instead of, as with some other possible and historically existent systems, coming into conflict with it. To one whose general bias is, like Marshall's, in that direction in any case, this fact causes no particular difficulty. But Souter entirely fails to see that Marshall in dealing with "activities"[32] is thinking on

---

tion. But refusing, as he does, to lay down any principles in terms of which either economics or the others are to be defined, this admission cannot be held to meet the demand for a systematic outline of the society of the sciences of action which the present discussion attempts to supply. It is one thing to admit something exists, and quite another to give a satisfactory account of what it is. See *Prolegomena*, 37, 38.

31. Cf. the writer's article, "Wants and Activities in Marshall," [*Quarterly Journal of Economics* 46 (1931): 101–40].

32. There is only one reference to Marshall's "activities" in Souter's book which only confirms this statement. *Prolegomena*, 55. In my own previous plea for an abstract science of economics ("Economics and Sociology: Marshall in Relation to the Thought of His Time" [chapter 8 of this volume]) I did not adequately see the necessity of relating the economic to the other elements of the means-end chain and hence put forward a view of economics open to some of the objections here advanced against Robbins's position. I certainly shall maintain the essential correctness of my critical analysis of

an entirely different plane from that of his "utility" theory; and this is one of the most striking symptoms of the strong empirical bias of his own thought.

The qualitative variation in history of ultimate value systems is more than a mere a priori deduction. It is one of the fundamental facts of empirical experience, and has come increasingly to be recognized as such. And it is a fact of such overshadowing importance that there is no escape from the conclusion that really consistent empiricism leads inevitably to *Historismus*.[33]

Of course this set of ultimate ends impinges on the economic element most obviously in the concrete structure of the demand pattern of a society. It also impinges in the type of action which attempts directly to put such values into practice and requires scarce resources for that purpose. But for our present discussion the most important point of contact is still another. It should be clear that "economic action" cannot be conceived as taking place in a social vacuum, but that since it involves the exclusion of certain highly useful (from the point of view of the actor) means to acquisition, there must at the very least be some system of control over activities which eliminates or keeps within bounds the use of such means as force, fraud, and strategic position (e.g., monopoly). Beyond this necessary minimum for order in any society, it will be necessary, according to the kind of ultimate values present in such a society, to exercise a further control over economic activities to prevent those values from being impinged upon in various possible ways.[34] This control operates essentially in the form of a set of normative rules, obligatory on the participants (quite different from norms of "efficiency") and governing the whole complex of economic activities of a society. This system of normative rules I should call its economic institutions insofar as they are effectively embodied in actual activities and relationships.[35] Now this implies that economic institutions are in the causal sense a specifically *non*economic factor. But they form at least one fundamental element in accounting for the specific qualitative form of organization of any

---

Marshall but not without some qualifications, the suggested way of escape from his difficulties. Pareto, whose position I used as a model, is also in some respects tarred with the same positivistic brush as Robbins.

33. Outside German thought, where this view is indigenous, it is strikingly attested by Pareto, Durkheim, Sumner, in the "autonomy of the mores," MacIver, in his theory of "culture," and certain important trends of thought among "institutionalist" economists.

34. Cf. Plato's and Aristotle's well-known arguments against excessive wealth on account of its danger to the "good life."

35. The mode of enforcement is irrelevant for the general concept of institution.

particular "economy." It is, in fact, above all the qualitative differences of institutional structure which mark off one "economy" from another. But neither Robbins nor Souter, though both vaguely note their existence,[36] have any clear conception of the relation of institutions to economic activities, nor any systematic place for a theory of institutions in their scheme of the social sciences. In my own opinion it is one of the central elements of sociology. Souter in fact, though he does not explicitly admit it, is continually driven by his empiricist tendency in the direction of the inclusion of institutions as an economic factor in the causal sense.[37]

Since institutions rest essentially on the ultimate value attitudes of a community, insofar as institutional control plays a part in concrete "economic" life, in "business," a sociological element must be considered to be there, beyond the range of economic theory. And the empirical evidence is strongly in favor of a very great importance being attributed to this factor.[38] As it has also been noted above, this is not the only possible "sociological" influence on "economic" life. And furthermore similar reasoning will soon demonstrate that concrete "business" is by no means free from what I would term political,[39] technological, and even the positivistic factors of external environment and man's inherited nature.[40]

36. Cf. Robbins, 92–94, 128.

37. Souter does, to be sure, once refer to "Institutionalism" as "Economic Sociology," but fails to elaborate. The mere statement is not enough. Cf. *Prolegomena*, 85.

38. Cf. Durkheim, *The Division of Labor in Society*, trans. by G. Simpson, New York, 1933.

39. Cf. Veblen's views of "business enterprise," to mention only one case.

40. Though it does not fit directly into the present context I cannot refrain from taking this opportunity to note and protest against Robbins's treatment of the so-called "materialistic interpretation of history" by which he clearly means the Marxian. (See Robbins, 41–44.) Without the slightest attempt at proof or even a single reference to the works of Marx and to only one secondary critical analysis of Marx (Strigl), he roundly asserts without qualification that it is a purely technological interpretation of history and hence deserves the epithet "materialistic," but is in no sense "economic." Apart from the question whether materialistic and technological can be equated, which is highly dubious, there is no warrant either in Marx himself or the secondary sources for this facile assumption. Though some interpreters have held that Marx's view was mainly technological, not even those on the whole hostile to Marx are predominantly of that opinion. (Cf. Bober, *Karl Marx's Interpretation of History*.) It seems clear that in view of the central role of the class struggle Marx did not altogether neglect the factor of coercive power. In fact, in the light of Marx's background in Hegelian philosophy, the most reasonable interpretation seems to be that Marx had in mind the whole of the "intermediate" sector of the means-end chain. (This is the German-Hegelian meaning of "material" as opposed to "ideal.") Thus his conception of "economic" as equal to "material" was too broad rather than too narrow. Robbins presents no evidence of

The logical conclusion of this is that any "empiricist" doctrine of the subject matter of economics, any position which like that of Souter refuses to think in terms of an abstract "aspect" of concrete life, must necessarily end up, from the theoretical point of view, not as a *specific* economic theory but as an encyclopedic sociology in the broad sense. The history of economic thought fully bears out this view. One by one every one of the factors we have discussed has been brought into the forefront of "economic" theory and held to be the key to it.[41] If there is to be *any* theoretical division of labor between the social sciences at all, it must be on the basis of some form of the *aspect* view. This is the dilemma into which Souter will find himself driven if he only follows his position out to a final conclusion.

There is more than a question of scientific expediency involved. Souter, following Marshall and many others, in spite of his "encyclopedic" view of the scope of economics, clings to the traditional "economic" scheme of analysis of supply and demand curves. There is nowhere in his book the suggestion that this general scheme is inadequate to any of the tasks of analysis it is called upon to perform, though he gives some very acute criticism of certain of its previous uses. To a sociologist, however, it is quite clear that institutions, for instance, cannot be analyzed theoretically in terms of supply and demand curves but require an analysis of a totally different kind.[42] It is of course true that institutions, like every other factor in the concrete reality, *affect* the forms of the concrete schedules. But it does not follow that they can be understood in terms of the same analysis. Thus the real result of Souter's empiricism, like Marshall's, is the tendency to attempt to extend "economic" categories to cover the whole of concrete life. This is the objectionable "economic imperialism" of which I spoke above. If pushed far enough it will result in the same kind of harmful lack of perspective of which Marshall was guilty. (He thought of India simply as a "backward country" for instance.) It is a tendency against which the sociologist, as well as other scientists, must stand up and fight for his scientific life.

---

having devoted the careful study to the question, which would be necessary to justify any such sweeping assertion. This facile and plausible way of sliding over difficult, subtle, and controversial questions is unfortunately to be found at a number of points in his book.

41. In an as yet unpublished paper, "Sociological Elements in Economic Thought" [chapter 17 of this volume], I have entered into a full discussion of this point.

42. Essentially because the kind of "quantification" inherent in the scheme is not applicable to institutional structure.

III

Having set forth this central point I now wish to turn to a series of questions a lack of clarity on which, on the part of one or the other of these writers, contributes greatly to the main difficulty. In the first place the failure of Robbins and Souter to attain a satisfactory position is considerably facilitated by the ambiguity of the term "formalism" as used by both. The initial fault seems to lie with Robbins who rather glories in it, and likes to refer to economic theory as a "purely formal science of implications."[43] But as has been shown by much philosophical discussion, and also that over the "formal" school in sociology, the distinction of "form" and "content" is a slippery and dangerous one. For present purposes, however, two different meanings are sufficient to distinguish. Putting the most favorable interpretation on Robbins's use of it, it means nothing more than "abstract." "Form" is what is retained from the concrete for purposes of a particular theoretical analysis; "content" is what is left behind.[44] Souter on the other hand persistently interprets "formal" to mean "having no reference whatever to empirical facts."[45] Mathematics and pure logic are in this sense purely formal sciences.

It is clear, however, that, in spite of his unguarded way of expressing himself, Robbins cannot possibly mean what Souter takes him to mean. Scarcity, which is at the very basis of his discussion, is not a mere "mathematical assumption," but a fact of the real world.[46] Robbins's economics is only formal in the sense that it is interested in the implications of a relatively simple and general set of facts, which represent a relatively high degree of abstraction.[47] But every scientific proposition is formal in this sense. It is the proposition if A then B (as Souter himself remarks). That is merely to state that scientific theory involves the use of logical reasoning. But the difference between an empirical science, and a formal discipline in the strict sense is precisely that A and B are not in the former case mere "assumptions" but refer to real elements in the world of concrete fact.[48] It is only in establish-

43. Robbins, 98, 109. Souter, *Quarterly Journal of Economics*, 379.
44. Robbins, 108–10.
45. Souter, *Quarterly Journal of Economics*, 385, 397.
46. Robbins, 45, 76–77, 96–97.
47. Another motive of Robbins seems to be to call economics formal because it deals with relations rather than intrinsic properties of things. This is a highly relative distinction. See 21, 37.
48. Another way of putting the point is that *all* theory is formal. The formalism of pure logic and manipulation of symbols is only transcended when the question of the factual reference of the symbols is raised.

ing some kind of correspondence between the symbol or concept of the theory and something beyond itself that any theory becomes more than an exercise in logic.

But unless we are to go all the way in an empiricist direction, and repudiate the legitimacy of analytical abstraction to any degree or for any purpose whatever, no general railing against "formalism" is of any use in establishing a science. What kind and degree of abstraction is valid and useful cannot be settled a priori in advance, but only in terms of a knowledge of the problems of the science in question and its bordering sciences. Certain of Robbins's abstractions, for instance that from the existence of a system of ultimate ends, I consider unfruitful. But Souter is in grave danger, with his blanket denunciation of "formalism," of falling into a radical empiricism which would only result in the crippling of science.

In this connection it is worthwhile to point out another line of thought in which I cannot follow Robbins. He is quite clear that economic theory is abstract, and with that view I have no quarrel. But while this abstract economic element is held by him to be subject to necessary law, he seems to imply that the elements from which it is abstracted are outside the realm of law altogether, are completely "adventitious" or "random." [49] Obviously such a view is totally incompatible with the position taken up in this paper. The total concrete reality is to be conceived, not as made up of the area of law (= economic) plus the area of chance (= noneconomic), but as the result of the synthesis of all the different groups of forces concerned. Each of these is subject to laws of its own. To be sure, since political forces cannot be analyzed in terms of economic categories, from the point of view of "economic law," they are in a certain highly relative sense "irrational." But the same is true of economic forces seen from the point of view of "political law," and so on.

Back of this curious view seems to be the assumption already discussed, that the abstractness of economics consists in the assumption of an abstract, "purely economic" society.[50] Then for purposes of economic analysis the other forces are not merely set aside and ignored as variables, they are assumed *not to exist*. Hence anything noneconomic which does exist is totally "irrational"; that is, not subject to law at all.[51] This is the old idea that economic action can be conceived as taking place in a social vacuum. The preceding analysis has at-

49. Robbins, 99.
50. Especially that wants of individuals are distributed and vary at random.
51. Ibid., 98, 111–15.

tempted to show that this view is untenable. True scientific abstraction always consists in making certain factors vary (experimentally or analytically) *independently* of others. The others are excluded from the specific *problem* in hand but are most emphatically not thought of as absent from the concrete situation being studied. That situation is rather inconceivable without the presence of the other forces.[52] The independence of economics is founded not on the separate existence of economic forces, or even actions, but on the fact that the economic elements in action are subject to different causal laws from the other elements—that is, vary independently of them.[53]

One of the reasons why Robbins can fall into this peculiar kind of error, really a particularly insidious variety of that of "misplaced concreteness," is that while on the one hand he is greatly impressed with the rigorous necessity of his economic laws, on the other he must somehow leave room for the freedom of human choice. But his attitude seems to involve a misconception of the nature of "law" as applied to the sciences of action. As already pointed out, its necessity is not descriptive, but "normative." It is not that given certain data men necessarily *must* act in certain ways, but that *if* they would achieve certain kinds of ends which we assume do serve as motives to them, the *most rational* way of doing so is that formulated in the law. The concrete relevance of the law depends on the "fact" of experience that men do *try* to attain such norms of efficiency, of course with varying degrees of success. The necessity of economic law lies in its logic, not in the "facts." There is always an "if" attached to it. There is no reason why the same should not be true of the other elements of action. This "necessitarian" view of economic law seems to be a survival of the older dogmatic positivism[54] which ignored the role of ends in action.

Thus the sciences of action may be viewed on the one hand as con-

52. It follows from these considerations that insofar as the pure "individualistic" order of the laissez-faire economists is conceivable at all, it is to be thought of not as free from any relation to the noneconomic factors, but as only possible in one very particular combination of them. Put somewhat differently it exists not insofar as economic action is free from all "control," but only insofar as it is subject to one particular kind of control. Or, still differently, laissez-faire implies a particular set of economic institutions in the sense already set forth.

53. Such independence must, of course, always be thought of as relative, not absolute.

54. It is well known that many methodologists of the physical sciences have become sceptical of the ironbound necessity of physical law. For our purpose it is unnecessary to inquire whether the basis of their scepticism is the same as ours. But *we* must certainly throw off the older materialistic metaphysics.

cerned with a study of the conditions of the situation in which choices are made—insofar as they are relevant to the choices—on the other of the consequences of choices once made. But since the *standards* in terms of which they are made must be assumed, rather than proved necessary, there is no warrant that any particular course of action must be considered absolutely necessary.[55] Only in two cases is this true: when the conditions are so narrowly limited that only one course of action is objectively possible, and when (on psychological or other grounds) only one end is conceivable. But these are limiting cases, not type cases, and we must not elevate them into norms for our sciences. In the sciences of action the "if" becomes of very particular importance as the hiding place for the freedom of human volition.[56]

One of the issues on which Souter most vigorously attacks Robbins is that of the precision of economic theory. While I cannot pretend to enter into a thorough discussion of the point here, one or two remarks may be made which fit into the present argument. Of course one of the major aims of all science is precise formulation of its theory. But exactly insofar as a given body of theory is abstract, no matter how precise a formulation of its theoretical propositions may be, it cannot be a precise description of the concrete reality. Theoretical precision must be carefully distinguished from empirical precision.

Souter very acutely demonstrates that except under certain very specific assumed conditions,[57] namely those of stationary general equilibrium, the whole system of an economy in all its interrelations cannot be formulated with perfect precision. For the processes of adjustment to a change in the data occurring within the system will in turn result in an alteration of the data, resulting in an imprecise picture. But in this whole argument Souter is speaking on the empirical plane. Any given *concrete* system of curves will, except under very specific con-

---

55. A further element of determination arises from the fact that once choices are made the actions following from them become part of the conditions of further action by the same individual, and by others. While from the point of view of the *general* analysis of the elements of action only nonhuman environment and human nature form true "conditions," from the point of view of any individual acting in a *social* environment the actions of others are perhaps the most important conditions of all. In economic analysis, of course, this element is central. Once the choices are all made their consequences follow with rigorous necessity; but that does not eliminate the element of choice at one crucial stage. These considerations should be kept in mind all through this essay.

56. Here again we see how confusing the inclusion of both "ends" and "conditions" of action without distinction in the one blanket category of "given data" can be.

57. As he quite correctly states: "The quest of precision leads inevitably to the whole." *Prolegomena*, 78. See also 77, 83.

ditions, be incapable of precise formulation in purely economic terms precisely because the economic element, while on the one hand dependent on certain noneconomic conditions, is at the same time a factor in the total situation, and hence in turn influences the conditions. The area of imprecision in the formulation of an empirical system of curves in economic terms is just that in which the concrete facts are determined by the interaction between economic and noneconomic factors. From a wider point of view such as to include both it would disappear. This imprecision is a difficulty which is bound to arise whenever the attempt is made to interpret empirical data entirely in terms of an abstract theory.

An opening is given for Souter's remarks on this issue by the fact that Robbins himself does not really make this fundamental distinction between theoretical and empirical precision. His conception of economics as the science of an abstract type of society is, as has been shown, not true abstraction but a pseudo-empiricism. He also is talking about empirical curves, even though they be hypothetical. His system is not really a theoretical system but a hypothetical concrete system. On these assumptions, of course, it can be precisely formulated as a closed system. But Souter is equally entitled to ask whether any empirical system of curves is likely to meet these hypothetical conditions and to reply in the negative.[58] The whole argument is really on the empirical plane. I submit that the position here taken avoids the difficulty.

Our final issue may be briefly discussed in conclusion—that of the relation of dynamics to economic theory. Souter makes a great deal in his criticism of the static aspect of "static formalism." Insofar as this implies the conception of a system of instantaneous curves eliminating the element of time altogether the criticism is wholly justified. We must accept Souter's correction that only the long-period curve is truly static and that a system as a whole can only be conceived as static in terms of a *period* long enough to permit the whole system to adjust to a change in the data.[59] But this does not touch the deeper question of economic dynamics—whether all economic changes are "adjustments" to changes in the "data" of economic action—its ends or conditions—or whether there are purely economic causes of dynamic change.

From the position here taken I think it is quite clear that from the pure concept of "economy," that is on the Crusoe level of analysis, no

58. See, for instance, ibid., 72.
59. Ibid., 69.

dynamics can be derived. For given Crusoe's scale of valuations and given the nature and quantity of resources available to him, there is only one truly "economic" solution of his problem and so far as he acts rationally he will always be approaching this solution. Any change in the *direction* of his activities could only be due to a change in the data.

But still, on the purely economic theoretical plane, there is room for possible dynamic elements in the interrelations of the actions of a plurality of economizing individuals connected by markets and a monetary mechanism. Certain changes for instance in the monetary mechanism, or in the production of durable goods in anticipation of demand, appear to function not merely as adjustments to changed data, but to be subject to cumulative changes in certain directions. Whether these changes would eventually stop, whether they go on indefinitely or are cyclical and hence from the point of view of a long enough period in a sense static, I do not attempt to decide. All I wish to do is to point out that it is only in the field of changes of this order that purely economic causes of change in the concrete economy are to be looked for. Of course even such changes would only occur in certain specific combinations of the noneconomic factors, such as that of "laissez-faire individualism." But, given this combination, the *causes of the changes* would be purely economic.

This order of dynamic factor, whether it actually exists or not, must be clearly distinguished from another—those changes in the concrete economy due to the interaction of the economic with the noneconomic factors.[60] Considering the concrete importance of these noneconomic factors in any given empirical economy it is likely that the most important causes of its changes are of this order. This is certainly the type with which Souter is most concerned. He repeatedly points out the ways in which internal adjustments of an economic system will react on the data of the system. Unfortunately, with his empiricist bias, he fails to distinguish the two kinds of dynamic causes, implying that both are "economic dynamics" in the same sense. His "expanding economic universe," if it exists, expands only in part from purely economic causes; mainly, it is probable, from the interaction of economic with other causes.[61] The importance of this kind of factor is precisely

60. Of course to complete the classification we must include those factors of change in the concrete economy consisting of one-way action *upon* the economic by the noneconomic element. This type is of no theoretical interest in the present context.

61. As an example of Souter's tendency to fail to make this distinction note the following: "The progressive development of economic theory *is* that of the *inter*relations of economics with its fellows" (in the corpus of the sciences). Ibid., 63. See also 130.

a measure of the indissoluble unity of man's social life, and of course of the futility of Robbins's assumption of a purely economic society. Economic theory alone can only partially solve such problems.[62]

To summarize the main argument of this paper. The aim has not been to criticize the work of either Robbins or Souter in detail, but rather to discuss in general terms some of the central methodological questions about which their thought revolves. My central thesis is that the two are caught in a false dilemma. In order to avoid the difficulties of Robbins's "atomistic, exclusionist positivism" it is not necessary, as Souter tends to think, to abandon the attempt to draw any methodological boundaries between economics and its neighboring sciences altogether, in favor of a radical empiricism. What is needed is not the abandonment of this attempt, but rather its prosecution on a more highly critical plane.

The initial trouble is that Robbins puts the case for a logically independent science of economics badly. In his eagerness to remain "positive" in the sense of the natural sciences, he fails to clarify the implications of attempting to center his economics on the conception of rational action in terms of the relation of means and ends. He is thus continually forced in the direction of what I have called the radical positivistic position, which results in the elimination of ends as a real factor in action altogether. This appears on one plane in his tendency to think of behavior as a resultant of "conflicting psychological pulls." Essentially the same "atomistic" tendency on the social level forces him to ignore the integration of ends of individuals in a social system, and to think of the economic activities of a society as merely the resultant of the independent activities of individuals in pursuit of their private ends.

But this failure to place the economic element of action in relation to other parts of the means-end chain presses him to think of economic action as concretely existent by itself in an environment of random "data." This forces Robbins continually to think of the subject matter of economics not as an abstract element of action, but as a hypothetical concrete purely economic society. But such a society is unreal in a far more radical sense than as an abstracted element, for it assumes the other elements not merely as constant, but as nonexistent. This abstract society has a continual tendency to become a norm of practical policy.[63] Souter clearly sees most of these weaknesses in

62. Very many business cycle theories, especially those of Marxian origin, invoke various such elements. The Marxian type, dwelling as it does on the implications of the class struggle, may be called mainly a politicoeconomic theory.

63. See Souter, *Quarterly Journal of Economics,* 400.

Robbins's position, though rather empirically than in terms of such a systematic scheme of the elements in action as has been essayed above. But in trying to avoid them he reacts in a manner not novel—indeed frequent among previous critics of views like those of Robbins. He moves in the direction of an empiricism which, if followed through to its logical conclusion, would altogether eliminate systematic abstraction from the social sciences. The essential subject matter of his economic theory becomes the whole concrete "economy." While vaguely recognizing that other social factors than the economic exist, his failure to present a systematic account of their relation to the economic element—rather worse, his definite refusal to admit the legitimacy of such an attempt[64]—results in a confusion of categories. The main manifestation of it is the attempt to draw into his economics problems which are beyond the scope of such a narrow analytical apparatus. Some modification of the apparatus is indeed indicated, signalized by such catchwords as "organic," "biological," and "dynamic." But its central element, never questioned, remains the analysis in terms of supply and demand schedules, so that the net result of this empiricism is, as it was with Marshall, an unfortunate "economic imperialism" which insofar as it does not merely blur distinctions, imposes economic categories on elements, which, like institutions, are quite unsuited to their use.

Finally, I suggest that all Souter's essential criticisms of the "neo-Austrian" position can be met successfully, and the advantages of a clear-cut division of theoretical labor in the social sciences still be maintained, if the analysis is based on a systematic scheme of the elements of rational action, a bare outline of which has been presented here. Both Robbins's positivism and Souter's rather vaguely "organic" empiricism are obstacles to clarity on the basic problems.

64. *Prolegomena,* 61, 134. When Souter protests that the "notion of *completely* independent technological, political or social change is inherently illogical," he seems clearly to misunderstand the nature of scientific abstraction. There is never any question of complete, but only of relative, abstraction. In attacking a "*completely*" independent economics he is knocking over a straw man.

17

Sociological Elements in
Economic Thought

Part 1: Historical

The methodological battle between "orthodox" forms of economics and "institutionalist" or other unorthodox forms has been raging now for a good many years without much sign of a peace. The contestants are so deeply absorbed in pressing their own case that perhaps they do not often stop to try and see the issues in the perspective of the history of social thought. The present study is an attempt to appraise the question of the status of "orthodox" economic theory in terms of the history of economic thought since roughly the beginning of the nineteenth century. Taking what may be called the orthodox tradition as its starting point, it will attempt to trace some of the principal elements which have modified it, which have been put forward under the rubric of economic theory in the course of the last century, trying above all to determine their logical relations to the initial orthodox core. In the second part of the study, the attempt will be made to raise explicitly the question of the scope of economic theory in relation to the other social sciences. On the basis of the historical perspective furnished by the first part it will perhaps be possible to see the essential issues and the logical consequences of taking one or other of the alternatives open more clearly than has sometimes been the case.

As a preliminary it is necessary to sketch the general logical framework which may be called "orthodox economic theory" in order to have a scheme of analysis in terms of which to approach actual concrete theories. Direct discussion of the status of the other modifying elements will be postponed till the second part of the study. Any such scheme of analysis is necessarily a product of a rather highly sophisticated phase in the development of a science. The earlier phases are almost always concerned directly with the understanding of pressing concrete, though not necessarily practical, problems which are at-

Originally published in the *Quarterly Journal of Economics* 49 (1935): 414–53, 646–67. Reprinted by permission of John Wiley and Sons, Inc.

tacked in whatever way at the time promises results, without bothering very much about the exact logical nature of the procedures involved or the relation of various possible approaches to each other. The social sciences have now, however, reached a stage where such careful logical discrimination has become imperative and is in process of realization.

I

It is only in retrospect that we can see just what sort of a science the founders of economics were building up. There can, I think, be little doubt as to what is the main trend of development of economic thought. It is that which has rightly been called orthodox and which, whatever its variations at different stages of development, has certain definite elements of continuity throughout. It may be said to be the general tradition which, starting, for "modern" purposes, with Adam Smith, develops through the classical school, whose most important figures were Ricardo and Mill, down to the marginal utility economics and Marshall. The variations, especially in the later phases, between marginal utility theories, specific productivity theories, and mathematical equilibrium theories, are too numerous and complex to be entered into here. Fortunately they may all be regarded as family quarrels, too minor to be of real significance for the purposes of the present study.

What are the distinguishing principles of this orthodox economic thought? The question can, I think, best be answered with reference to its later rather than its earlier forms, since matters of principle come to be thoroughly worked out and clearly formulated only after the difficulties and ambiguities of earlier rough formulations have come to light. Since this essay is concerned with types of thought it is essential to achieve as clear-cut a formulation of the "ideal type" "orthodox economic theory" as possible.[1]

The central conception, perhaps, is that the science of economics is concerned primarily with the study of the processes by which individuals, living in society, secure the means for the satisfaction of their individual wants. In the abstract situation selected out of the complex whole of social life for special study by economics, there are, perhaps,

1. For the present purposes we are concerned with economic theory only in its aspect as a systematic *explanatory* theory of empirical phenomena. Other aspects of the same body of concepts, as for instance as a possible guide to public policy, are beyond the scope of this paper.

three main groups of elements. In the first place there are the wants of the individuals, or groups which may be taken as units for economic purposes, making up the society. While it is logically quite possible to enter into a very complex investigation in order to explain the nature and existence of the wants which in the last analysis motivate acquisitive activities, leading into sociology, psychology, biology, and what not, it may be safely said that orthodox economics assumes the wants as given data which the economist at most simplifies into relatively general types. Their explanation is left to other sciences. The quantitative measure of want-satisfaction on which most orthodox economists have agreed is utility. Thus it may be laid down as a fundamental proposition that the economic element of action is directed to the maximization of want-satisfaction or utility.

Secondly, the means required for want-satisfaction are not given in unlimited quantity, but must be acquired through a complex process: production. The productive process requires the ultimate expenditure and allocation between alternative uses of the economic resources of the community, which fall into the three great categories of natural resources, labor, and the ability to save. It is through the various combinations of these resources that satisfactions, utilities, are produced; and the production always involves cost, expenditure.

Finally, economics makes a definite assumption about the type of human behavior involved in the whole process—namely that it is, in limiting type, rational in the limited sense that, given the "end," maximization of utility through acquisition of the largest possible quantity of means to want-satisfaction compatible with the limitations of "cost," the adaptation of means to this end tends to be the best possible under the circumstances.[2] The end may thus, in the given circumstances, be held to determine the course of action. This rationality will hold equally of the individual's distribution of his income between his different wants, and of the processes by which he acquires his income.

While these essential elements will hold for an isolated individual, such a case has no more than an academic interest. The fact of a plurality of individuals living together in a society introduces the further complications of the division of labor and exchange. With these conditions and a general medium of exchange, money, the immediate end of individual economic action becomes predominantly the acquisition

2. For some of the reasons why this must be considered an ideal type and not a concrete description see Knight, "Relation of Utility to Economic Method," in *Methods of Social Science,* ed. S. A. Rice. The present sketch can in the nature of the case be only very rough. Really precise statement would call for much greater elaboration. It will, however, suffice for present purposes.

of money, and this fact makes a quantitative treatment of economic problems enormously easier. Economics is, in fact, the only social science which enjoys the advantage of an automatic quantification of its subject matter. The boon is not unspoiled, however, since the translation of money quantities into utility terms is not an easy matter.

Given the acquisition of means of want-satisfaction as the aim of economic action, there are three logical limiting types of sets of conditions under which the action can take place.[3] One, generally called competition, is where each individual works to satisfy his own wants under a given set of market and production conditions which he is unable to alter deliberately. The second, monopoly, is where there is more or less possibility of altering the conditions. The third, collectivism, is where the whole society is deliberately organized and centrally controlled for the acquisition of means. Historically, for important reasons, competition has been much the most-used assumption in developing economic theory. Only relatively recently has much attention been devoted to the theory of the other cases.

The existence of a complex system of division of labor and exchange and of a generally recognized medium of exchange creates certain possibilities of complication. The immediate "economic" motive of each individual may become the maximization of his money income. And what is from the point of view of the community as a whole and thus of the individuals in it taken together the "real" end of economic activity, the production of goods and services, becomes from the point of view of each individual a means, and money the immediate end. Thus the economic system as a whole may be looked at from two angles, one as an "earning" process, the other as a "producing" process. The coordination of the two becomes a major issue.

Theoretically perfect coordination is possible under certain very rigidly defined sets of conditions—those of the theorem of maximum satisfaction which is generally formulated subject to existing distribution of ownership. Perhaps the most important of these is that "purchasing power" should be power only over goods and services for consumption, not power over persons which is by its inherent nature cumulative. The line is a very difficult one to draw in concrete reality. In general the lack of coordination will be empirically as important as the extent of its existence.

Furthermore the very fact of the division of labor introduces a further complication. In the theory of competitive individualism every case of cooperation for a common end is insofar an element of mo-

3. See Pareto, *Manuel d'économie politique*, chap. 3, sec. 40ff.

nopoly, a disturbing factor. It is, except for the extent to which the family, not the individual, is the real unit of consumption, possible to eliminate this factor very largely on the "earning" side. But on the "producing" side organization may well be a fact of dominant importance. This was not true, of course, of the earlier formulations of the theory, which thought of exchange as the only "social" process while production was individual and solitary. But the facts of a changing society have forced a reconsideration in terms of a productive unit which itself is a complex organization of cooperating individuals. The polar antithesis of Locke's solitary Indian killing a deer is the modern giant corporation. It is quite possible that a whole series of such organization types of the unit of economic enterprise might each be taken as a basic assumption for purposes of theoretical reasoning. Marx, following up suggestions in Malthus and Ricardo, was perhaps the first to attempt to build a theoretical structure on the assumption of an organized producing unit.

The theories developed on this basis may, in certain ways, serve not merely as explanatory principles, but as norms of economic efficiency. Since the type case which economic theory makes use of is that of the norm of rationality in the adaptation of means, under given conditions, to given ends, thought of in practical terms, the theory expresses the best possible utilization of the given resources to satisfy the given wants. This aspect of the theory has, for the case of competition, been formulated particularly in terms of the doctrine of maximum satisfaction, which, under the assumptions of rationality, independence of wants from the processes of their satisfaction, and mobility of resources, states that the pursuit by each individual of his own interests in competitive production will result in the maximum of want-satisfaction for all the individuals in the society.

The leading elements studied by orthodox economics thus formulated form an abstract "ideal type." On this basis a theory has partly been developed, partly awaits elaboration, which by itself says nothing as to the concrete relevance of the assumptions on which it is based. The problems of the relation of economics and the other social sciences and the various possible concepts of the scope of economics arise out of investigation into the concrete significance of these assumptions and the relation of the factors specifically dealt with in this theory to the others which may be held to play a part in social life and which may or may not be dealt with by other sciences.

II

We shall make use of a double classification of the possible ways in which this "ideal type" of economic theory may be related to the concrete reality. The first distinction involves the general conception of science entertained by the writers concerned. On the one hand they may adopt an "empiricist" view, that any science, or at least economics, has the task of delivering a full and complete explanatory account of a given sector of concrete reality. In terms of this attitude two basic alternatives are possible: Either the principles of economic theory as above outlined are directly, without essential qualification for other factors, applicable to concrete "economic activities," to "business," in which case the orthodox theory will be held to be satisfactory by itself, or they are not so applicable. In this latter case, two further alternatives are open—they must be supplemented by other elements, still dealt with within the framework of economic science, or, in the more radical view, they are definitely wrong and economics must build anew from the start. If any departure from the "narrow orthodoxy" sketched above be held to be a "sociological element" [4] then the earlier theories introducing such elements have employed mainly the supplementary method; a root and branch criticism of the whole thing and a tendency to throw it all out is relatively recent. The great bulk of "unorthodox" movements have belonged in this general "empiricist" category.

On the other hand, one may take a view of a science that its specific subject matter is not concrete phenomena as such, but a logically defined abstract element or set of *elements in* the concrete. If this position be adopted, criticism of the direct concrete applicability of economic principles ceases to be so disturbing. Divergences may be explained as due to other factors—and the corrective is no longer necessarily alone the remodeling of economic theory to take account of them but rather the synthesis of its results with those of other sciences in the final full explanation of the concrete. The latter is a path explicitly and consciously taken only in relatively recent times—some outstanding examples of it will be discussed in the second part of the study. Its path consists not so much in emphasizing sociological or other elements within economics, as in working out a sociological supplement to an avowedly abstract economics. In certain respects this has formed one of the most important trends of recent sociologi-

---

4. Whether this view is justified will be discussed in the second part of the study.

cal thought which, to a very important degree, has been determined by this means of defining its relation to economics.[5]

The other main line of distinction of theories will concern the character of the elements invoked to supplement or replace, as the case may be, the central element of rational economic action. This, like all "action" (as distinct from "behavior" in the technical behaviorist sense), is and must be analyzed in terms of some form of the schema of the relation of means and ends. The peculiarity of "economic" action is its situation in an intermediate position in the great chain of means and ends, where its "ends" are by definition only means to other ends of a more ultimate nature. The ultimate ends motivating the action, as well as the main facts of the situation, the "conditions" of the action, are taken for granted as data. Looking at the thing, as this schema does, from the "subjective" point of view, i.e., that of the individual acting, the supplementing of the "economic" element can take place in two directions. One or other or both of these sets of data can be turned into problems and their explanation made an obligation of the economic theorist.

Historically, in the tradition of Anglo-Saxon economics, by far the greater part of the unorthodox movements have concentrated their attention on the "conditions," rather than the "ends." In this manner attention is thrown to such factors as the external environment, the ultimate source of natural resources, population and the laws of its growth, scientific knowledge and its resultant technology, or finally the "social environment"[6] consisting above all of forms of business organization. Since the bulk of these thinkers are empiricists in the above sense their treatment must also be accompanied by some positive means of eliminating the element of ends from consideration. For this purpose various psychological assumptions like hedonism, the instinct of acquisition or other constant instincts or, finally, a "habitual" standard of living have proved most serviceable. Marshall was, to my knowledge, the first English economist explicitly to make "wants" a variable category, an innovation the implications of which certainly led farther than he realized.

From the formal point of view of the logical structure of scientific theory, the empirical "supplement" to abstract economics consists

5. The present part of the study will be concerned with theories on the empiricist basis. The second part will take up the alternative of an *abstract* economic theory in relation to other abstract social sciences.

6. The methodological status of this element raises important problems. They will be discussed in the second part of the study.

merely in narrowing the range of the "data" accepted without inquiry by economics, and a corresponding widening of the range of "problems" included within its scope.

Given, as any empiricism of the above type must assume, the constancy (for scientific purposes at least) of the ultimate ends of action, it is inevitable that there should be a general tendency to measure means in terms of the degree to which they realize these ultimate ends. Hence a continual bias toward a linear evolutionary view of the process of "economic" development, laying stress, as the case may be, on biological selection, accumulation of scientific knowledge and resulting technological improvement, or better adaptation of social organization, i.e., its becoming more "economic." To account for a long period of time in achieving a relatively high degree of such adaptation it is convenient to invoke retarding influences, so that the process may be conceived as one of emancipation from them. "Ignorance" and "custom" are by far the most pervasive of these, though others such as Veblen's "anthropomorphism" and "predation" may also enter.

But in the face of this logical situation it is natural to suspect that the appearance of *qualitative* rather than quantitative differences between economic epochs and systems indicates the presence of elements of a different sort, even if they are arrayed in a single irreversible temporal order. There is one great body of economic "empiricism" in which this insistence on qualitative differences is most conspicuous: the German historical school. It is in fact the antithesis to the Anglo-Saxon "positivistic" empiricism. It either assumes as constant, or tends to ignore or minimize, such factors as external environment, even science and technology, as well as man's bio-psychological equipment. The emphasis on the other hand is on the specific totality of a "culture" and above all on the integration of its economic organization and activities with its religious and ethical values, or more vaguely its "Geist" or spirit.

The difference made by the abstract as opposed to the empirical view of economic science is that the "ends" and "conditions" of action, instead of modifying or replacing the "economic" element, are held to supplement it in a wider synthetic view. On the one hand economics is held to be abstract because it neglects the "conditions" of economic action, on the other because it neglects the specific nature of its ultimate ends.

Finally, criticism may attack the economic conception of the process of economic action itself. This attack has from the positivistic side centered above all on the rational element. In its extreme form positivistic anti-intellectualism has held the rational element in any action to be either nonexistent or negligible. To find a substitute for the logical role of rational action the positivist is driven in the first instance to some form of anti-intellectualist psychology, usually in instinct or behaviorist form, and ultimately to a biological explanation of this in turn. This path has above all been taken by the school of empiricists who have argued first that all economics is dependent on psychological assumptions; second, that the older economics was eventually an application of hedonistic psychology; and third, that modern psychology has disposed of hedonism.

The "historical" opposition on the other hand has attacked not so much the conception of rational action itself in its broader sense but rather its specific economic form as dominated by "calculation of advantage." As against this it has urged the individual's incorporation in the larger groups and his subordination to superindividual ends.

The theories to be taken up explicitly in the remainder of this study will be chosen with a view not to encyclopedic completeness, but rather to illustrate each of the principal logical possibilities inherent in the situation just sketched. Omission of particular names does not indicate an adverse judgment on the thinker "slighted" but rather limitations, on the one hand of space, on the other of the writer's interest in and knowledge of particular theories. Obviously a complete discussion would require an extended treatise rather than a moderate essay.

III

The simplest position of course is that which takes the ideal type of "economic" action and relationships and maintains its direct and unqualified applicability to concrete "economic" phenomena. This position may be called "empirical orthodoxy" as opposed to the "abstract orthodoxy" of Pareto for instance. It involves one of two assumptions. The less radical is that there is a concrete "sphere" of activities, a "department" of social life in which these abstractly defined relationships are substantially true in concrete fact. The more radical is the generalization of this view to include not merely the one "department" but virtually (or in limiting type, absolutely) all of social life. This latter makes economic theory the central element in, if not the whole of, a system of general social theory; in perhaps the strictest sense of the expression it is the "economic interpretation of history."

In fact such a view, wavering as between the less and the more radical of the above assumptions, has played a very great part in the

history of economic thought. In general the tendency has been to con-
centrate on the analysis of a limited sector of concrete relationships—
those roughly of market value, price, and the distribution of wealth—
with a certain indefiniteness as to how far it was legitimate to push
the analysis out into the peripheral questions of factors impinging
upon but not so directly involved in these relationships. This is substantially true of that element of the utilitarian tradition which, following Locke and Adam Smith, rested on some form of the postulate
of the "natural identity of interest." [7] It is at least one main strain in
the "classical" economics and the later thought of Jevons and Marshall.

Historically the theory was arrived at mainly by considering how
the harmony of a beneficent state of nature could be translated into
the conditions of a society characterized by the division of labor and
exchange. The fundamental concept is that of the quantitative equivalence of exchange relations so that it can still be said that in a "virtual" sense every individual receives in exchange only the product of
his own labor. The absence, on the one hand, of the concept of marginal utility and hence the emphasis on a "real" cost of production
theory of value, the derivation, on the other, from the conception of a
nonsocial state of nature, where the productive functions of land, capital, and business management are not in evidence, led to the main
peculiarities of the classical system centering about the role of labor
in production and value. The internal logical difficulties growing out
of this situation can be said to have been substantially overcome in
the later marginal utility and opportunity cost theory, so that the
theory of a competitive economic order expressed in the propositions
involved in the modern doctrine of maximum satisfaction constitutes
the most sophisticated and logically satisfactory formulation of economic theory in this sense. Insofar as this theory has been held to be
substantially true of any considerable section of concrete reality, "orthodox empiricism" has existed.

Analysis of the logical conditions necessary for the formulation of
such a theoretical system, however, soon reveals the necessity for the
existence of a very definite set of corresponding concrete conditions
for the working of the real system. If then the theoretical analysis is
to apply directly to the concrete reality these conditions must be
proved to exist and be accounted for. This above all involves the fac-

7. Cf. E. Halévy, *La formation du radicalisme philosophique*, 3 vols. This is incom-
parably the most extensive and penetrating analysis of the interrelated currents of English social and economic "individualism" in the late eighteenth and early nineteenth
centuries.

tual conformity of the competitive process to rules which prevent its divergence from the assumed end. It is not difficult to show that the use of either physical violence or deception as means of attaining "economic" ends, on the one hand, or of economic resources and strategic position in economic relations as instruments of power over others, on the other, will upset the conditions for the working of such a system. How then is their absence accounted for?

The simplest and least convincing solution is simply to assume that they are in some sense contrary to the nature of things, or a variant of the same view, that the enlightenment of self-interest will cause each individual to see that his own interest is so bound up with that of the system as a whole that it does not "pay" to do anything detrimental to the latter. Among other things this would involve the assumption that the length of time entering into the calculations of one's own "long-run" interests so far transcended the span of a single human life as to become essentially meaningless. It is difficult to see how acts the benefit of which will accrue to posterity of only the fourth or fifth generation can be construed as motivated by self-interest. The general social theory underlying this view is of course anarchism, and strictly speaking the theory of a system of "pure" economic individualism operating without control by any other agency is a form of anarchism.

But relatively few economists have been so "tender-minded" as to believe seriously in its possibility. On the "periphery" has almost always been found a noneconomic controlling agency. The most pervasive of course has been the state whose "minimum" functions—external defense, maintenance of internal order and enforcement of contracts (now almost all economists would add provision of a monetary standard)—have very generally been held to be necessary. In general the "laissez-faire" economists' objection has not been to the state having anything to do with the economic system, but to its doing the wrong things. This view of the necessity of the state may be said to be common ground for all economists except the extreme anarchistic wing.

In addition to this, various other regulatory mechanisms have made their appearance from time to time. Besides those to be discussed specifically later, two may be mentioned here: Adam Smith's "moral sentiment," and that vague but nonetheless important factor invoked by Ricardo to fill in some of the gaps left open by his economic analysis, the "habits and customs of the people." [8]

By and large though, while such factors as this have served to fill

8. Cf. *Principles of Political Economy*, Everyman edition, 55.

the chinks along the outside walls of economic science, they have not been made the subject of systematic analysis, as distinct from more or less casual citation, by economists themselves, and above all have not been built into the body of economic theory—Adam Smith's "moral sentiments," for instance, were dealt with in a separate work and not as part of the *Wealth of Nations*. The first major change in this situation which deeply shook the optimistic laissez-faire individualism of the late eighteenth and early nineteenth centuries came in with the doctrines of Malthus, which gave new turns to thought in at least three different directions.

The "pure type" of economic theory is after all pretty narrowly defined—it may be compared to the crest of a narrow knifelike ridge. Once having made a step off it on either side it is by no means easy to stop, for the empiricist, at least. And it is all the more difficult to avoid making such a step to one side when one is primarily preoccupied with avoiding a step down the other. This in essence is what happened to Malthus. He fully realized the indistinctness of the boundary between the laissez-faire doctrines of his time and anarchism. The latter in the form of Mr. Godwin's *Political Justice* he was above all concerned to combat. But to exorcise an evil spirit it is sometimes necessary to call in the devil himself. Malthus in fact slipped over heavily down the opposite slope into three main lines of thought, all of dubiously "economic" parentage.

The devil in this case was, of course, the "principle of population," in essence the view that the main lines of our social situation are determined by the (nearly) uncontrollable propensities of "human nature" on the one hand, the unalterable niggardliness of an unkind physical nature in the form of diminishing returns on the other. This is the first major beginning of the linking of economics with biological theories of survival, a trend which will be entered into more at length below.

But this devil also has offspring who are not to be ignored. As Malthus says to Godwin, imagining his anarchistic idyl once realized, the growth of population would soon lead, as the only alternative to chaos and general starvation, to the spontaneous reestablishment of the institutions of property and marriage and the division of society into classes of employers and laborers.

The first two items form perhaps the first appearance in economic thought of an independent role of social institutions as regulators of economic life—in this case with specific reference to the growth of population. As distinct from the more usual position these institutions are not for Malthus "instituted" by the state, but arise spontaneously in the processes of social life itself. The state merely sanctions them. This independence is the new note. It is true that Malthus shared the view of his contemporaries that the pursuit by each individual of his own self-interest was beneficial to the whole—in fact it was the *vis mediatrix rei publicae*, the very life principle. Ill-advised interference with it, as in Pitt's poor law, could only have disastrous consequences. But this was true only *within* the framework of institutional control. Without such control it is quite safe to assume that for Malthus, as for Hobbes, self-interest could only lead to social chaos, a *bellum omnium contra omnes*.

But the further development of the independent role of institutions as a regulator of economic activities belongs to a much later date in the history of social theories. The thing of by far the most important immediate influence was the third consequence of the principle of population, the division of society into classes. The original starting point of individualistic economics, the conception of a state of nature, had no place for a division into classes. All men were by nature equal. And this natural equality was carried over into the division of labor as necessary to preserve equivalence in exchange. The only differences were those due to the greater "quantity of labor" performed by one man as compared with another. The typical division of labor thought of was where each man produced and exchanged the products of his own labor, the deer and beaver of Adam Smith's and Ricardo's examples.[9] But for Malthus the pressure of population drove the division of labor farther, to the splitting up of processes within the same productive unit and a division between those supervising and those carrying out the process.

Malthus was so concerned with the greater productivity of this more minute division of labor as a means of supporting population that he did not draw the crucial theoretical consequences of the fact that the division into classes meant an inherent and cumulative inequality between the classes, both as to wealth and, more important, as to economic power. The basis of this inequality had been clearly seen by Adam Smith in his analysis of the conditions of the labor contract,[10] but not used for theoretical purposes. Ricardo went a step farther in his statements about the precariousness of the standard of living and the greater likelihood of its being lowered than raised.[11] But for Ricardo the "capitalist" was primarily the one who supported la-

9. *Wealth of Nations*, 41; *Principles of Political Economy*, 6, 15, 16.
10. *Wealth of Nations*, 58.
11. *Principles of Political Economy*, 75.

borers, and who took the residual share of the income. So in spite of the clear-cut conflict of the interests of the classes in his theory of distribution the *differences* of power with their implications for the stability of the competitive system were not prominent in his thought. It was Marx who took the decisive step in this direction. Assuming the organized capitalistic enterprise as the unit of his system, he laid the principal stress on its control by the owner-manager, particularly through his ownership, and the resultant cumulative process of "exploitation" of labor leading finally to the overturn of the whole structure.[12] Thus the introduction of this power element within the economic system and its crystallization, by virtue of the advanced division of labor and the resulting structure of the organized productive unit, about the division into classes, led to a basic reconstruction of economic theory itself. A very great amount of subsequent economic discussion, particularly "unorthodox" theories of the business cycle, goes back ultimately to differences over this point.[13]

Whether the power element and the class difference are or are not "economic" factors cannot be said to be agreed today. What is popularly called the "economic interpretation of history," being of Marxian origin, naturally includes them. It can be said to shade off into the narrower version referred to above by imperceptible degrees. A great deal of misunderstanding in discussion would be avoided if people would make their position on this point clear in their arguments.

The introduction of the power element through Malthus led to an internal reorganization of economic theory. We have now to note two movements which while leaving the theory intact (in either of the above versions) have attempted to give it a more secure underpinning and a more certain and extensive concrete application by supplementing it with certain theories not inherently logically implied in it, nor involved in its internal structure. The first movement is psychological hedonism. Finding its most famous and influential formulation in Bentham's "felicific calculus" it became so intimately associated with the classical economics in the system of "philosophical radicalism" that some later critics have (erroneously) held them to be logically inseparable.

Hedonism accepts the rationality of the processes of action. What it does is to put in the place of the diversity of wants, assumed as data

12. Part of the Marxian theory of "exploitation" is based on the erroneous classical view of the role of labor in production referred to above. But even in the more correct modern formulations the introduction of cumulative differences of power will lead to substantially similar results, though differing somewhat in detail.
13. Outside Marxist circles, cf. Hobson.

by the economist,[14] one all-pervading psychological motive, the pursuit of pleasure. This gives an appearance of completeness of explanation of the totality of action, which cannot but be of great comfort to the empiricist with his inability to rest content with abstractions. Since there seems to be one direction of economic activity—acquisition—and this is thought of in quantitative terms, it is logically very satisfactory to have one quantitatively variable motive explaining it all.

It is only natural that the wide currency of hedonistic psychology as an integral part of the "philosophical racialism" of the earlier nineteenth century should have greatly aided in giving generality and philosophical sanction to the classical economics, especially in the then prevailing empiricist atmosphere. Even later in the new impetus given by Jevons by his discovery of the principle of marginal utility the connection remained very close indeed, perhaps closer than it has ever been.

It is true that in an empiricist view economics must have a psychological foundation, and that hedonism is the one by far best adapted to the rational-individualistic economics. But the advance of an abstract factor view of the scope of economics has made it possible to separate it from hedonism. This is possible because it is no longer necessary to postulate that "economic motives" are ultimate motives in any sense, but that acquisitiveness, in the sense of a tendency to maximize utilities, is a simple deduction from the general postulate of rationality of economic action. The possibility of quantitative treatment of utility arises not from the fact that it reflects a single ultimate motive, but that, remaining on the level of means, its immediate object is generalized purchasing power, that is command over the means to the satisfaction of all wants whatever their ultimate nature. It is merely a truism that the "satisfaction" of wants is greater the greater the means available for their satisfaction.

It is further worthwhile to point out that the confusion over the relation of economics to psychology in general and hedonism in particular has been greatly increased by the very prevalent identification of all elements of behavior seen from the "subjective" point of view, i.e., that of the acting individual, with "psychological" elements. Since the latter category refers to one factor in concrete behavior, the former to the *whole* of behavior seen from one aspect, they can be the same

14. Or perhaps somewhat better stated, in place of the generalized immediate "economic" goal of action, the acquisition of "purchasing power," the quite different psychological motive, pleasure.

only if there is only the one factor. The economic category of utility is certainly a "subjective" category—outside the "subjective" means-end relation economics in the factor sense has no meaning whatever, but it does not follow that it is a psychological concept at all.

Finally from a strictly empiricist point of view hedonism itself scarcely constitutes a sufficient basis for economics. It leaves unanswered the question why pleasure has come to be associated with certain forms of activity and not with others. The pursuit of such questions inevitably leads far beyond the mere hedonistic postulate itself into questions like that of biological survival, which will form the subject of our next treatment.

We have already seen that Malthus was one of the first to invoke biological considerations in the explanation of the "economic" facts confronting him. In fact the Malthusian theory and, more generally, the whole classical economics form a main element in the background of one of the greatest intellectual movements of modern times: Darwinism. In practically all thought concerned with man in the second as distinct from the first half of the nineteenth century and having any kind of a positivistic leaning, it has had a major role.

On the one hand Malthus's conception of the vast potential fecundity of man, generalized to include all organic species, provided the surplus on which natural selection could operate—on the other the theory of economic competition as a means of promoting efficiency provided a model for the conception of the process itself. In fact so striking was the analogy that Keynes has remarked, "The Principle of Survival of the Fittest could be regarded as one vast generalization of the Ricardian Economics." [15] To be sure there are difficulties in the analogy with the organic structure. As Malthus so clearly recognized, competition to be beneficent must proceed according to rules of the game which in the conception of "Nature red in tooth and claw" were conspicuous only by their absence. Moreover to retain a direct connection with the older economics it was necessary to leave a place for a limited role of rationality of individual action.

However, while Darwinism may be considered both the mother and the goal of practically the whole of the positivistic phase of the modern anti-intellectualist movement, it is only relatively recently that it has penetrated economic thought in this radical form—on that we shall remark briefly below. Its first effect was undoubtedly to bolster up the classical view of the economic process by tending to widen it out into one of cosmic significance.

15. *The End of Laissez-Faire,* New Republic edition, 17.

The earlier phase was perhaps best represented by what was hardly explicitly an economic theory at all—the individualism of Spencer. On the one hand his extreme negative position on the outside control of this competitive process came so close to anarchism that the necessity of controlling rules for the economic as distinct from the biological struggle scarcely even occurred to him. On the other the Lamarckian element in his biology made it easier to maintain the postulate of economic rationality than strict Darwinism would have done.

But perhaps the most notable attempt by an economist to relate the conception of an individualistic competitive order to the general conditions of biological survival in Darwinian terms has been that of Professor T. N. Carver.[16] Starting from the economic doctrine of maximum satisfaction and its implication that an individualistic competitive order is the most efficient possible, he has maintained that for this reason its adoption constitutes the most powerful factor in the chances of survival of a group. It thus becomes, as for Spencer, the logical end of the great process of social evolution which in turn is the continuation of biological evolution.

It is, however, interesting to note that Professor Carver somewhat modifies the "pure" conception of "economic" society, partly to bring it successfully into this wider framework. It is for his purposes no longer adequate to consider the "end" of social organization as merely the maximization of individual want-satisfaction. It is necessary to show that a competitive order contributes more than any other to "survival value." As a means of maximizing the economic power of such a society, and of guaranteeing against its resting on its oars in the ultimate struggle for survival, he invokes the "workbench philosophy," the devotion to work for its own sake—a motive entirely outside the logical necessities of the older system. Also he goes rather farther than some of his predecessors in conceding that the correct rules of the game need to be laid down by an agency outside the competitive process itself, notably as regards the unearned increment from land, monopoly, and inheritance of property. In many ways Professor Carver's theories are directly reminiscent of those of Herbert Spencer, who has the same combination of orthodox economic individualism and biological evolutionism. But being free from Spencer's naive Lamarckian biology, and considerably more clearheaded in meeting objections to unmitigated laissez-faire, it serves as a better example of this type of theory.

16. See especially *Essays in Social Justice, The Religion Worth Having,* and his recently published *Essential Factors of Social Evolution.*

IV

The "unorthodox" elements entering into economics in the theories so far discussed have consisted in modifications in and supplements to the "orthodox" theories due to the *addition* of factors not considered by the latter. Still remaining on positivistic ground there is another class of theories which go farther—they do not merely add to the orthodox theory, they reject it as positively wrong and substitute other positivistic elements in its place as explanations of the concrete facts of economic life.

(*a*) As pointed out before, the "ideal type" of economic action concerns a relatively narrow sector in the whole long chain of relations between ultimate ends and "ultimate means." Without attacking the validity of the basic scheme of means-end relationships it is possible to object to the emphasis on the specifically "economic" element in it, and bring out others instead. This is essentially the position taken by Veblen.

The general framework of his theoretical structure is essentially very simple. In the typical fashion of positivistic empiricism he disposes of the problem of the role of ultimate ends by assuming them to be given as constant factors in the form of four basic "instincts": the "parental bent," "predatory bent," the "bent of workmanship," and "idle curiosity." Unlike the instincts of the main type of anti-intellectualist psychology, however, Veblen's are explicitly "teleological"; they are "ends" of action rather than "tendencies." The processes of their expression or attainment, on the other hand, he thinks of as rational, resting on a knowledge of the conditions under which action takes place.[17]

Secondly, Veblen criticizes the orthodox economics as logically dependent on hedonistic psychology. Since he holds the latter to be positively unsound[18] and fails to make the separation just discussed,[19] he is forced to throw out the type of "economic action" altogether. One may say that in so doing he throws out the "baby with the bath." He is then left with two main types of rational action in fulfillment of the instincts, each resting on a type of knowledge and of interest. On the one hand there is the "predatory" type, concerned with the promotion of egoistic interests and resting on pragmatic "worldly wisdom," a knowledge of men, their weaknesses, susceptibilities, etc., that is

17. Cf. *The Instinct of Workmanship*, chap. 1.
18. "Preconceptions of Economic Science" in *The Place of Science in Modern Civilization*.
19. Sec. 3.

everything about them which may be turned to the advantage of the agent dealing with them when he tries to use them as means to his own ends. This in turn is subdivided into the explicitly "predatory" type, making use of violence and outright fraud to attain its ends, and the peaceful "pecuniary" type making strategic use of economic power, especially as given in monopoly position and the command over large masses of property, to attain ends always at the expense of others.

On the other hand there is the "workmanlike" type of action, resting on knowledge of "opaque fact" and "mechanical sequences," such knowledge being essentially the product of "idle curiosity." The interest in this case is in the workmanship itself, in the best possible performances of the technical task on hand, with a rather vague (and untenable) implication that such devotion to workmanship works out to promote the general welfare while "pragmatic" action in terms of self-interest is always essentially predatory.

This being the case Veblen sees the main line of continuity in the process of social development as that of workmanship or essentially industrial technology. The pragmatic type does not figure as an "evolutionary" factor because it is, on the one hand, destructive—it is the Hobbesian element; on the other hand there is no such cumulative development of "worldly wisdom" as there is of "matter-of-fact knowledge."

There have been three eras relatively favorable to workmanship: the "savage" era of peaceful industry, held back, however, by the "self-contamination" of workmanship—its tendency to turn to magical manipulations, the era of handicraft when peace was established but pecuniary interests were not yet predominant, and finally the modern era of the "machine process." The modern economic situation Veblen interprets mainly in terms of the inharmonious relations, on the one hand, of the "machine process" and the "industrial employments" that go with it, on the other, of the essentially predatory and self-inhibiting strategic maneuvers of the business men in their "pecuniary employments."[20]

Veblen's whole treatment of the latter centers around an emphasis on the power factor which brings him in this respect close to Marx. Also in a rather vague way he conceives of the working classes as concerned with workmanship as against pecuniary strategy (a conception a little hard to reconcile with certain phases of trade union activity) and hence tends to identify his division with the Marxian class

20. *Theory of Business Enterprise*, chap. 1.

division. In his conception, however, the working class is a passive factor in the struggle for power in a way quite foreign to Marx. Veblen's struggle is essentially between businessmen. Moreover, for Marx the machine technology is mainly significant as influencing the structure of the business unit and setting the stage for the particular modern class conflict, while for Veblen it is itself the central and the *only forward-moving as against inhibiting element in the economic process.*

Veblen's principal catchword for use against the older economics is "institutions." Nowhere to my knowledge does he clearly define the concept, usually employing such vague expressions as "habits" and "modes of activity." Where does it fit into his general theoretical scheme?

There is one almost universal connotation of the term "institutions" which certainly also applies to Veblen—a certain relativity. Institutions are not one of the elements which may be held to remain constant at all times and places. One of Veblen's main indictments against the orthodox economics was that it was a "taxonomic" science, interested mainly in classification. For our purposes this may be taken to mean that it thinks in terms of a few fundamental and unchanging categories—value, cost, production, distribution, etc. As against this Veblen sets the ideal of an "evolutionary" science, one which explains things genetically in terms of temporal antecedents with the implication of an irreversible process of change in time. It is mainly as this changing, "evolutionary" element in economic life that Veblen thinks of institutions.

Given his general theory, the constancy of the four instincts excludes the possibility of this element being attributed mainly to the varying ends of action,[21] it must have to do with the processes of attaining ends themselves. The doctrine then seems to be that these processes are not settled ad hoc in each case by new rational considerations, but that they get crystallized into relatively well established and settled modes of doing things and of thinking about them. Variations take the form of alterations, in each case relatively slight, of these settled modes, due to new exigencies of the situation or the inherent process of advancing matter-of-fact knowledge—a truly Darwinian conception. While continually changing there is in every society at every stage a relatively stable pattern of such institutions, which forms the main basis of its specific structure.

---

21. Such variability is brought in on various occasions by talking of the temporary "predominance" of one or the other instinct.

Since there are for Veblen two principal categories of action—the workmanlike and the pragmatic—there are correspondingly two main groups of institutions, regulating these two respectively. But since society is one, they have to stand in some sort of relation to each other. In general they will tend to harmonize, but, especially in the later stages of social evolution, since the most important dynamic factor is the technological process, the institutions directly associated with it tend to change more rapidly and those of the "pragmatic" type tend to lag behind and to represent a set of habits formed in connection with an earlier technological stage. This will be the more true the farther removed the persons and groups concerned are from direct contact with the everyday technological process.[22]

Thus, in addition to his complete rejection of the concept of "economic action" in the strict sense and his consequent concentration of attention on predation and technology, Veblen has invoked a further element—"institutions." Though never very explicitly stated it is to be inferred that its importance goes back mainly to a psychological thesis—that of the very great importance of "habit" in concrete action. Thus Veblen's theory of institutions is the expression mainly of one element of psychological anti-intellectualism, though it is confined to the retarding, lag element, while social change is essentially due to rational adaptation. This psychological element, and the fact that, having assumed ultimate ends as constant, institutions concern only the processes of action, marks Veblen's "institutional" theory off sharply from others to be discussed later.[23] As opposed to them it may be called "positivistic institutionalism."

Thus, in Veblen, empiricism has born the curious fruit that the science of economics has become a complete philosophy of history emphasizing everything in human life, ultimate ends—to be sure in terms of a very special theory of them—predation, technology, science, even institutions accounted for by habit, leaving out only the specifically economic element. It is carrying the revolt against the orthodox economics about as far as it can be done—by throwing out its own positive conceptions root and branch—and putting in its place almost every other conceivable element. Surely the sin of committing the fal-

---

22. This is the essential theoretical argument of Veblen's celebrated theory of the leisure class. In our society the leisure class and its institutions form one great "archaic" survival of the "predatory culture."

The most recent variant of the general theory is the "culture lag" theory of Professor Ogburn. The resemblance is so striking that it almost certainly owes much to Veblen. See Ogburn, *Social Change*.

23. In the second part of the study.

lacy of "misplaced concreteness" on the part of the older economists has been amply avenged.

(*b*) In Veblen's theory of institutions the psychological factor of habit has made its appearance in economic thought. It is an element of psychological anti-intellectualism whose derivation from Darwinism is very evident. One further step in this general direction is possible. Veblen, after all, repudiated only the specifically economic form of rational action, retaining the predatory and the technological. One may go a step farther and repudiate the role of rationality altogether. This step has not been made the basis of any really well worked-out "economic theory," in fact has hardly gone beyond methodological discussions and scattered, unsystematized appeals to certain nonrational psychological factors to explain certain concrete phenomena— such as "crowd psychology" as a factor in bank runs, etc. Nevertheless two anti-intellectual psychological movements have had enough influence to merit at least mention.

The one most closely related to the Veblenian point of view and most in vogue among his followers is behaviorism. Their principal conception for the interpretation of behavior, the "conditioned reflex," is a more precise and physiological formulation of what Veblen more vaguely had called "habit." With the extension of the reflex mechanism to cover the areas of rationality still allowed by Veblen, the "institutional" element in his theory easily passes over into a generally behavioristic social theory. In addition, Veblen's conception of science as "matter-of-fact" knowledge of "opaque fact" and its distinction from the "worldly wisdom" of insight into human motives fits into the behavioristic stress on "objectivity" and its abhorrence of contact with the "subjective." Finally the common filiation from Darwinism is very clear indeed. The conditioning of behavioristic reflexes is clearly the application of the idea of natural selection to the acts of the individual, while the random movements are the analogue of Darwinian variations. Given the empiricist starting point, it was out of the question that economic thought should have remained immune from the great current of positivistic "objectivism," of which radical behaviorism is the logical culmination.

In going over to behaviorism economics approaches the final term in departure from its "classical" starting point. Not only has it, as with Veblen, thrown out the particular central category of rational economic action on the grounds of its alleged dependence on a particular unsound psychological theory, but it has on psychological grounds thrown out the whole great category of rational action in general, thus shutting out radically any possibility of a return to the older ways even in a modified form.

The other main psychological movement to come under consideration is the "instinct" psychology. In reality it was a twin brother of behaviorism, differing from the latter essentially in the emphasis on heredity as against environment. The most notable case in economic literature, perhaps, is Professor Mitchell's pledge of allegiance to MacDougall.[24] Arguing, more radically than Veblen, that the assumption of rationality itself and not merely hedonism was the core of the difficulty of the classical theories, he proposed the adoption of MacDougall's scheme of instincts in its stead. He never, to my knowledge, attempted to build a scheme of economic theory on this basis. The insecurity of the whole thing is evident both from the transitoriness of the psychological theories on which Professor Mitchell and other economists have rested their hopes and from the inability to distinguish even a real psychological theory from others. Professor Mitchell's inclusion in a later article of Sombart, along with MacDougall and Thorndike, as a man attempting to supply a psychological foundation to economics shows nothing less than a complete misunderstanding of Sombart's work, as the following discussion will show.[25] In general, the extension of positivistic empiricism in economics to such extremes of logical conclusion as these psychological theories seems to have involved the science in far more difficulties than it has extricated it from.

V

Thus far we have been concerned with theories which in their supplements to or substitute for orthodox economic theory have remained on "positivistic" ground. That is, they have, on the whole, tended either to ignore the problem of ultimate ends or, like Veblen, to assume them constant. They have invoked, on the other hand, such factors as the external "conditions" of action, technology or biological or psychological properties of the human individual. There is another group of theories which, while still remaining on an empiricist basis, trying to explain the whole of concrete "economic" reality, have invoked quite a different order of considerations centering mainly in the

24. W. C. Mitchell, "Rationality of Economic Action," *Quarterly Journal of Economics*, 1911.

25. Sec. 5, c.

role of ultimate ends and values in human action, and concentrating their critique of orthodoxy mainly on the predominant concrete role it assigns to "economic motives." As a whole, this group may be termed the theories of "romantic empiricism."

(a) While the main home of these views has been Germany, strange as it may seem Marshall also may be placed in this category. Of course, Marshall is generally regarded as the very ideal type of orthodoxy. Examination of his theory, however, shows that besides the element of "utility theory" there is in his work a second most important theoretical strand.[26] It is noteworthy, in the first place, that his definitions of economics are highly imprecise—the usual one is "a study of man in the everyday business of life." When it is inquired more closely what this involves we find it bifurcating into two main branches: the "study of wealth" and its "more important side, a part of the study of man." This latter concerns the "ways in which man's character has been formed in the conditions of his work."[27] The "study of wealth," developed by Marshall in terms of the marginal utility principle and the "Principle of Substitution," is essentially "orthodox economic theory"; the "study of man" is something quite different.

It is noteworthy that Marshall accepts on the whole the underlying assumptions of the doctrine of maximum satisfaction such as competition, mobility, rationality, and, with certain qualifications, the doctrine itself, with one, from the point of view of *utility* theory, basic exception—he refuses to accept the independence of wants from the processes of their satisfaction. Here he classifies[28] wants into three categories: biological needs, which he sometimes refers to as "wants" without qualification, "artificial" wants, and wants "adjusted to activities." Action connected with the first two categories may be understood directly in "utility" terms, but in the last case the wants and the activities form an inseparable unity which cannot be broken down even for analytical purposes.

Thus in the "activities" in a state of mutual adjustment with wants Marshall has introduced a factor quite outside the scope of the ordinary utility theory. This is what he means when he says that "much that is of most interest in the science of wants is borrowed from the

26. See the writer's articles: "Wants and Activities in Marshall" [*Quarterly Journal of Economics* 46 (November 1931):101–40] and "Economics and Sociology: Marshall in Relation to the Thought of His Time" [chapter 8 of this volume].

27. *Principles of Economics*, 8th ed., London, 1925, 1.

28. The classification is nowhere explicitly worked out but must be inferred from his treatment. See my article of November 1931 referred to [in note 26] above.

science of efforts and activities," and "if either, more than the other may claim to be the interpreter of the history of man, whether on the economic side or any other, it is the science of activities and not that of wants."[29] This factor is thus conceived by him as an integral part of his economic theory.

Concretely the activities and qualities of character he has in mind are those embodying the virtues, on the one hand, of energy, initiative, enterprise; on the other rationality, industry, frugality, honorable dealing. In such activities these virtues, the typical "economic virtues," are thought of as practiced not for ulterior motives on the principle "honesty is the best policy" but strictly as ends in themselves without thought of reward. They, as much as competition and the other "utility" elements, characterize the modern system of "free enterprise."

The role of these "activities" may be followed straight through Marshall's thought, starting with the internal structure of his more technical theory and branching out into his general social philosophy. It is their part which primarily prompts his defense of the Ricardian labor theory of value against Jevons. Only by its introduction does he maintain the classical doctrine that the total supplies of the factors of production (other than natural agents) are direct functions of their prices. At the other end of the scale, correlative with the doctrine of maximum satisfaction, this forms the basis of Marshall's strong defense of freedom of enterprise, and finally, along with the process of developing rationality and emancipation from custom, it is the center of a linear theory of the process of social evolution as a whole, culminating in the development of "free enterprise."

This element of a definite type of activities pursued as ends in themselves not only is something different from the orthodox theory we have discussed, it supplements it in a way radically different from the "positivistic" theories treated above. It brings in ends, not the immediate end of economic acquisition but ultimate ethical values, as a basic *variable* which must be taken into direct account in economic explanations.

It is possible, however, for it to harmonize with the "utility theory" element, and to cause relatively little disturbance of the main outline of the competitive individualistic picture—and thus largely to have escaped detection—because it fits directly into a single logical whole with the other element. To the empirically minded the conspicuous thing in Marshall is his use of the utility analysis and his general sup-

29. *Principles*, 90.

port of competitive individualism[30]—not the logical grounds involved in the latter. But if Marshall broadened his perspective to include a general comparative study of the relation of different systems of ultimate values to economic activities the picture would be very different and would bring out unmistakably how radical his theoretical departure from orthodoxy really is.

(*b*) Marshall, like the first group of positivistic empiricists we dealt with, supplements his pure utility theory with another factor—in his case, "activities." As in the other case, there has here been a group who have gone farther radically to repudiate the factors formulated in orthodox theory.

The German Historical School in its various ramifications is the principal representative in this view. Going back as it does very largely to Hegelian idealism and to historical jurisprudence for its roots, it is distinguished by two main features. On the one hand, it maintains on the whole a radical historical relativism. The attempt of orthodox theory to build up a general economic science universally applicable is held from the outset to be foredoomed to failure. The classical system was held to be simply the economics of one historical epoch and its analysis to have no validity for other times and places. Each economic organization must be considered as a reality "sui generis," as a thing by and for itself, without essential connection with others. Economics cannot hope to set up a universal system of analytical concepts but must attack each period as an entirely new problem.

Secondly, in looking for the order of reality responsible for this radical historical relativity, the Historical School has tended to find it in an ethico-spiritual factor, the *Volksgeist,* which is an irreducible entity, above all not a psychological factor in the positivistic sense. It is fundamentally because the spiritual constitution of societies, above all their ultimate values, differ, that their economic organizations also differ. From their empiricist point of view any system of theory which attempts to abstract from these differences is necessarily inadequate.

With the general empiricist tendency predominant, and hence a propensity to become immersed in historical detail, and on the other hand the impact in Germany, which though weaker than elsewhere was by no means negligible, of Western positivistic thought, the clear-cut features of this Historical empiricism tended, especially in the later Historical School, to become blurred over. Above all, in the work of Schmoller there are large positivistic elements; he has a great deal to

30. Both in positive definition and in their use to support individualism Marshall's "activities" bear a striking resemblance to Professor Carver's "work bench philosophy."

say about climate, geography, race, and other such factors. But nevertheless the difference of emphasis is always marked. No German Historical economist ever placed the exclusive trust in a positivistic biological or psychological theory which has been fairly common in our own thought, and the *Volksgeist* has always been there, even if pushed from the place of exclusive interest.

(*c*) It is worthwhile to discuss at some length, perhaps, the most important contemporary heir—rather than a representative—of the Historical School, Werner Sombart. Sombart has, on the one hand, reacted away from the positivistic tendencies of the later historicism back to a definite if not extreme "romanticist" position. At the same time, as against the extreme empiricism of Schmoller, he has attempted not merely to write economic history but to develop a systematic theory.

True to the historical position his theory is not universal, except in the most formal sense, but is the theory of a particular historical economic system, that of modern capitalism. Only one other, the precapitalistic, is dealt with at all, and that principally in order, through contrast, to throw the characteristics of capitalism into clear relief.

In his treatment of capitalism, Sombart's principal predecessor is a thinker not usually reckoned to the Historical School, Karl Marx. Marx as an economic theorist in the narrow sense belonged mainly to the classical school, differing from his predecessors in that tradition mainly by his explicit recognition of the power factor and the resultant class struggle. But at the same time his economic theory was worked into a dialectical philosophy of history mainly of Hegelian origin. The most important point is that he considered capitalism a definite and specific *system* of economic organization, marked off sharply in *principle* from its predecessor and successor in the dialectical process. From the point of view of the individual participants in the system it is thought of as one of compulsion, by which the individual entrepreneur is forced above all to pursue a path of unlimited acquisition. Acquisition is indeed the dominant principle of the system but not because of an inherited acquisitive propensity of men—rather because placed in certain competitive situations there is no other type of conduct possible.

The class conflict, arising out of the structure of the capitalistic enterprise which crystallizes differences of power about the class line, reinforced by the competitive pressure which keeps individuals in line, provides for Marx a dynamic element which forms the main bridge between Marx's classical economic theory and his dialectic theory of social evolution, giving a result notably different from all positivistic theories of economic change. By introducing instability into the very heart of the capitalistic system it facilitates the conception of it as a unique system, peculiar in its principles of organization and limited in temporal duration.

Sombart freely acknowledges his debt to Marx, stating that his own work[31] is to be regarded as a continuation and he hopes completion of that of Marx. But it is very largely done by drawing Marx away from his affiliations with the English economics and laying the main stress on the "romantic" elements in the theory of capitalism. In general Marx's principal element of continuity from system to system, the class struggle, recedes far into the background and is replaced by a *Wirtschaftsgeist* peculiar to each system, and in each radically separated from that of the last.

In fact, aside from what Sombart would regard as quite secondary elements, such as the physical conditions of economic life (limitation of natural resources, etc.), all the elements of his theoretical analysis are peculiar to the one system under consideration. His departure from pure history writing is apparent in that his controlling concept, that of the economic system (*Wirtschaftssystem*), is explicitly abstract, an "ideal type." Its concrete counterpart, the economic epoch, is a period of history in a given area when such a system is predominant, with no attempt to deny that elements of other systems are present. In particular the period of concrete transition from one system to another is always one of mixture in concrete fact. Though the distinction in principle between two such systems is always sharp and clear, in concrete fact they shade off almost imperceptibly.

Such an economic system has, in Sombart's view, three main aspects: a *Geist* or "spirit," a "form of organization," and a "technique." Each aspect is characterized by certain principles which distinguish it sharply from the corresponding aspect of other systems. In form of organization the capitalistic system has as its unit the capitalistic enterprise which is internally organized by the division into the two classes of owner-managers on the one hand and propertyless wage workers on the other. The different elements within it are brought into relation with each other through one market, the labor market. At the same time enterprises are related to each other and to the ultimate consumers through other markets. The whole thing is based on private initiative and competitive production for market exchange. With it is contrasted the precapitalistic handicraft form of

31. *Der moderne Kapitalismus*, 2d ed., 6 vols. This statement is to be found in the foreword to vol. 5.

industrial organization, differing primarily in the absence of a division into the owner and laborer classes.

The connection of enterprises in competitive relations through the market makes the system as a whole acquisitive. While the "ultimate" cause of an enterprise's activity lies in the demand for its product, the immediate end of every enterprise *must* be the making of profit, regardless of the personal motives of individuals. Money is the quantitative common denominator of the economic order and money profit both the immediate aim of economic activity and the measure of its success. This gives the possibility of acquisition losing its connection with the satisfaction of wants and becoming an end in itself. It is the "tendency of capital to reproduce itself" which Sombart takes over from Marx.

To this peculiar form of organization corresponds the "spirit of capitalism" [32] which, indeed, Sombart holds primarily responsible for its creation. This he divides into two main elements, the "spirit of enterprise" and the "bourgeois spirit." The former is a product of the Renaissance, essentially a phase of the individual will to power. Capitalistic acquisition because of its essential lack of limitation and its impersonality offers an exceptionally favorable field for the search for power. The real creative force behind modern industrial development is this restless search for power, harnessed to acquisition. It is inherently competitive, for power of its very essence is something we can hold only insofar as others do not hold it. At the same time there has grown up from other sources a rational, disciplined element in the capitalistic spirit, what Sombart calls the "bourgeois spirit" (*Bürgergeist*). This is characterized by the typical "economic virtues" of industry, frugality, thrift, careful counting of the cost. Only the coalescence of the two gives the complete picture. The three principles of the spirit of capitalism are thus acquisition, competition, rationality.

With it is contrasted on each point the "precapitalistic" economic spirit. In place of acquisitiveness it has the principal of needs (*Bedarfsdeckung*) traditionally fixed for each according to his status in the social hierarchy. Once these needs are cared for, acquisitive activity stops. Competition to the point of yielding power over others is severely repressed. Finally in place of rationality is the traditionalism of the precapitalistic economy—acceptance of the ways of the fathers without question.

Finally the capitalistic technology is not merely more "advanced" than the precapitalistic—it also is different in principle. That of the

32. Cf. besides the *Kapitalismus*, *Der Bourgeois*.

precapitalistic era was traditional, and empirical—its procedures were accepted from the past and the knowledge on which it rested was won from the concrete experience of the particular case. Technical knowledge was that of rules learned from a master. Capitalistic technique, on the other hand, is both rational and scientific. It is based on a rational examination of each situation and thus a new solution of its problems. Nothing is taken for granted. At the same time its intellectual basis is knowledge of scientific laws based on analysis *applied to* the particular case, and not rules *derived from* experience of particular cases. Perhaps nowhere does the radical nature of Sombart's thesis of the discontinuity of economic systems stand out with such startling effect as in his attempt to push it into the field of technique, where continuity of development has seemed to most to be too obvious even to need discussion.

Of the three elements of the economic system it is quite clear that Sombart gives priority to the "spirit." To be sure, once the system of capitalism is fully established it tends to be self-sustaining regardless of the mental attitudes of its participants—as it was for Marx from the beginning. Each individual finds himself in a situation where it is impossible for him to act counter to the system. His existence as a member of the society would in that case be impossible. Sombart speaks of the "objectification" of the principles of the spirit of capitalism in the capitalistic enterprise itself.

But these considerations do not account for the genesis of the system out of one radically different. That, Sombart holds in direct opposition to Marx, is only conceivable on the assumption that men's mental attitudes had changed and that the changed attitudes have created the form of organization. From this point of view it is to be noted that Sombart views the capitalistic order *not* primarily as a mechanism of want-satisfaction but as the result of men's direct pursuit of *non*economic ends, the quest of power and the exercise of the rational bourgeois virtues.

Professor Mitchell's unfortunate confusion, mentioned above, makes it necessary to emphasize in conclusion that Sombart's "subjective" theory of capitalism in terms of men's mental attitude toward their economic activities is *not* a "psychological" theory. It is not an explanation in terms of the *general* properties of the human mind, but of a *particular* set of value attitudes specific to modern Western culture and not derived from the racial heredity of its population. The term *Geist* should not be allowed to deceive. This is no more individual psychology than Hegel's philosophy of the *Weltgeist* is behaviorism. In fact, far from being a case of the psychological factors which Professor Mitchell invokes to help him out of his economic difficulties, Sombart is, in terms of our classification, the extreme polar antithesis of such views. While radical behaviorism and instinct psychology throw out, in the explanation of concrete behavior, everything, including the "economic" element, except psychological mechanisms, whether acquired or inherited, Sombart radically minimizes *everything* at the positivistic end of the scale, including both the "economic" element and such mechanisms of behavior, in favor of the most radically "romantic" element of all, the unique "spirit" of a culture. It is an element the very existence of which Professor Mitchell's friends do, and to be consistent must, deny.[33]

This completes our sketch of theories of economics put forward on an empiricist basis. It is in many ways a hasty sketch, but is, I think, sufficiently full to justify drawing a few general conclusions. It may be said in the first place that these writers have all taken it for granted that the task of economic science was to supply the full theoretical explanation of a body of concrete facts, the facts of "economic life" or of "economic activities." Secondly, it may be concluded that the narrowly defined body of concepts included within orthodox economic theory, the modern "utility theory," is inadequate to this task. The attempt to rely upon it alone inevitably involves the "fallacy of misplaced concreteness," taking the part for the whole. I cannot agree with the contention of some of the extreme unorthodox schools that this element has no important concrete relevance at all. But neither is it possible to maintain that it is alone adequate to the task imposed upon it by an empiricist methodology.

Thirdly, a striking conclusion emerges from the consideration of the character of the elements invoked by one or another of the unorthodox schools. That is, seen from the subjective point of view of the means-end schema, *all* the elements of human action which are theoretically distinguishable from each other have found a place in "economic" theory at one time or another. The "positivistic" theories tend on the whole to reduce economic activities to terms of biological heredity or the external environment or some combination of both. Short of this is the tendency to emphasize technology. Then there is an important body of thought which invokes the element of coercive power in one form or another. Finally another body rests on the role of a system of ultimate values directly expressed in economic activities.

33. For a more detailed account of Sombart's theory of capitalism, cf. the writer's article "'Capitalism' in Recent German Literature" [chapter 1 of this volume].

What is the significance of this fact? There can, I think, be no doubt that in large measure these unorthodox theories are empirically right. While many of their contentions are open to criticism in detail, it seems to me quite impossible to deny in principle that any or all of these factors are relevant to the understanding not merely of concrete social life in general but of concrete economic activities. In principal *all* the elements of human action in general are involved in its "economic" phase—that is concrete acquisitive activities.

If this conclusion be accepted it follows that an economics which adopts the empiricist position must include in its *theoretical* principles all the elements which are relevant to the understanding of human conduct in general. Then economics, regarded as a theoretical discipline, loses its separate identity from the other sciences dealing with human conduct. It becomes the application to a particular body of concrete facts of the body of principles which is equally applicable to any other phase of human life in society. But economics has no special title to be the final authority in the formulation of this body of principles. It is rather what has generally been called an "encyclopedic sociology," [34] a general synthesis of the theoretical results of all our knowledge of social life. Economics is then a branch of applied sociology.

Short of a radical "economic interpretation of history," this conclusion is indeed inescapable on an empiricist basis. It is not, however, the only possible alternative. At the beginning of the second section of the study I shall take up a group of writers who have abandoned the empiricist basis altogether. Then, following up the implications of their work, I shall attempt to sketch the outline of an alternative conception of the scope of economics, and the corresponding conception of sociology, which will preserve the theoretical independence of each and yet not be in danger of succumbing to the fallacy of misplaced concreteness as the older orthodox economics so frequently did.

Part 2: The Analytical Factor View

I

In the first part of this study we have seen that in attempting to construct a science of economics on an empiricist basis the whole gamut of possible factors in concrete social life from the physical environ-

34. This is not the view of the scope of sociology to which I subscribe. The question will be entered into in the second part of the study.

ment and man's biological necessities in adaptation to it on the one hand to his independent ethical attitudes on the other has been run. In turn each one of the possible factors has been made the cornerstone of an "economic" theory. The most conspicuous result is the tendency to submerge what we have started out to call the economic element altogether, so that we have the curious spectacle of the science of economics being derived from the principles governing every other element of human action except the economic.

It remains to ask whether it is not possible to take a radically different course from any of these previously discussed theories, to abandon the empiricist basis altogether, admitting frankly that economics should not and cannot be concerned with a full explanation of concrete facts, whether they be those of "economic activities" or any others, but must reconcile itself to be limited to the analytical abstraction of one of the fundamental factors in human action and its study for the purposes of the systematic formulation of theory[35] in "artificial" isolation from the rest.

The group of theories to be discussed in this section have, explicitly or by implication, taken this course. More specifically they stand upon the common ground that even in concrete economic activities are involved other than economic elements and that it is not within the competence of the science of economics, out of its own theoretical resources, to supply the principles in terms of which to account for these other elements.

Though Emile Durkheim never pretended to be a professional economist and never called anything he wrote "economics," his whole sociological theory is so largely oriented to the problems under consideration here that he merits a place in the discussion.[36] His original interest was in the understanding of concrete "economic" activities and he was a pioneer in the clear realization of the importance of the "noneconomic" elements present there.

The starting point of his thought in this field is his study *De la division du travail social* (1893),[37] a work which has received far less

35. Not of the concrete division of labor of scientists. It seems to me that all important concrete research problems cut across several of the divisions between theoretical sciences. I see no reason why this should not be true of the social as much as, for instance, of the biological sciences.

36. He has fathered a school of "economics," of which perhaps the most conspicuous representative is F. Simiand.

37. Now translated into English by G. Simpson, under the title *The Division of Labor in Society*, New York, 1933.

attention than it deserves from economists of the empiricist persuasion. Durkheim's primary concern is with the understanding of a society characterized by "economic individualism." He chooses the division of labor as his subject because of the central place occupied by that conception in individualistic economic thought. His fundamental thesis is that a highly differentiated economic order cannot be understood as resting entirely upon "contractual relations" (in Spencer's phrase), that is, on the determination of the concrete relations of the individuals alone by the direct and immediate economic interest of each. There is, on the contrary, present in all *concrete* contractual relations a qualitatively different element which may be called the *institution* of contract, a body of rules and norms, both legal and informal, determining the conditions according to which contracts are and may be entered into. While some of the terms of each specific contract are agreed upon *ad hoc* by the parties, and it is a matter of their voluntary choice whether or not to contract at all, there is present, *if* they so choose, a whole set of conditions which may be regarded as involuntary and obligatory, as "constraining" their actions.

It is only, in Durkheim's view, by virtue of the presence of this "noncontractual" element that a *system* of contractual relations is possible at all. The very practical difficulties of settling all the implications of a contract ad hoc anew would make it necessary. But more important, it is the normative rules of the institution of contract which account for the principal element of order making the stability of the system possible. Durkheim's most fundamental thesis is that individual interest alone does not provide a basis for such order but if left to itself a system of "contractual relations" would result in a state of chaos, a war of all against all.[38]

The institution of contract is not for Durkheim merely a complex of habits. Already in the *Division du travail* he speaks of it mainly as a body of normative rules—no one ever claimed that habits were normative rules. Later in *Le suicide* he specified this further by developing the view that the principal factor of stability in modern individualistic society was the common ethical valuation of individual personality as such. The main content of the normative rules of contract is the obli-

38. It should be noted that it is not the legal possibility of enforcing contracts by the courts on which Durkheim lays the principal stress. It is the effective functioning of a body of normative rules involved in all contractual relations, whether they come before the courts or not. The particular *ad hoc* provisions of each separate contract are as subject to enforcement as the rules of the institution. "Sanctions" are only one element in the functioning of social institutions and for Durkheim, I think, not the most important. Durkheim here differs profoundly from the individualistic economists.

gation to respect the rights of others, not merely the other party to the contract—so that an agreement obtained under duress or by fraud is void—but the rights of third parties as well. This is not merely an extension of individual self-interest but a qualitatively different element, social in character. It means subordination of every individual to common norms. Durkheim called it the factor of "organic solidarity."

In *Le suicide,* which, though the title does not indicate it obviously, is very much concerned with the problems of economic individualism, Durkheim goes a step farther than in the *Division* to doubt the efficiency of this character of norm in securing social stability. He finds that one type of suicide, the *anomique,* because of absence of normative control over individual activity, is peculiarly prevalent in the most "individualistic" elements of the economic system, above all in commerce and urban industry, and that a permanent stability of economic relations implies a greater part played by the integrated social group than is possible in a highly individualized order. It is from this motive that he proposed a revival of the occupational group,[39] based on the analogy of the medieval guild. It is to be noted that he conceived these groups, contrary to the syndicalist-guild socialist idea, not as a channel for the expression of interests but as a curb upon them. It was as an instrument of control that he was interested in them.

Thus Durkheim has clearly seen (in my own opinion, demonstrated) the presence in concrete "economic" life, to say nothing of other parts of social life, of elements other than the economic in the narrow sense. In this he agrees with Veblen and other empiricists of the unorthodox school. He also agrees to call this factor "institutions." But he differs profoundly in his view of the essential nature of institutions. Instead of being mere habits they are normative rules ultimately dependent on common ethical values. Thus Durkheim's "institutionalism" leans to the "romantic" not the "positivistic" side of the "economic" factor.[40] Secondly, the study of this institutional factor is for him the business not of economics but of sociology, which he goes so far as to define as the "science of institutions." [41] This view is at least consistent with the maintenance of "orthodox" economics, provided it is recognized to

39. Most fully developed in the preface to the second edition of the *Division du travail.*

40. Durkheim himself was, especially in his earlier phases, a strong and self-conscious positivist. He reached his sociological views rather in spite of than through his positivistic scientific methodology. Especially in the later stages of his work this led into methodological difficulties too involved to enter into here.

41. Preface to second edition of *Les règles de la méthode sociologique.*

be an abstract science. Here is where Durkheim in his study of "economic" activities breaks radically with all the empiricist schools of economics.

While the abstract "aspect" view of the role of economic science was implicit in Durkheim's sociological treatment of "economic" activities Pareto was one of the first to make this view definitely explicit. He was himself a professional economist whose central interest as such was the systematic formulation of the general theory of economic equilibrium, especially in mathematical terms. He very soon, however, became aware of the abstractness of this general theory and the necessity, before it could be made applicable to the understanding of concrete, even "economic," phenomena, of its being supplemented by other theoretical principles.[42]

This realization of the concrete inadequacy of economic theory centered above all around the interpretation of two concrete "economic" phenomena—the protectionist movement and the socialist movement. In his earlier years Pareto was a prolific writer in the protectionist controversy in Italy on the free trade side, but it became evident to him that he was fighting a losing battle. During that time, mainly the 80s of the last century, the protectionist movement was steadily gathering force. But from the point of view of abstract economic theory protection must result in economic loss,[43] and hence on economic grounds alone it is impossible to explain why governments should adopt a protectionist policy. But not only had they very generally done so in Europe, but the expected detrimental effect of protection on wealth had not appeared. On the contrary, the period was one of generally increasing prosperity.

The explanation of these concrete phenomena Pareto found primarily in the relation of the economic order to government and the structure of the governing classes in Europe. Protection was one principal phase of a relation of reciprocal usefulness to each other of business and government. It is primarily as a means of maintaining and extending their power, not of promoting the economic welfare of the community as a whole, that governments adopt protection. At the same time the shelter of protection provides a peculiarly favorable opportunity for the rise to positions of control in economic life of a type particularly fertile in "combinations," as Pareto puts it. The increased

42. See *Manuel d'économie politique,* and, especially, *Traité de sociologie générale* (now translated into English as *The Mind and Society,* New York, 1935).

43. Except in certain special cases, which it has taken all the ingenuity of protectionists to think up.

productivity due to the change in the character of the entrepreneur class overbalances the direct loss due to protection itself.

Similarly in the case of socialism. From the strict economic point of view, the harmonious cooperation of the classes in the productive process is the obvious way of maximizing productive efficiency.[44] But in spite of this fact a powerful movement based on the antagonism of classes has grown up. Its primary basis is the tendency for a certain type of persons, those strong in the "persistence of aggregates," to be excluded from the governing classes and to such the road to power lies not through the selective process *within* a competitive order but by the overturn of those in command of the order itself.

In neither case does Pareto see in the failure of his economic theory to give a satisfactory complete explanation of these concrete economic phenomena a valid reason for discarding the theory itself.[45] It is rather that the factors formulated in the theory cannot be alone at work in the concrete situation. The correct procedure then is to supplement it by other theories which in synthesis with the economic will give a more adequate account of things.

But Pareto does more than merely point out the necessity of such a theory. In his sociology he undertook to supply it himself. Thus at least one main motive of Pareto's becoming a sociologist late in life was the attempt to do in another way what he felt could not be done within the limitations of economic theory. While he himself was far from claiming finality for his sociological theory, and analysis shows that he was justified in this modesty, the general direction of his thought with relation to economics was a most promising departure.

Into his general sociological system Pareto fits the factors dealt with by economic theory as one main element of the category of "logical action," including principally beside the "economic," the technological and the "Machiavellian" type of political action. The primary analytical task of his sociology on the other hand Pareto sees in the analysis of the residual category of what he calls "nonlogical" action.

Nonlogical action, that is action insofar as the "logical" elements have been abstracted from it, Pareto studies by a peculiar procedure of his own. That is, of the two concretely observable sets of data, "overt acts" and "linguistic expressions," involved in nonlogical ac-

44. It is clear that in excluding both business influence on government and class antagonism from "purely economic" considerations Pareto is, with the competitive individualists, shutting out the "power" factor from economics. Thus he praises Marx as a *sociologist* for emphasizing the importance of the class struggle, not as an economist.

45. See *Traité*, secs. 33ff.

tion, he confines himself to the latter. As a result of inductive analysis he arrives at the two concepts, the "residues" and "derivations," which constitute respectively the relatively constant and variable elements of the "theories" associated with nonlogical action.

These theories are specifically contrasted with those which guide "logical" action, scientific theories. While the principal element of the latter is a statement of observable fact, in the nonlogical case the corresponding element, the residue, cannot be this but must be the "manifestation of a sentiment."

As is likely to happen with residual categories this "sentiment," of which residues are a manifestation, turns out not to be a homogeneous category but, on further analysis, to bifurcate into two main elements. One is the psychological instinct or drive element which determines action apart from any subjective intent of the actor—from one point of view the ultimate conditions of action and the sources of departure from a "logical" norm, of ignorance and error. The other is the ultimate value element coming out most strikingly in Pareto in his concept of the "end a society should pursue." [46] This latter element may be regarded as a phase of the role of "ideas" in social life, but ideas which Pareto insists are to be clearly distinguished from those of science.

The residues are divided by Pareto into six classes, of which only the first two, the "Instinct of Combinations" and the "Persistence of Aggregates," need be mentioned here. The two may, in one main aspect, be interpreted as the states respectively of absence and presence[47] of "ideal ends." The first is characterized by a mobility and ingenuity of action in the pursuit of immediate ends, tending, however, to instability; the second by a concern for more remote ends and the interests of the group rather than the individual, combined with a certain rigid lack of adaptability to immediate exigencies. Thus ideal ends are thought of as exercising a discipline over individual conduct, in the absence of which stability is jeopardized. It is a view strikingly akin to Durkheim's treatment of the role of normative rules.

Pareto proceeds further to analyze a cycle of the alternate predominance of these two classes of residues, and works above all, through the influence of the "circulation of the elite," on the residue composition of the governing classes. The beginning of such a cycle is the advent to power, usually by force, of an elite strong in the persistence

46. Ibid., sec. 2143.
47. That is, it is here that the "value" element of the sentiments is most strongly manifested.

of aggregates. They are strong but inclined to rigidity. The exigencies of maintaining power on the one hand, the conditions favorable to vertical mobility in peaceful times on the other, lead to a dilution of these residues in the governing classes. For a time this leads to a state of greater flexibility and mobility and hence increased economic prosperity, but eventually the relaxation of discipline goes so far as to involve instability and, above all, the danger of overthrow of the governing classes by force. In the economic field the latter part of the cycle is characterized by the predominance of a type he calls the "speculators." It is because protection creates opportunities for this type that it leads to increased prosperity.

Thus Pareto achieves a high degree of realism, combined with a retention of orthodox economic theory, by supplementing it with a broadly conceived system of sociology. It is further significant that Pareto, like Durkheim, finds one of the most important qualifications of the concrete applicability of the economic factor to be the role of ideal ends as agencies for effecting discipline over individual interests. Thus as a sociologist he shows important "romantic" elements, even though, again like Durkheim, his background is mainly positivistic.

We turn finally to Max Weber, who shares with Pareto this self-conscious attitude toward the abstractness of economic theory, combined with eminent achievements in the field of the sociology of "economic" life. This coincidence on the part of two men with such diverse intellectual backgrounds and apparently with no mutual influence on each other's work cannot but be significant.

Weber began his intellectual career in the field of historical jurisprudence as a student of Mommsen, turning then to economics, where his earlier work was chiefly in the historical field and strongly under the influence of the Historical School, and also of the economic interpretation of history.

A new phase was marked by his most famous study *The Protestant Ethic and the Spirit of Capitalism*. For present purposes this essay may be thought of as attempting to do something very similar to Durkheim's *Division of Labor*. In the "economic" aspect of modern life it attempts to demonstrate the existence of a noneconomic, ethical element, the idea of selfless, disinterested devotion to a "calling," i.e., any ordinary occupation, as an end in itself. This attitude toward work, conspicuous for the absence of calculation of personal advantage, Weber finds to be both a most prominent element in the modern economic world and indispensable to its functioning. This attitude toward acquisitive occupations, and not any avaricious interest in gain as such, is what Weber calls the "spirit of capitalism." While

Durkheim maintains the indispensability for the "division of labor" of a set of normative rules governing "contractual relations," i.e., essentially the relations of exchange, Weber concentrates on the other principal aspect of modern economic life, productive labor, finding it to depend on a similar factor.

In both cases the distinguishing characteristic of this factor is its radical difference from the pursuit of individual economic interest. From the point of view of such interest it is a controlling, disciplining factor.

On this account Weber goes so far as to call it an "ascetic" element and it is this which gives him the clue to connect it with a religious ethic, that of the "ascetic" branches of Protestantism, notably Calvinism. By maintaining the ascetic ideal of exclusive devotion to religious interest, yet rejecting monastic separation from the world in favor of an active rational discipline of it into a Kingdom of God on earth, the Puritan ethic combined a rational yet selfless devotion to worldly "callings" with an ascetic inhibition on the spending of wealth as a dangerous concession to the weakness of the flesh, to self-indulgence. Thus the traditionalism of the medieval economic order was broken through without relaxation of ethical control—rather an intensified control which placed a dynamic force behind acquisitive callings, entirely lacking when they were looked upon as necessary evils from the religious point of view.

Weber, like Marx and Sombart, thus emphasizes the compulsive disciplinary side of the modern economic order, above all maintaining that its acquisitiveness is not primarily a matter of the assertion of individual propensities brought out by the breakdown of a previous control—as is the prevailing Anglo-American view.[48] But unlike Marx, and even more decisively than Sombart, he holds it is a matter, in origin at least, not of the "material" conditions of production but of positive ethical valuations of men, however far the objective result may be from what the original Protestants intended. Thus the principal modifying element of the narrow economic factor is found by Weber, as by Sombart, Durkheim, and Pareto, to lie in the field of ethical valuations independent of utilitarian advantage.

But like Pareto and unlike Sombart, Weber recognizes the legitimacy and importance of the narrower economic factor. It is highly noteworthy that, starting from essentially the same "romantic-historical" position as Sombart, instead of attempting like the latter to develop a

48. Even a writer generally so closely linked with Weber as R. H. Tawney lays his principal stress on this process of emancipation. See his *Religion and the Rise of Capitalism*. H. M. Robertson (*The Rise of Economic Individualism*) can see nothing else and entirely misses the "ascetic" element of capitalism which is Weber's principal concern.

"historical" economic theory to account for the concrete facts, involving the total rejection of the traditional economic theory, he took the same course as Pareto in accepting this theory. But he built it into a wider system of sociology, characterized above all by the important place assigned in it by Weber to the element of action regarded as a direct expression of ultimate values.[49]

Weber's sociology did not rest for its empirical basis merely on an analysis of the modern economic order; he pushed his researches into an extraordinarily comprehensive comparative study of many different societies. The result of these researches is recorded above all, though by no means exclusively, in the unfinished series on the sociology of religion.[50] The general thesis of the series may be said to be that the principal factor in the *differences* of economic life of the great civilizations of modern western Europe, China, India, and Mediterranean antiquity lies in the influence of the economic *ethics* of the great religions which in the first case has directly fostered, in all the others powerfully inhibited, the kind of economic development which so many of our writers have simply taken for granted as "natural."

Thus Weber may be placed with Pareto as a professional economist who, while recognizing the validity of the orthodox economic analysis, found it necessary to escape from its limitations in concrete interpretation by a very extensive excursion into general sociology, to which both have made outstanding contributions. It is further noteworthy that both, while approaching their subjects from the radically different points of view of, on the one hand devotion to the model of the physical sciences, on the other to that of German idealism and "historism," have found a principal defect of the orthodox economic analysis as a concrete theory to lie in its neglect of the role of common ethical and religious values and have in turn both made the analysis of this role the *pièce de résistance* of their sociological theories.[51]

II

We have now completed the survey of "economic" theories from the point of view of the relation of the rigidly defined narrow "orthodox"

49. What Weber termed *wertrationales Handeln* and sharply distinguished from *zweckrationales Handeln*, under which category the orthodox type of "economic action" fell in his sytem. Cf. *Wirtschaft und Gesellschaft*, chap. 1.

50. *Gesammelte Aufsätze zur Religionssoziologie*, 3 vols. The essay on the Protestant ethic was reprinted as the first part of vol. 1.

51. A fuller discussion of Weber's treatment of capitalism, with a very brief sketch of his general sociological system, is to be found in the writer's "'Capitalism' in Recent German Literature" [chapter 1 of this volume].

economic element in them to other "sociological" elements. It remains to sum up the results of the survey and to point its moral for the systematic theoretical work of economics in relation to other social sciences.

As was pointed out in our introductory remarks the subtler questions of the scope and methodology of a science do not usually play a very great part in the earlier stages of its development. Hence it is not surprising that whatever methodology is implied in the work of the earlier economists should in general be of a rather naive empiricist variety. They were concerned with concrete problems and naturally tended to follow them wherever they led. Since the actual economic order of their time was one in which individual competitive enterprise played a very prominent part relatively unhampered (at least by very obvious forms of control) it is not unnatural that the individualistic competitive analysis should have been applied directly and literally, especially since certain aspects of the philosophical tradition in which they lived, roughly summed up as utilitarianism, on the whole predisposed them pretty definitely in this direction.

But further empirical investigation plus changes in concrete economic life itself soon brought to light other factors. It is not surprising that the attempt should be made to modify the simpler theory to take account of these factors, especially as they could, perhaps, like the power factor of the Marxian theory, be built directly into the older scheme, with, to be sure, very important differences in the concrete results. Or, like the Darwinian principle of natural selection, they could be used to fit the theory of economic competition itself into a wider theoretical framework of cosmic significance and thus confirm its essential soundness. Or finally, the modifying elements, like "custom," could be thought of as part so to speak of the "environment" of economic action, but not as entering into the concrete individual actions themselves. In all these cases the older theory could be thought of as an essential part of a more complex "economic" theory, including other elements as well.

But the progress of empirical investigation was sooner or later bound to bring out the fact (which such studies as those of Durkheim and Weber, to mention no others, have established beyond doubt) that in concrete "economic" actions themselves, not merely in their "environment," other than "economic" elements were involved—even in individualistic competitive action itself. Moreover, some of these were of such a radically different nature, impugning either the rationality of the action itself or its subordination to "economic" ends, that the Marxian expedient of internal modification of the theory to meet them was no longer possible.

The inevitable reaction to this discovery, so long as the empiricist position was maintained, was an attack on the validity of the older economic analysis itself for any scientific purposes whatever. Hence the charges that it was abstract (that is, in empiricist terms, false), metaphysical, deductive. Economic theory would then be required to undertake a radical reconstruction from the very beginning.

In treating some of the outstanding attempts to achieve such a reconstruction we have noted the striking fact that economic theorists have at times emphasized as the main basis of economic theory every major factor around which any of the social sciences has built its own theory. Thus biological evolution is taken to be the key; or the psychological factors of instinct or habit; or rational technology; or the "predatory" quest of power (both these last in the case of Veblen); or finally ethical and religious values. Thus in theoretical principles, if not in concrete subject matter, economics would appear to become identical with sociology,[52] if that term be applied to the science which attempts to synthesize in one system the principles in terms of which the whole of concrete social life is to be understood.[53] From this point of view there is no such thing as economic theory as a theoretical discipline distinct from others dealing with human action. The economist is distinguished from other social scientists only by his greater knowledge of the concrete facts of what he chooses to call "economic activities."[54]

This consequence is indeed inescapable for the consistent empiricist. For there is absolutely no reason to suppose that concrete human action is divided up into water-tight compartments, each dominated by radically different principles. Only the relatively high degree of differentiation of modern Western society has enabled this illusion to stand up as long as it has, and now it has definitely broken down. Human life is essentially one and no concretely possible degree of functional differentiation can destroy its unity.

But though its concrete reality is a unity, it can, like all other complex phenomena, be broken down for purposes of analysis into different factors. However predominant any one of these factors may be in

52. Just as in the opposite case, the tendency of some of the older economists to extend their principles to cover the whole of social life in effect made sociology identical with "orthodox" economics—or rather the application of economics. Professor Carver—alone to my knowledge—explicitly maintains this position, and quite consistently.

53. As will be noted presently the writer does not accept this conception of sociology, though it has been the predominant one in the past.

54. The really consistent empiricists among economists in fact maintain this position, if indeed they do not go further and deny the place in science of theoretical principles altogether, except as "empirical generalizations."

a particular set of concrete activities, it is never present to the complete exclusion of the others. The only way of maintaining a positive role for economic theory as a systematic generalizing science is to make it the science of *one* of these factors in concrete human action, to be sure more conspicuous in those concrete activities we call "business" than elsewhere, but neither confined to them nor excluding others there. From this point of view no one social science is capable of giving a theoretical explanation of concrete social facts but only a synthesis of the principles of various of them.[55] Thus economic theory is necessarily and by its inherent nature abstract. But so, according to the best modern methodology, is all scientific theory. The earlier economists strongly tended to be guilty of the "fallacy of misplaced concreteness,"[56] of taking the formulations of a set of abstract principles applying to some of the factors in concrete reality for a complete description of the whole of that reality.

This fallacy gave the empiricist criticism its opening, and it has had little difficulty in making a decisive case. Empirically, discounting the one-sided biases of emphasis resulting from the empiricist's own non-empirical (and therefore from their own point of view illegitimate) theoretical preoccupations, the empiricists are undoubtedly right. But that does not make them any the less disastrously wrong theoretically. Their view has quite definitely resulted in "throwing out the baby with the bath." Indeed, my own considered opinion, which cannot be further justified here, is that a thorough-going empiricism is inconsistent with science itself. The essence of science, the *understanding* as distinct from the mere photographic reception of concrete phenomena, is theory and the essence of theory is analytical abstraction. Whatever its dangers, there is no other way.

The only other course for economic theory as distinct from a scientifically fatal radical empiricism is that taken by Sombart. On the basis of German "historism" he has maintained a greater degree of concreteness for his economics than the orthodox school, but at the heavy cost of sacrificing forever its claim to generality and of limiting its

55. As has already been noted this does not mean that the systematic theoretical division of labor of the social sciences should be translated directly into a concrete division of labor of scientists. The theoretical subject matter of his science should define a scientist's central focus of interest, but the exigencies of concrete research are such that he inevitably ventures across the borderlines, probably in several directions. The important thing is not that he should stick to his own theoretical field, but that he should know what he is doing when he goes outside it. But there is no more reason why an economist should fail to know something about sociology than why a physiologist should ignore chemistry.

56. Cf. Whitehead, *Science and the Modern World*.

applicability to a particular culture limited in time and place. In his conceptional scheme there is no such thing as general economic theory, but only the economic theory of capitalism, of the handicraft system, etc. This involves an abdication on the part of science of its claims to generality in which most economists are not willing to acquiesce.[57]

In science the first criterion is the pragmatic one of success—in explanation. Perhaps Sombart's will prove the best road after all, but the other, taken self-consciously and critically above all by Pareto and Max Weber, still seems to be open. To save the generality of economic theory it involves the relegation of the factors which above all account for the specific peculiarities of an "economic system" on Sombart's theory, its "economic spirit" or in other words its ultimate ethical values, to another science, namely sociology. The importance of this element in the work of Sombart, Weber, Durkheim, and Pareto, insofar as they were concerned with "economic" problems in the concrete sense, invites further discussion.

The present study is entitled "Sociological Elements in Economic Thought." Thus far it has left the first term of the title purposely undefined. But both in the interest of completeness and clarity and because the writer considers himself a sociologist, the treatment cannot be complete without a brief consideration of its implications for the status of sociology in relation to economics.

The central theme of the preceding exposition has been the status of "orthodox" economic theory through the history of more than a century. Insofar as its exclusive concrete adequacy has been questioned it has been in the name of every major factor which the history of the social sciences of the period shows to have been emphasized anywhere in them as of fundamental importance for social life in any of its phases. The treatment of all these together as "sociological" elements clearly implies the so-called encyclopedic conception of the scope of sociology as the final synthesis of all our scientific knowledge of man in his relations with his fellows. This has in fact been so predominantly the accepted conception as fully to justify the use of the term "sociological" in the title of this essay. Some sociologists, however, have themselves raised their voices against this view and the present writer shares the protest.

It has been shown that if we look at human action from the "sub-

---

57. Which is not of course to be taken to mean that Sombart's method is incapable of making *any* significant contributions. The issue is its adequacy as a general methodological basis for economics.

jective" point of view of the means-end relationship, economic theory occupies an intermediate position in the chain from ultimate means to ultimate ends. The deepest division between theories which have disputed its claim to concrete adequacy has been according to whether the factors lying to one or the other side of the "economic" element of the chain were thought of as being slighted. The empiricist position, as we have seen, does not alone decide which; empiricist theories have emphasized both.

In the traditions of Anglo-American economic thought it has been predominantly the factors "below" the economic which have been emphasized—from the "subjective" point of view, the "conditions" of individual action. Insofar as thought has tended in this direction it has ended up in biological and psychological theories which attempt either to provide a more solid because more concrete foundation for orthodox theory or to replace it entirely. In the "encyclopedic" sense, of course, this is sociology, but not in the sense that the sociological elements embody new principles not brought to light by any other science. They are rather the result of the application of biological and psychological principles to the particular concrete subject matter.

That our economic (and sociological) thought has so strongly emphasized these factors is not in my opinion due primarily to their overwhelming intrinsic importance. It is not a matter of sheer empirical generalization, but rather of a definite theoretical bias due primarily to our predominantly positivistic tradition of thought. The factor of ultimate ends has not been *proved* to be constant[58]—but assumed so either tacitly or, as in the case of Veblen's "instincts," explicitly. The empiricist tendency of our thought has served merely to obscure the presence of these theoretical preconceptions and delay the ultimately necessary realization of their role.[59]

The most striking feature of recent sociological thought has been a slow, and even as yet not frequently clear, realization of the concrete importance of the principal factor lying to the other side of the economic, the "value" factor. Its emergence into prominence has been embodied in a remarkable process of the development of thought, in which the question of the role of "economic action" in the strict sense has played a central part. We may note briefly what has happened in

58. And hence of no theoretical importance, since scientific theory is concerned with the *behavior* only of variable elements.

59. With many empiricists it has been a popular sport to lay bare the "preconceptions" of opposing theories (cf. Veblen) but as against this they have uniformly set up the claim to be entirely free from any themselves. But a theory free from "preconceptions," i.e., fundamental categories, is a contradiction in terms. It is not a theory at all.

the case of the writers treated here who have most strongly emphasized it.

In what we have called the "romantic" tradition of thought, this
emphasis has naturally been indigenous. In its earlier stages it is a
form of empiricism, but because of the theoretical "preconceptions"
underlying it, its views have been so radically opposed to those of
positivistic empiricism as to have been for the most part flatly rejected
in that quarter as "mysticism." Sombart, as we have seen, emerged
from the methodological empiricism of Schmoller, but by making his
theory one of historical particularity rather than analytical generality.
Weber, on the other hand, by taking the "value" element out of economics and placing it in his comparative sociology is enabled to avoid
Sombart's repudiation of orthodox theory and to achieve a far wider
perspective.

The emphasis on the value element would be under considerable
suspicion had it occurred only in the "romanticist" camp whose scientific hardheadedness has not been excessively admired in positivistic
circles. But perhaps the most striking development of modern social
thought is its emergence from the positivistic camp itself with unmistakable clarity—thus giving a remarkable case of convergence of
thought starting as it were from opposite poles.

The two leading cases in this category are Pareto[60] and Durkheim.
Pareto, working with high self-consciousness on the model of physical
science, came to the double result of decisively rejecting an empiricist
view of economics, and finding a main supplement to it in a theory of
the "residues" as systems of nonscientific values held in common by
the members of a society. This is in Pareto definitely an emergent element, not clearly distinguished from other radically different ones
such as psychological "drives," but perhaps we may on that account
hold it to be all the more significant.

Durkheim starts from a more definitely positivistic position, but
with a "collectivist" bias derived largely from Comte. He is clear from
the start that his "social" factor is radically different from the "economic" as here defined. He plays for a while also with bio-
psychological factors[61] but soon abandons them. His *conscience collective* reached, at the end of a process of thought too long and complex to be traced here, a point where it turned out to be precisely this

60. Pareto can scarcely be said to have held a definitely positivistic philosophical
position, but insofar as he had any philosophical biases they were strongly in this direction.

61. Especially in his explanation of the "causes" of the division of labor in terms of
population pressure. Cf. *Division du travail*, part 2, chap. 2.

same element of common values.[62] Thus the same element that the "romanticists" Sombart and Weber have emphasized has also emerged as central to the sociological theories of the "positivists" Pareto and Durkheim.

It is a striking fact that all of these men have been deeply concerned with concrete economic problems. All of them are agreed about the concrete inadequacy of orthodox economic theory, and further that the main reason for its inadequacy lies in its neglect of the role of ultimate common values. Yet only one, Sombart, sees in this fact a reason for its total rejection. All the others agree in leaving a place for the orthodox theory, Pareto and Weber explicitly, Durkheim implicitly. They also agree to treat the value factor in terms of a sociology.

I submit that this is the most promising view both in doing justice to the concrete facts and in providing for a satisfactory treatment of the systematic relations of the social sciences. It avoids the necessity the extreme unorthodox schools feel themselves to be under of sacrificing entirely the theoretical work of generations of economists. It removes the danger that, by trying to assimilate their treatment of these factors too closely to their own view of the economic element, economists will end as Marshall did, with a very striking lack of perspective on their general role.

Finally, it points the way to a specific theoretical subject matter for sociology which enables it to escape from the (to other social scientists especially) irritating pretentiousness of the encyclopedic view of its scope.[63] The concrete importance of the common ultimate value factor

62. Clear only in his last work, *Les formes élémentaires de la vie religieuse,* especially bk. 2, chap. 7, sec. 4, and bk. 3, chap. 3, sec. 3. Durkheim's theory on this point has been grossly misunderstood. I hope to deal with it in detail in a work to be published soon.

63. This conception of sociology as a systematic theoretical discipline which is concerned with the common ultimate value element in human action is not generally accepted among sociologists, most of whom lean toward the "encyclopedic" view. The nearest approach to it which enjoys recognized standing in the literature is that of the so-called formal school, of which Georg Simmel is generally regarded as the founder. I regard it as a way of retaining the principal advantages of the "formal" approach without being open to many of the very serious criticisms which have been leveled at the latter.

The issues involved are obviously far too complex to be entered into here. Such an essay as the present one can only point a very general direction. The history of economic thought, however, in the aspects treated here seems to me to provide one exceedingly important element of the logical situation out of which such a conception can be built. In a forthcoming volume I shall deal with the question in a still wider perspective of the history of thought which will place the question of the status of economic theory more accurately in its larger context of the methodology of the social sciences as a total group.

in relation to the economic and the biological and psychological as well as others[64] naturally cannot be settled a priori—it must be the result of empirical investigation. But there is already quite enough empirical evidence that it is sufficiently important to be the basis of a major science. In the past, in the theoretical sense, there has been both too much sociology (as well as biology, psychology, etc.) in economics and too much economics in sociology. There is, however, a vast field for their fruitful cooperation, again with other sciences, in the solution of concrete problems beyond the scope of one or the other taken alone—as almost all really important concrete problems are.[65]

64. I should leave a place for a theoretical political science centering around the "power" factor which among economists preeminently Marx and Veblen have emphasized, and perhaps a science or a group of sciences of technology. In the sense of systematic generalizing empirical sciences I am inclined to think these cover the field of human behavior. The "science of law" is of a different logical order.

65. Dr. R. W. Souter (*Prolegomena to Relativity Economics*) protests against the view that one social science is logically independent of another in the sense that it can do without assumptions drawn from the fields of the others. Of course the ultimate concrete unity of human social life implies that the division of fields of the social sciences is only possible in terms of a coherent analysis of the whole into primary elements which must be thought of as related to each other in definite ways. If the "independence" of economics be meant to imply that economic action can be conceived as taking place in a social vacuum, Dr. Souter's protest is quite justified. For purposes of its own analysis it assumes the other factors constant, not nonexistent. Thus certain general assumptions are always found. But if this be pushed too far into the specific logical structure of economic theory it soon lands one in all the empiricist difficulties we have discussed. I think Dr. Souter goes rather far in this direction. The exact line, however, must be expected to shift somewhat with the development of science. See, for a detailed criticism of Dr. Souter's position, my article "Some Reflections on 'The Nature and Significance of Economics'" [chapter 16 of this volume].

It is evident that the issues with which the present study has been concerned are closely related to those involved in the so-called institutionalist controversy over questions of the methodology of economic science. I have, however, preferred not to deal in terms of that controversy directly because it seems to me that a number of different issues have become confused in it, and it is necessary to develop some such analytical apparatus as that attempted here in order to disentangle them. Its application to the discussion would require a separate essay, which I hope to be able to present at a future date.

18

The Place of Ultimate Values in Sociological Theory

The positivistic reaction against philosophy has, in its effect on the social sciences, manifested a strong tendency to obscure the fact that man is essentially an active, creative, evaluating creature. Any attempt to explain his behavior in terms of ends, purposes, ideals, has been under suspicion as a form of "teleology" which was thought to be incompatible with the methodological requirements of positive science. One must, on the contrary, explain in terms of "causes" and "conditions," not of ends.

Of late years, however, there have been many signs of a break in this rigid positivistic view of things. The social sciences in general have been far from immune from these signs, and in sociology in particular they have combined to form a movement of thought of the first importance. One main aspect of this movement has been the tendency to reopen the whole question of the extent to which, and the senses in which, human behavior must or can be understood in terms of the values entertained by men. In the present essay I wish to attempt a formulation of the kind of conception of human action which I take to be implied in some of these recent developments of sociological theory. In particular, what is the status in that conception of the element which may provisionally be called "ultimate values"? I shall not attempt here to trace the process by which this conception of human action has been built up, but merely to outline the conception itself.[1]

Originally published in the *International Journal of Ethics* 45 (1935): 282–316.
1. For this reason I shall not attempt to give detailed references to the literature. My own views have taken shape mainly in the course of a series of critical studies in European sociological theory. The important writers for my purposes may be divided into two groups—those starting from a positivistic and those from an idealistic background. I should maintain the thesis that the two groups have tended to converge on a conception somewhat like that which I shall outline in the present essay. Of the writers starting from a positivistic basis, two have been most important to me—Wilfredo[!] Pareto and Emile Durkheim. Of the other group, the most important have been Max Weber,

One of the most conspicuous features of the positivistic movement just referred to has been the tendency to what may be termed a kind of "objectivism." Positivism, that is, has continually thought in terms of the model of the physical sciences which deal with an "inanimate" subject matter. Hence the tendency has been to follow their example in thinking of a simple relation of observer to externally observed events. The fact that the entities observed, human beings, have also a "subjective" aspect has a tendency to be obscured, or at least kept out of the range of methodological self-consciousness. The extreme of this objectivist trend is, of course, behaviorism which involves the self-conscious denial of the legitimacy of including any references to the subjective aspect of other human beings in any scientific explanation of their actions. But short of this radical behaviorist position, the general positivistic trend of thought has systematically minimized the importance of analysis in terms of the subjective aspect, and has prevented a clear-cut and self-conscious treatment of the relations of the two aspects to each other.

Of course the results of analysis of human behavior from the objective point of view (that is, that of an outside observer) and the subjective (that of the person thought of as acting himself) should correspond, but that fact is no reason why the two points of view should not be kept clearly distinct. Only on this basis is there any hope of arriving at a satisfactory solution of their relations to each other.

End and value are subjective categories in this sense. Hence it is not surprising that the objectivist bias of positivistic social thought should tend either to squeeze them out altogether or to militate against any really thoroughgoing analysis of them in their bearing on action. For the same reasons the present attempt to present at least the foundations of such an analysis must be couched mainly in subjective terms. The implications of the analysis for the objective point of view can at best be only very briefly indicated.

There seems to be no evading the fact that the subjective analysis of action involves in some form the schema of the means-end relation-

---

George[!] Simmel, and Ferdinand Tönnies. The reader who is interested in these problems in more detail may be referred particularly to the following of their works: Pareto, *Traité de sociologie générale;* Durkheim, *De la division du travail social, Les règles de la méthode sociologique, Le suicide, L'éducation morale,* and *Les formes élémentaires de la vie religieuse;* Weber, *Wirtschaft und Gesellschaft* and *Gesammelte Aufsätze zur Wissenschaftslehre;* Simmel, *Soziologie;* and Tönnies, *Gemeinschaft und Gesellshaft.* In a forthcoming volume I am attempting, mainly in terms of the works of these writers, to trace the genesis of these ideas in detail. The study as a whole has been aided by the Harvard Committee on Research in the Social Sciences. I am happy to take this opportunity of acknowledgment.

ship. We must be careful to avoid any arbitrary assumption that this schema can exhaust the subjective aspect, but for various reasons it is the most favorable starting point of such an analysis. Hence, after some introductory definition of concepts, the second part of this essay will be concerned with an outline of the principal elements of action so far as it can be understood in terms of the means-end relationship, and with the main sociological implications of this analysis. Then, in the following parts we will proceed to a consideration of the possible relations of this schema to other aspects of the subjective, and in turn the sociological implications of these.

I

It is necessary in following out this program to point out an ambiguity in the concept of "end" which may cause serious confusion. One possible definition would be the following: An end is the subjective anticipation of a desirable future state of affairs toward the realization of which the action of the individual in question may be thought of as directed. The thing to note is that this definition makes the "real" reference of an end—that is, the future state of affairs—a *concrete* state of affairs. But only *some* of the elements in that concrete state of affairs can be thought of as being brought about by the agency of the actor. Part of it consists of a *prediction* of what the future state of affairs will be, independently of his action. Thus, if I say it is an end of my present action to take a vacation in New Hampshire next summer, the concrete state of affairs I anticipate—vacationing in New Hampshire in the summer—will, if the end is realized, only to a certain extent come about through my own agency. The fact that it is *I* who does it will, to be sure, be attributable to that factor—but the geography of New Hampshire and the fact that it is summer will not be my doing—I merely predict, on the basis of my knowledge of the circumstances, that the former will remain substantially the same as now for another year, and that the cycle of the seasons will, by July, have brought summer in place of the present fall weather.

Ends in this senses may be called *concrete* ends. Our concern in this discussion is not, however, with concrete ends, but with ends as a *factor* in action. That is, it is with the prevision of a future state of affairs *insofar as* that future state is to be brought about through the agency of the actor—it is the alterations from what his prediction, if accurate, would yield as the future state without his agency which constitutes the end. Thus I can "see" New Hampshire next summer without my vacationing there. I can also "see" myself at that future time not in New Hampshire, but, for instance, perspiring over my work in Cambridge. It is the peculiar elements of *myself, vacationing* in New Hampshire, which may be considered my end. Thus, ends in this discussion will be used as an analytical category—a *factor* in action, and this sense of the term will be implied throughout unless otherwise stated. It is highly important not to confuse it with the concrete reality I have referred to.

If the means-end relationship involving this sense of the term "ends" is employed in this analysis, it is clear and should be pointed out at the outset that the whole analysis involves a metaphysical position of a "voluntaristic" character. That is, the analysis has empirical significance and is more than a mere exercise in logic only insofar as subjective ends in this sense do actually form an effective factor in action. This postulate a materialistic metaphysics would roundly deny. The metaphysical implication of the analysis is, however, thus far only negative—at the pole of materialism it ceases to have empirical meaning. But on the other hand, short of that pole, the analysis by itself does not beg the question of the quantitative empirical importance of the factor of ends. So long as it is not negligible, we may go ahead with a good conscience. But insofar as positivistic social theory has involved a genuinely materialistic metaphysics (which I believe it very generally has), it has quite rightly shied away from this type of analysis. For it, "ends," insofar as they exist at all, must be epiphenomena. Hence the importance of the foregoing distinction. Some concrete ends *may* be epiphenomena to us also, but to postulate this of the *factor* ends in general is naturally a contradiction in terms.

Before entering on an analysis of the means-end relationship itself, one more preliminary question should be called attention to. The means-end schema is, in type, at the rationalistic pole of the analysis of action. An end is thought of as a *logically formulated* anticipation of certain elements in a future state of affairs, and the relation of means to end is thought of as based on knowledge of the inherent connections of things. This is, in its type form, a *scientific* statement couched in the conditional, or, as it is sometimes put, the virtual form. That is, *if* I do certain things, bring about certain conditions, I will achieve my end. But this rational schema of the relation of means and ends is not to be arrived at by empirical generalization from the crude facts of experience. It is not only an analytical schema, but one of a peculiar sort. What it formulates is a *norm* of rational action. Its empirical relevance rests on the view, which I believed to be factually borne out, that human beings do, in fact, strive to realize ends and to do so by the rational application of means to them. This involves what I just called a "voluntaristic" conception of human action. Neither the knowledge of the relation of means and end on which action is based nor application of that knowledge comes automatically. Both are the result of effort, of the exercise of will. Hence the probability that concrete action will only imperfectly realize such norms. Ignorance, error, and obstacles to the realization of ends which transcend human powers will all play a part in determining the concrete course of events. While, on the one hand, the concept of action itself has no meaning apart from "real" ends and a rational norm of means-end relationships (it dissolves into mere "behavior"), on the other hand it equally has no meaning apart from obstacles to be overcome by effort in the realization of the norm. The concepts built up on the basis of the means-end schema are thus not empirical generalizations but, to use Max Weber's term, "ideal types." But, precisely insofar as this voluntaristic conception of action holds true, they are indispensable to the understanding of concrete human affairs.

I have said that the rational norm of action implied in the means-end schema constitutes a *scientific* statement in conditional form. Indeed, insofar as it has been concerned with the subjective aspect of human action, the whole of modern social theory revolves about the question of the relation of science and action: In what sense and to what extent may action be thought of as guided by scientific knowledge?

It should be clear that the creative, voluntaristic element which we have found to be involved in the factor of ends precludes action ever being *completely* determined by scientific knowledge in the sense of the modern positive sciences. For the business of science is to understand the "given"—its very essence is a certain objectivity, that is, an independence of the "facts" from the will of the scientist. In action, therefore, the element of scientific knowledge may have a place in imparting accurate understanding of the conditions in which action takes place—and in forecasting the results of such conditions whether independent of the actor's agency or not.

But *ends* are not given in this sense—they are precisely the element of rational action which falls outside the schema of positive science. Indeed, many positivistic theorists, by trying to think of rational action as the type *entirely* determined by scientific knowledge, and attempting thus to fit ends into the scientific schema, have in fact squeezed out the *factor* of ends altogether. For concrete ends could only be scientific facts in so far as they constituted scientific predictions from present and past facts. The creative element has no place.

But although we must reject this narrow interpretation of rational action, nevertheless the scientific schema is basic to what is historically (in terms of the history of modern thought) the main type of means-end relationship—what I shall call the *intrinsic* relationship. It is that which can be analyzed in terms of scientific knowledge (or its commonsense predecessors), with the one exception of the *determination* of ends.

The factor of ends may be fitted into this schema in the following way. Though what concrete ends should be striven for cannot be determined on the basis of scientific knowledge alone, once the end is given the means to its attainment may be selected on that basis. Moreover, though an end cannot itself be determined by scientific knowledge, the fact or degree of its attainment may, after the time to which it refers has arrived, be verified by scientific observation. Insofar as this is true of an end, I shall refer to it as an empirical end. Then action is rational in terms of the intrinsic means-end relationship insofar as, on the one hand, its ends are empirical, and on the other, the relations of means and ends involved in it are the intrinsic relations of things as revealed by scientific knowledge of the phenomena. Once he knows the end, the rationality of such action can be judged by an external observer, both before and after its completion, in terms of his own scientific knowledge.[2] Deviations from the rational norm will be explicable in one or more of three sets of terms: ignorance of intrinsic relationships, lack of effort, or presence of obstacles beyond the power of the actor to remove, whether they be obstacles in the actor's own constitution and character or in his environment.

But does this type exhaust the logical possibilities of the means-end relationship? By no means! First, as to ends: Here it is necessary to enter into definitely philosophical questions. What is the implication of what I have called the creative character of the factor of ends, and hence of the impossibility of fitting it, for the actor, into the category of facts of the external world? It is, I think, a negation of the positivistic view that the "realities" which can be studied by empirical science are the sole realities significant for human action. I have purposely defined ends in terms of a vague phrase, a future "state of affairs." It is now necessary to define more closely what the phrase means.

It is clear that insofar as an end is, in the foregoing sense, an empirical end, the future state of affairs is to be thought of as a state of the

---

2. Before, in terms of *probability* of success, of course.

scientifically observable external world.[3] But there is a certain diffi-culty in thinking of this as alone involved. For the ends of action are not, in fact, to be based on the mere arbitrary whims of a once popular "libertarian" philosophy. Overwhelmingly the realization of the ulti-mate ends of action is felt to be a matter of moral obligation, to be binding on the individual—not, to be sure, in the sense of physical necessity, but still binding. The ubiquity of the concept of duty is per-haps sufficient proof of this.

But whence this sense of binding obligation? The source of specific moral obligations cannot be derived from the empirical properties of "human nature" as revealed by scientific psychology—for this is part of the same external world as the environment—the subjective point of view is that of the *ego* not of the body, or even the "mind." Psy-chology may reveal man as a creature who obeys moral obligations—but not as bound by his nature to *one* particular set of such obliga-tions. Moreover, this explanation would violate both the inner sense of freedom of moral choice, which is just as ultimate a fact of human life as any other, and its consequent moral responsibility. In fact, a psychological explanation of moral obligation really explains away the phenomenon itself. Finally, also there is a very large body of em-pirical evidence indicating that specific moral values are not com-pletely correlated with "human nature."

If this explanation is rejected, it seems to me that there is only one other avenue left open. The world of "empirical" fact must be only a part, only one aspect, of the universe insofar as it is significant to man. The "external world," i.e., that of science, is as it were an island in a sea the character of which is something different from the island. Our relation to the other aspects of the universe is different from that of scientist to empirical facts. It will be noted that all these characteri-zations are negative—it is something transcending science.

The ultimate reason, then, for the causal independence of ends in action, the fact that they are not determined by the facts of human nature and environment, is the *fact* that man stands in significant re-lations to aspects of reality other than those revealed by science. Moreover, the fact that empirical reality can be modified by action shows that this empirical reality, the world of science, is not a closed system but is itself significantly related to the other aspects of reality.

Now it has been stated that the concept of end involves logical for-mulation. Does this mean that empirical ends are the only possible

3. To both actor and observer after completion of the act.

ones? While our logical formulations of nonempirical reality differ
from those of empirical reality—that is, are not *scientific* theories—
they exist nonetheless. They are metaphysical theories, theologies, etc.
Now such theories may be thought of in relation to ends in two ways:
They may constitute the terms to be used in justifying empirical ends;
this is, in fact, an empirically important case. At the same time, however, they may lay down, as desirable, ends of action altogether outside the empirical sphere—that is, ends the attainment of which cannot be verified by empirical observation. Such an end is, for example,
eternal salvation. This class, the attainment of a "state of affairs" outside the realm of empirical observability, I should like to call "transcendental ends."

We may then put the situation somewhat as follows: Ultimate empirical ends are justified to the actor in terms, not of scientific, but of
metaphysical, theories. He may, however, by virtue of his metaphysical theories pursue not merely empirical but also transcendental ends.
It is conceivable that there should be a system of empirical ends justified directly by a metaphysical theory without reference to transcendental ends. That is the case, for instance, with the ideal of socialism—it refers to a desired future state of affairs in this world only. But
in general such a metaphysical theory at the same time enjoins transcendental ends. Whenever that is the case, empirical ends are also
present; otherwise there is no relation to action as an empirical reality.
The relation will in general be such that a transcendental end is
thought logically to imply as a means to it a given empirical end.

One further distinction in the realm of ends remains to be made.
Some empirical ends refer to a state of affairs differing from the merely
predicted state by more than a changed state of mind of the actor. On
the other hand, one may think of the actor as attempting to attain
only a subjective state of mind—happiness, for instance. In these
terms I should like to distinguish "objective" empirical ends from
"subjective" empirical ends.[4] The attainment of both is verifiable, but
in different ways. This is to assume, as we do throughout, the anti-
behaviorist position that scientific observation of an individual's subjective state of mind is possible and valid. It is necessary, of course, to
distinguish an altered state of mind as a *result* of action from its role
as an end. "Happiness" or "satisfaction" may be thought of as, in
general, a result of the attainment of objective ends—empirical or

---

4. This is, it should be repeated, *not* a classification of *concrete* ends, but of *elements*
in concrete ends. Both are often combined in the same concrete end.

transcendental. But on occasion it is thought of as an end in itself—whether attainable or not is another question.

The attainment of a transcendental end should not be thought of as that of a state of mind. What is true is that the only empirical evidence we have of its attainment is *through* the statements and the state of mind of the individual actor. Religious persons may state that they are saved, or that they have attained Nirvana. Scientifically, such statements are not verifiable. But we may verify that persons who *believe* they have attained such a transcendental end do *in fact* typically attain certain subjective states of mind.

Now to return to the element of means. We have given as the kind of means involved in the scientific norm of rational action those which are *intrinsically* related to their ends. This relation is a normative type which may be further defined as follows: The relation between end and means is intrinsic insofar as the employment of a given combination of means will bring about the realization of the end by processes of scientifically understandable accusation. There is, however, a large category of means employed in human action of which this is not true. From the point of view of a scientific analysis of the relation of means and end, the connection is arbitrary—therefore from the scientific point of view the action is "irrational." Insofar as this arbitrary relationship is not due merely to ignorance, i.e., inadequate scientific insight, but to a definitely nonscientific "ritual" attitude[5] toward the means, I should call this a symbolic means-end relationship.[6] It is possible that there are other types of means, but for present purposes I shall limit myself to the two categories of intrinsic and symbolic.

II

Having detailed the principal types of elements of the means-end relationship, we may now proceed to inquire into their interrelationships in *systems* of action. We may start with the intrinsic means-end relationship. This may be thought of as constituting a "chain" of such relations. At one end will be those elements which are ultimate means or conditions of action but not, from any point of view, ends. These

5. A term used by Professor A. R. Radcliffe-Brown. See his paper "The Sociological Theory of Totemism," *Proceedings of the Fourth Pacific Science Congress,* Java, 1929.

6. Symbols may, of course, also be used as intrinsic means—e.g., linguistic symbols to convey meaning. Whether a means is intrinsic or symbolic is to be judged in terms of its relation to the particular end—not of its general inherent "nature."

will, on analysis,[7] turn out to constitute the two categories of heredity and environment—the cosmic and bio-psychological factors of human life. Positivistic social theories always attempt to elevate these into the sole factors and thus, as we have noted in another connection, squeeze out that of ends. Action, whether rational or not, is thought of as a process of adaptation to these factors.

At the other end of the chain is the factor of ultimate ends, which are, looked at in intrinsic terms, ends in themselves and not means to any further ends. The ultimate ends of the *intrinsic* chain must, it is apparent, be empirical ends, but may be either objective or subjective. The existence of such an element of ultimate ends is a logical necessity for any view which allows a place as a real factor in action for ends in any sense whatever.

In between these two extremes with indefinite possibilities of ramifications will be an "intermediate" sector of the intrinsic means-end chain. These elements are both means and ends at the same time— ends when looked at from "below," e.g., from means to ends; means when looked at from "above," from end to means. This intermediate sector can be analyzed, it seems to me, into three subsectors—the technological, the economic, and the political, respectively. The technological element exists, insofar as action is concerned, with the choice and application of means for a single end in abstraction from others. The economic element enters when the question of the alternative uses of scarce means for different ends arises. The economic problem is essentially that of the allocation of these scarce means as between alternative uses in terms of the relative urgency of the ends— that is, of marginal utility.

Finally the political element is specifically concerned with the relations of individuals to each other as potential means to each other's ends. It is present insofar as authority over others and control of their actions for one's own ends is secured by means of coercive power. The state is the focus of the political element because it is the association which attempts to regulate the power relationships of the community in the general interest, partly by its monopoly of the *legitimate* exercise of physical coercion.

The standard of rationality applicable to the intermediate sector of the intrinsic means-end chain is that of efficiency. It is a matter of the intrinsic adaptation of means quite apart from other considerations.

Now we must return to the factor of ultimate ends, which is our main concern. So far nothing has been said of the relation of ultimate

7. Unfortunately, there is no space here to present the details of this analysis.

ends to each other. One possible view is that they form a random plurality, with no connections whatever. The element of order in human action would then be restricted to the relations of means to these ends. This has been, indeed, the position implicit in at least certain trends of utilitarian thought. There are, however, cogent reasons for rejecting it.

Taken first on the individual level, reflection will show that this doctrine is fatal to the conception of rational choice, which is in turn essential to the whole voluntaristic conception of action put forward here. For a choice between ends implies that they are related to each other, that they are true *alternatives* in terms of a wider system of principles. It is, indeed, no wonder that utilitarianism shows such a strong tendency to slide off into some form of positivistic determinism, for once rational choice is eliminated in this fashion there is nothing left to determine action but biological and psychological drives. It can safely be concluded, then, that precisely insofar as the action of an individual is guided by rational choice, its ultimate ends are to be thought of as constituting an integrated system. Rationality of action for an individual implies just as much the working-out of such a coherent system of ends as it does a rational selection of means.

But then is it not conceivable that though individuals must be thought of as acting in terms of such integrated systems of ends, the systems of different individuals should, within the limits of biological survival at least, be thought of as varying at random? It is, indeed, *logically* possible but not, I think, empirically. For such a statement there are two kinds of evidence. In the first place it may be argued in general and abstract terms that this random variation of systems of ends would be incompatible with the most elementary form of social order. For there would be no guaranty that any large proportion of such systems would include a recognition of other people's ends as valuable in themselves, and there would thus be no necessary limitation on the means that some, at least, would employ to gain their own ends at the expense of others. The relations of individuals then would tend to be resolved into a struggle for power—for the means for each to realize his own ends. This would be, in the absence of constraining factors, a war of all against all—Hobbes's state of nature. Insofar, however, as individuals share a *common* system of ultimate ends, this system would, among other things, define what they all held their relations ought to be, would lay down norms determining these relations and limits on the use of others as means, on the acquisition and use of power in general. Insofar, then, as action is determined by ultimate ends, the existence of a *system* of such ends common to the members of the community seems to be the only alternative to a state of chaos—a necessary factor in social stability.

In addition, there is much empirical evidence that such systems of ultimate ends exist and play a decisive role in social life. This evidence is derived from many sources. One is the comparative study of actual historical societies and their functioning. Thus Greek society would appear to be scarcely understandable without reference to the peculiar conceptions of what human relations should be, centering about the idea of the *polis*. So much were these values common to all Greeks that persons who did not share them were unhesitatingly stigmatized as barbarians, and their values dismissed from serious consideration. Similarly in the Middle Ages with the values clustering about the church. Another very impressive source of evidence derives from the study of the processes of child development which brings out the enormous importance in the formation of individual personality of the child's "socialization" in terms of the values of the group.[8] But perhaps the most impressive evidence of all is Durkheim's empirical demonstration that even the modern individualism to which the utilitarians have pointed as the main confirmation of their thesis involved highly important *common* values, centering, above all, in the common ethical valuation of individual personality as such.[9]

It is advisable, though it should scarcely be necessary, to point out once more that we are merely arguing for the necessity of assuming that a common system of ultimate ends plays a significant part in social life. We are not arguing that the concrete reality may be understood completely, or even predominantly in such terms. Nor that the *common* system exhausts the genuinely ethical element. Thus, criticisms to the effect that there was in the Middle Ages anti-Christian action or sentiment, or that, after all, Socrates resisted the populace of Athens on ethical grounds, are not relevant unless the critic can prove not only that phenomena not fitting into this scheme *exist* but that those formulated in the scheme do not, which is an entirely different matter.

If the place for a common system of ultimate ends be granted, a further question arises: Is there inherent in our relations to nonempirical reality only *one* such system, are we in the normative sense subject to a unitary Law of nature or not? Almost all philosophers have pictured the scheme of values they themselves formulated as the one eth-

---

8. Brought out notably in the works of Jean Piaget.

9. Cf. *Division du travail social,* especially book 1, chap. 7; *Le suicide,* especially book 3, chap. 1.

ically possible one. I do not propose even to attempt to enter into the philosophical question at issue. It is quite possible that there "is" only one such system. On the other hand, looked at empirically, which is, after all, the point of view of sociological science, this would seem to be a dangerous assumption. For the first thing that strikes the observer of values in history is the very great diversity of such systems. To take only one instance, the values embodied in the Indian doctrines of karma and transmigration and the empirical ends associated with them seem utterly incompatible with those inherent in our Western individualism. The former yield a direct sanction of caste; whereas caste is utterly unacceptable to even the highest of our high Tories. The safest procedure for sociologists would seem to be to take this historical diversity of value systems as a starting point, first to attempt to determine what are the ultimate value systems relevant to understanding action in a given society at a given time. From that starting point, then, it is quite legitimate to proceed to attempt to discover relationships between such systems—to classify them according to types, to establish genetic relationships. But all this should be done with the greatest of care to avoid the common fallacy of reading arbitrarily into the facts a tendency to the ultimate realization of the investigator's own particular values. The fallacy is, of course, only too prevalent. It may be said to be involved in virtually every current doctrine of social evolution and progress.

We may now consider the modes in which the ultimate common system of ends is related to action in the intrinsic means-end chain. There are, I think, two modes. Either an ultimate end is also the immediate end of a given train of action or it is not. In the former case the logical situation is very simple—it is merely a matter of an ordinary means-end relationship.[10] Its rationality is to be judged by the ordinary standards of efficiency once the end is given. The standard of efficiency is, of course, applicable only insofar as the end is an empirical end; but this may in turn be derived from a system of transcendental ends. But the strategy, for instance, of a general in a religious war is to be judged in exactly the same terms as though the sole aim of the war were aggrandizement. Such a coincidence of ultimate with immediate ends occurs generally at times of critical decision—for individuals, societies, and social movements.[11]

But most of our action is not directly concerned with critical deci-

10. This is the type which Max Weber has called *wertrationales Handeln*. See *Wirtschaft und Gesellschaft*, chap. 1.

11. For a great social movement this has been called by my colleague, Professor Crane Brinton, the stage of "active religion." It is a useful term.

sions between conflicting ultimate ends. It is rather a matter of the pursuit of immediate ends which may be removed by a very large number of intermediate links from any system of ultimate ends. The miner mining coal, to smelt iron to make steel to make rails, etc., is contributing to railway transportation, but at a point very far removed from the question of the ultimate value of railway transportation. These very facts of the remoteness of such action from ultimate ends, of the latency of such ends in relation to it, create a problem of control. There would, to be sure, be no such problems were the rationality of action automatic. But such is not the case. This is true neither of the rational formulation which transforms what may be called "value attitudes"[12] into specific ultimate ends, nor of the knowledge of relation of means to these ends, nor finally of the actual application of this knowledge to action itself. The voluntaristic conception of action implies that there is resistance to the realization of the rational norm—partly the resistance of inertia, partly that of factors which would tend to divert the course of action from the norm. We will not here inquire into what these factors are—merely call attention to their presence.

This problem of control tends to be met by the subjection of action in pursuit of immediate nonultimate ends to normative rules which regulate that action in conformity with the common ultimate value system of the community. These normative rules both define what immediate ends should and should not be sought, and limit the choice of means to them in terms other than those of efficiency. Finally, they also define standards of socially acceptable effort. This system of rules, fundamental to any society not in the state of "active religion," is what I call its institutions. They are *moral* norms, not norms of efficiency. They bear directly the stamp of their origin in the common system of ultimate ends.

The question of the modes in which institutional norms become enforced on individual actions is a complex one and cannot be entered into here. Suffice it to say that there are two primary modes, first, by the inherent moral authority of the norm itself due essentially to its derivation from the common system of ends to which the individuals obeying it subscribe. Second, there is the appeal to interest. That is, conformity to the norm may, apart from any moral attitude, be in the given concrete situation a means to the realization of the actor's private ends apart from the common value system. This type may in turn be divided into two main types—where conformity is due to the pos-

12. See below, section IV, for a discussion of this term.

itive advantages attached to it—as social esteem, and where it is due to a desire to avoid the unpleasant consequences of nonconformity— its sanctions.

Thus to sum up—the analysis of the intrinsic means-end chain yields the necessity for the existence of a class of ultimate ends which are not means to any further ends in this chain. Partly a priori and partly empirical considerations lead to the view that these ultimate ends do not occur in random fashion, but that both in the case of the individual and of the social group they must be thought of as to a significant degree integrated into a single harmonious *system*. In the case of the social group, which mainly interests us here, this is to be thought of as a system of ultimate ends held in common by the members of the group. Insofar as these common ideal ends concern, directly or by logical implication, the relations of members of the group to each other, the norms of what these relationships are thought should be are understandable in terms of the common system of ultimate ends.

This common system may be thought of as related to the rest of the intrinsic means-end chain—above all, the intermediate sector—in two main ways. In the first place the immediate end of a particular concrete complex of actions may be, in this sense, an ultimate end. In the second place the actions in pursuit of nonultimate immediate ends may be thought of as governed by normative rules, institutions. Institutions may be classified as technological, economic, and political, according to what elements of the intermediate chain they govern.

Because of the great intricacy and subtlety of the possible relationships between action and moral rules, it is primarily, in connection with the institutional aspect of ultimate ends that the important sociological problems arise. The theory of institutions will indeed form one of the most important, as well as difficult, branches of sociological theory. But in order to see its role in perspective, it is necessary to place it in terms of a coherent scheme of the elements of action, as we are attempting to do. It is this which has, more than anything else, been lacking in previous attempts to formulate a theory of institutions.

III

Near the beginning of this paper it was stated that the logical starting point of the subjective analysis of action in our own (i.e., modern Western) thought was the "scientific" standard of rationality—the intrinsic connection of means with empirical ends. An outline of the main elements in action as far as this standard will reach has just been completed. It has already been made clear, however, that this does not exhaust the analysis of elements possibly significant for human action. On the contrary, the factor of ultimate ends necessarily points beyond this schema. It is now our task to enter explicitly into the realm of this "beyond." Fortunately, it is not necessary at once to abandon familiar landmarks. While we have, without going farther into detail, exhausted the logical possibilities of the *intrinsic* means-end chain, that is not true of the means-end schema altogether.

One resource is left which has not been made use of at all—the symbolic means-end relationship. In many societies, especially (though not exclusively) the so-called primitive societies, we find very conspicuous an element of action which in terms of the standard of intrinsic rationality somehow ought not to be there. That is, we find the attempt to secure empirical ends—such as a large crop, seaworthiness in a canoe, victory over an enemy—by symbolic, ritual means. That is, instead of performing technical operations (or rather, in addition to performing them) men perform ceremonies, say spells, invoke the aid of nonempirical agencies. This is in a field where rational techniques exist and where, according to rational standards, there is no intrinsic connection between the (symbolic) means and the end. This elment may be called magic.[13] It is a spurious practical technique. This does not in any sense mean that magic is of no importance in social life. It is true that it cannot by definition be effective as a rational technique by acting directly on external phenomena. But our voluntaristic conception of action opens the door to understanding the role of magic. For action involves effort, and effort demands something more than an end and knowledge of means—it demands a certain state of mind, a will to overcome obstacles. While magic can have no effect on action directly, it may well be highly important in determining this state of mind, and thus indirectly be a major factor. And, in fact, there is much positive evidence that this is so.[14] Magic is essentially a tonic, a bracer to self-confidence.

But magic is not of central interest to us. A brief reference to it is included for the sake of completeness and to mark the line of distinction between it and other forms of the symbolic means-end relationships. Magic is not an inherently necessary form of action, for it

13. The most illuminating theoretical discussion of magic I know is Malinowski's essay on "Magic, Science, and Religion" in *Science, Religion, and Reality,* edited by J. Needham.

14. See, for example, R. Firth, *Primitive Economics of the New Zealand Maori,* chap. 7, "Magic in Economics."

occupies a place from which it may be ousted by rational techniques—it is inherently in competition with them. But what of action in pursuit of transcendental ends? We have pointed out the logical possibility of a whole system of action without them—with a system of ultimate empirical ends self-contained—the only nonempirical element being a metaphysical theory justifying these ends.[15] But in spite of this logical possibility it would be highly arbitrary to deny the role of transcendental ends in history or from their comparative inconspicuousness in recent times to conclude that they are destined to disappear.

But by what means can transcendental ends be pursued? There are two logically possible modes. First they may, by real or supposed logical implication, obligate their adherents to pursue certain ultimate empirical ends, which are then capable of attainment by intrinsic means. Then the analysis falls into the grooves already discussed. But such an ultimate empirical end is only a means to a transcendental end—unless it be the direct command of a transcendental being. In any case, there is still the possibility that people attempt to attain transcendental ends by direct action. But since they lie, by definition, outside the empirical world, the relation of means to them cannot be intrinsic—that is, must be symbolic. That is to say that *from the intrinsic point of view* the relation is arbitrary and the action irrational. Then we get complexes of action which, again from the intrinsic point of view, do not serve any (i.e., empirical) end, but are ends in themselves. But to the actor it is in the strictest sense action—that is, the attainment of ends.[16] That means it is governed by norms which enjoin the *right* selection of means. This action is religious ritual—distinguished from intrinsic rational action by the character of both end and means, from magic by that of ends only. Hence the very close relation of religion and magic. It is only natural that means believed efficacious in attaining transcendental ends should also be applied to empirical ends.

Insofar as the common system of ultimate ends involves transcendental ends, it is then to be expected that it will be expressed in common ritual actions. From the empirical point of view the question whether such actions in fact attain their ends is irrelevant, for there is

15. It is clear that this metaphysical element is the minimum possible unless one denies the independent role of ends. The "scientific" theories such as socialism, liberalism, etc., which purport to justify such ends in purely scientific terms, always contain metaphysical elements such as, for instance, the famous utilitarian postulate that each individual shall count as one and only one.

16. "C'est de la vie sérieuse," says Durkheim. See *Les formes élémentaires de la vie religieuse,* 546.

no possible means of verification. But that is again, as in the case of magic, no reason whatever for denying a priori any functional importance in society to religious ritual. On the contrary, there is ample evidence that people's states of mind depend very much indeed on what they *believe* to be their status with reference to the attainment of transcendental ends. And inasmuch as their action, taken as a whole—above all, its energy—depends very much indeed on their general state of mind, there is every reason to believe that religious ritual is a very important phenomenon and cannot be simply suppressed without serious social effects.

The special character of the symbolic means-end relationship helps to explain two peculiar features of religious ritual. Since it is a form of action, of the *vie sérieuse,* it must be thought of as governed by norms. So far we have encountered two types of authority in norms— efficiency and moral obligation. There may be others conceivable in relation to action,[17] but they are not so conspicuous as these two. Anyway, the norm of efficiency is excluded in the nature of the case. Thus there tends to be a certain moral obligation to employ certain ritual means. Our attitude to ritual hence tends to be that kind of respect which we give to moral rules rather than the utilitarian attitude which predominates in attempts to realize a norm of efficiency. The same situation accounts, at least in part, for a second peculiarity: the prominence of traditionalism in ritual. For there is, insofar as the symbolic relation exists, no intrinsic reason why *one particular* symbol rather than another should be employed. But the idea that it does not matter what means is employed to achieve an end is repugnant to the very idea of action. Hence the tendency for certain particular ritual means to become traditionally stereotyped. Tradition is, as it were, the substitute for intrinsic requiredness in determining the choice of particular means. This situation may help to explain certain complex repercussions, for instance, of technological advance. For insofar as that technological advance may be due to a certain type of "scientific attitude" which is hostile to traditionalism in general, the same attitude may serve to undermine the basis on which ritual rests, and in turn destroy the social functions ritual may perform.

Of course this element of "religious action," insofar as it takes the form of a means-end schema, involves a rationalization in several senses—a rational formulation of ends, an explanation of why these ends should be sought and of why the particular symbolic means en-

17. Two other types of norm *not directly* related to action may be mentioned—that of *logical* correctness and the "requiredness" of a given aesthetic style.

joined in ritual are thought to serve to attain the end. But for the same reason that symbolic means are resorted to in attaining transcendental ends, symbolism plays a peculiarly important part in the ideas associated with religious action.

All thought, to be sure, takes place in terms of symbols—linguistic symbols, visual images, and others. But *scientific* thought makes use of concepts which contain, as it were, only a simple symbolic reference—directly to the empirical content of the concept. But the entities dealt with in religious thought are not empirical realities in the same sense. Hence, not only does the thought employ symbols; but insofar as there is an attempt to "visualize" the entities to which religious concepts refer, it must be in terms of symbols again—except to the extent to which, as mystics claim, we have direct insight into the nonempirical aspects of reality. Hence in this field there is a double incidence of symbolism.

Religious action thus forms, along with action in immediate pursuit of ultimate empirical ends and with institutions, a third aspect of the incidence of ultimate ends on social life. One fundamental element in it is certainly the ritual expression, both individually and collectively, of the common ultimate value attitudes of the community.[18] As such it may, as we have noted, have highly important social functions. These three phenomena are not to be understood primarily as three separate "factors" in social life, but rather as three modes of expression in different relations to action, of the same fundamental factor— the ultimate common value system.

IV

The element of the religious ritual, although falling outside the realm of applicability of "scientific" norms of rationality in the full sense, is still, as we have seen, subject to analysis in terms of what are, in a sense, rational norms. It is still capable of being cast in terms of the means-end schema which itself implies rationalization in the three senses just mentioned. It is now necessary to raise the question whether it is only insofar as this kind of rational norm is applicable that action can be understood in terms of ultimate "value" elements at all. If that is so, any element in action not so understandable must be relegated to the category of ultimate conditions, which we have,

18. It was Durkheim in *Les formes élémentaires de la vie religieuse*, who, from a sociological point of view, first strikingly brought out this aspect of religious ritual.

though without full justification on account of limitations of space, identified with the positivistic factors of heredity and environment.

This is the most difficult question this paper has to face. There are, I think, two possible positions. First, that the extent to which human action is in fact independent of positivistic determinism is a matter solely of the degree to which man has achieved logical formulation of his ends—and that so far as he falls short of this norm he is the "dependent variable." The alternative is the view that this logical formulation (that is, an "end" in the strict sense) is the specification, the fixation in certain forms and directions of something vaguer, less determinate which is, however, of the order of a value element and not a psychological drive.

I have no hesitation in taking the latter view. But I have equally no hesitation in admitting the extreme difficulty of finding adequate formulations for any scientific analysis of the implications of this view. The best I can do at the present time is to call attention to two types of phenomena in social life which it seems to me impossible to analyze either in terms of pure positivism or of the view that value elements exist only in so far as they are rationalized.

First let us dispose of a matter of terminology. True to our starting point, we have in general used the term "end" to designate the value element (that is, the nonpositivistic element) in action. This arises from our departure from the means-end schema. An end, it will be recalled, is a logical formulation of the anticipation of a desired future state of affairs insofar as it is to be brought about by the actor's own agency. But from the present point of view it turns out that ends do not constitute the value element *in toto,* but only one part of it.[19] It is in turn a rationalized expression, a manifestation of something else, something vaguer, less defined. This "something," of which an end is a logically formulated specification, I call a "value attitude."[20] This conception is, it is evident, arrived at negatively—it is the name for an unknown.[21] Further analysis may well reveal many things about it of which I do not here take account. But, if only negatively, our analysis

19. I wish to use the term "value," as suggested, to designate the creative element in action in general, that element which is causally independent of the positivistic factors of heredity and environment.

20. There is a direct parallel, I think, between my terms "end" and "value attitude" and Pareto's "residue" and "sentiment." I do not, however, adopt Pareto's terminology because he did not clearly draw the line between positivistic and value elements in action which is absolutely essential to me. His terms include both categories. See my brief article, "Pareto," in the *Encyclopaedia of the Social Sciences* [chapter 12 of this volume].

21. The fact that some of its relations to other categories of action are known prevents it from being itself entirely unknown.

has defined it in relation to a number of other important entities. Hence it does not seem to me that the conception is, recognizing its provisional character, altogether valueless. It follows from these considerations that the three elements of social life which we have already traced to common ultimate value elements are better designated as manifestations of common ultimate value attitudes, than of ends. For neither institutions nor ritual *need* be derived from the logical formulations of ends and the rationalized metaphysical theories associated with them. They may be direct manifestations of the same ultimate value attitudes of which ultimate ends are also manifestations. The question of the exact relationships is one which should be left open for empirical determination.

Let us turn now to the two phenomena which fall, I think, in the main outside the rationalized means-end schema but at the same time have a great deal to do with value attitudes. I am not, be it noted, advancing any claim that they are the *only* phenomena of which this is true. But they illustrate adequately, I think, the kind of problems our analysis must face if it is to get beyond the strict means-end schema.[22]

The first of these is art. There are, of course, many complex phenomena which go under that name. I do not propose even to attempt to exhaust them. But it can scarcely escape the most elementary observer, I think, that for example the Greek architecture of the fifth century has something to do with the value centering in the *polis,* or that medieval gothic has something to do with the church and its place in people's lives. This may be only one kind of art, but it is unquestionably art. Where can it be made to fit into our scheme?

Perhaps the first thing that strikes one is the close relation between art and religious ritual on the one hand, and practical techniques on the other. But there is a highly important difference from ritual. There is lacking the binding character of the relation of means to end which is so conspicuous in ritual.[23] The artist is, in a sense, free in his choice of means in which the performer of ritual is not. It is true that he is subject to norms—the norms of a style, of harmony, beauty, taste. But they are norms of a different character from those of ritual obligation. To be sure also, the action of the artist has, like all action, an end; but this is more diffuse and less definite than the end of a specific ritual— it is glorifying the gods, the *polis,* etc. This situation may be put by

22. That is a schema in terms of which an action or a complex of actions can be understood as attempting to achieve a specific end.

23. Note, again, that we are dealing with analytical *elements* not *concrete phenomena*. Temples, statues, churches, are all involved in concrete ritual.

saying that artistic creation is not so much the attainment of a specific end as the expression of an attitude, or a complex of attitudes. The form, the style, the means, must be in general harmony with the attitude—with its "end"—but this does not bind the artist to any specific means. Hence the difficulty of finding critical standards by which to judge artistic achievement.

It is, of course, true that artistic creation involves the use of techniques—often highly complex and rationalized techniques. Insofar as this is true, the artist's action may be analyzed in terms of the intrinsic means-end relationship. But taken as a whole, artistic work is not a technique, because it is not a means of attaining any specific end. In terms of the ordinary means-end analysis, art is a "luxury," it is unnecessary.

If we adopt this formula that art is a form of the "expression of attitudes,"what attitudes? In principle it may be any attitudes, but on empirical grounds it seems quite clear that a great deal of art, as in the examples adduced, is primarily an expression of the common ultimate value attitudes of the community. As such it may, like ritual and magic, have an important functional relation to action—that is a matter for investigation. In any case, it is a highly important index of these value attitudes—the existence in a community of common art styles and tendencies in subject matter would seem to indicate that they should be given a high degree of importance, while the lack of such things would argue the opposite.

The line between art and ritual is, as we have seen, a fluid one. To a believing Catholic the mass is a form of action—it is a means of getting something done. To me, a Protestant, with skeptical tendencies, it is primarily a work of art. It is something I can "appreciate" not only as beautiful but as significant. But I am not, like the Catholic, bound by it in terms of a rigid means-end schema. There is, indeed, with the change of values a tendency for the value expressions of the past to take on an aesthetic significance, to be looked upon with the attitude of artistic appreciation rather than strictly as actions in the pursuit of specific ends. Thus art, both to the artist and his audience, falls outside the means-end schema in its strictest sense altogether. While these other manifestations of the ultimate value attitudes *may* be thought of in its terms, to do so in the case of art involves forcing the facts into an analytical straitjacket which they do not fit.

We have seen that, although the technical operations of the artist may be analyzed in terms of the ordinary means-end schema, the same is not true of the complex of actions taken as a whole. This case well illustrates the difficulty, and importance, in this kind of analysis, of defining the unit of analysis. There is, I think, no one obvious and necessary unit. The schema is applicable all the way from the simplest individual act to the most extensive complexes of action—provided, of course, that proper precautions are taken to introduce the additional complicating factors that enter in. It is true, however, that the starting point of the means-end analysis is the individual act with a single well-defined end. The case of art well illustrates the "organic" nature of the phenomena of action, that certain characteristics only become visible when we look at a complex of actions as a whole rather than at the simplest analytical "atoms" which make it up, simple means-end relationships.

The same is true of the other phenomenon I wish to call attention to. Actions in society give rise to relationships of the actor to other human beings and in turn become dependent on these relationships. The "extensive" view of social life which looks upon it as a web of relationships between individuals may have something to teach us not revealed by the study of action elements alone. And, in fact, we find a striking distinction between two fundamental types of relationship.[24] Putting it in one way, we may say that in the one case these action elements—the particular means and ends of the individual actors— are primary, and that the relationship is to be understood as resulting from the interaction of these elements. It is a relation of the type generally known in the English literature as "contract." It is true that a system of such relationships is not conceivable without governing institutional norms—the rules of contract. But these norms are, as it were, "external" both to the action elements and the particular relationship of the parties. In the actions which lead to, and result from, a contract there is implied no further permanent relationship than that of the ad hoc contractual relationship itself.

This is not true of the other type. Here the primary element is an (at least relatively) permanent personal relationship between individuals. Their individual acts, while analyzable in terms of means and ends, can only be understood as in a sense subsidiary to the relationship. The classical example of this type is that of relationships within the family. Husband and wife exchange services. Many of these at least are concrete services which might perfectly well be bought on the market. But, while functionally they may be the same, their meaning in terms of human motives and interest is very different. They are "manifestations" of a permanent relationship. It is a type of relation-

24. The distinction I am about to develop is substantially that to which Tönnies's name will always be attached—between *Gemeinschaft* and *Gesellschaft*.

ship which excludes the same kind of calculation of advantages which we think of as a normal adjunct of contractual relationships.[25]

This kind of a noncontractual *Gemeinschaft* relationship is very difficult, if not impossible, to fit into the means-end schema. Marriage has highly important social functions, and the parties entering into it may have some specific ends. But marriage itself has *no* specific end; whatever specific ends the parties may have are subsidiary to the main thing—when it is thought of as *only* a means to them, we think of it as a perversion. What is that main thing? It is difficult to express it accurately. It is a community of life, a sharing of the daily routine of rewards and obligations, a fusion of interests over a wide area so that the parties are, for certain purposes, a single inseparable unit. It shares with other phenomena we have discussed the prominence of a *common* element between individuals. But it is not a specific common end. It is rather common attitudes and general unspecified interests. The rights and obligations of marriage are to a certain extent specified, but for the most part negatively. On the side of obligation for instance, a husband is bound by any obligation to his wife which may arise unless there are special *value* reasons (that is, conflict with a higher obligation) for releasing him from it. That such and such was merely "not in the contract" is never an excuse.

Above all, the basis of such a relationship is a *value* element. The relationship is a focus and expression of value-attitudes. And the particular acts incident to the relationship are in turn also "expressions" of these attitudes; in marriage we should most generally say, of "love" or "affection." These value attitudes naturally have, in turn, a very close relation to the other manifestations of the ultimate common value attitudes we have discussed—particularly, to religion. I think it is safe to say that there is no case in history known where religious attitudes were *indifferent* to family relationships. There is often the closest integration and sometimes acute hostility, but never indifference.

Finally, it is by no means necessary for the "principles" underlying these *Gemeinschaft* relationships to be explicitly and rationally formulated, though it is certainly possible. But perhaps more often they are implicit; such relationships are simply taken for granted as the natural and inevitable way of living.

We have thus here again a most important element of social life—in fact, an absolutely fundamental one in all societies which cannot,

25. Professor Sorokin has called this type "familistic" relationships. It is, however, by no means restricted to the family.

at least in the majority of cases, be thought of as a whole in terms of a rationalized course of action directed toward specific rationally formulated ends. But it is quite illegitimate on that account to exclude value elements from its understanding, and fall back on positivistic factors. On the contrary, there is every reason to believe that such relationships are as intimately bound up with value elements as anything in our lives; but it is in the form of the more diffuse value attitudes, rather than the more specific ultimate ends, that they can best be brought in. These two cases do not, I am quite sure, exhaust the possibilities of social phenemona where the diffuse value attitude is more relevant than the end; but they will suffice, I think, to illustrate the general character of problem involved. The discussion of them serves both to indicate the limitations of analysis in terms of the means-end schema, and to throw into bolder relief its peculiar characteristics and merits.

This paper has attempted in very brief compass to cover an enormous amount of ground. As such it suffers from the limitations of all such attempts: it is a sketch rather than a detailed and thorough analysis. Furthermore, it very greatly oversimplifies problems. I am fully aware that the concrete problems of social science are of a degree of complexity which makes such a simplified scheme seem almost hopelessly inadequate. Limitations of space have naturally prevented me from presenting more than the boldest outline and from entering into many of the ramifications which might have made the concrete usefulness of the scheme far more evident to the reader. With all these limitations, however, it does to me provide a series of threads which do run throughout social life and which may, if followed carefully, reveal a good deal of the pattern of order underlying the apparently haphazard chaos of human history.

Like most Americans growing up in the social sciences since the war, my starting point has been what may broadly be called the "positivistic" movement in those fields—the tendency to imitate the physical sciences and to make physical science the measuring rod of all things. I quite early reached a conviction of the inadequacy of these current views.[26] That conviction centered primarily on the vague realization that these positivistic theories somehow, by a kind of logical jugglery rather than by empirical proof, were squeezing what I have here called the "value" elements out of their interpretation of social life.

26. In particular, "institutionalist" economics and behaviorism.

But such a vague general conviction of the importance of values is clearly not enough. It is necessary first to enter into an exhaustive critique of these theories to uncover the exact points at which they go wrong, to determine what unacknowledged assumptions and non-sequiturs are responsible for their confident denials of the position I have taken up. I have not attempted to present that critique here, but it must obviously underlie the second task which I have, in outline, attempted here. That is to go beyond critique and the general conviction of the importance of values to an analysis of the specific ways in which values enter into social life and in which they are related to the "positivistic" factors.

It is a tentative outline of the latter which I have attempted to present here in the most general terms. Its point of departure is the means-end schema which plays such a prominent part in positivistic thought (short of behaviorism). The method is essentially to see what, after dropping the arbitrary assumptions which squeezed out values altogether, are the logical implications of this schema, calling in general observation of actual social life as an aid. This has led us first to the various ramifications of the intrinsic means-end relationship. Then, with the aid of both observation and at least semiphilosophical reasoning, we have proceeded to consider the possible extension of the basic schema beyond the intrinsic type which positivistic social science has come fairly near doing justice to. Finally, we have explicitly questioned its universal applicability and tentatively suggested modes of analysis of social phenomena involving value elements but which cannot be considered simple and direct applications of the means-end schema. As it has departed from the main core, the analysis has necessarily become more and more halting and tentative. That is an inevitable result of departing from familiar territory on an expedition into the unknown.

Recognizing all its limitations, I submit that this is more than a mere argument for admitting values to a place in social theory. It is not, to be sure, a system of sociological theory embodying the value factor. It is rather a methodological prolegomena to such a theory, clearing the way and indicating some directions of fruitful analysis. It is, as such, that I should like to have it received by the reader.

In conclusion I should like to say a brief word about science and philosophy. The task of sociology, as of the other social sciences, I consider to be strictly scientific—the attainment of systematic theoretical understanding of empirical fact. The failure of the positivistic schools of sociology to attain such a goal I do not attribute, as so many do, to the inherent impossibility of the goal, but rather to their own inadequate methods of approaching it. Their inadequacy consists essentially in trying to apply both modes of thought and substantive concepts developed in the study of and suited to one kind of empirical fact—mainly that of the physical world—to quite another, human action in society. It is surely not altogether heterodox to say that the basic conceptions of a science should be developed in connection with a study of its own subject matter—not imported from other sciences.

Thus I hold the goal to be scientific. But I do not believe that there is in social or any other science a rigid line between science and philosophy. The positivists, while officially denying it, have most certainly made very far-reaching philosophical assumptions about social life, if not as to the "ultimate nature" of it, at least as to what was "ultimately" capable of scientific analysis. Thus for my scientific purposes it is essential to be a philosopher at least in the negative sense—it is necessary to uncover and criticize on philosophical grounds the assumptions which block the way to doing justice to the empirical facts as I see them. Beyond that it is necessary to be clear about the philosophical implications of one's own positive concepts. In this sense the role of philosophy in science is merely a consequence of the rationalism inherent in science. The concepts of science must attempt to be consistent with each other and with the known facts of experience, whether in its own concrete field or not. In this sense science must be able to meet the criticisms directed against it from the people who attempt a rational apprehension of reality as a whole, the philosophers. But equally the philosophers must be, in ideal, ready and able to meet the criticism directed at their views from any of the sciences.

In spite, however, of this necessary interpenetration of philosophy and science, there remains, I think, a fundamental difference between them. The scientist *starts* always from the empirical facts of a certain area of experience. Philosophy is to him only an aid to the understanding of these particular empirical facts. The philosopher, on the other hand, goes directly to the whole. His interest in particular empirical facts is limited to their significance for his view of the whole. If he has a social theory it is as an *application* to a particular set of facts of a general philosophical theory. This paper has unavoidably entered into philosophical questions. I recognize that quite frankly. I even hope it may prove of some interest to the philosophers. But at the same time it is not a philosophical essay. I stand squarely on the platform of science. The philosophical problems involved are approached from a scientific point of view in the sense just outlined. It is in these terms that I should like to have this effort received by both philosophers and social scientists.

19

On Certain Sociological Elements in Professor Taussig's Thought

It is a fact scarcely to be doubted that a principal origin of all science lies in commonsense concern with the exigencies of practical life. Even an appreciable degree of rationality of action is impossible without a fund of empirically valid knowledge and insight into the phenomena to which the actor must adapt himself if he is to attain his end. In this sense there has existed a not inconsiderable fund of rational knowledge of human behavior since time immemorial, since other human beings constitute perhaps the most important part of the environment in which anyone must act.

A further step in generalization of this knowledge comes when the practical exigencies are such as to involve judgments on the probable behavior of large numbers of human beings in various circumstances. This is preeminently true of the practical necessities of public policy. Hence it may be said that one of the main origins of social science lies in men's reflections about the probable practical effects of various measures in this field. This is very particularly the case with the science of economics, where discussion of policy in the two closely related fields of international trade and of monetary problems formed perhaps the central breeding ground of modern economics.

In the course of discussion and reflection of this sort, however, another phenomenon appears. It is quite possible to have sound and therefore useful insights in the form of relatively disconnected aphorisms, of general statements about what experience has taught men to expect. It is, however, equally possible that this level should be transcended by the development of a relatively integrated body of concepts which transforms knowledge from a series of wise insights and practical precepts based upon them into a *system* based on a rounded conceptual scheme, a "theory" in the specific scientific sense. It happens that this stage emerged in the development of the science of economics far earlier than in any of the other sciences concerned with human behavior to anything like a comparable degree of logical and systematic refinement. A theoretical system in this sense was well developed in the classical economics of the early nineteenth century, and was being widely, and to a large degree successfully, applied to the understanding of important empirical and practical problems.

Once this development of a theoretical system, a well-integrated conceptual scheme, has occurred, sooner or later the problem of its relation to the concrete empirical reality in the study of which it has been built up, and to which it is to be "applied," will have to be raised. But at the same time there is strong resistance against its being explicitly raised; the whole situation in which such a scheme is developed biases its proponents in the direction of assuming one solution of this problem as too obvious to need explicit justification at all. This is what may be called the "empiricist" solution. It is the view that the concepts included in the system are by themselves adequate to explain all concrete phenomena within the range to which the theory is applicable at all. Or, put somewhat differently, the concrete course of events which the theory enables one to deduce as the outcome of any initial state of affairs should, insofar as the theory itself is "correct," correspond exactly to the actually observed course of events. Any failure for this to occur is ascribed merely to the fact that the theory is not as yet sufficiently developed and refined.

The more rigorously such a theoretical system is developed, in the sense of drawing all the logical implications of the propositions included within the system, the more it tends to become a "closed" system. That is, so long as the underlying methodological position is "empiricist" in the above sense, the more it comes to be a methodological requirement that all facts ascertainable about the concrete phenomena in question should "fit" the categories of the system.

It is the present writer's view of the relation between scientific concepts and empirical reality that at least in the field of human behavior and probably more widely, no one system of theoretical concepts is in this empiricist sense adequate to the explanation of most concrete things and events. On the contrary a scientific theory must in this field be abstract in the sense that it can take account only of certain limited "aspects" or "elements" of the concrete situation, and therefore needs to be supplemented by other theories taking account of other aspects, before a satisfactory complete interpretation is attainable. The common appearance to the contrary is due to the existence of what may be called "experimental conditions." For the purpose, that is, of understanding certain *changes* in concrete phenomena, a given theory may sometimes adequately formulate the important *variable* elements. It is the function of experimental techniques to create conditions in which this is true. Where, as in the field of human behavior in the mass, this possibility is excluded by practical considerations, it may still happen that fortuitously "nature" has arranged a set of conditions which approximate these logical requirements. This is roughly what happened at the time that the classical economics was developing. The founders of the theory were living in and observing a society which, within a certain area of its activities, approximated to the experimental conditions required by the conceptual scheme with which they were working.

This is particularly true so long as the conceptual scheme itself is developed only in broad outline, so that all that is required for its verification is the demonstration of very general factual trends, especially since at this stage there is in the nature of the case little attempt to attain numerical exactitude in quantitative results. But three things may cause difficulty in this situation. The process of progressive refinement of the conceptual scheme itself may uncover factual discrepancies which remained concealed when only the broad outline was being considered. This is particularly true since refinement of a theory is generally concomitant with greater and greater attention to detail in the study of the facts. Secondly, the tendency mentioned above for such a system of theory to become closed leads to a process of widening the area of empirical study from the original focus of attention as investigation progressively demonstrates the functional dependence of phenomena within the area upon those outside it. But the latter are, though obviously relevant to the empirical problems of the science, on the whole less likely to meet the experimental conditions which make an empiricist interpretation of the theory itself plausible. Finally, the phenomena within the original focus of interest itself may undergo change in the course of generations which makes them less adequate experimental situations from the point of view of the theory. All three of these processes have with little doubt been going on apace in the development of economic science since the classical era.

So long as the empiricist interpretation of the nature and function of a theoretical system in science remains unquestioned there are two possible extreme reactions to the difficulties which emerge as a result of these processes. One is what may justly be called the dogmatism of the theory, the attitude that since it is helpful in explaining some things it must therefore be adequate for all things that in any sense come within its range. Insofar as the difficulties are real and not imaginary this leads either to blindness to the facts which will not fit in this sense, so that they and their implications are totally ignored, or to an arbitrary twisting of the facts so that they will fit. It is but natural that this dogmatic tendency should develop and that it should be most prominent among those who take the theory most seriously and who contribute most to its development, elaboration, and refinement. Largely in reaction against this dogmatic tendency comes the other extreme solution. Since the theory fails to fit some of the facts which are incontestably relevant to its empirical problems, then the theory itself not merely falls short of complete adequacy but is held to be totally inadequate. Then one of two consequences follows; either it must give way to a theory which will comprehend both the facts adequately dealt with by the older one and those which will not fit it, or theory itself is held to be scientifically mischievous on general methodological grounds and must give way to mere fact-finding without benefit of theory. Largely no doubt because of the inherent difficulties of turning the former alternative from a program into actuality, this extreme of the reaction has predominantly taken the latter and become antitheoretical on principle.

Both extremes, however, are apt to appeal to a type of mind which delights in logical consistency for its own sake and which is largely antithetical to the commonsense empiricism which remains steadily interested in the facts and at the same time is ready to accept any conceptual aid which seems useful in the immediate context without too much regard for the remoter logical implications of the procedures involved. This cast of mind has been particularly conspicuous among the Anglo-Saxon peoples who have played the leading role in the development of economics in the classical tradition. Hence it is not surprising that between the radical extremes just outlined there has been a middle ground maintained which refuses to be pushed all the way in either direction. It is as perhaps the most eminent exponent of this middle path in his generation, as John Stuart Mill was in his, that the work of Professor Taussig, so far as it concerns the relation of economic theory to concrete economic activities and their social framework, is to be placed.

Certainly before the development of a pronounced dogmatism in the above sense it was not uncommon for an economist to realize that phenomena in which he was interested depended on factors which if not in principle unamenable to economic analysis at least had not thus far been so analyzed, and which he himself did not attempt to analyze. A conspicuous example is Ricardo's use of the "habits and customs of the people" as an important factor in the regulation of wages through the mechanism of the standard of living. One may say that the necessity of the middle-ground position we are concerned with is to keep continually adding to the roster of conceptions of this sort, which recognize and name features of the total social situation impinging on concrete economic processes, but which at the same time are, at least in any obvious sense, not amenable to explanation in terms of the traditional categories of economic theory.

To one who has the interests of social science in general as well as economics at heart, and who is at the same time cognizant of the extreme importance of theory for its fruitful development, it cannot but appear a fortunate circumstance, in the situation in which economic science has been placed in the last generation, that so strategic a position in the field, above all as a teacher influencing the younger generation, has been occupied by a man of Professor Taussig's cast of mind. For there has been real danger that between the upper millstone of dogmatism and the nether one of a negativism in all matters theoretical economic theory should have been ground down to a state where for a very long time it could not become the concern of a reasonable quota of the active and inquiring minds of the time. In the range of alternatives which have been open in this passing generation an open mind and a judicial appraisal of the importance of things not readily amenable to economic analysis, combined at the same time with a steady insistence on the fundamentals of the traditional analytical scheme itself, has been the only way in which a just balance between the empirical and the theoretical interests of the field could be upheld.

A further aspect of the matter is worthy of mention. It has been remarked that the original concern of the economist as of other scientists has been with matters of practical urgency. In particular he has been concerned with the grounds in favor of and contrary to various proposals in the field of public policy. In such a field it goes almost without saying there is a close intermixture of considerations of a factual and of an ethical nature. Indeed the empiricist bent of social science has for the most part strongly inhibited any very rigorous attempt to separate even logically the two orders of considerations bearing on a matter of policy. But in the process of evolution of the dogmatist dilemma this could not but have a highly unfortunate result. For there has been a marked tendency for what has here been called the dogmatic interpretation of economic theory to become linked with the defense of a particular empirical social order, in general terms, that which realized an approximation to the ideal experimental conditions of the theory. Thus added to the scientific dogmatism that things actually did work out according to the expectations of the theory, was the ethical dogmatism that it was just and right that they should, and anyone who proposed an attempt to modify the social order away from this pattern was not only foolish but vicious as well. Undoubtedly this ethical dogmatism has contributed in no small measure to the general discredit of economic theory at the hands of those at the other extreme, and their moral indignation at this, to them ethically objectionable, attitude has blinded them to the scientific possibilities of economic theory, since the indissoluble connection of the two has not been questioned. Opposition to economic theory as "capitalist apologetics" has been almost as important as on grounds of empirical inadequacy, though of course the two have generally been combined.

In view of this situation it has been doubly fortunate that a voice has been heard which defended economic theory but which was at the same time ethically and politically in the best traditions of a tolerant liberalism, which above all was not deaf to the cry for social justice and the corresponding indictment of certain features of the existing order. In this respect as in the other it seems fair to say that Professor Taussig has been in his generation the leading exponent of the same admirable tradition as John Stuart Mill.

Indeed it seems probable that this liberal open-mindedness both in the more strictly scientific context and in the ethico-political one, was in Professor Taussig's case considerably promoted by the sheer facts of his earliest chosen field of empirical investigation, international trade. For on the one hand this is a field where certain of the noneconomic modifying elements of economic processes are peculiarly conspicuous. Thus differences in the standard of living in different countries as affecting the actual course of trade, and nationalistic sentiment as an influence in the determination of national policies in this field, are often in direct conflict with the clear economic interest of the country. Similarly, apologetic dogmatism was, to one trained in economic theory, peculiarly difficult in this field at a time when the protectionist movement was steadily gaining force, since the latter did not very obviously conduce to the maximum economic welfare of all. Indeed so far as economic interests played a part it was not on the whole as guided by an "invisible hand" in the general interest, but rather as a case of special interests gaining their end at the expense of the majority, as in the logrolling process so conspicuous in the process of tariff making in the United States.

These insights may be generalized. In Professor Taussig's work we find, elaborated and illustrated in many different directions, the recognition that under actual social conditions the free play of individual economic interest works out at best very imperfectly to the maximum benefit of all. He has done much to make problematical again what has been but too facilely assumed in so much of economic thinking which leans in the dogmatic direction, the question of how it is that even the extent of coincidence of private interests and the common good which actually exists, has come about, as well as to recognize the many points at which, as over a large part of the tariff field, the correspondence breaks down. For on the one hand he emphasizes again and again that men's realizations of the remoter consequences of their actions and policies are very limited. Every protectionist sees the effect of a tariff on the imports which compete with his product, but few its relation to exports and the balance of trade and payments. At the same time there is no guarantee that in pursuing their interests men will always adhere to the limited range of means which are compatible with the general interest. The whole range of "predatory" activities, in the business field as elsewhere, which has been a conspicuous blind spot for many economists, is a matter of much concern for Professor Taussig. From this follows of course a vivid realization of the difficulty of controlling these tendencies, and the bearing of this difficulty on many phases of social policy.

Professor Taussig's insight into the reasons why actual conditions fail to conform with the assumptions of the doctrine of maximum satisfaction may be elaborated somewhat further. In the first place there are the predatory means of gaining ends in the narrower sense, force and fraud. It is clear to almost anyone that they are incompatible with the free play of interests working out to the general benefit. The difference of Professor Taussig's treatment from this bare realization is his keen sense of the reality and practical importance of these phenomena, especially perhaps the fraudulent or semifraudulent abuse of fiduciary positions on the part of directors and officers of corporations for which opportunity is so conspicuously created in the present economic order, and which is so extremely difficult to regulate.

Second, there is the problem of the role of the state. It will generally be agreed that the beneficial play of self-interest depends on the political power of the state being used entirely impartially in the struggle. But on the one hand it is inevitable that the state should have an enormous degree of control over economic opportunity: this also would be generally agreed. At the same time Professor Taussig has been keenly aware of the extreme difficulty, especially perhaps under modern democratic conditions, of guaranteeing that this control shall in fact be used impartially. Indeed acquiring in one way or another influence over the actions of the state, or any political bodies, in this way must constitute one of the principal "illegitimate" means of gaining economic ends. The possibilities of special interests in protected industries playing a disproportionate role in the determination of tariff policies is only one, if a particularly vivid, illustration. The state cannot in fact be completely insulated from the struggle of interests in the society in which it exists, and this fact is one of the principal modifications which must be made in the ideal picture of the dogmatists of economic theory.

Finally there is a third category of elements modifying these ideal conditions, which do not involve resort to means the community generally condemns as illegitimate, but which are probably in the aggregate of greater concrete importance than those which do. These are the many ways in which there may exist inequalities in the terms on which different individuals and groups of them enter into the competitive struggle, even though the latter be limited to bargaining in terms free of force or its threat, fraud, or the intervention of a powerful outside agency like the state. One example is that of monopoly and the other ways short of out-and-out monopoly in which a strategic position in the bargaining process may be taken advantage of. It is interesting to note that Professor Taussig's interest in these phenomena is not so much the technical theoretical one in their modifications of the competitive conditions of price determination, but rather the broader social interest in their implications for social stratification and the problem of inequality. A second illustration is his admirable account of the conditions of the labor contract, emphasizing as he does the inherent bargaining disadvantage of the laborer so long as he is isolated. In particular the employer's power of discharge, though nominally merely the power to terminate a contract at will which can equally be severed by the other party at any time, is in effect a very formidable coercive weapon against which the ordinary worker has no adequate defense. Indeed in this sense the strike is its coercive counterpart though formally an act of quite a different order. Finally a somewhat similar situation leads still further afield. Professor Taussig's well-known analysis of the vicious circle of low wages, low standard of living, lack of social ambition, and large numbers.

This last point brings out strongly a matter of principle which is stated many times. These various possible disadvantages of one party to a competitive bargaining relationship are, in their social significance, to be sharply distinguished from another class of handicaps which may burden individuals. For their consequences are not exhausted by the immediate unfavorable effects on the position of the individual concerned, but are cumulative. It is, I think, largely by this road that Professor Taussig comes to what is, it appears, the dominant social problem of his work, which runs through his whole treatment of economic science, the problem of inequality. His deep concern with it, its causes and consequences, is perhaps the sharpest difference in the impression given by his work as against that of writers who have been called the dogmatists of economic theory. It goes almost without saying that the competitive process will not equalize individual rewards in money income, but that differences in economic efficiency will be reflected in a corresponding scale of different incomes. This will inevitably be the case so long as conditions of earning are competitive on the one hand, and so far as there are inborn differences of abilities relevant to earning on the other. But this is not the essense of the problem of inequality as Professor Taussig sees it. It is rather the superposition upon these elements in the situation of two others. While he fully recognizes the extent to which differences of business ability are probably hereditary, he is equally insistent upon the fact that the hereditary component does not account for all the actual differences of men in their earning capacity. For other things being equal the man who has had environmental advantages, a better education and training, better health and the like, will be more efficient than the one who has been denied them. In the second place pecuniary success, though powerfully affected by sheer ability, is by no means solely conditioned by it. The man born in the classes used to directing industrial operations will have an advantage in getting a start which means that, other things equal, apart from differences of ability however accounted for, there will be an element in the differentiation of income due to environmental advantages which do not act to increase personal efficiency, especially "capital and connection." In addition the existence of possibilities of securing property incomes and the institution of inheritance introduce a still further factor in favor of perpetuating the high incomes of the rich and even adding to them.

The net effect of all these factors taken together is a cumulative tendency to inequality, which would not be present were inborn differences of ability the sole determinant of inequality. Indeed in this particular context inborn differences, although they go some way toward explaining, and for the ethical feeling of our time, justifying existing inequalities, at the same time serve to complicate the problem. For so long as inequalities arise from this origin the cumulative forces will be set in motion which will tend to accentuate them still further to the point of a major cause of social instability and hence an urgent social problem.

The general outline of social stratification insofar as it is on the one hand relevant to economic problems, on the other determined by factors other than the hereditary component in ability, Professor Taussig has formulated in his doctrine of noncompeting groups. According to this, while there is undoubtedly a considerable volume of mobility between groups, there is a significant balance of difficulty in making the transition upward, so that, in effect the upper groups obtain a monopoly advantage in that actual numbers competing for the economic opportunity open to members of the group are not so great as the distribution of hereditary traits in the population as a whole would justify if all could be given the environmental advantages in fact open to members of the upper groups. One interesting aspect of this monopoly advantage, which Professor Taussig develops as an application of the theory of international trade, is the more favorable terms which members of the upper income groups are able to secure in the exchange of their services for those of the lower.

Particular emphasis is laid by Professor Taussig on the outcome of this situation at the two extreme ends of the scale. The underlying ethical attitude by which we on the whole justify differences of income insofar as we justify them at all is our feeling that high individual achievement should have a corresponding reward. But even though the *origin* of large accumulations may be predominantly accounted for in these terms—the degree is certainly highly problematical—in the present institutional situation the result is the creation of a leisure class of large means maintained through property income and inheritance, which in our society tends to be divorced from any important social function except as a goal of ambition. Though we may feel that the founder of a fortune has on the whole earned it, the same surely cannot be said of the other members of his family and his descendants, who are in a position to enjoy the proceeds more or less in perpetuity. This development Professor Taussig views with serious concern, as likely to throw discredit on the system as a whole.

At the other end of the scale is the vicious circle we have mentioned of poverty, low wages, large numbers, and low standard of living. In both cases it is scarcely possible to contend seriously that the situation is in its main outlines the simple result of hereditary differences in ability.

In this connection it is interesting to note the way in which he deals with the population problem. This is a particularly crucial point because of the prominent place of the Malthusian doctrine in the thought of the classical economists, to whose views in technical theoretical matters Professor Taussig adheres perhaps more closely than any other equally prominent contemporary economist. But in spite of this background and the fact that he was brought up at a time when Malthusian views were far less generally questioned than they are now, Professor Taussig gives one of the most judiciously balanced reviews of the population problem to be found in the literature. Above all, writing in the first decade of the century, when the Malthusian bogey of general overpopulation was beginning to be revived, he was one of the very few to see the significance of the tendency to a declining rate of population growth, which now occupies the center of the stage in all discussions of population. Above all he was certainly one of the first to point the direction of explanation of the phenomenon which has come to be recognized as most fruitful, the prevalent "social ambition" of our era. The only point at which he accepts anything like a literal Malthusian view is in application to the vicious circle of poverty and numbers at the bottom of the social scale, where it is certainly more nearly applicable than anywhere else in contemporary society. But his view even here is tempered by the realization of the many other factors beside the biological urge behind population growth on which this situation depends.

The range of problems just outlined constitutes, it seems to the present writer, one of the two main areas in which Professor Taussig has broadened the perspective of economics by paying careful and explicit attention to aspects of the social environment of economic activity which do not fit readily into the rubrics of traditional economic theory. The other field in which he has made similar ventures is the subtle and difficult one of human motivation. This rather obviously presents crucial problems to the economist in the orthodox tradition. So long as he has been concerned with the functioning of an individualistic competitive order some such concept as the "rational pursuit of individual self-interest" has inevitably crept in as descriptive of typical individual action in the competitive situation. The question is as to the interpretation of such phrases and their relation to the various possible elements into which motivation may more generally be analyzed.

It is comprehensible that the tendency of economics in becoming a closed system in the sense outlined above is very strongly to press for a clear solution of this problem. The one which received the widest vogue in the earlier nineteenth century was of course hedonism, according to which the pursuit of economic self-interest was but a phase and the inevitable outcome of the deeper human necessity to seek pleasure and avoid pain. This solution was beautifully fitted logically to the requirements of economic theory since it disposed of the whole problem with a simple formula. Most economists of the more dog-matic persuasion, if they have thought of the problem at all, have been disposed to accept this simple formula, at least so far as "economic" activities were concerned, that is, the activities of the shop and the marketplace. Hedonism, it may be remarked, was a theory which fit-ted into a broader framework, the distinguishing feature of which was a dichotomy between egoistic and altruistic motives. Hedonism be-longed of course clearly on the egoistic side, and hence even apart from strict hedonism there has been a strong tendency for economists to think of "economic motives" as necessarily and always egoistic or "self-regarding."

Professor Taussig has taken an important step beyond this position. He has on the one hand not been content to ignore the problem of motivation nor on the other to accept any such simple solution as the hedonistic formula. His clear grasp of the concrete reality of economic life has made him realize that of the motives important to the concrete results of business and industrial activities, many would not fit, not only into strict hedonism, but into any form of the self-regarding type in the ordinary sense. Thus we find in his work a clear recognition of the importance of "domestic affection" among the motives to accu-mulation, of social ambition which, even if in a sense self-regarding, is not merely a desire for the intrinsic utilities which can be com-manded by money income, of the "instinct of contrivance" to which he assigns a prominent role in the process of invention, and many others. It is altogether understandable that in harmony with the cur-rents of thought of the time he should have invoked, in *Inventors and Money-makers*, a tentative and undogmatic version of the instinct theory of psychology as his vehicle for ordering these insights. Espe-cially with his avoidance of a certain type of psychological dogmatism corresponding to the economic, this has meant an immense broaden-ing of perspective on the range and variety of human motives as they affect the economic order, especially as compared with anything pos-sible within the framework of economic dogmatism. Above all he has been able to assimilate many of the empirical insights of so-called anti-intellectualistic psychology without abandoning the sound emphasis on the existence of a kind of rationality which, even though limited and qualified, is essential to economic theory and its explanatory value.

Closely connected with this is another dominant note of Professor Taussig's work. One prominent result of the dogmatic position is to lead its exponents in the direction of a sort of mechanistic automa-tism, as though the human individual were as inert a link in the chain of economic causation as the atom or particle is in a mechanical system. As against this tendency he asserts again and again the importance of effort, of the active participation of men in their affairs. There is nothing inevitable under any and all conditions about the level of productive effort which we are apt to take for granted. Above all is leadership important in human affairs of all sorts, not least in the field of business and industry. Its changes and accomplishments cannot be accounted for in terms of any stereotyped average of ability or effort, but only of the leadership of the extraordinary and rare individual.

It has been the thesis of the above discussion that so long as the empiricist view of the relation of economic theory to the concrete phenomena the economist studies has, explicitly or implicitly, held sway, as has in fact been the case with few exceptions down to the present moment, certain difficulties have inevitably appeared of which the dogmatist dilemma is the expression. It has, furthermore, been the thesis that on this methodological basis the middle-ground position held by Professor Taussig has, in general terms, been far preferable to either of the two extremes. Only by virtue of it has it been possible to hold a just balance between the empirical and the theoretical interests of the science, and thus to serve the progress of economics as an integral discipline rather than any special aspect of it.

Nevertheless it is the opinion of the present writer that at the stage which economics has reached in its recent development, these basic virtues of Professor Taussig's work must be purchased at a price, and that the price is by now becoming so exhorbitantly high that the time has come to look closely for new inventions which may serve to lower the cost of production of economic truth. And this is the point where one who is not technically an economist but a sociologist who has yet been through the mill of economics and has been much concerned with the relations of the two sciences may be in a position to suggest a direction of development worthy of the economist's consideration, yet not so easy to see without the perspective lent by intensive concern with an explicitly noneconomic field *in relation to* the economic. But first a word may be said as to the price of adhering to the older order.

In the first place to anyone acquainted with the history of science it seems almost obvious that scientific understanding has, beyond a quite elementary stage, advanced in proportion to the possibility of bringing facts into relation with a systematic theoretical scheme. This is, in the writer's opinion, the great, almost overwhelming, source of the preeminence of economics among the social sciences. But from this point of view it is one of the striking things about Professor Taussig's work that, in spite of his recognition of the empirical importance of so many noneconomic factors in social life, he has had relatively little success in bringing them into a degree of theoretical systematization at all comparable with the more technically economic aspect of his work. Of those phases discussed above two things may be said. All the factors bearing on the cumulative tendency to inequality are formulated essentially negatively, as elements modifying the expectancies of the working of more strictly economic factors. There is practically no evidence of the emergence of an independent conceptual scheme which would justify their treatment as independent factors. It is not meant to be implied that this means that the treatment is valueless, on the contrary it is most valuable, but only that the possibilities of the situation are not fully realized. So far as the economic scheme is not the source of understanding, it remains on the level of wise empirical insight on the part of a man of broad culture and knowledge of human affairs.

The case of the problem of motivation is somewhat different. Here the noneconomic elements are not so readily treated as merely modifying, but certain of them seem directly antithetical to those closest to the economic. Hence the double tendency to think in terms of the egoism-altruism dichotomy, and the resort to an explicit noneconomic conceptual scheme, that of instinct psychology. The latter is, however, used as by its own proponents essentially in an empiricist sense, and hence it is well that Professor Taussig does not attempt to apply it very rigorously but only as a loose framework of order for his facts. Even so it may be very strongly doubted whether instinct psychology constitutes the most promising framework, taken at least by itself, in which to set "economic motivation" in a proper perspective.

But perhaps because the conceptual scheme is here more definite than in the other case, and at the same time because the pressure inherent in any empiricist interpretation of the economic analysis for a solution of the motivation problem is so strong, in spite of Professor Taussig's eminently judicial sense of reality there appears a bias which in the writer's opinion is definitely harmful to the empirical interests of economics and leads to untenable views of empirical issues. For the empiricist, for every concrete act there must correspond a concrete motive. And since the typical economic act is in the pursuit of "self-interest" the tendency is to regard motivation in the economic sphere of activity as "egoistic." This, fitted into the dichotomy of egoism and altruism, throws most noneconomic elements of motivation over into the antithetical category of altruism. In the interests of empirical accuracy the rigidity of the dichotomy is somewhat mitigated by treating such motives as family affection, which are not obviously egoistic in the strict sense, as still predominantly "self-regarding." The main point is the strong tendency, which this hardly mitigates, to force the interpretation of concrete economic motivation into the egoistic pattern. In Professor Taussig's case this tendency is accentuated by his very realism in connection with the problem of inequality and all the related modifications of the theorem of maximum satisfaction in concrete application. For, once having rejected the literal acceptance of the "invisible hand" thesis, a whole range of grave defects in the individualistic competitive order appears, as well as of equally grave difficulties in the way of realization of any alternative. This circumstance throws a strong emphasis on the problem of the maintenance of productive efficiency through effort and saving, and the direction of solution, repeatedly brought forward, is that these things are heavily dependent on the "material reward" of labor and saving since men are predominantly in these matters actuated by egoistic or self-regarding motives. This position is open to serious criticism for reasons which will be brought forward presently, but there is one more item in the price of even liberal, open-minded empiricism in economics.

The third point is that in the dilemma which has been characterized as the dogmatic, the liberal attitude, which makes possible a high degree of just appreciation of the importance of noneconomic elements, itself acts as a serious inhibition on the technical theoretical development of the conceptual scheme itself. For in an empiricist interpretation, the scheme can appear to such a liberal mind as tenable at all only in a very broad and general sense. As soon as the attempt is made to push its refinement very far empirical difficulties appear which violate a vivid appreciation of the facts. It may be surmised that this circumstance goes far to explain what has been to many a puzzling feature of Professor Taussig's work. He belongs to a generation in which there occurred the most important theoretical advance in economics since the time of Ricardo, the whole development growing out of the discovery of the principle of marginal utility. But, while accepting the new doctrine in principle, he goes much less far than some even of his older colleagues like Marshall and John Bates Clark in working out its remoter consequences for systematic theorizing. The result is that he has adhered much more strictly to the letter of the classical system than they, or than to many appears scientifically fruitful in the present situation. The explanation may be offered that, in the nature of the case in the situation of the time, this theoretical development biased its proponents in the dogmatic direction, and that it was predominantly fear of these consequences, which he clearly saw, which inhibited Professor Taussig from participating in the development to the extent to which he might have done it.

The question then unavoidably obtrudes itself whether all these difficulties are unavoidable, inherent in the subtle and complex nature of human behavior, or whether, building on the foundations which men like Professor Taussig have so solidly laid and carrying on what I conceive to be the essence of their spirit, a just balance of the empirical and the theoretical aspects of social science, it is not possible now, as it was not at the beginning of the century, to strike a new path which will open out new possibilities not hitherto realized. I should like to close with the affirmation that we now have available the fundamentals of such a new position which avoids the major difficulties of all three of the positions here treated, above all which carries on the spirit of the middle-ground position but at the same time appreciably lowers the price it has to pay for maintaining the wisdom of its balance.

The essence of the matter may be put in the form of two propositions, which are closely interdependent. First, the empiricist conception of the role of economic and any other systematic theory in the social sphere must be abandoned. It must be realized that it formulates only a limited number among the variables which must be studied to account for human behavior, even within the range traditionally called economic. Concrete conclusions over any wide range can only be safely derived when the others have been adequately accounted for. Secondly, the others cannot be adequately accounted for by a series of logically unsystematized observations of the limitations of the economic scheme. This step, though historically indispensable, must be superseded by the explicit relation of economic theory to other, logically comparable *theoretical* systems in terms of which these other elements receive the same kind of systematic analysis as do the economic elements.

This whole development has obviously been retarded in the past by the fact that the other social sciences have on the one hand shared the empiricist bent with economics, perhaps even more strongly; on the other have not had anything like equally well-developed conceptual schemes of their own which, by extension into the field of traditionally "economic" phenomena, could serve to sharpen the issue. Hence it is not altogether surprising that the development under consideration has only begun to take definite shape in quite recent times. Perhaps the first major figure is that of Pareto, in a phase of his work to which, unfortunately, little attention has been paid. Though himself an eminent economic theorist in the "neoclassical" tradition he explicitly held that economic theory was insufficient alone to explain certain concrete phenomena in which it was yet unmistakably involved. It is interesting to note that one of the main ones was one to which Professor Taussig also devoted much attention, the growth in the latter years of the last century of the protectionist movement. But from this he not only concluded that other, noneconomic elements were in fact involved, but proceeded to attempt to develop a theoretical scheme in terms of which these elements could be dealt with as adequately as the economic. This is, in brief, the logic of the genesis of Pareto's venture into general sociology. How far he may have fallen short of reaching a definitive solution of the problems inherent in such an attempt is of secondary importance in the present connection. The important thing is that he should have made the attempt, involving as it did a conception of the role of economic theory relative to the concrete phenomena to which it applied, radically different from any to be found in the empiricist tradition. This general type of relation of economics to sociology, and the cooperation between the two which would result in the solution of empirical problems, seems the most fruitful line of work open at the present time to the theoretically minded who yet cannot be indifferent to the empirical applicability of their results.

Lest the foregoing theoretical considerations seem too abstract and their implications hence not clear, a few brief remarks may be made in closing on their relevance to the problem of motivation of so-called economic activities. Once the abstract analytical interpretation of economic theory is accepted and its consequences developed to a certain point, it becomes evident that while the economic is an indispensable element of all human motivation in the general sense of an orientation to the phenomenon of scarcity of desired things, at the same time there is and can be no such thing as an "economic motive" in the concrete sense. All concrete motivation of concrete activities involves other elements which cannot possibly be adequately dealt with in the framework of economic theory. Apart from the usual sense in which the economic is a rational element and hence nonrational elements fall outside it, there are two particularly important points to mention. Economic analysis deals with motivation on the level of means, not of ultimate ends. The desire for things, for goods and services, or for command over them in certain respects, with which the economic theorist is concerned, is the proximate one as means to the individual's ends. The point is that for purposes of economic analysis it does not matter what the character of the ultimate end is, whether egoistic or altruistic, for instance. It makes no difference to his problem whether one who buys stocks in the expectation of a speculative gain intends to use the proceeds to endow a hospital or for sensual indulgences.

The consequences for the mechanism of the capital market are the same. In this sense it is possible to abstract the proximate, economic elements of motivation from another, that of ultimate ends, to which the egoistic-altruistic dichotomy, whatever validity it may turn out to possess, properly belongs.

In the second place, on the "supply" side of the analysis, that is, in the question of the motivation of productive activities, the economic element turns out to be, as it may be put, a differential element. People may be said to be economically motived *insofar as,* other things being equal, they *prefer* among the directions of activity open to them that which yields the greatest "advantage." In technical economic terms it is that which maximizes utility, in commonsense terms, that which yields the largest monetary reward. But the fact that, in actuality, large numbers of men prefer a line of activity which yields a higher monetary reward to an alternative with a lower prospective reward proves nothing one way or another about the other elements in the motivational situation. Above all, the fact of monetary reward being the decisive differential factor as between two alternatives proves nothing about what would happen were the choice something radically different from that between the given alternatives. It does not follow that the level of effort is primarily dependent on the level of monetary reward.

This may be illustrated by two other elements of motivation to productive activity about which we have considerable knowledge. One is what Veblen vaguely called the "instinct of workmanship" and Max Weber the idea of a "calling." It is essentially a case of "disinterested" application to a task for its own sake, apart from any consideration of reward. It is clearly of great importance in the activities of the liberal professions, and, one may surmise, of greater importance in the performance even of routine industrial labor than Professor Taussig's insistence on the irksomeness of labor would lead one to suspect. It is not in the least a proof of the nonoperation of this motivational element that, among two lines of work approximately equally attractive from this point of view, the more remunerative should be preferred. Above all there is no reason to believe that if choice were so limited that no more remunerative line were available, productive effort would slacken disastrously. Most proposals to modify the individualistic order consist essentially in a limitation of choice in this sense. It is not of course to be inferred, either, that this would *not* have any such effect. The fact is we do not know and cannot without explicit investigation of this, and of course other, elements. No a priori conclusion about the relation of reward and productive effort either way is justified, and Professor Taussig's view is in this sense essentially an a priori one.

The other element is one to which Professor Taussig gives considerable attention, and on which he throws a good deal of light, yet fails to relate satisfactorily to his own conception of economic motivation; it is that of emulation and social distinction. The need to be respected by one's fellows and the related desire to excel as many as possible of one's fellows in the qualities, possessions, and achievements which are valued in the community is indeed one of the most deep-seated of human needs. But there may be enormous variations from one society to another in the concrete content of these qualities, possessions, and achievements. The error enters in when pecuniary reward and income are taken to be inherently the objects of emulative effort. So far as productive activities are oriented to pecuniary reward as more than a means to acquiring desired goods and services, but rather as an end in itself, it is generally as a symbol of success and achievement, as Professor Taussig himself often remarks. But symbols are notoriously lacking in intrinsically necessary connection with their meanings. Insofar as money income has become, as is largely the fact in our society, the dominant symbol of achievement and social status, the explanation is not to be looked for in any intrinsic nature of economic motivation, which if interfered with will bring disaster, but in what may roughly be called "institutional" causes which are historically variable.

Such questions as these, that is, the essential thing, cannot be decided without the careful factual investigation which, on the whole, it is not unfair to say, the older economics has not devoted to them. It has rather, guided largely by the logical exigencies of an empiricist economic theory, tended to give us a priori, essentially dogmatic solutions of the problems. When a writer so free from bias in general as Professor Taussig gets involved in serious difficulties of this sort it is indeed strong evidence that the situation is in need of attention. But, further, the way out of such a situation does not lie alone in wise empirical observations of the factors modifying the economic picture. It is necessary in addition to attempt to develop an explicit analytical theory of human motivation in which the economic elements will have a highly important place but will of course not stand alone. Moreover, not only will the other elements receive explicit theoretical formulation, but above all it will be possible to state their relations to the economic in terms of a systematic conceptual scheme. The only approach to this in the older tradition is the old egoism-altruism dichotomy which is empirically quite unsatisfactory.

Unfortunately it is not possible here even to sketch the outline of such a scheme, which does justice to the economic elements in substantially the form they have been developed in the classical tradition, and to the others as well. Suffice it to say that the beginning of such a scheme is now available. It is not, in the ordinary sense a "psychological" scheme, but one which comprehends the categories of all the analytical sciences dealing with human behavior. In the opinion of the present writer it is in this direction that an escape from the dogmatic dilemma of the last generation of economic science is most likely to be found, and in terms of which the spirit of the middle-ground position, so admirably maintained by Professor Taussig under the conditions of his own generation, can be made to continue to bear significant fruit for the future.

20

Review of *Economics and Sociology,*
by Adolf Löwe

Professor Löwe's little book is a most welcome addition to the literature of a crucially important but somewhat neglected subject. It is one of the most penetrating discussions available and should be carefully read by economists and sociologists alike.

Its position relative to the methodological controversies over the status of economic theory is, from the present reviewer's point of view, highly commendable. It will, however, be pointed out later that Löwe neglects certain analytical considerations which could serve to clarify the problems still further.

In the first place, Löwe successfully transcends the old dilemma which has plagued so much of the methodological discussion of these problems between, on the one hand, the dogmatic "reification" of a system of individualistic, competitive economic theory on the classical model and, on the other hand, the tendency to repudiate theory altogether, which has been typical of the German historical and the American institutionalist schools.

He also recognizes that in avoiding the fallacy of reification it is not satisfactory merely to introduce specific empirical ad hoc qualifications on a series of particular points. It is necessary to place the categories of economic theory in a generalized setting of theory in order to lend them concrete relevance. In Löwe's terminology, realistic economic theory, implicitly or explicitly, always involves reference to categories of "sociology." From "pure" economic theory alone it is never possible to deduce empirically important and usable conclusions.

With respect to "pure theory" he apparently accepts the rather common definition that "economic behavior is concerned with disposing of scarce means for given ends." Within its particular sphere it is possible for pure theory to work out certain aspects of this process with mathematical exactitude. This nonsociological side of economic behavior "in charge of the nasty business of fighting the stinginess of

Originally published in the *American Journal of Sociology* 42 (1937): 477–81.

nature" deals with problems of more and less and nothing else. Löwe remarks quite rightly that for purposes of the logic of this theory the fact that "every real economic action is always a part of man's social activity" does not matter. It is an avowedly abstract analysis, self-consciously neglecting certain fundamental elements of concrete human action.

But this "pure theory" does not suffice to cover even the ordinary classical "laws of the market," to say nothing of other realms of activity usually thought of as remote from economic considerations, such as man's religious life. The conception of a system of exchange relations functioning smoothly over time could not be analyzed in terms of pure theory alone. As actually used by the classical economists, it involved at least two crucial noneconomic assumptions—the "economic man" and competition. By the economic man in this context he does not mean an "egoist" but merely one who in the actual situations of exchange can be counted on to act so as to maximize his immediate economic advantages, regardless of ultimate motivations. Under the conception of competition, in addition to economic rationality in this sense, he includes above all a private-property system, giving every individual the right to dispose freely of his means, and a state of social organization which makes this formal right actually effective.

Modern realistic economic theory differs from the classical system and cannot be said to have reached any similar agreement on the relevant sociological "middle principles" like the economic man and competition, which gave a unity of empirical interpretation to the work of the classical economists. But its relation to such principles is, as opposed to that of the "pure theorists," similar. The main point of the present agreement is that we cannot assume a general equilibrating tendency like that of the classical school, but economic society must be assumed to be undergoing a process of dynamic development. In other words, the social data of economic theory are not constant but are changing in a process of interdependence with the economic process itself. Löwe regards Marx as the first to give theory this new direction. Further, there is coming in this connection to be more and more focus of attention on the processes of the business cycle and on the role of technological organization and change. This type of thinking is following, methodologically, the classical model, even though it is quite conscious of the extent to which many of the classical substantive views are inapplicable under the changed conditions of the present.

It was said in the foregoing that it was one of the great merits of

Löwe's book to have avoided the common tendency to try to meet the problems of the empirical inadequacy of pure economic theory by mere ad hoc empirical qualifications. He is, rather, attempting to relate economic theory systematically to a neighboring social science—sociology. It is, indeed, the present reviewer's opinion that a good deal of the lack of fruitfulness of the discussion of the relation of economic theory to empirical reality has been due to the fact that this approach has not been taken. It has, rather, been assumed that economic theory was the *only* theory which had to be considered in the discussion—what was problematical was only its relation to fact. Löwe's approach to the problem is a very great advance on this older type. But it still does not seem fully satisfactory in the sense of taking advantage of all the analytical tools available in the social sciences. In closing, I should like briefly to attempt to justify this statement and to indicate what seems to me a way in which it is possible to remedy this shortcoming.

Economic theory has pretty generally come to be recognized as an analytical system which is logically similar to the theory of mechanics. It has, however, by now also come to be pretty generally realized that it depends for its concrete relevance on noneconomic data, the behavior of which is not capable of being deduced from the laws of the system alone. Furthermore, it is a fairly well recognized methodological principle of general application that data are not simply "facts" but that, like all the facts of science, they are stated "in terms of a conceptual scheme." The statement of such data involves noneconomic theory.

As Löwe himself remarks, many of the pure theorists in economics have maintained that they could carry out their reasoning without any concern whatever with what he calls the "structure" of the data. This tendency has given rise to some very serious fallacies connected with the implicit assumption that, so far as the theoretical concerns of economic theory go, these data may be assumed to vary at random. Löwe has, it seems to me, conclusively shown that this cannot be so and at the same time have economic theory lead to empirically useful results. It must assume data which have a determinate structure. The question is, "On what level should this structure be described and analyzed?"

Löwe states and analyzes them in terms of what he calls "sociological middle principles." What are these? The economic man, competition, and modern industrial technology are examples prominent in his discussion. It seems clear what their general status is. They are descriptions of the main outline of the particular concrete society in which the economic processes being analyzed take place. The classical economists assumed a fundamentally static individualistic competitive society; the modern realistic economist assumes a different kind, above all a dynamic society. I do not wish in the least to question the importance of the economists' having a clear idea of these matters, or the extent to which his assumptions in this regard may influence his empirical conclusions. What I do wish to question is whether this mode of theoretical "supplement" to economic theory is the only possible or important one, or whether, even, it is analytically the most fundamental.

It must be clear that there is a fundamental logical lack of symmetry between the two sciences of economics and sociology as Löwe conceives them. Economic theory is an abstract analytical system of general applicability. Sociology, on the other hand, consists, in its relevance to economic theory, in a series of discrete sets of "middle principles," of general descriptions of particular concrete social structures, each explicitly differing from the others. Historical relativity is fundamental not only to concrete societies, which are individually unique, but also to sociological principles. Is it not possible to attack the problem of the theoretical supplement to economic theory on a higher plane of generality than this?

I am quite convinced that it is. "Pure" economic theory, even as a generalized analytical system, is not *the* theory of a class of concrete phenomena but is part of a broader system of analytical theory on the same level of generality—the "theory of action." It focuses attention only on one limited part of the structure, not of a specific concrete society but of a generalized system of social action. Basic to economic theory is the conception of a "rational" relation of means and ends. Economic theory really deals with one mode of normative orientation, the "rational," in the sense of that involving valid empirical knowledge as defined by the criteria of scientific methodology and, in one aspect, defined by the role of scarcity. But, as Löwe himself remarks, it is not concerned with the specific content of ends, of the ultimate means and conditions of action, or with many other structural elements of a generalized social system.

But these other elements, which must enter into the data of the concrete problems of economics, are not random relative to those dealt with by economic theory. They can, however, be analyzed in terms of a conceptual scheme on the same analytical level as economic theory and directly articulated with it in such a way as to fill the empirical gaps left open by economic theory.

Löwe's "middle principles" can be derived from such a general analytical theory of action by working out its implications for certain kinds of concrete situations on a more concrete level than that of the generalized theory, that is, by making certain additional assumptions. But, as in all such cases, the generalized theory forms a more important means of critical check on the formulation of such "middle principles" and, with its development, more and more should provide a basis for the formulation of the complex modes of interaction between the economic elements and their noneconomic data.

It is to be hoped that Löwe will not leave the problem of the relations of economics and sociology at the point to which this book has brought it but, with his eminent theoretical ability, will attempt to explore the possibilities of a more generalized theoretical statement of the problem.

APPENDIX

A Word from Amherst Students

with Addison T. Cutler

The Meiklejohn affair, as it has come to be called, is an extremely complicated piece of business. No simple formula of Upton Sinclair's will quite cover the case, and it certainly would appear that any alumni statements to the effect that "it was simply a matter of maladminstration with no issues of policy involved" do not strike bottom.

Parts of the affair are still clouded with mystery, and it is probable that very few individuals hold all the threads of the tangle in their hands at the present time. Neither the trustees nor the alumni fully understood the character of the Meiklejohn teaching. In fact it looked as if certain individuals in these groups had not the slightest conception of what the liberal college was trying to do; witness the charges that "atheism and Bolshevism" were being taught.

It would be unreasonable to expect a full knowledge of the educational processes of here and now from trustees and alumni who are tied up with practical affairs of business and who have received their own education under another tradition, be the differences ever so subtle. And if the elders were unfamiliar with what was going on in the college, it was no less true that the students were ignorant of the administrative questions involved and of the endless diplomacy which went on behind closed doors both before the denouement and during it. Rather it would be better to say that the students were ignorant of the content of the secret diplomacy, but not of its existence. From the beginning of our college careers it had been common knowledge to the members of our class that a struggle to oust President Meiklejohn was going on, and occasionally bits of news about it would leak out, as such things have a way of doing.

Our impressions of freshman year were of course very vague on the subject. Mr. Meiklejohn, himself, was abroad on a year's leave of absence and Dean Olds, who is now Mr. Meiklejohn's successor, was acting president. With one exception the studies of the freshman year are drill subjects, highly uncontroversial. That one exception is a

Originally published in *The New Student*, 20 October 1923, 6–7.

287

course called "Social and Economic Institutions," which was introduced into the curriculum by President Meiklejohn and which has
served the double function of an introduction to the social sciences,
and a solvent for that stock of preconceptions and prejudices which a
freshman brings to college along with his other baggage. The large
majority of our class took this course and profited from it, probably
more than we realized at the time.

Our sophomore year was quite different in many ways from the
preceding one. "Prexy" was back from his year's absence and among
other things he taught the sophomore course in philosophy with the
aid of Professor Ayres, a younger man of considerable brilliance and
a strong liberal leaning. The latter was one of Mr. Meiklejohn's
staunchest supporters throughout, although he differed with him on
many points of philosophy. This course in philosophy together with
an "introductory" course in history given by Professor Laurence J.
Saunders, struck the keynote of our sophomore studies, both of them
being chosen by almost the entire class.

The history course was a most unorthodox affair. In fact it was
almost the antithesis of the usual "cram" course in names and dates.
Not only did it stress the social, economic, and geographical factors
involved rather than the military-parliamentary ones, but the subject
matter was dealt with topically rather than strictly chronologically.
Mr. Saunders could jump from prehistoric movements of population
in the steppe-desert belt of Asia to a discourse on the probable future
of the Irish Free State with more agility than most historians show in
making the grade between James the First and the Long Parliament.
All of which was done to the tune of a personality and a Scotch wit
which made the subjects studied seem somewhat more alive than a
well-embalmed mummy, which so frequently symbolizes historical
teaching. The net result for us of this introductory course in history
was a considerably changed notion of historical process. Specialized
knowledge in any one field of history was left for subsequent courses.

Campaign for Real Sport

Now, while these courses and others were making some changes in
our intellectual horizon, a large number of our class became very
much tied up with athletics and college activities, as of course is always the case. A good test of the Meiklejohn influence was whether
or not it would spread to these men or be limited to the so-called
"intellectuals" who always have been the strongest supporters of Mr.

Meiklejohn's liberal ideals. The metal of the athletes was tried when "Prexy's" campaign for the deprofessionalization of college athletics came along.

This campaign it will be remembered crystallized in a conference of twelve New England college presidents called by President Meiklejohn for the purpose of devising ways and means of getting college athletics away from the vicious circle of professionalism into which it had fallen, and back to a basis of "sport for sport's sake." The first step of the program which this conference decided upon was a change of the coaching system from the employment of highly paid, seasonal, professional coaches, to that of permanent faculty coaches.

President's Step Wins Favor

When this proposition was laid before the student body of Amherst, there was some natural hesitation on the part of the more athletically inclined students. Amherst athletics had been in something of a slump and the prospect of a change to faculty coaching did not look toward an increase in the success of the teams. Some of the athletes looked on the idea with very much disfavor. On the other hand, however (and here it is that the influence of the Meiklejohn ideals is seen to be increasingly strong), there were some athletes who championed the proposition with enthusiasm, and when it came to a vote in the Student Association meeting the decision of the college body was overwhelmingly in favor of the president's step, provided the other colleges would agree to do the same.

Third Year Brings Awakening

The junior year saw a great intellectual change in most members of the class of 1924. It is often said that the sophomore year is one of the breaking down of illusions and prejudices and that the rebuilding must come in the later years. During the last year, after having many of our old ideas very completely shattered, we had a chance to see what the Amherst of President Meiklejohn had to offer in their place.

For the first time a large proportion of us came under the influence of Professor Walton H. Hamilton in economics, and continued under Professor Ayres in philosophy. And most of us can say that what these two men in particular gave us in the way of solid ground on which to build our social, ethical, and economic ideas was not only very satisfying but also exceedingly stimulating for further thought and investigation. From them we got the point of view that the economic and social order was a matter of human arrangements, not one of inevitable natural law, and hence that it was subject to human control.

It has seemed to us that the teaching of those ticklish subjects was as nonpartisan and disinterested as is humanly possible. In economics neither socialism nor any other radical system was either directly or indirectly advocated but at all times the discussion was perfectly free and open. Any point of view was welcome to be thrashed out thoroughly, and as far as possible the facts were made to speak for themselves.

Students Plan Own Course

Of course by the junior year everyone has begun to specialize to some extent and by no means all the class were so strongly impressed by the social sciences, economics, philosophy, and political science, but a large number of the best men were attracted to this field from others. An example of the enthusiasm for this sort of thing was the group major which was arranged in "Control in the Economic Order" by a group of these men for their senior year. This was to consist of Professor Hamilton's course in economic control, a political science seminar under Professor T. R. Powell of Columbia University, and a course in the history of European industrial expansion under Professor Saunders. It was to be accompanied by a large amount of independent research work in individual problems in this field. After the resignation of President Meiklejohn, Professor Powell has declined his invitation to join the Amherst faculty and Professors Hamilton and Saunders have also resigned so that this group major cannot be given.

All through the year the student body was conscious that there was friction in the faculty and among the alumni and trustees over the administration, but it was almost impossible to secure any definite information. We did know that there was a very definite split in the faculty and we got to think of the members as Old Guard, New Guard, and middle-ground men. We had no doubt that as a group the men whom we knew to be pro-Meiklejohn were the most stimulating and able men of the faculty.

The first rumbling of the actual explosion was the presence in town of a number of younger alumni to confer with a committee of trustees, and it came as a surprise to us. This occurred less than two weeks before commencement. A number of seniors at once circulated their petition asking the trustees about the authenticity of the information

which they had, and in the event of Mr. Meiklejohn's resignation as a
result of the charge which they understood had been brought against
him, refusing to accept their degrees from the college.

Juniors Circulate Petition

In spite of the fact that final examinations were almost over and a
large number of the junior class had already left town, a similar petition was circulated among the remaining members to the effect that
we would not return to Amherst for our senior year if the president
were forced to resign. No difficulty was encountered in securing over
twenty signatures in one morning's work. Many men did not sign the
petition because of the specific way in which it was worded, but very
few were encountered who were not in thorough sympathy with the
cause of Mr. Meiklejohn.

With the sending of the senior committee to New York for information from the trustees, both petitions were stopped for purely tac-
tical reasons. Neither was ever submitted to the board of trustees.

Since our petition was binding only in the event of its being submitted, there was no obligation on anyone not to come back this year,
and as it has turned out most of us have done so. The principal reasons seem to be the difficulty of getting anything worthwhile out of
another institution for only one year, and the fact that with such a
nucleus of men back, it might be possible to help out the cause of
liberal education at Amherst quite appreciably.

This article is only the personal opinion of two men, both of whom
were strong supporters of Mr. Meiklejohn, and it does not officially
represent the attitude of the student body, or of the class of 1924 as a
whole. However, we have attempted to estimate the influence of the
Meiklejohn administration upon our entire class, not simply our-
selves.

Loyal to Meiklejohn Idea

We know for a fact that there are a great many of the men of the class,
probably a majority, who feel essentially the way we do about the
situation. Those men are not by any means of any one type, or centralized in any one fraternity. They are representative of the best element, and are pretty widely scattered throughout the college. They
include the "intellectual" element almost to a man, and it is our opinion that they are in general the men who have really come to realize

what Mr. Meiklejohn and his associates were trying to do for Amherst, and who have come to place the primary value of a college in its opportunities for education rather than in the many extraneous activities of the campus. We are looking, not for controversy, but to the maintenance of the general educational policy for which the Meiklejohn administration stood. And for a very considerable group of the present senior class, those educational ideals have become so supremely worthwhile as to be the issue on which we will stake a great deal.

Index

Action, 20–21, 47, 51, 74–81, 83, 88–
93, 106–7, 119–20, 136–50, 154–72,
179–80, 182–83, 187, 204–5, 212,
217–18, 222–23, 225–26, 231–57;
Parsons's view of, discussed, xliv, l–lv,
lxii, lxvi
Amherst College, xi–xvi, xvii, 287–92
Analytical method, 21, 63, 89, 93–94,
105–6, 124–28, 130, 134–36, 159–
60, 168, 172–77, 180, 186–87, 195,
213, 216–17, 219, 221, 223–25, 228–
29, 257, 260, 272, 274–77, 279, 281–
83; Parsons's exposure to, xxxii–xxxv,
lvi; Parsons's view of, discussed, xliv–
xlv, li–lii, liii–liv, lvii–lxiii. See also
Empiricism
Anarchism, 191–92, 197
Andreas, Willy, xxiii
Anthropology, xvi, xvii, xviii, xxxix, 95,
149 n.48
Anti-intellectualism, 75, 79–80, 88–90,
106, 117, 150, 188–89, 196, 201–2,
270
Aquinas, Thomas, 49, 50, 112
Aristotle, 53, 109, 112, 170n.34
Art, 251–53
Aspects, analytical. See Analytical
method
Atomism, xxi, lvi, 73, 143, 145, 154,
157–59, 178–79, 253, 270–71. See
also Individualism
Ayres, Clarence, xv, xvi, xviii, xxxii, 288,
289–90

Barnes, Harry Elmer, lix
Baxter, Richard, 59
Becker, Howard, xlix
Behaviorism, xvi, xxxviii–xl, xliv, lv,
lxvii–lxviii, 79, 88, 90, 154–56, 160,
187, 189, 202–3, 210–11, 232, 238,
255n.26, 256

Bentham, Jeremy, 77–78, 194
Bierstedt, Robert, xliiin.120
Bigelow, Karl, xxxi
Biologism, xvi, xxiv, xxxviii, xl, xliv,
xlvi, xlvii, 72, 78–81, 83, 86, 95, 189,
196–97, 226, 229, 241, 267–69
Bodin, Jean, 117
Boehm-Bawerk, Eugen, 4n.1, 17n.21, 23
Brentano, Lujo, 30n.44
Brinton, Crane, xxxviii, 243n.11
Burbank, H. H., xli
Bureaucracy, 24–27, 33–35, 36, 70

Calling, 28–29, 42, 48, 49, 53, 59–60,
71, 114, 219–20, 276
Calvin, Jean (Calvinism), 41–43, 45, 49–
50, 53, 63, 114–15, 220
Cannan, Edwin, xvii, xlv
Capitalism, origins of. See Capitalist society
Capitalist society, 42, 54–55; Hamilton's
analysis, xv; Marshall's analysis, 72–
73, 84; Marx's analysis, 9, 17–19, 103,
207–10; Meiklejohn's view, xii; Edward Parson's view, x; Parson's view
of, discussed, xxiii–xxx, xliv; Robertson's analysis, 60–65; Sée's analysis,
39–40; Sombart's analysis, 3–19, 26,
27, 30, 33; Taussig's analysis, 264–69,
271; Veblen's analysis, 199–200; Weber's analysis, 9, 22–36, 40, 57–65,
70–71, 93, 219–20
Carver, Thomas Nixon, xxxi, xxxv–
xxxvi, 10n.15, 62n.15, 197, 223n.52
Catholicism, 29, 42, 48–49, 53, 54, 58–
59, 63–65, 110–13, 252
Chamberlin, Edward, xxxi
Character, 46, 69, 81, 83, 84, 85, 90, 92,
204–5
Charisma, 32–33
Choice. See Voluntarism

Clark, John Bates, 273
Classes, social, 8, 17, 26, 45–46, 48, 51–
  55, 59, 90, 101–2, 107, 120, 171–
  72n.40, 192–94, 199–200, 207–8,
  216–29, 264, 266–68
Committee on Sociology and Social Ethics (Harvard University), xxxvi, xli
Communism, 166, 287
Comte, Auguste, 134, 227
Conant, James, xliii, xliv
Conditions (of action), 53–55, 74–77,
  83, 86, 95, 116–19, 141–43, 155–56,
  158, 162–63, 169, 171, 176, 187–88,
  203, 218, 226, 235–36, 239–40, 249–
  50; Parsons's view of, discussed, xlvi–
  xlvii, xlix, l, liv, lv, lviii
Convergence (in social theory), 14, 71–
  72, 87–93, 119, 186–87, 213–21,
  226–28, 231, 231–32n.1; Jasper's
  view, xx; Meiklejohn's view, xii; Edward Parsons's view, x; Parsons's view
  of, discussed, xxvi, xlii, xlv, xlvii, lix–
  lx, lxiii, lxvi, lxvii–lxviii
Cooley, Charles Horton, xvi
Culture, xvi, xviii, xxi, xxxviii, xlix, lv,
  lxiv, 12–13, 17, 120, 188
Cutler, Addison, xiii, 287–92
Cyclical theory (of social change), 90,
  107

Darwinism, xxxvi, xlvi, 75–77, 79,
  89n.49, 103, 117, 163, 196–97, 200,
  202, 222
Davis, Kinsgley, xliiin.120
Depression, xxvii
Determinism, xxvi, xxxix, xlv, lxiii, 18,
  32, 77n.18, 116, 241, 250, 270–71
Devereux, Edward, xliiin.120
Dewey, John, xvi
Dialectic, 7, 18, 82, 91, 207
Diversity, societal, xvi, xxv, li–lii, lxii–
  lxiii, 3–14, 17–19, 33, 36, 47–50, 51–
  55, 70, 82–83, 91–92, 120, 124, 126,
  169–71, 188, 200, 206–10, 221, 225,
  226, 243, 277, 281–83
Durkheim Emile, 50, 96, 119, 120, 121,
  129, 146, 149n.48, 170n.33, 171n.38,
  213–16, 219–20, 222, 225, 227–28,
  231–32n.1, 242, 249n.18; Parsons's
  exposure to, xvi, xxxix, xxxixn.104;

Parsons's view of, discussed, xlix, lix–
  lx, lxi, lxiii, lxvi, lxvii
Duty. *See* Obligation, binding

Economic dynamics, 177–78, 280
Economic imperialism, 153, 162, 172,
  180
Economic interpretation of history. *See*
  Materialism
Economic motivation. *See* Interest
Economics: as capitalist apologetics,
  263–65; classical, 3, 14, 55, 74, 80,
  102–3, 116–17, 181–82, 190–96,
  206, 207, 212, 222, 259–62, 279–81;
  impasse in, xxxiii, lvi–lxiii, lxvii,
  87n.43, 181, 229n.65, 279; legitimate
  domain of, 119, 164, 165, 168, 175,
  223–24, 229, 240, 282. *See also* Institutionalism; Neoclassical economics;
  Utilitarianism
Economics Department (Harvard University), xxii–xxiii, xxx–xxiv, xl–xli
Economic sector. *See* Means-end chains
Effort, 149, 160, 175, 235, 236, 246,
  248, 271, 273, 276. *See also* Voluntarism
Elements, analytical. *See* Analytical
  method
Empiricism, xxxii, li, lvi, lxiii, 95–96,
  124, 130, 135, 136, 168, 170–80,
  186–89, 211–13, 222–27, 260–63,
  272–74, 277, 290; middle-ground,
  262–74, 279, 281; orthodox, 190–98;
  positivistic, 198–203; romantic, 204–
  11. *See also* Analytical method
Emulation, 277
Encyclopaedia of the Social Sciences,
  xxviii, xxix, l
Ends, ultimate. *See* Value elements
Enlightenment, 12
Environment. *See* Conditions (of action)
Evolutionary theory, 7, 12–13, 15, 18,
  27, 32–34, 36, 75–84, 90, 91–93, 103,
  117, 169, 188, 199–201, 205, 207–8,
  243; Parsons's exposure to, xvi, xviii;
  Parsons's view of, discussed, xxv, xxvi,
  xlv, xlvii

Factors, analytical. *See* Analytical
  method

Facts. *See* Analytical method; Empiricism
Fallacy of misplaced concreteness, xxxiv, lv, 159–60, 175, 201–2, 211–12, 224
Family, 47–48, 51–52, 54, 55, 102, 109, 253–54, 270, 272–73
Fascism, 108, 166
Feuerbach, Ludwig, 6
Firth, Raymond, 246n.14
Force, and fraud, xxvi–xxvii, 74–75, 84, 89, 107, 165, 166, 170, 199, 218–19, 241, 265
Formal school (of sociology), xlix, 95–97, 167, 173, 228n.63
Free enterprise, 27, 55, 69, 71, 81, 116–17, 158, 166, 170, 175n.52, 184–85, 191–93, 197, 205, 264–66, 273

Gay, Edwin, xxviii, xxxi, xli, xliv
Gemeinschaft, 31, 47–48, 54, 55, 97–98, 120, 253–54
Genetic method, xv, xvii, xxv, xxx, li–lii, 4–5, 20, 36, 61, 126, 200
Geographical factors, 81–82n.31, 83, 95, 163, 207
Gesellschaft, 31, 48, 50, 97–98, 110, 116, 120, 214, 253
Gestalt psychology, xxxix, 77
Giddings, Franklin, xlviii
Ginsberg, Morris, xvii, xxxixn.104
Godwin, William, xlvi, 12, 74–75, 102, 192
Groups, social, 47–49, 54–55, 95–96, 110–14, 117, 120, 215, 245, 253–54, 268

Habit, 101, 187, 200–202, 214–15, 262
Halévy, Elie, 104, 121, 190n.7
Hamilton, Walton, xv, xviii, xix, xxv, xxxii, xlv, xlvi, 289–90
Hankins, Frank Hamilton, xlviii–xlix, 95–96
Harris, Seymour, xxxi
Harvard University, xxx–xliv
Hedonism, 28, 42, 71, 73, 80–81, 106, 187, 189, 191–96, 198, 203
Hegel, G. W. F., 3, 6–7, 14, 18, 75n.14, 82, 84, 91, 118, 171–72n.40, 206, 208, 210
Henderson, Lawrence J., xxxiii, xxxiv–xxxv, xxxviii, xliv, li, 133n.1

Heredity. *See* Biologism; Conditions (of action)
Historical school (of economics), 3–37, 82–83, 123–24, 126–27, 169–70, 188, 206–11, 219, 279
Historiography, xxv, xxxii, 5, 6, 40, 60–61, 127, 208, 288
Hobbes, Thomas, xlvi, 73–80, 102, 115, 116, 119, 158, 199, 241
Hobhouse, L. T., xvii, xviii–xix, xxxix, xlviii, lviii, 73n.11, 121
Horace Mann School for Boys, xi

Idealism, xx, 6–7, 118, 206, 221
Ideal-types, xxv, xxx, lii, 5, 17n.21, 20–23, 34–35, 37, 127–28, 182–86, 208, 235
Individualism, xv, xxi, xxix, xlvi, xlvii, lvi–lvii, 16, 42, 45, 47, 48, 55, 61–64, 73–75, 77n.21, 79, 109–10, 113–17, 119, 143, 145, 150, 164, 191, 195, 197, 205–6, 214–15, 222, 242. *See also* Atomism
Inequality, xxvi, lxii, 193, 266–68, 272
Instinct psychology, 79, 140–41, 150, 187, 189, 198–201, 203, 211, 270, 272
Institutionalism, 9, 87n.43, 135, 170n.33, 181, 198–203, 210–11, 215, 229n.65, 225n.26, 276, 279, 288–90; Parsons's critique of, xxiv, xxxiii, li, lx–lxi; Parsons's embrace of, xxiii–xxx; Parsons's exposure to, xiv–xv, xvii, xxi, xxii, xxxii, lvi–lvii, 288–90
Institutions, social, xii, xiv, xv, xxxvii, xlviii, lxi, lxiv, 24–25, 41, 97, 102, 115, 120, 170–72, 175n.52, 180, 192–93, 200–202, 214, 218, 244–45, 249, 251, 253, 277
Interaction, 86
Interest (self-interest), 47, 50, 54, 58, 60–62, 65, 74, 119, 191–93, 198–99, 214–15, 244–45, 264–70, 272–73, 275–77. *See also* Wants
Iron cage, 11–12, 13, 18–19, 25, 27, 30–31, 33–35, 71, 207, 210, 220

Jaspers, Karl, xx, xxiii, xxvi, xxxixn.104, xlvii, 1, 20n.24
Jevons, William Stanley, 190, 195, 205

Kant, Immanuel, xiv, xx, 6
Keynes, John Maynard, 73, 75, 80, 196
Knight, Frank H., xxix, xxxix–xl, xlii,
　lii–liii, liv, lxiii, lxiv, 22n.29, 78n.24,
　183n.2
Koffka, Kurt, xxxix
Köhler, Wolfgang, xxxix, 77n.19

Laissez-faire. *See* Free enterprise
Laski, Harold, xvii
Laws, scientific, xxxiv, xxxv, lvi, 127–28,
　159–60, 174–75; Pareto's view, 135;
　Sombart's view, 4–5; Weber's view, 20,
　124–26
Lederer, Emil, xxi
Lévy-Bruhl, Lucien, 129n.1
Liberalism, 77–78, 80, 83, 91, 166,
　247n.15, 264, 273
Locke, John, xlvi, 73–75, 77, 103, 116,
　185, 190
London School of Economics, xvii–xviii,
　lxii
Löwe, Adolf, lxii–lxiii, 279–83
Lowell, A. Lawrence, xxx, xxxvi, xlii,
　xliii
Luther, Martin (Lutherianism), 41, 49,
　50, 113–14

McDougall, William, 79, 203
MacIver, Robert, xxxix, 50, 121,
　170n.33
Magic, 246–48, 251
Malinowski, Bronislaw, xvii, xviii,
　xxxixn.104, 149n.48, 246n.13
Malthus, Thomas (Malthusians), xlvi,
　xlviii, lx, 74–76, 101–4, 185, 192–94,
　196, 268–69
Mannheim, Karl, xx, 129–30
Manthey-Zorn, Otto, xiv, xix, xxi–xxii,
　xxiv
Marshall, Alfred, 69–73, 80–94, 162,
　168–69, 172, 180, 187, 190, 204–6,
　228, 272; Parsons's exposure to, xvii,
　xxxi–xxxii; Parsons's view of, dis-
　cussed, xlv–xlvii, lii–liii, lx, lxvi, lxvii
"Marshall and Laissez-Faire," xlv
Marx, Karl, xxi, xxv, xxvi, lx, 3, 6–7, 9,
　12, 13, 17–19, 27, 30, 36, 82, 91, 96,
　103, 171–72n.40, 185, 194, 200–201,
　207–10, 220, 222, 229n.64, 280
Mason, Edward, xxxi

Materialism, 6, 12, 18, 27, 30, 32–34,
　36, 40, 175n.54, 189, 194, 212, 219,
　234
Mayo, Elton, xxxixn.104
Means-ends chains, li, liv, lvii–lviii, lxiv,
　119, 141–45, 162–68, 179, 187, 198,
　239–40, 243–45, 253
Means-end schema, lxiv, 51–52, 88–93,
　118–20, 136, 138–49, 154–72, 182–
　85, 187, 196, 198, 211, 225–26, 232–
　56. *See also* Action
Meiklejohn, Alexander, xxii–xiii, xxvi,
　xliii, xlvii, 287–92
Meiklejohn affair, xiii, 287–92
Meriam, Richard, xxii
Merton, Robert, xliiin.120
Metaphysical elements, 119–20, 237–39,
　242–43, 247–49. *See also* Value ele-
　ments
Methodology. *See* Analytical method;
　Empiricism
Michels, Roberto, 32n.48, 108
Mill, John Stuart, 76n.17, 182, 262, 264
Mitchell, Wesley, xxiv, lxi, 203, 210–211
Mobility, social, 268
Mommsen, Theodor, 219
Monopoly. *See* Free enterprise
Moral sentiments, 75n.14, 191–92

Nazism, xx, xxvii
Neoclassical economics, 5, 9n.13, 19, 22,
　36–37, 79–80, 85–89, 92–93, 105–6,
　135–36, 143–44, 149–50, 153–61,
　163–64, 166, 169, 172, 173–75, 182–
　86, 189–90, 204–5, 211, 228, 259,
　271–75, 280; critiques of, xv, xxi, lvi–
　lvii, lx; Parsons's exposure to, xxii–
　xxiii, xxxi–xxxiii, xxxix–xl, lvi; Par-
　sons's view of, discussed, xxv–xxvi,
　xlv, xlvi, lvii–lxii
Neo-Kantianism, 124, 127
New Student, The, xiii
Normative elements, xv, xlvi, xlix, l, lxi,
　lxiv, 97–98, 115, 118–20, 145, 160–
　61, 170, 175, 185, 197, 214–15, 234–
　35, 244–45, 248, 251, 253. *See also*
　Value elements

Objectivity, scientific, 21, 84, 124–25,
　128–30, 202, 235, 290
Obligation, binding, 237, 244, 248, 251

Ogburn, William F., 201n.22
Olds, George, 287
Order (moral, social). *See* Problem of order
Owen, Robert, 74

Pareto, Vilfredo, 79, 96, 105, 108, 119, 121, 133, 216, 219–21, 225, 227–28, 231–32n.1, 274–75; analysis of action, 87–93, 106–7, 136–50, 189, 217–18; methodology, 105–6, 134–36, 150, 216–17; Parsons's exposure to, xxxiv, xxxix; Parsons's view of, discussed, xlvii–xlviii, xlix, lii–liv, lvii, lix–lx, lxiii, lxvi, lxvii
"Pareto and the Problems of Positivistic Sociology," liii
Parsons, Edward Smith, x, xi, xix, xliii, xlvii
Parsons, Helen (Helen Walker), xvii
Parsons, Mary A. Ingersol, x
Parsons, Talcott: at Amherst College, xi–xvii, xxiii, xxxii–xxxiii, xxxviii, 287–92; at Harvard University (Economics Department), xxiii, xxxi–xxxvii, xl–xli, lxvii; at Harvard University (Sociology Department), xxx, xxxvii–xliv; at London School of Economics, xvii–xix, lxvii; at University of Heidelberg, xix–xxii, lxvii; birth of children, xlii; childhood and adolescence, x–xi; conception of society discussed, 1; dissertation, xxi, xxii, xxiii, xxiv, xlv; efforts to legitimate sociology, xxxvi–xxxviii, xl, xliv–xlv, xlvi–xlviii, liv, lvi, lvii–lix, lxvii; phases in early work of, xxiii–xxiv, xliv–xlv, lv–lvi, lxv–lxvii; political views of, xiii–xiv, xvii, xxvi–xxvii, xxix, lxii; religious background and views, x, xx, lviii, lxiv, 252; student papers, xvi–xvii, xxxii–xxxiii; style of thought, xii, xxvii–xxviii, lxvii–lxviii; teaching activities, xxii, xxxvi, xxxvii, xli, xlii–xliii, xliii in.120
Pattern variables, xxix
Perry, Ralph, xli
Philosophic radicalism, 194–95
Philosophy, 256–57
Philosophy of science. *See* Analytical method; Empiricism
Piaget, Jean, 242n.8

Plato, 109, 170n.34
Poincaré, Henri, 96
Political sector. *See* Means-end chains
Politics, legitimate domain of, 166, 171, 220n.64, 240
Population, 74–76, 89, 95, 101–3, 187, 192, 196, 266, 268–69
Positivism, 76, 108, 116–19, 150, 154–56, 169, 171, 175, 179–80, 188, 196, 198–203, 205–7, 211, 215, 226–28, 231–32, 234–36, 240–41, 249–50, 255–57; Jaspers on, xx; Parsons's view of, discussed, xlvi–xlvii, l, lvii, lxiii, lxviii
Powell, T. R., 290
Power, 89, 107, 119, 165, 166–67, 171–72n.40, 191, 193–94, 199, 207, 209, 218–19, 222, 229n.64, 240, 241, 265
Pragmatism, 78n.24, 130
Problem of order, 74–75, 77, 102, 107, 119, 145, 158–59, 170, 193, 199, 214, 218, 241–42, 244–45, 267; Meiklejohn's view, xii; Edward Parsons's view, x; Parsons's view of, discussed, xvi, xlv, xlvi, lxiv
Protestantische Ethik und der Geist des Kapitalismus, Die (The Protestant Ethic and the Spirit of Capitalism), xx, xxvii, xxix, 22n.29, 27–30, 43, 50, 55–56, 57–65, 70–71, 219
Protestantism, 28–31, 40, 41–42, 45, 49–50, 53–55, 57–65, 71, 92, 113–15, 220, 252
Psychologism, xvi, xxiv, xxxvii, xliv, xlvi, xlviii, 78–80, 83, 86, 87n.43, 88–90, 95, 150, 157–58, 160, 179, 187, 201–3, 226, 229, 241
Psychology, 9, 23, 163, 195–96, 210–11, 237, 278

Radcliffe-Brown, A. R., 149, 239n.5
Randomness of events, 72, 75–76, 79, 83, 115, 145, 174, 179, 240
Rationalistic positivism, 130, 154–57
Rationality: of action, 20, 29, 51–52, 83, 88, 90, 106, 125, 136, 149–50, 154–55, 157, 160, 175, 183, 185, 188–89, 194–95, 202–3, 222, 234–36, 239–41, 244–47, 255, 259, 270, 282; of capitalism, 7–8, 10–11, 14–16, 23–27, 29, 31, 32, 40, 70–72, 209

Rationalization, 32–35, 52, 65n.19, 71, 248–49, 255
Reason, 74–75, 80, 102, 142
Relativism, scientific, 124–25, 128–30
Religion: Edward Parsons's view, x
Religious factors: effects of, 42, 45, 48–50, 53–55, 65, 72, 73, 90, 96, 110–15, 119–20, 239, 242, 247–49, 251–52, 254; Pareto's analysis of, 146–49; Parsons's view of, discussed, xvi, xxix, xxx, xlv, lviii, lxiv; Weber's anslysis of, 27–31, 57–65, 71, 81–82n.31, 92, 220–21
Ricardo, David, 69, 75, 102–3, 182, 185, 191, 193–94, 205, 262, 273
Rickert, Heinrich, 127
Riley, John, xliiin.120
Ripley, W. Z., xxxi
Robbins, Lionel, lvi–lviii, 153–80
Robertson, H. M., xxix–xxx, 57–65, 220n.48
Romanticism, German, xxi, 3, 7, 11–12, 18, 204–11, 227–28
Ross, Edward A., 50
Rousseau, Jean-Jacques, 75n.14, 116, 118

Salin, Edgar, xxi–xxii, xxiii, xxiv, xxv, xlv, xlvi, 5n.3
Saunders, Laurence J., 288, 290
Schmoller, Gustav, 206–7, 227
Schumpeter, Joseph, xxxi–xxxii, xxxiii, xli, 9n.13, 17n.21, 27n.28, 104
Science, modern, 14–15, 25, 70, 96, 120, 210, 235–37
Secularization, xxix, xlvii, 10, 15, 31, 45, 49, 50, 52, 55, 63–64, 65, 71, 96, 115, 147, 247–48
Sée, Henri, xxvii–xxviii, 39–40
Service, xxviii–xxix, 47–50
Simiand, F., 213n.36
Simmel, Georg, xlix, ln.140, lxiii, 121, 167, 228n.63, 231–32n.1
Sinclair, Upton, 287
Smiles, Samuel, 45–46, 55
Smith, Adam, 102–3, 182, 190, 191–92, 193
Social Ethics Department (Harvard University), xxxv, xxxvi
Socialism, x, xii, xxi, xxvi, 4, 8, 13, 17, 26–27, 41, 45, 81–82, 88, 215, 216–17, 238, 247n.15, 290
Socialization, 242, 267
Social relations, 98, 109, 112, 115–16, 120–21, 253–55
Social sciences: at Amherst College, xii, xiv–xvi, 288–90; at Harvard University, xxx–xliv, lxvii; at London School of Economics, xvii–xix, lxii; at University of Heidelberg, xx–xxii; in America, xxxviii, 96, 255
Social structure, 120
Society, 98, 120–21
Sociology, 9, 12, 27–28n.40, 36, 60–62, 64, 65n.19, 77n.20, 78–80, 85–93, 95–96, 98, 106, 108, 135–37, 144, 164, 167, 171, 172, 186–87, 212, 215–17, 219, 221, 223, 225–26, 228–29, 256–57, 275, 279, 281–83; Parsons's exposure to, xvi, xvii, xviii–xix, xxxv–xxxvi, xxxviii–xxxix; Parsons's view of, discussed, xxxvi–xxxviii, xlviii–l, lii–liv, lviii–lxiii
Sociology Department (Harvard University), xxxvi–xliv
Sociology of knowledge, 129–30
Sombart, Werner, 3–19, 22, 24, 26, 27, 30, 33, 35–36, 40, 56, 83, 91, 169, 203, 207–11, 220, 224–25, 227–28; Parsons's view of, discussed, xxiv–xxvi, xxviii, lx; Salin's view, xxi
Sorokin Pitirim, xxxvi, xxxvii, xli, xlii, xliv, xlix, 108, 121, 140n.23, 254n.25
Souter, Ralph W., lvi–lvii, 153–80, 229n.65
Spencer, Herbert, 73, 76n.16, 108, 197, 214
Spengler, Oswald, 17, 91
Spirit of capitalism, xxv; Sombart's view, 5–15, 209–10; Weber's view, 23, 27–31, 33, 40, 42, 60, 62, 72–73, 219–20
Spiritual factors, 5–8, 10, 12, 18, 27–28, 33–34, 97–98, 188, 206–11. *See also* Value elements
State, 16, 25, 26, 41–42, 49, 50, 74, 77, 107, 109–20, 158, 191, 193, 240, 264, 265–66
Structure of Social Action, The, ix, xxiii, xxxv, xliv, xlv, xlvii, liii, lxv, lxvii, 228n.62, 228n.63, 231–32n.1

Subjective elements. *See* Value elements
Sumner, William Graham, xvi, 170n.33
Survivalism, 76–78, 80, 83, 87n.43, 88
Systems of actions. *See* Means-ends chains

Taussig, Frank W., xxxi, xxxiii, xli, xlv, lxi–lxii, 76n.17, 84n.36, 262–78
Tawney, Richard H., xvii, xxvii, 43, 50, 56, 220n.48
Taylor, Overton, xxxi, 77n.18
Technological sector. *See* Means-end chains
Technology factors, xvi, 14–15, 26, 119, 164–65, 171, 201, 209–10, 240, 246, 252
Teleology, 198, 231
Theory, scientific, 5, 96, 173–74, 224, 226n.59, 259–62, 271–72, 282–83. *See also* Analytical method; Empiricism
Thorndike, Edward, 203
Thrift, xxviii–xxix, 10, 11, 30, 42, 51–55, 71, 209, 273
Time factor, 155–56, 177
Tolman, Edward, xxxix
Tönnies, Ferdinand, xlviii, xlix–l, ln.140, lxiii, 31, 50, 97–99, 120, 121, 231–32n.1, 253n.24
Traditionalism, 42, 47–50, 52, 53, 112, 118; Sombart's view, 7, 12, 13–14, 209–10; Weber's view, 28, 33, 70, 91, 220
Transcendental elements. *See* Metaphysical elements
Troeltsch, Ernest, 43, 50, 56, 65n.19, 121

University of Heidelberg, xix–xxii, xxiii
Utilitarianism, xv, xxi, xxix, 1, 28, 50, 75n.14, 85, 102, 115–17, 118, 143, 164, 169, 190, 222, 241, 242. *See also* Economics, classical
Utility theory. *See* Neoclassical economics
Value attitudes, 244, 250–55
Value elements, xxix, xlvii, liv, lv, lviii, lxiii–lxiv, 27–28, 47–50, 51–55, 69, 71–72, 89, 91–92, 97, 101, 107, 108–

20, 124–25, 140–49, 157–59, 169–70, 188–89, 197, 198, 203–6, 210–11, 214–15, 218–21, 226–29, 231–56, 275–79. *See also* Normative elements
Veblen, Thorstein, xvi, xxiv, lxi, 52, 55, 56, 62n.15, 171n.38, 188, 198–203, 215, 223, 226, 229n.64, 276
Verstehen, 128–29
Vierkandt, Alfred, xlix
Voltaire, 12
Voluntarism, xxxix–xl, lvii, lviii, lxiii–lxiv, 142, 158, 169, 175–76, 214, 231, 233–37, 241, 244, 246, 250, 251. *See also* Effort
von Jaffe-Richthofen, Else, xx
von Schelting, Alexander, xx, li, liv, 21n.28, 27–28n.40, 123–31
von Wiese, Leopold, xlix

Wants, 72–81, 83, 88–92, 102, 107, 115, 144–45, 160, 182–85, 187, 194–95, 204–5. *See also* Interest; Randomness of wants
"Wants and Activities in Marshall," xlvi
Watson, John B., xxxviii
Wealth, 119, 193
Weber, Alfred, xx, xxiii, 34n.52
Weber, Marianne, xx, xxvii
Weber, Max, 3, 9, 19–36, 40, 57–65, 70–71, 90–93, 96, 98, 120, 121, 219–21, 222, 225, 227–28, 231–32n.1, 235, 243n.10, 276; methodology, xxv, xxx, li–lii, 20–22, 34–37, 60–61, 123–30; Parsons's exposure to, xx; Parsons's view of, discussed, xxiv–xxvi, xxvii–xxviii, xxxix, xlvii–xlviii, xlix, li–lii, lix–lx, lxiii, lxvi, lxvii; Salin's view, xxi
Weber circle, xx
Whitehead, Alfred North, xxxiii–xxxiv, xlix, lii, 96, 224n.56
Will, human, 11, 31–32, 235. *See also* Voluntarism

Young, Allyn, xxxi, 36n.53

Znaniecki, Florian, xxxix